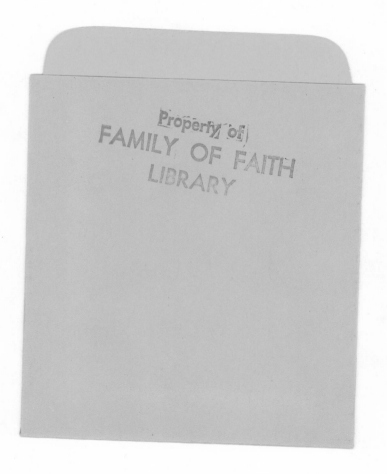

PRACTICAL
MANAGEMENT
COMMUNICATION

▲

VICKIE JOHNSON STOUT

THE UNIVERSITY OF GEORGIA

EDWARD A. PERKINS, JR.

THE UNIVERSITY OF GEORGIA

E56

Published by

SOUTH-WESTERN PUBLISHING CO.

CINCINNATI   WEST CHICAGO, IL   DALLAS   LIVERMORE, CA

PREFACE

The development of communication skills is a continuous process in which people strive to understand and in turn be understood. Through the use of effective communication, organizations have a sense of direction; and people are stimulated to action.

We have designed *Practical Management Communication* for use in a managerial communication course or a traditional business communication course; it may also be adapted for use in a short course that covers only selected chapters or topics. The book is suitable for students in universities and senior colleges; community or junior colleges; private business schools; technical institutes; and special management training programs in business, industry, government, and the military. It is useful to anyone interested in improving his or her management communication skills.

Purpose and Approach

Practical Management Communication was written because of a need for a balanced text to use in managerial communication courses. This book addresses the systematic development of critical communication skills.

Effective management communication interrelates all the communication skills—listening, speaking, reading, and writing. Researchers say that oral communication skills are primary vehicles for management communication and that writing is the least relevant communication activity. Analyses of contemporary business communication texts, however, show that writing is the major communication skill emphasized in a majority of texts.

Practical Management Communication meets the need for a text with a balanced view of management communication. The book covers just enough communication theory to establish the groundwork for communication skills that form the core of the text. It places a realistic emphasis on the skills of listening, speaking, reading, and writing. Moreover, these communication skills are prioritized and presented in order of their importance to the users of the text.

The approach used in *Practical Management Communication* is workable. It has been field-tested extensively by collegiate business communication students as well as management and management support personnel from business, industry, education, and government.

Distinctive Features

Several distinctive features are incorporated in *Practical Management Communication,* including the following:

1. *Concise format.* Since we planned and wrote each chapter together, the book maintains a concise, consistent format. It emphasizes the mechanics of good writing and reflects the language used in today's business organizations.
2. *Research base.* Resources are included which reflect the most recent developments and practices in the field of management communication.
3. *Technology.* Significant technological innovations in management communication are identified and interwoven with text material.
4. *Practical business examples.* Extensive examples of actual business situations provide ample opportunities to assist in the learning process.
5. *Chapter objectives.* To give the book the highest degree of relevance to students, major learning objectives are placed at the beginning of each chapter.
6. *Full-sized illustrations, cartoons, and graphic displays.* Numerous full-sized illustrations, cartoons, and graphic displays are used throughout the book to heighten student interest and promote maximum learning opportunities.
7. *Two-color format.* A two-color format and attractive page layout enhance the readability of the book.
8. *End-of-chapter activities.* Questions, Problem-Solving Experiences, and Cases at the end of each chapter challenge and encourage students to make communication skills a part of their daily lives.
9. *Marginal notes.* Notes are placed in the side margins of each chapter to summarize points and encourage students to think beyond the chapter concepts.
10. *Key terms and concepts.* All key terms and concepts are italicized and set in bold type. To be of maximum help to students, key terms and concepts are defined in the Glossary in Appendix B.
11. *Selected Readings.* A collection of durable articles on practical communication matters are in Appendix A. These readings reinforce and broaden the text material and provide a basis for class discussion of timely and thought-provoking management communication topics.

Instructional Materials

The following supplements have been prepared to make *Practical Management Communication* more sensitive to the needs of instructors:

1. *Teacher's manual.* This manual provides instructors with assistance in the presentation of the text material, including

   ▲ Teaching suggestions.
   ▲ Chapter and part overviews.
   ▲ Chapter outlines for teaching suggestions and lecture notes.
   ▲ Solutions to the end-of-chapter activities, with text page references.
   ▲ Thirty-seven Enrichment Activities and solutions.
   ▲ A set of 40 Transparency Masters.
   ▲ A test bank for all 17 chapters comprised of
   170 multiple-choice questions.
   170 true/false questions.
   170 essay/short-response questions.
   ▲ A key for each test bank, with text page references.

2. *MicroSWAT.* Computerized diskette versions of the text test banks are provided to help verify student mastery of terms and concepts and to ease the chore of test preparation. MicroSWAT enables the instructor to generate tests from the text test bank and allows the instructor to control the content and form of generated tests. The instructor may select individual test questions from the test bank, or the computer will randomly select questions for the instructor. Microcomputer knowledge is not essential for using MicroSWAT; the program will prompt the instructor every step of the way.

Message to the Student

Practical Management Communication is student centered. Special features of this book have been designed to enhance your acquiring effective communication skills. These features include objectives which clarify the purpose of each chapter, marginal notes, key terms, a succinct summary for each chapter, practical application experiences, and a glossary. The practical application experiences are particularly important in the improvement of communication skills for business-related and personal applications.

A Note of Thanks

The development of *Practical Management Communication* was facilitated by many highly-skilled, special people. We want to acknowledge their contributions to this book.

Our reviewers provided invaluable insight concerning text content and organization improvements. They are Dr. John E. Gump, Eastern Kentucky University; Dr. Phyllis Gump; Ms. Donna N. Newhart, West Georgia College; and Dr. Thomas L. Means, Louisiana Tech University. "The Importance of Manuals" section of Chapter 17 was contributed by B. L. Johnson, Sr., of Martin Marietta Energy Systems, Inc., who has special expertise in the subject matter of manuals. We appreciate his assistance.

Ms. Deidra Thomas served as our graduate research assistant for *Practical Management Communication*. We would not have completed this book without her help. Special thanks go to Mr. Fred Stout for his computer programming assistance and business insights. We also appreciate Mr. Jeff Perkins and Mrs. Peggy Perkins's computer program assistance. We are indebted to Mrs. Beverly Snyder Cormican and Mrs. Theresa LaValley Jarrels for their library research assistance.

We appreciate the content preparation contribution made by the following University of Georgia personnel: Ms. Karen Martin, Ms. Martha Eaton, Mrs. Mary Alice Simpson, and Dr. Alphonse Buccino. A deep expression of gratitude is due Mrs. Sue A. Johnson and Mrs. Marilyn Apted Perkins for their noteworthy assistance to the development of this book.

Vickie Johnson Stout
Edward A. Perkins, Jr.

CONTENTS

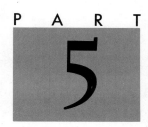

1

THEORETICAL BASE

When you complete this chapter, you should be able to:

▲ Explain the basic managerial functions performed by all managers.

▲ Discuss the importance of management communication.

▲ Explain the working roles performed by every manager.

▲ Compare the five basic forms of organization.

▲ Contrast internal and external communication.

The field of management has received a great deal of attention during the second half of the twentieth century. Perhaps this increased popularity of the study of management can be attributed to the realization that effective management skills can be learned. Being an effective manager is not dependent upon innate qualities or characteristics; it is possible to learn how to achieve organization objectives through people. Based upon this belief, companies throughout the world have spent large sums of money on human resource development programs to train managers. The development of communication skills continues to be an integral part of managerial training.

Effective management skills can be learned.

▲ WHY COMMUNICATE?

Communication is the process of passing knowledge from person to person. Good communication is the means by which management is achieved.

Effective management is accomplished through communication.

> In the management process, communication is a means, not an end—a lubricant for the effective operation of the system in which we as managers work. It is the means through which managerial planning is performed, organization is carried out, and management direction and control are achieved.[1]

Much of a manager's success is based on communication. Thus, management and communication are inseparable. The study of managerial communication consists of the oral, written, and nonverbal communication skills needed by today's manager. What does today's manager do? A clear understanding of *managerial functions* is needed if specific communication skills are to be developed.

Managerial communication involves oral, written, and nonverbal skills.

Managerial Functions

A *manager* is a person in charge of or having authority over an organization or one of its units. The major responsibility of a manager is to ensure that the company efficiently produces its goods or services. Fulfilling this responsibility involves proper planning, organizing, leading, and controlling. These functions are not performed in isolation.

A manager plans, organizes, leads, and controls.

Source: From THE WALL STREET JOURNAL—Permission, Cartoon Features Syndicate.

Planning

Planning involves setting goals and developing strategies to attain goals.

The *planning* function involves developing goals and objectives to be attained by the company under the manager's control. It also involves the development of strategies for attaining goals and objectives. Proper planning draws upon knowledge of the past, present, and future. The time span for which plans are made varies among management levels. *Supervisory or first-line managers* engage in short-range planning. *Middle-level managers* are responsible for intermediate-range planning. *Top-level managers* assume responsibility for long-range planning. Poor planning can hinder the attainment of company goals; it can create confusion and frustration among workers. It is important that managers allow workers to participate in the planning process when possible. Planning with employees not only makes plans acceptable but also helps employees know what to expect and what is expected of them. Time spent in planning is time well spent. A common criticism of management in America as contrasted with management in other countries is that more time is spent in implementing plans rather than in planning. Good planning can shorten implementation time.

Organizing

Organizing involves the orderly arrangement of resources needed to achieve what has been planned. There is no one best way for a manager to organize. The appropriateness of organizing depends on the situation.

The size of a company, its formal organization structure, and its management leadership styles are among the factors that make organizing a managerial function.

Organizing consists of arranging resources in an effective, cost-efficient manner.

Leading

The managerial function of *leading* encompasses staffing and directing. Staffing may consist of recruiting, hiring, and training human resources within a firm. Directing entails motivating personnel so that company and employee goals can be met. Leading is the most delicate managerial function. Increased attention is being given to human resource development within firms—and for good reason: it is through people that plans are implemented and company goals are attained.

Leading involves recruiting, hiring, training, and motivating.

Controlling

The *controlling* function of management consists of measuring or evaluating progress made toward planned goals and objectives. Through the controlling function, managers are able to compare projections and actual results. Efficiency and effectiveness are taken into account when processes and products are evaluated.

Controlling allows for measurement of goal attainment.

The amount of time spent performing any one function will vary depending upon the manager's position within the formal organization and the specific situation in which the manager serves. Communication is vital in the performance of each managerial function. Table 1–1 shows examples of the types of communication needed to fulfill each managerial function.

Table 1–1   Types of Communication to Fulfill Managerial Functions

Planning	Organizing	Leading	Controlling
Formulating objectives	Giving instructions	Delegating responsibility	Completing employee performance appraisals
Sharing plans	Scheduling work loads	Training personnel	Monitoring production rates
Conducting job	Reclassifying positions	Interviewing recruits	Writing progress reports

Mintzberg identified ten roles commonly assumed by today's managers. Each role has implications for how a manager communicates. These roles are[2]

▲ Figurehead.   ▲ Spokesperson.
▲ Leader.   ▲ Entrepreneur.
▲ Liaison.   ▲ Disturbance handler.
▲ Monitor.   ▲ Resource allocator.
▲ Disseminator.   ▲ Negotiator.

In addition to being a problem solver, today's manager must be a problem preventer.

Several principles of management also have a bearing on how managers communicate. These principles include clearly defined objectives, responsibility for organization, unity of functions, delegation of authority commensurate with responsibility, unity of command, and span of control. The *unity of functions* principle is of special importance; it represents the interdependence of parts within a firm. All parts of a firm must work and communicate with one another if mutual goals are to be realized.

The unity of functions principle depicts the interrelatedness of units within an organization.

Importance of Managerial Communication

Communication is the nervous system of a firm; without it, workers do not know what is expected of them. The need for strong communication skills among managers is not restricted to their respective work groups. Figure 1–1 reflects the extended communication requirements for an individual within a firm. Communication can extend to the organization at large and to its external environment.

Recent research confirms the importance of management communication. A survey of senior managers revealed that employee communication ranks second among the most important human resource activities; productivity improvement ranks first. According to one senior manager, "Any problem can be alleviated through better communication."[3]

In 1981, a study of administrative managers was conducted to determine their perceptions of their most important and most enjoyable job functions. Data were obtained from over 750 managers. These data showed that a majority of managers viewed oral communication as their most important and most enjoyable job function. They rated written communication as their fourth most important and most enjoyable job function.[4]

Good communication skills are timeless. In the 1950s and again in the 1970s, Robert Katz pointed out the need for such skills among managers.

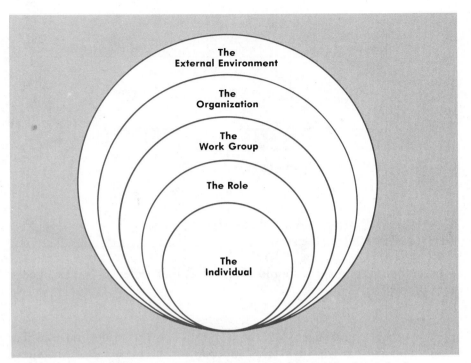

FIGURE 1–1   The Interaction of the Individual with the Organization and the External Environment

Katz advocated that managers develop three kinds of personal skills: technical skills for one's job, human or communication skills to work with others and build cooperation, and conceptual skills for problem solving. Katz suggested that the importance of these skills varies with the levels of management. As shown in Figure 1–2, supervisory managers need strong technical skills and some human skills.[5] Middle-level managers depend on technical, human, and conceptual skills; top-level managers draw most heavily upon human and conceptual skills.[6]

▲ WHO COMMUNICATES?

Successful managers are good leaders, peers, and followers. To achieve these three working roles, astute managers use formal and informal communication channels to their advantage.

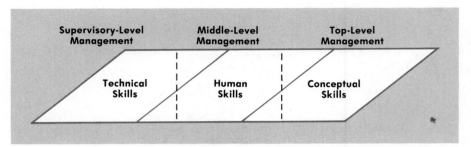

FIGURE 1-2   Model of Important Managerial Skills[7]

Common Communication Roles
Played by Managers

A good manager is a leader, peer, and follower.

Contemporary managers should understand their roles as leaders, peers, and followers.

Leader

One aspect of management communication is the leadership role that every manager has with workers. *Leadership* is the means used to achieve company goals by motivating and controlling workers to high levels of performance.

Considerable efforts have been made to define effective leadership. Effective leadership traits are essentially the same regardless of the particular work environment. Good leaders, no matter where they work, possess the ability to:

Do good leaders have these traits?

▲ Understand the feelings, problems, and needs of employees.
▲ Let employees participate in decisions that affect them.
▲ Create opportunities for employees to succeed.
▲ Deal with employees in an objective, nonemotional manner.
▲ Understand the kind of influence they are having on employees.
▲ Adapt to a constantly changing work environment.
▲ Understand their own strengths and weaknesses.

Good leaders will use a leadership style appropriate for the situation.

Leadership can also be viewed as a range of styles available to a manager. Tannenbaum and Schmidt portray leadership styles as a continuum. The styles range from the *autocratic leader,* who makes decisions without the advice of workers, to the *democratic leader,* who involves workers in making decisions. The continuum, as shown in Figure 1-3, also accounts for external forces—both in the organization and in the larger society—that affect the relationship between managers and employees. There is no one best leadership style. The effective leader is ". . . one who maintains

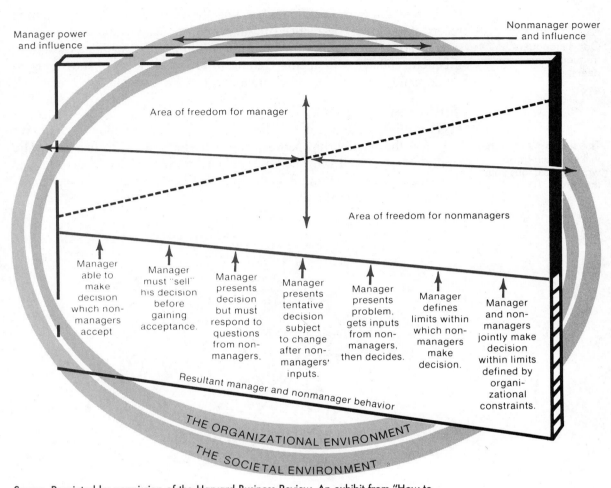

Manager power and influence

Nonmanager power and influence

Area of freedom for manager

Area of freedom for nonmanagers

Manager able to make decision which non-managers accept

Manager must "sell" his decision before gaining acceptance.

Manager presents decision but must respond to questions from non-managers.

Manager presents tentative decision subject to change after non-managers' inputs.

Manager presents problem, gets inputs from non-managers, then decides.

Manager defines limits within which non-managers make decision.

Manager and non-managers jointly make decision within limits defined by organizational constraints.

Resultant manager and nonmanager behavior

THE ORGANIZATIONAL ENVIRONMENT

THE SOCIETAL ENVIRONMENT

Source: Reprinted by permission of the Harvard Business Review. An exhibit from "How to Choose a Leadership Pattern" by Robert Tannenbaum and Warren H. Schmidt (May–June, 1973). Copyright© 1973 by the President and Fellows of Harvard College; all rights reserved.

FIGURE 1–3   Leadership Continuum

a high batting average in accurately assessing the forces that determine what his [or her] most appropriate behavior at any time should be and in actually being able to behave accordingly."[8]

Peer

Another working role a manager must play is the role with peers. A *peer* is a co-worker or colleague of roughly equal rank or status. Relationships with peers are an important part of company success and worker satisfaction.

Good managers frequently interact with peers.

The successful manager will maintain good working relations with the boss.

Peer relations in companies are not always smooth. Conflicts among peers at work can be reduced through proper organization and development. To achieve good working relations with peers, a manager must have frequent contact with them. Getting to know one's peers and trying to understand their problems are important steps for managing peer relations.

Follower

The third working role of the manager is that of follower. *Follower* refers to the relationship between the manager and his or her boss. The ability to relate well with the boss is crucial to the manager's success. The boss may determine promotional opportunities, salary and benefits, transfer possibilities, and the like.

THE WALL STREET JOURNAL

"It is lonely at the top. On the other hand, it's lonelier at the bottom."

Source: From THE WALL STREET JOURNAL—Permission, Cartoon Features Syndicate.

The skilled manager may favorably influence the boss by applying insights gained from Abraham Maslow's concepts of human motivation. Maslow held that human needs exist at five basic levels. As shown in Figure 1–4, these needs are presented in ascending order, starting with primary needs and going to secondary needs. Once the primary needs have been satisfied, the secondary needs become the dominant motivating factors.

Research shows that managers who are high achievers are driven mainly by the need for *self-actualization,* or the need to realize their full potential. Managers who are average achievers are concerned with *esteem*

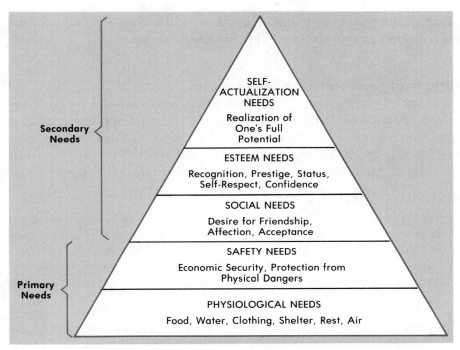

FIGURE 1–4   Maslow's Hierarchy of Needs

needs, or the need to feel important and to receive recognition from others. Low-achieving managers are equally preoccupied by esteem needs and *safety needs,* or the needs for economic security, for protection from physical dangers, and for the desire for an orderly, predictable environment.[9]

The manager may contribute to the satisfaction of the boss's primary needs by helping the work unit meet its goals and objectives. Giving sincere praise on tasks well done, providing constructive feedback when problems arise, and striving for personal compatibility are ways in which the manager may help the boss satisfy secondary needs.

The boss's leadership style may also suggest ways in which the manager can relate to the boss. The autocratic boss defines the procedures for upward communication and expects the manager to respond accordingly. The democratic boss expects the manager to initiate a constant upward flow of ideas, opinions, recommendations, and reports.

The boss has needs that must be met.

Insights gained from the leadership continuum can be useful in relating to the boss.

Roles Played Based upon Communication Structure

Within a firm, communication flows downward, upward, and horizontally through formal organization channels and in many directions through informal channels. Communication also flows externally as part of the firm's public relations and marketing functions.

Internal Communication—Formal

In formal company structures, communication moves up and down the **chain of command,** which links managers at the top levels with managers and workers at the lower levels. Communication problems increase with the complexity of the chain of command. Even the simple chain can cause communication breakdowns as illustrated in the following anecdote.

A colonel issued the following order to his executive officer:

Tomorrow evening at approximately 2000 hours Halley's Comet will be visible in this area, an event which occurs only once every 75 years. Have the men fall out in the battalion area in fatigues, and I will explain this rare phenomenon to them. In case of rain, we will not be able to see anything, so assemble the men in the theater and I will show them films of it.

Executive officer to company commander:

By order of the Colonel, tomorrow at 2000 hours, Halley's Comet will appear above the battalion area. If it rains, fall the men out in fatigues, then march to the theater where this rare phenomenon will take place, something which occurs only once every 75 years.

Company commander to lieutenant:

By order of the Colonel be in fatigues at 2000 hours tomorrow evening; the phenomenal Halley's Comet will appear in the theater. In case of rain, in the battalion area, the Colonel will give another order, something which occurs once every 75 years.

Lieutenant to sergeant:

Tomorrow at 2000 hours, the Colonel will appear in the theater with Halley's Comet, something which happens every 75 years. If it rains, the Colonel will order the comet into the battalion area.

Sergeant to squad:

When it rains tomorrow at 2000 hours, the phenomenal 75-year-old General Halley, accompanied by the Colonel, will drive his comet through the battalion area theater in fatigues.[10]

Closely related to the chain of command are the principles of unity of command and span of control. The **unity of command** principle states that a worker should report to only one boss. With too many superiors, the worker's communication problems grow. **Span of control** is the number of workers who are directly managed by one person. While research

The chain of command links top-level managers with lower-level managers and workers.

Unity of command means that a worker should report to only one boss.

THE WALL STREET JOURNAL

Source: From THE WALL STREET JOURNAL—Permission, Cartoon Features Syndicate.

results are mixed concerning the best number for span of control, the size of a manager's work group will affect communication effectiveness.

The five basic forms of organization are line, functional, line-and-staff, committee, and matrix. There is no best organization form; each form has advantages and disadvantages.

Line Organization. In a *line organization,* direct authority flows downward from top-level managers, through middle-level managers, to lower-level managers and workers. Each follower is responsible to only one leader. A clear-cut flow of formal communication lines exists in this structure; the organization relationships and duties are easily understood by all people. The weakness of this structure is that line managers may have to perform specialized duties, since staff help is not available. Figure 1–5 depicts the line organization.

Functional Organization. The *functional organization* is built around specialized areas such as sales, marketing, and production. A manager

Span of control refers to the number of people that a manager directly supervises.

Every manager is an expert in the line organization.

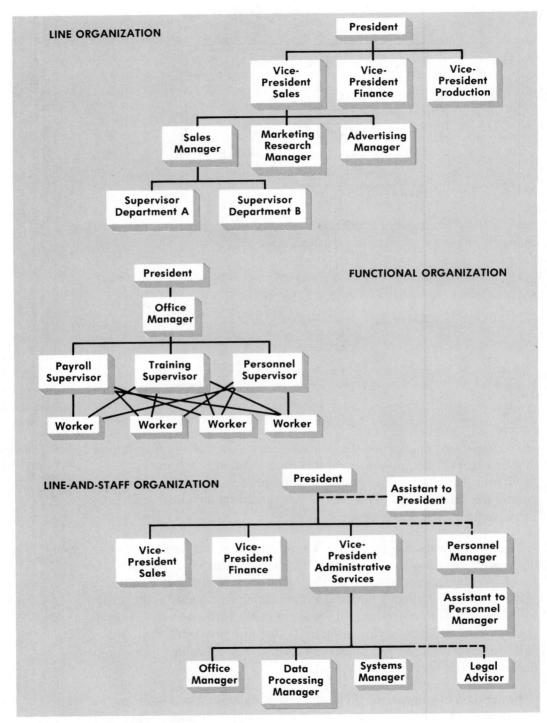

FIGURE 1–5   Three Forms of Organization

specialist is in charge of each function. Thus, each manager in this structure has line authority over all employees in the work unit. Even though the functional structure overcomes the line organization's lack of specialization, it creates a difficult situation where workers report to more than one boss. An example of the functional organization plan is shown in Figure 1–5.

Functional organization features specialization; workers may have more than one boss.

Line-and-Staff Organization.   The *line-and-staff organization* combines the direct flow of authority of the line organization with the specialized feature of the functional organization. Line positions are retained from the top to the bottom of the firm. Staff personnel are added to the line organization to give advice and specialized assistance to line personnel. Staff personnel have no authority over line personnel. Figure 1–5 shows a line-and-staff organization. The solid lines denote line positions; the broken lines depict staff positions.

The line-and-staff organization combines the strengths of line and functional structures.

Committee Organization.   The *committee organization* provides a structure for pooling ideas and coordinating plans and policies among workers across departmental lines. Authority and responsibility are jointly held by a group of people rather than by a single manager. Committees are often used to supplement the line-and-staff structure. The success of any committee depends on member involvement.

The committee organization combines the thinking of managers in diverse areas.

Matrix Organization.   The *matrix organization* uses a dual command system to work on complex projects or products. Workers with special expertise are temporarily borrowed from various functional areas of the firm; they are assigned to work either full-time or part-time on a project. Each worker in the matrix reports to two bosses. While the matrix structure tends to cause communication problems, it does offer the best of two worlds for dealing with projects requiring both functional specialization and product expertise.

Each worker in the matrix organization has two bosses—one functional manager and one project manager.

Internal Communication—Informal

Informal channels of communication exist along with formal channels. Informal channels move in many directions. Informal channels are not planned; they grow out of the interaction of groups of people drawn together by common interests. Membership in an informal group often cuts across the formal organization. For example, the company bowling team may be comprised of workers from many departments and levels in the firm. Team members get together informally; company operations as well as personal interests may be discussed. Company car pools, coffee breaks, and lunchtimes often result in associations of diverse people who develop informal channels.

Informal networks among employees develop over time.

The best known
informal communication
system is the grapevine.

The informal communication network that exists in every firm is known as the **grapevine.** The grapevine tends to get important information to people much faster and more directly than formal channels. Depending upon the people involved, the grapevine can result in garbled and distorted messages or accurately transmitted messages. According to Davis, the most common grapevine channel is the ***cluster chain*** in which information is selectively distributed.[11] Figure 1–6 shows how the cluster works. A tells selected people B, C, and D the message. Only B and C pass the message on to selected persons E, F, and G; and only F passes it on to others.

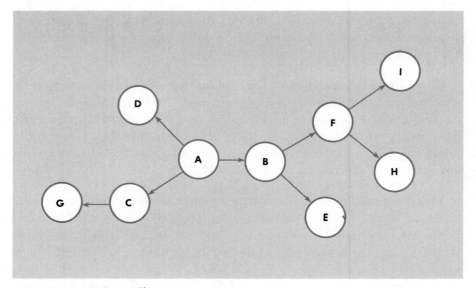

FIGURE 1–6   Cluster Chain

External Communication

While communication constantly flows through the internal channels of a firm, communication must also flow between the firm and the major elements outside it. The external environment includes clients, suppliers, competitors, the local community, the general public, government bodies, and international contacts. Some outside elements are more vital to the company's success than others. A successful manager relates to and communicates with the proper mix of external components. The manager who fails to act as the key communication link between the company and its external environment gets left behind.

The manager must be
able to relate to
elements outside the
organization.

▲ HOW PEOPLE COMMUNICATE

The development of communication skills is a continual process in which people try to understand and in turn be understood. Through the use of good communication, companies have a sense of direction; people are moved to action. Although the major responsibility for leadership in communication rests with managers, all people should recognize the value of and need for communication skills.

Good management communication blends listening, speaking, reading, and writing skills. Research studies about the relative importance of communication skills show that oral communication (listening and speaking) requires more job time than written communication (reading and writing).

Effective oral and written communications are vital management skills.

Oral Skills

The large portion of time spent communicating on the job through non-writing activities has been well documented. To achieve a balance among the critical communication skills, this book includes an appropriate emphasis on oral skills. Chapters 3 and 4 cover listening skills. Chapters 5 through 8 cover speaking skills—speaking person-to-person, speaking in group situations, and making speeches.

Six chapters of this book are devoted to oral communication.

Written Skills

Reading and writing can be grouped as written communication skills. Both areas are discussed in Parts 4 and 5 of this book.

Reading
Reading is addressed in Chapters 9 and 10 so that managers can acquire methods for improving reading skills. Reading is one of the few remaining avenues available for professional development after managers have completed their formal training.

Writing
Written communication is the most tangible of the communication skills. Although managers spend a small part of their communication time writing, the majority of communication training tends to focus on the enhancement of written communication skills. The documentation aspect

Written communication is tangible.

of written communication causes some people to approach writing more methodically than they do other areas of communication. Chapters 11 through 17 address the major aspects of writing skill development.

Nonverbal Skills

Body language is unspoken communication.

Sometimes the unspoken word, or one's body language, speaks more loudly than spoken words. The power of nonverbal communication is presented for each of the four communication skills—speaking, listening, reading, and writing.

Influence of Technology

Technology is interwoven with text material.

New technology is changing the communication process. Vast changes now taking place or being planned will bring about a world unlike the one known today. Trends in communication technology are blended in the text.

SUMMARY

Communication is a crucial part of management. It is through communication that information is passed among people. Good management is based, in part, on good communication. Managers communicate while performing the functions of planning, organizing, leading, and controlling. How much a manager communicates during any function varies in direct proportion with the time spent on that function.

Research studies show that communication is one of the most important human resource activities within firms. It is also one of the most enjoyable functions for a manager. Effective communication skills allow a manager to serve as a good follower, peer, and leader. A manager's leadership style can affect how she or he communicates as a leader and how others communicate in return.

A manager may play many roles based upon the communication structure within a firm. Internal communication is shaped by both the formal and the informal organization structures. The formal organization is usually shown by a line, functional, line-and-staff, committee, or matrix design. In formal structures, communication moves up and down the chain of command; it is affected by unity of command and span of control.

External communication occurs as a firm relates to outside elements. Managers are key links between their firms and outside people and groups.

Although the major responsibility for leadership in communication rests with managers, all people in a firm should recognize the value of and need for communication skills. Major skills include listening, speaking, reading, and writing. Nonverbal communication usually accompanies each of these skills.

QUESTIONS

1. Describe the relationship between communication and the principle of unity of functions.

2. How can effective management be learned?

3. Oral, written, and nonverbal communication skills are needed by today's manager. Give examples of how a manager might communicate verbally, in writing, or nonverbally.

4. Why is leading the most delicate of the managerial functions?

5. Contrast the communication skill requirements of a supervisory manager with those of a middle-level manager.

6. Contrast the autocratic leadership style of management with the democratic leadership style of management. Which style of leadership would you follow? Why?

7. Is it possible for a manager to have both line authority and staff responsibilities? Explain.

8. Why does committee effectiveness depend on participation?

9. Comment on this statement: "If managers want to communicate an important message quickly, they should not use the formal organization."

10. How would you establish a good relationship with a peer? Cite personal examples.

PROBLEM-SOLVING EXPERIENCES

1. Observe the styles of leadership used by three leaders to whom you report or with whom you come in contact; for example, a boss, professor, living group head, or student activity group head. Prepare a report of your observations for the class.

2. Participate in a group brainstorming session on communication skills needed to recruit, hire, train, and motivate workers.

CASE 1–1

Bob Dineen is a senior engineer at Strategic Designs. He has worked in the Systems Engineering Department for seven years. Marsha Temples, the systems engineering department head, relies heavily on Bob's expertise when new contract bids are needed. Currently, Bob is working on a systems project contract bid for the Foralite Corporation. The bid must reach Chicago by October 15. Yesterday Tim Mahaney, the plant manager, asked Marsha to assign Bob to a plant-wide project for one-third of his working time. The assignment is temporary and will run only through Wednesday, October 13.

Reluctantly, Marsha called Bob into her office to discuss the part-time assignment. During the discussion, she explained to Bob that work to be completed in the remaining two-thirds of his time must take priority over the plant-wide project. Later the same afternoon, Bob received a call from Tim. Tim made it clear that the plant-wide project should receive top priority.

1. What communication problems do you foresee for Bob?
2. Which job should take top priority? Why?
3. How can Bob improve his communication with Marsha and Tim?

ENDNOTES

[1] George Miller, "Management Guidelines: Being a Good Communicator," *Supervisory Management*, Vol. 26, No. 4 (April, 1981), p. 20.

[2]Adapted from Henry Mintzberg, "The Manager's Job: Folklore and Fact," *Harvard Business Review*, Vol. 53, No. 4 (July–August, 1975), p. 55.

[3]Roy Foltz and Karn Rosenberg, "Senior Management Views the Human Resource Function," *Personnel Administrator*, Vol. 27, No. 9 (September, 1982), p. 47.

[4]Donald W. Jarrell, "Administrative Managers Profiled in Study," *Management World*, Vol. 11, No. 10 (October, 1982), pp. 19, 26–27.

[5]Robert L. Katz, "Skills of an Effective Administrator," *Harvard Business Review*, Vol. 33, No. 1 (January–February, 1955), pp. 33–42.

[6]Robert L. Katz, "Skills of an Effective Administrator," *Harvard Business Review*, Vol. 52, No. 5 (September–October, 1974), p. 100.

[7]Based on Robert L. Katz, "Skills of an Effective Administrator," *Harvard Business Review*, Vol. 52, No. 5 (September–October, 1974), pp. 90–102.

[8]Robert Tannenbaum and Warren H. Schmidt, "How to Choose a Leadership Pattern," *Harvard Business Review*, Vol. 51, No. 3 (May–June, 1973), p. 167.

[9]Jay Hall, "What Makes a Manager Good, Bad, or Average?" *Psychology Today*, Vol. 10, No. 8 (August, 1976), pp. 52–53, 55.

[10]From a speech by Dan Bellus, Didactic Systems, Inc., Cranford, NJ, *DS Letter*, Vol. 1, No. 3 (1971).

[11]Keith Davis, "A Method of Studying Communication Patterns in Organizations," *Personnel Psychology*, Vol. 6, No. 3 (Autumn, 1953), p. 306.

SYSTEMS APPROACH TO COMMUNICATING EFFECTIVELY

When you complete this chapter, you should be able to:

▲ Differentiate between a closed system and an open system.

▲ Discuss the relationship between a super system and subsystems.

▲ List the main components of a business system.

▲ Explain how the communication system works in a business organization.

▲ Describe the relative importance of the basic components of a management communication system: input, process, and output.

Communication is a process that needs continual attention. A systems approach to communicating involves patterning after a model or conceptual framework.

▲ WHAT IS A SYSTEM?

Practical, effective communication does not occur by chance; it is a system. The term *system* can be defined as the orderly arranged parts of a whole. Effective communication results when the parts or components of communication are analyzed, organized, implemented, and monitored.

A system represents the orderly arranged parts of a whole.

Types of Systems

Systems may be grouped into two categories—closed or open.

Closed System
A *closed system* does not interact with the environment in which it exists. It is self-contained and automatically controls its own operation. Examples of closed systems are

A closed system controls its own operation.

- ▲ A battery-operated clock.
- ▲ A furnace or air conditioner with a thermostat that automatically controls room temperature.
- ▲ A computer-based inventory system that automatically generates a purchase order when the current inventory level falls below a specified level.

In reality, the completely closed system does not exist. Over a period of time, batteries lose their power and mechanical parts break down. The system cannot repair itself—it requires a force from outside the system to do the job.

Open System
An *open system* does not exist in isolation. Its operation requires the interaction of the system with the environment. The open system has the capacity for making the adjustments required to adapt to changes in the external environment. Examples of open systems are

The operation of an open system requires interaction with the outside environment.

- ▲ A windup clock.
- ▲ A heating or cooling unit with a switch that is controlled by a person as circumstances dictate.

▲ A computer-based inventory system that produces an inventory-on-hand report for review by a stock clerk who prepares a purchase order.

Super Systems and Subsystems

A super system contains many smaller systems called subsystems.

Most systems can be described as one *super system* comprised of many *subsystems* or smaller systems. The success of the super system is based upon the success of the subsystems. The unity of functions principle is an integral part of the super system/subsystem concept. Interdependence must be realized and maximized if the total company or super system is to attain its goals. Close to 2,000 years ago, the structure of a super system containing many subsystems was described this way:

> . . . the body is one, and hath many members, and all the members of that one body, being many, are one body . . . for the body is not one member, but many.[1]

The apostle Paul was describing the structure of the church to Corinthian Christians. The super system of an organization and its subsystems are shown in Figure 2–1.

Components of a System

The business organization is an open system.

The main components of a business system are input, process, output, feedback, and controls.

The business organization is an open system. Its survival depends on receiving input from and sending output to the external environment. The five main components of a business system include input, process, output, feedback, and controls.

Input refers to the elements that enter a system from the external environment. Examples of input are raw materials, human resources, energy, and information. *Process* is that phase of the system that changes inputs into outputs. *Output* refers to the goods and/or services produced by a company. *Feedback* seeks to provide managers with information about the quality, quantity, and cost of the goods or services produced. It is the process whereby output can be compared with established goals and standards. *Controls* are the policies, rules, and regulations that monitor the various components of the system. Each major component of the communication system will be examined in detail later in this chapter.

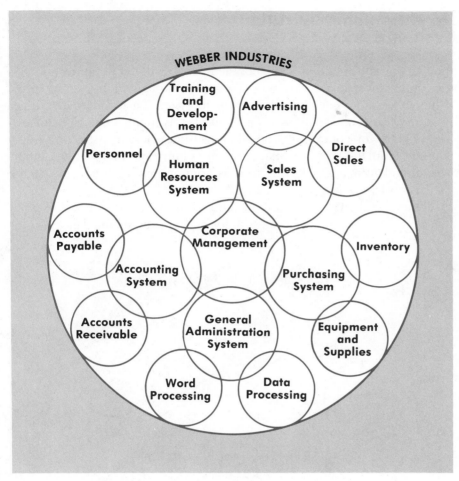

FIGURE 2–1   Subsystems Within a Super System

▲ COMMUNICATION SYSTEM

The **communication system** within a firm may not be readily recognized as a system because it is not always tangible. The communication system is invisible during some stages because it occurs at the same time as other activities within a firm. However, skilled managers recognize and use the communication system. A good communication system can improve business activity. A poor communication system can hamper or even sabotage business endeavors; it can abort future business activity.

The communication system is not always visible.

How the Communication System Works

Interaction within and among subsystems makes the communication system an open system. This system reaches throughout the entire firm. When necessary, interaction occurs with systems external to the super system. Clear, concise information is needed as input. Objective processing provides for controlling and filtering extraneous or distracting information. Thinking skills are vital to understanding and interpreting output. Meaningful feedback confirms what is communicated. Each part of the system must work if the system is to be successful.

Figure 2–2 shows how communication is infused throughout the super system, thereby serving as a network for all the subsystems. The commu-

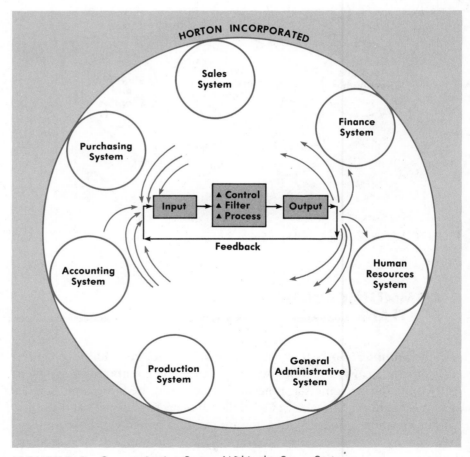

FIGURE 2–2   Communication System Within the Super System

nication system transforms information into communication much like the nervous system transforms nerve impulses into knowledge, action, or attitude.

Reasons for communicating vary, but people communicate to yield desired results. Ideally information is communicated as intended by the sender. Breaks or distortions in the communication of information can occur if any part of the communication system fails to work properly. These breakdowns can be costly. They can cause loss of time, money, and work as well as misunderstandings, injuries to team effort, and damage to morale.

Components of the Management Communication System

The focus of all human-to-human and machine-to-human communication is the human mind. The complexity of the human communication process can be appreciated by examining the basic components of the management communication system.

Input

Input comes to the conscious part of the brain from the external environment in the form of stimuli which activate the body's sensory systems. In the business environment, information is transmitted among people as oral, written, and nonverbal communication.

Input comes from the environment, including messages from other people.

Oral Input.   Oral input in business primarily consists of face-to-face or telephone communication. The face-to-face two-way situation is the best method of sending information because it allows the sender to make sure the receiver understands the message. Telephone communication is also very common in the business environment, but it is less effective than face-to-face communication because nonverbal cues are not visible.

Face-to-face and telephone communication are the main forms of oral input in business.

The primary skill used to improve oral input capability is listening. Listening skill development is explained in Chapters 3 and 4.

Written Input.   Written input consists of letters, memos, reports, manuals, and other documents. Written input is usually handwritten, typewritten, or printed. Since one-way written communication is read without the assistance of nonverbal cues and instant feedback, it is frequently necessary for the sender to clarify a written message with an oral explanation.

Written input can take a myriad of forms.

The primary skill used to improve written input capability is reading. Reading skill development is discussed in Chapters 9 and 10.

Nonverbal Input.   In face-to-face communication, at least half of a message's meaning is received as nonverbal input. Nonverbal communication, or communication without words, consists of facial expressions, gestures, voice fluctuations, and other means of signaling one's feelings. Nonverbal cues are powerful forms of communication input because they help to reinforce the accuracy of verbal messages.

Nonverbal communication is expressed in several ways:

1. Body language—Information sent by parts of the body.
2. Space—Messages communicated by the use of space.
3. Touch—Messages transmitted by touching.
4. Object language—Meaning communicated by different objects.
5. Time—Information transmitted by how time is used.
6. Sound—Meaning sent by the manipulation of voice and other sounds.
7. Color—Messages transmitted by different colors.
8. Smell—Information communicated by odors.
9. Taste—Meaning transmitted to the taste buds.

Nonverbal input is used to get a message across.

Process

Verbal and nonverbal inputs received from the external environment are processed by the brain. The primary processing phases are decoding and decision making.

Decoding.   The received message is changed from words, sounds, or nonverbal cues to mental images within the brain. In an effort to give meaning to the message, the brain supplements the new input with information previously stored in memory. This interpretational function of the brain is called *decoding.*

Since a person's senses are constantly bombarded by information, the mind automatically screens out unnecessary and unwanted data. Through personal experience and training, a person focuses on input data that are considered important and ignores other pieces of information. This mental process of interpreting information by focusing on some input and ignoring other input is called *filtering.*

Decoding is the process of deciding what a message really means.

Filtering means intentionally focusing on some input and ignoring other input.

Decision Making.   After a message has been interpreted, the receiver decides to either respond or not respond. If the receiver decides to respond, additional decisions are made concerning *what* to respond and *how*

The receiver decides either to respond or not to respond to a message.

to respond. The medium through which the response travels is called the communication *channel.* The channel may be a written memo, a sound wave, or a handshake.

The control component of the communication system is implemented during the decision-making phase. Output is controlled through the decision to respond or not respond and through the selection of a channel that may increase or decrease communication efficiency. The primary skills involved in improving input-processing capability are logical thinking and memory.

> The channel carries the sender's message to the receiver.
>
> Controls are implemented in the decision-making phase of the process stage.

Output

Output is the actual response to processed input. As soon as the message has been processed in the receiver's mind and a response is made, the original receiver becomes the new sender; the original sender becomes the new receiver. The major aspects of output are creation and feedback.

Creation of Output.   The muscle system is used by the sender to formulate a response into meaningful sounds, symbolic words or pictures, or nonverbal cues. This process of selecting or converting thoughts into a message is called *encoding.*

> Encoding means using the right words to reach the receiver.

Common forms of oral output in business are speaking face-to-face, dictation, telephone calls, teleconferencing, speeches, and meetings. Forms of written output include letters, memos, reports, manuals, handbooks, posters, and in-house newspapers. Forms of nonverbal output include facial expressions, body movements, and intentional silences.

Feedback.   Feedback, the response to a message, is the last step in the communication system and the first step in a new communication cycle. Feedback may include a verbal or written reply, a puzzled look, a raised eyebrow, a nod of acceptance, a smile, or silence. Feedback serves the critical need in the communication process of checking the results of one's message or one's response to a message. A crisp, candid explanation of the significance of feedback is offered by Staley:

> Feedback is used to evaluate the effectiveness of communicated ideas.

> Feedback is a relatively new term for an old phenomenon. A synonym for feedback could be "reaction," and there certainly isn't anything new about folks "reacting" to each other. So why all the fuss about "feedback"? The fuss concerns the philosophy that supports our reactions. The whole idea is that feedback should be given and received in such a way that we improve our communications. Unfortunately, for a great many of us, the basic idea of feedback is discomforting. As a rule, superior-subordinate relationships generate such a smoke screen of phony reactions that we find it a real challenge to close the communication loop.[2]

The primary skills used to improve output capability are speaking, writing, and gesturing. Speaking skill development is discussed in Chapters 5 through 8. Writing skill development is discussed in Chapters 11 through 17. Nonverbal skill development is interwoven throughout each of the four communication skills.

The communication system in a business must be ongoing if the business is to succeed. Roles among communicators change. One moment a sender might provide input; the next moment that sender might be the receiver of input or output from another sender. The continual nature of the system can change yesterday's output into today's input. Advances in communication technology make it possible for some changes to occur in minutes.

A strong system is built on strong individual components. A break can occur anywhere in the system, and in some cases, a break can have a domino effect in creating other breaks. Inferior or inadequate input can cause faulty processing, which in turn can produce meaningless or uninterpretable output.

Communication Climate

Organizational climate is linked to communication.

The related goals of high employee motivation and company success depend on the *climate* of the organization. Climate within a firm has a lot to do with communication. A company's climate or atmosphere affects the degree of openness with which people communicate. Climate is shaped in large part by management. Thus, the climate itself nonverbally communicates the availability, accessibility, and approachability of managers. As mentioned in Chapter 1, a manager's willingness to communicate reflects his or her leadership style—whether positive or negative. Likewise, climate is affected by a manager's leadership style. The upper portion of Figure 2–3 shows the benefits of a positive leadership style.

The by-products of a negative leadership style are also significant. The lower portion of Figure 2–3 depicts the relationship between a negative leadership style and poor communication. Managers can affect the climate within their respective work units. In essence, managers are responsible for setting the stage for practical, effective communication.

Barriers

Barriers to good communication can creep in despite the use of positive leadership styles and the fostering of a positive climate for communication.

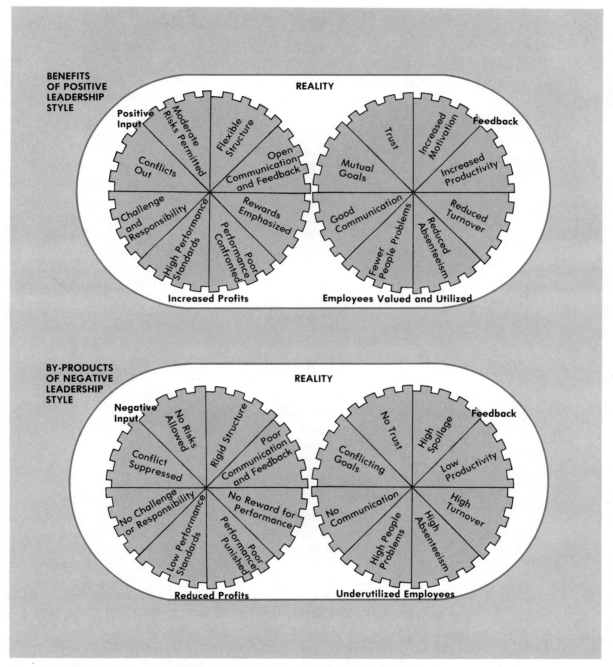

Source: Joan K. Cannie, *The Woman's Guide to Management Success: How to Win Power in the Real Organizational World* (Englewood Cliffs, NJ: Prentice-Hall, Inc., 1979), pp. 55, 57.

FIGURE 2–3   Influence of Leadership Styles on Communication Climate

Potential Barriers to Communication

External and internal factors can become barriers.

Managers are not solely responsible for good communication. External and internal factors also exist and can become *barriers.* These barriers tend to be controlled more by the communicator.

External factors exist outside and internal factors exist inside the sender and/or receiver.

External factors include organization structure, surroundings, circumstances, and communication resources such as hardware, software, and other office equipment. *Internal factors* exist within the sender and/or receiver. The "baggage" that people bring to a relationship are considered internal factors. Specific examples include prejudice, close-mindedness, lack of trust, and physical impairments. Frame of reference, selectivity in perception, retention, transmission, and serial communication can be major internal barriers to communication as well. *Frame of reference* pertains to a communicator's background or life experiences. *Selectivity in perception, retention,* and *transmission* involve a person's choosing what is perceived, retained, or transmitted. *Serial communication* occurs when several messages are grouped in a single message.

The nature of some messages can create barriers to communication. Consider the following examples:[3]

1. Mixed message—A message in which verbal and nonverbal communication or written and nonverbal communication conflict.
2. Sarcastic message—A taunting or ridiculing message.
3. Meta-talk message—A two-part message in which the preface, or first part, is used to make the second part more acceptable or the true message more credible.
4. Judging message—A message that projects discrimination, authoritative opinion, lack of approval, or disbelief through word choice or tone.
5. Incomplete message—A message that contains assumptions and hidden expectations.
6. *Should* message—A message that implies personal expectations.
7. Irresponsible message—A message in which the pronouns *it, you,* and *we* are used to express what *I,* the communicator, believe.
8. *But* message—A two-part message in which the first part is cancelled or diluted by the second part, or *but* portion, of the message.

Prevention and Elimination of Barriers

Barriers may cause conflict.

Some barriers lead to *conflict.* In such cases, managers should eliminate or encourage the elimination of barriers. Unfortunately some managers just try to eliminate conflict. But conflict can be an outgrowth of different or new ideas being generated. In such cases, conflict can start a search for change and make change more acceptable.[4] However, although conflict can lead to positive change, not all conflict is productive. It can also be detrimental or even devastating to the communication process. An example might be a dissatisfied worker who gets even by withholding valuable information.

Managers should analyze whether barriers or conflict need to be removed. Although managers influence climate, they have limited control over eliminating other external or internal factors that pose as barriers to the communication process. The major responsibility of removing barriers rests with the people who communicate.

Communication training can help workers to identify and eliminate barriers. On-the-job communication training should address the removal of barriers. Communicators should be trained to treat the causes of problems rather than just the symptoms. Communication skills grow, but they require continual practice and discipline. Periodic refreshers are appropriate for all communicators.

Managers serve as role models for their subordinates. It is important that managers be open-minded, clear, concise, accurate, and positive in their communication with others.

Communication training can eliminate barriers.

SUMMARY

Practical management communication is an open rather than a closed system; it does not exist in isolation. Communication can be the glue that connects the subsystems within a firm.

The main components of any system are input, process, ouput, feedback, and controls. Although the communication system may not always be tangible, it exists and contains all five components. Each part of the system must work if the system is to function properly. Breaks in the communication of information can be costly.

Information is transmitted by oral, written, and nonverbal communication. Oral input consists of face-to-face or telephone communication. Listening is a form of oral communication and is the primary skill used to improve oral input capability. Written input includes letters, memos, reports, manuals, and other media. Reading is also a part of written communication. The development of strong reading skills will enhance written input capability. Nonverbal input includes facial expressions, gestures, voice fluctuations, and other means of signaling one's feelings. They help to reinforce verbal messages.

Input is processed by the brain. Decoding and decision making are the major phases in processing information. The interpretational function of the brain is called decoding. The mental process of selecting, weighing, and ignoring input is called filtering. Message interpretation is followed by a decision to either respond or not respond. The decision to respond carries with it the selection of a channel for that response. Improvement of logical thinking and memory will yield improvement in processing capability.

Output is the product of processed input. Encoding is the process of selecting symbols to formulate a message. Output can be oral, written, or nonverbal. Feedback is both the last step in the communication system and the first step in a new communication cycle. Feedback enables the sender to check the results of a message or to evaluate the response to a message. Skills used to improve output capability are speaking, writing, and gesturing.

Roles among communicators change. As roles change, output may become input. Good communicators are aware of potential breaks in the communication system. They strive to maintain a positive climate in which workers can communicate.

External and internal factors that can become barriers to communication tend to be controlled more by the communicator. Senders should study the nature of their messages to avoid sending messages which are barrier oriented.

Managers should promote the elimination of barriers. Communicators need training to bring about continual growth. Some of the most valuable training occurs when managers assume responsibility as communication role models.

QUESTIONS

1. Describe the relationship that exists
   a. between a subsystem and a super system.
   b. among subsystems.
2. Explain how the communication system and other systems in an organization operate simultaneously.
3. Give an example of yesterday's output becoming today's input.
4. Contrast external and internal factors that could become communication barriers.

5. What should communication training include?

6. If every organization has a communication system like the one shown in Figure 2–2, why are so many organizations unable to achieve their desired goals?

7. In face-to-face communication, can one person transmit two messages simultaneously to another person? Explain.

8. At what point in the communication system in Figure 2–2 would the last communication breakdown occur? Explain.

9. What is the significance of feedback in the communication process at the interpersonal level?

10. Comment on this statement: "Output itself is not communication."

PROBLEM-SOLVING EXPERIENCES

1. Select an event that has received considerable news coverage in the past year. Prepare a brief report that includes (a) a description of the event and (b) specific references to communication problems involved.

2. Reflect on your affiliation with various organizations. Share occurrences you have witnessed in which conflict produced positive growth.

CASE 2–1

A year and a half ago, Rolf Carlson became acting division head of the Cotton Fabrics Division of Deltalite Corporation. Ordinarily the search for a permanent division head would have been completed by now; several employees are concerned about the delay. Rolf had been the protégé of the previous division head, Gloria Medina. Gloria retired after 27 years of service at Deltalite; 15 years as division head. Before she left, she wrote a memo to Fred Baker, the president, recommending Rolf as her replacement. Mr. Baker named Rolf as acting head but has not yet started the search for a permanent head. Rolf is expected to have an advantage in the selection process, if it ever takes place.

Some employees are concerned about Rolf's leadership style. He worked under Gloria for so long that he tends to do everything exactly as she did. He has not been able to solve some lingering efficiency problems and has been indifferent to modernizing equipment. Several employees see Rolf's continuing temporary status as a sign that the end is near.

Sales are off in cotton goods, and several workers are idle. The competition from polyester is stiff. A feasibility study on converting the plant to polyester production has been made, but the results have not been announced. Rumors have circulated that the whole plant may shut down rather than be renovated if profits do not improve. Even Rolf is wondering about his status.

1. Identify the kinds of communication used at Deltalite.

2. Can the climate be improved in Rolf's division? Defend your response.

3. Explain the power behind top management's nonverbal communication in this case.

ENDNOTES

[1] 1 Cor. 12:12, 14.

[2] H. A. Staley, *Tongue and Quill: Communicating to Manage in Tomorrow's Air Force* (3d ed.; Montgomery, AL: Air Command and Staff College, Maxwell Air Force Base, 1977), p. 99.

[3] Joan K. Cannie, *The Woman's Guide to Management Success: How to Win Power in the Real Organizational World* (Englewood Cliffs, NJ: Prentice-Hall, Inc., 1979), pp. 96–106.

[4] Joseph A. Litterer, "Conflict in Organization: A Re-Examination," *Academy of Management Journal*, Vol. 9, No. 1 (September, 1966), p. 179.

3

THE
IMPORTANCE
OF
LISTENING

When you complete this chapter, you should be able to:

▲ Define listening.

▲ Discuss the importance of listening as it relates to the communication skills of speaking, reading, and writing.

▲ Identify several cost-reducing benefits associated with good listening.

▲ Explain the three major types of listening: concentrated, attentive, and casual.

▲ Discuss the influence of nonverbal messages on listening.

The mastery of listening eludes some managers because listening is more qualitative than quantitative in nature: listening is intangible. Although it is the least researched and least understood communication skill, it provides the greatest potential for managerial success.

Managers who listen well stand out among their peers. They are better liked, and they wield greater influence than managers who possess average or poor listening skills.

▲ WHAT IS LISTENING?

Listening is more than just hearing; it involves discipline. The use of the word *discipline* in the definition of listening implies that listening is an acquired skill rather than an inherent skill. Good listeners train themselves to be attentive to verbal communication. Thus, listening requires both mental and physical preparation.

Mental preparation is needed because listening is a conscious act. A successful listener develops and practices a mind-set for listening just as a contending athlete develops a mind-set for a race. Mental obstacles and hindrances are identified and eliminated.

Likewise, physical preparation is important. Physical channels such as eye contact and hearing are cleared and prepared for receiving communication.

As shown in Figure 3–1, the listening process begins when speech sounds (in the form of sound waves) enter the ear of the listener. The listener then identifies and recognizes the speech sounds as words. The final stage in the listening process is translating the words into meaning. At this point, listening becomes more complex because the translation into meaning also involves memory and experience.

Listening is the process of converting sounds into meaning.

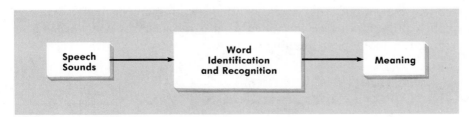

FIGURE 3–1 The Listening Process

▲ LISTENING AS A MANAGERIAL TOOL

Listening is one of the communication skills that ties together the tasks of planning, organizing, leading, and controlling—the tasks of managing people. Managing depends more on oral communication than on written communication. The effectiveness of oral communication depends on how well people speak and on how well they listen.

Relationship of Listening with the Communication System

Poor listening input leads to poor oral and written output.

The input-process-output components of the communication system are interdependent. Poor input can lead to faulty processing which, in turn, produces meaningless output. Research shows that the refinement of inputs results in improved forms of output and feedback.

Several factors influence listening.

Listening is one of the critical skills used to refine input capability. To enhance this capability, a program to improve one's listening skills must be conscientiously designed. When developing this program, a number of factors which influence listening must be considered:

1. Masking—Background noise or nearby conversation that may drown out the voice of the speaker.
2. Auditory analysis—The listener mentally compares the sounds heard with familiar sounds.
3. Mental reorganization—The listener employs a system that will aid retention, such as mentally rehearsing a word, name, or telephone number.
4. Rate of input—Messages that are received in sound units, such as words per minute.
5. Indexing—The listener mentally ranks and outlines the information received according to importance.
6. Sequencing—The listener mentally arranges the material received according to some logical sequence, such as the order of events.

Since the output skills of speaking and writing are no better than the quality of the input received, often what is mistaken for poor speaking or writing is actually poor listening or reading.

Relationship of Listening with Other Communication Skills

As early as 1926, research has established listening as a vital communication skill. Paul Rankin, a Detroit educator, selected 21 adults in 1926 and 47 adults in 1929, all of different occupations, and asked them to record on a log sheet, in 15-minute intervals, the amount of time spent talking, reading, writing, and listening. These observations were made over a 69-day period. Rankin found that the 68 adults spent an average of 9 percent of their communication time writing; 16 percent, reading; 30 percent, talking; and 45 percent, listening.[1]

The Rankin surveys show that oral communication skills (listening and speaking) account for 75 percent of a person's waking hours while written communication skills (reading and writing) account for only 25 percent of the time. The results of Rankin's work alerted educators for the first time to the importance of the listening skill.

During the spring of 1974, Weinrauch and Swanda surveyed 46 business personnel in the South Bend, Indiana, area. Thirty-eight of the respondents were business managers, including one in top-level management, 24 in middle management, and 13 in low-level management. The respondents were asked to keep a careful record (on a log sheet) of their time spent in communication during a typical workweek. Weinrauch and Swanda found that the respondents spent 19 percent of their communication time reading; 22 percent, writing; 26 percent, speaking; and 33 percent, listening.[2]

In terms of time consumed, research indicates that listening is the primary communication activity. In view of today's mass communication sources and tomorrow's far-reaching potential of communication technology, the amount of time spent in listening situations will most likely increase in the years ahead.

Research documents the need for effective listening. Yet for many people, listening remains the weakest link in the communication process. As shown in Table 3–1, a serious division exists between the need for developing effective listening skills and the actual amount of listening training received.

Research shows that listening is the dominant communication skill.

Most schools devote little attention to listening instruction.

Table 3–1   Communication Activities and Training

	Listening	Speaking	Reading	Writing
Learned	1st	2nd	3rd	4th
Used	Most (45%)	Next to most (30%)	Next to least (16%)	Least (9%)
Taught	Least	Next to least	Next to most	Most

Source: From Effective Listening: Key to Your Success, by Lyman K. Steil, Larry L. Barker, and Kittie W. Watson. Copyright © 1983 by Newbery Award Records, Inc. Reprinted by permission of Random House, Inc.

▲ LISTENING CONSEQUENCES AND REWARDS

History is filled with incidents where poor listening or not listening at all led to ill-fated consequences. For instance, poor listening was a contributing factor in the United States' involvement in World War II. Throughout 1941, Washington warned military commanders in Hawaii to expect aggressive action from Japan. Despite these warnings, the commanders failed to take steps to protect the United States Pacific Fleet at Pearl Harbor.

In the business world, poor listening may lead to the misunderstanding of critical plans and instructions. Efforts to improve one's listening skill or even to make managers and employees aware of the importance of effective listening should reduce communication costs and improve upward communication.

The Costs of Communication

The costs of communication are related to listening efficiency. Research by Nichols and Stevens shows that people listen at a 25 percent level of efficiency.[3] Thus, managers earning $60,000 a year who spend at least half of their working hours listening to people are paid half of their salaries, or $30,000, to listen. However, since the managers are effective listeners only 25 percent of the time, 75 percent of the $30,000, or $22,500, is paid for time spent listening ineffectively. Improving on-the-job listening skills will improve managerial performance and productivity.

When managers fail to listen effectively, the results can be costly.

The costs of communication are also related to the amount of paperwork generated. According to one estimate, 76 million letters are produced during a typical business day in the United States. For letters that are dictated face-to-face in the business office, the Dartnell Institute of Business Research in Chicago estimates the average cost of producing a business letter to be $8.52 for 1985.[4] For letters that are machine dictated or given to the secretary in rough-draft form, the cost of a letter drops to $6.22. Thus, the cost per day of writing business letters and memos exceeds $500 million. If improved listening skills resulted in a 20 percent reduction of written communication costs, about $100 million a day would be saved.

Poor listening skills increase the costs of generating paperwork.

Other cost-reducing benefits of good listening skills include

▲ Better use of time.
▲ Fewer mistakes.
▲ Improved work performance.
▲ Fewer complaints and grievances.
▲ Less stress in dealing with people.

Upward Communication _____

The flow of information from lower levels (employees) to higher levels (managers) is known as ***upward communication.*** Upward communication provides managers with feedback on the effectiveness of information sent downward; it also supplies managers with valuable information for making intelligent decisions.

Sources for upward communication include suggestion boxes, open-door policies, attitude surveys, and meetings. These communication sources are often ineffective because many employees are reluctant to say what is really on their minds. Upward communication is so poor in many firms that managers are not on the same communication level as the employees. The failure of upward communication is clearly noted in Table 3–2, which shows the results of a study in which both managers and employees were asked to rank ten factors leading to high job morale.

Another avenue for upward communication is relaying information through the human chain or the grapevine. Although this avenue has great potential, it seldom works well because the human communication chain is full of people who do not know how to listen. Refining manager and employee listening skills increases the possibility of improving upward communication channels in a firm.

Upward communication channels are ineffective in many firms.

Good listening skills improve upward communication.

▲ COMMON LISTENING PRACTICES ■■■■■■■■■■■■■■■■■■

Many people possess weak listening skills. A common characteristic among poor or weak listeners is "pretending" to hear; they pretend to be good listeners. Poor listeners may merely go through the motions of listening and at times mislead or deceive themselves. Thus, they may not always recognize their listening limitations. John Digaetani clusters weak listeners

Poor listeners may not recognize their listening deficiencies.

Table 3–2   What Do Workers Want from Their Jobs?

Morale Item	Ranking According to Managers	Ranking According to Employees
Good wages	1	5
Job security	2	4
Promotions and growth with company	3	7
Good working conditions	4	9
Interesting work	5	6
Management loyalty to workers	6	8
Tactful disciplining	7	10
Full appreciation for work done	8	1
Sympathetic understanding of personal problems	9	3
Feeling "in" on things	10	2

Source: Reprinted, by permission of the publisher, from "What Makes a Good Job?" by Lawrence G. Lindahl, *Personnel* (January, 1949), p. 265. © 1949 American Management Association, Inc. All rights reserved.

into five groups: the fidgeter, the aggressive listener, the pseudo-intellectual listener, the overly passive listener, and the inaccurate listener.[5]

Fidgeters are nervous listeners. They move or fidget while the sender transmits a message. Their restlessness is a barrier to communication. *Aggressive listeners* are so intent on receiving the correct message that they intimidate the sender. They project intense concentration. Concentration is a big part of good listening, but carried to the extreme, it impairs the flow of communication. *Pseudo-intellectual listeners* inhibit the sending of messages because they listen only to facts. They consider feelings and opinions of little value and, therefore, discourage a sender's interest in communicating. *Overly passive listeners* may be physically present to hear a message, but they are absent in spirit. They respond passively to a message. *Inaccurate listeners* alter the messages they receive. They are selective listeners; therefore, they do not retain the complete message.

According to Singleton, certain communication habits fuel poor listening. These habits are[6]

▲ Losing concentration.
▲ Criticizing speaker delivery.
▲ Prematurely judging a topic to be uninteresting.
▲ Avoiding difficult topics.
▲ Allowing distractions.
▲ Reacting to emotional words.
▲ Faking attention.
▲ Excessive outlining.

Good listeners avoid poor communication habits.

Listening can be affected by how the speaker delivers a message. Some speakers nurture poor listening by repeating a message until it is received. Thus, receivers may not feel obligated to listen to the message the first time if they know the message will be sent again. This is particularly true if instructions are being given. Speakers should avoid fostering poor listening by repeating messages.

▲ LISTENING REQUIREMENTS

Managers cannot be good communicators unless they are good listeners. Yet poor listening heads the list of major obstacles to effective management.[7]

Poor listening is an obstacle to good management.

Good listening requires **comprehension** and **retention.** A message does not become communication without comprehension. Retention is necessary if messages will be referred to or integrated with other messages in the future.

Comprehension transforms messages into communication.

Listening requirements vary depending on what is being communicated. The intensity with which one listens varies based on the expected or desired level of retention. People tend to listen more carefully if retaining the message is important. Unskilled or careless listeners make judgments about how important remembering a message will be before they start listening. They may know how closely they need to listen if the speaker's purpose or reason for speaking is known; however, this is not always the case. Speakers may have many reasons for talking, but they may not share that information in order of importance. Major points worth remembering may be embedded in less important thoughts or ideas. A wise listener understands that it is not easy to know in advance or to prejudge the value of what is to be communicated. Effective managers make such judgments as they listen rather than before the information is presented.

▲ TYPES OF LISTENING

The major types of listening are concentrated, attentive, and casual.

Concentrated Listening

Concentrated listening is sometimes referred to as critical listening or active listening. It involves concentration, analysis, synthesis, and evaluation. Concentrated listening draws upon memory and knowledge. It involves understanding and processing complex or abstract input into meaningful messages. Feedback such as questions and restatements enables the listener to clarify messages. A listener engaged in concentrated listening tries to retain the main idea and significant details of a message. Messages that require concentrated listening include contracts, status or progress reports, financial information, and the like.

Concentrated listening involves feedback.

Attentive Listening

Attentive listening resembles concentrated listening in that the main idea and the significant details of a message are retained. However, the subject matter to which a person listens is less complex or less abstract. Instead, the nature of the message is entertaining or interesting. Attentive listening requires less effort to be effective. Examples of messages that evoke attentive listening are avocational materials, personal letters, and the like.

Attentive listening requires less effort than concentrated listening.

Casual Listening

Casual listening or social listening[8] involves listening for overall content. Only the main idea or gist of a message is retained. Casual listening is popular among hearers because it is the least difficult kind of listening. Little evaluation skill is required. Examples of casual listening materials are sports-related information and greetings. People engage in casual listening to be pleasant, to pass time, to relax, and so forth.

Only the gist of a message is retained through casual listening.

Realistically managers do engage in communication that does not require concentrated listening. If only the gist of a message must be retained, a less-concentrated effort is needed. The typical listener has little difficulty in shifting from concentrated listening to casual listening. However, difficulty can be encountered when a message requires shifting from casual listening to concentrated listening. Ernest Fair suggests that managers listen closely and practice concentrated listening even when taking in casual comments. Why? Such comments can prove more valuable than responses to direct questions.[9]

▲ THE INFLUENCE OF NONVERBAL COMMUNICATION

Nonverbal communication complements speaking and listening. The nonverbal elements of body language, space, touch, object language, time, sound, color, smell, taste, eye contact, rate of speech, voice tone, silence, and posture are powerful—more powerful than verbal messages. Spoken messages are evaluated through nonverbal communication. However, nonverbal messages are complex to read because they occur in clusters rather than as isolated indicators.[10]

Nevertheless, nonverbal communication is valuable to the listener in confirming whether the speaker is sincere because speakers cannot mask nonverbal messages as easily as they can spoken messages. The expression "It is not *what* is said but *how* it is said that counts" is considered true. Since it is impossible to read the speaker's mind, nonverbal messages help the listener understand the real message that is being communicated.

Nonverbal communication enhances both speaking and listening.

"...Very concerned!"

Source: Reprinted with permission of THE SATURDAY EVENING POST Society, a division of BFL & MS, Inc. © 1984.

Speakers can also benefit from nonverbal messages. By observing the listener's nonverbal messages in conjunction with the verbal messages, speakers can determine whether their messages are understood.

SUMMARY

Listening is more than just hearing. It is an acquired skill that requires hearing plus discipline. It involves the development of a mindset that shuts out internal and external barriers. The listening process starts when speech sounds enter the listener's ear; the process continues as the listener identifies and recognizes the speech sounds as words. In the final stage, the listener translates the words into meaning. At this point, listening becomes more complex; it may also involve memory and experience.

Listening is a managerial tool that ties together the managerial functions of planning, organizing, leading, and controlling. A person's input and output capabilities can improve as a result of good listening.

Research shows that listening is the primary communication activity in terms of the time it consumes. Unfortunately some people never attain the level of listening skills that they really need. Poor listening habits can bring about costly consequences. They can lead to misunderstanding and misinterpretation. Improvement of on-the-job listening skills will improve managerial performance and productivity. Improved listening can also result in a reduction of written communication, and it can increase the quantity and quality of upward communication within a firm.

Even though possessing good listening skills is beneficial, many people possess weak listening skills; they do not recognize their listening limitations. Listeners and speakers need to monitor their communication habits so that bad listening habits can be eliminated.

Comprehension is an important part of good listening. Retention is also important if a message will be referred to or joined with other messages in the future. People tend to listen more carefully if messages are interesting or if retention is important to them. When possible, managers should decide the value of retaining messages as they listen rather than before they receive them.

People engage in three types of listening—concentrated, attentive, and casual. Concentrated listening involves understanding and processing complex or abstract input. A listener engaged in concentrated listening retains the main idea and major details of a message. Attentive listening involves understanding and processing entertaining or interesting input. Similar to concentrated listening, attentive listening includes the retention of the main idea and major details of a message. Casual listening involves understanding and retaining only the main idea or gist of a message.

Spoken messages are evaluated by nonverbal communication. Nonverbal communication benefits the listener by indicating the speaker's sincerity; it also benefits the speaker by helping to determine whether a message has been communicated properly.

QUESTIONS

1. At what point in Figure 3–1 would the last listening breakdown occur? Explain.

2. What is the significance of listening to management communication?

3. If you improved your listening skill by 50 percent, what personal benefits would you experience?

4. How do you account for the differences between managers and employees in ranking the ten job morale factors in Table 3–2?

5. What is meant by this statement: "Listening is more than just hearing"?

6. Contrast the behavior of an aggressive listener with an overly passive listener.

7. Describe several communication habits that fuel poor listening.

8. What are the requirements for listening? How do they relate to one another?

9. Define *concentrated listening*.

10. Can a speaker foster poor listening? Explain.

PROBLEM-SOLVING EXPERIENCES

1. Prepare a log sheet similar to the one shown here. Keep a record of your communication activities for one day. For every 15 minutes during a day place a check mark under the communication skill you are involved in at that moment. At the end of the day, determine the total time you spent listening, speaking, reading, and writing. Be prepared to discuss your observations in class.

Time	Listening	Speaking	Reading	Writing
8:00				
8:15				
8:30				
8:45				
9:00				
9:15				
9:30				

2. Observe and compile a list of the nonverbal communication used by your instructor during class.

CASE 3–1

Cy Jensen and Ellen Carpenter work together in the Finance and Materials Division of Capital Data. Cy is division chief and Ellen is his administrative assistant. Staff meetings for the Finance and Materials Division are held for one hour on a biweekly basis. In these staff meetings, ongoing projects and future plans are discussed.

Traditionally Mary Nell Kartt, division secretary, has been responsible for drafting the staff meeting minutes. Last month, Mary Nell injured her hip; she has been on sick leave for five weeks. In Mary's absence, Ellen has been delegated the responsibility of drafting the staff meeting minutes.

In her minutes of the last two staff meetings, Ellen tried to highlight the topics that were discussed. Ellen included detailed information in the opening and middle sections of the minutes, but the information in the closing section was so general that it bordered on being vague. Cy questioned Ellen about her lack of attention to the details discussed in the closing moments of both staff meetings. When confronted about the lack of detail in the last section of the minutes from both meetings, Ellen admitted that her listening skills were not what they could be. Cy encouraged Ellen to listen harder.

1. Speculate as to why Ellen has trouble listening during the staff meetings. Does her trouble focus on comprehension or retention?

2. Is Ellen's listening difficulty unique? Can her poor listening be detrimental?

3. What kind of listening should she practice during these meetings?

ENDNOTES

[1] Paul T. Rankin, "The Measurement of Ability to Understand the Spoken Language," *Dissertation Abstracts*, Vol. 12, No. 4 (1952), pp. 847–848; see also Paul T. Rankin, "Listening Ability: Its Importance, Measurement, and Development," *Chicago School Journal*, Vol. 12 (1930), pp. 177–179.

[2] J. Donald Weinrauch and John R. Swanda, Jr., "Examining the Significance of Listening: An Exploratory Study of Contemporary Management," *The Journal of Business Communication*, Vol. 13, No. 1 (Fall, 1975), pp. 25–32.

[3] Ralph G. Nichols and Leonard A. Stevens, "Listening to People," *Harvard Business Review*, Vol. 35, No. 5 (September–October, 1957), p. 85.

[4] The Dartnell Institute of Business Research, *Dartnell Target Survey* (Chicago: Dartnell Corporation, Spring, 1985).

[5] John L. Digaetani, "The Business of Listening," *Business Horizons*, Vol. 23, No. 5 (October, 1980), p. 42.

[6] John P. Singleton, "Managing Versus Management by Results," *Supervisory Management*, Vol. 22, No. 5 (May, 1979), p. 32.

[7] Ibid., p. 31.

[8] Digaetani, op. cit., p. 43.

[9] Ernest W. Fair, "Doorways to an Open Professional Mind," *Supervision*, Vol. 41, No. 2 (February, 1979), p. 15.

[10] I. George Parulski, "Silent Conversations: A Study of Nonverbal Communication," *Supervision*, Vol. 41, No. 1 (January, 1979), p. 7.

IMPROVING LISTENING SKILLS

4

When you complete this chapter, you should be able to:

▲ Evaluate your listening strengths and weaknesses.

▲ Explain how the speed differential between thinking and speaking inhibits good listening.

▲ Explain how internal and external distractions block effective listening.

▲ Explain how faking attention, a speaker's word choice, and physical factors influence listening ability.

▲ Describe the importance of the "Three *D's*" of good listening.

▲ List several aids for developing an appropriate listening mind-set and for controlling internal and external distractions.

The first stage to improving listening skills is to establish an awareness of the factors that affect listening ability. This awareness is achieved by identifying and analyzing one's good and bad listening habits. The second stage is to employ aids designed to eliminate or reduce the listening barriers that contribute to poor listening habits. A manager simply cannot afford to take her or his listening skills for granted. The development of good listening habits can mean the difference between a manager's success and failure.

Effective listening can be learned.

▲ LISTENING EVALUATION CRITERIA

To improve one's listening ability, a knowledge of good and bad listening habits is essential. *Listening habits* refer to the usual manner in which a person listens. These habits can be unconscious inclinations or acts. Through self-analysis and self-assessment, people can become more aware of their listening strengths and weaknesses.

Listening habits can be unconscious acts.

Self-analysis and self-assessment of listening habits do not have to be complex or involved. In general, listeners can measure their listening effectiveness by answering simple questions such as these:

Listening awareness involves self-analysis and self-assessment.

1. Do I desire to be a good listener?
2. Do I discipline myself to listen well?
3. Am I prepared to listen?
4. Do I listen or do I merely hear?
5. Do I consistently understand the messages to which I listen?
6. Do I properly interpret the messages to which I listen?
7. Do I practice good listening habits on a daily basis?

If listeners respond negatively to any of these questions, they need to take a closer look at their listening habits. Poor or weak listening habits can occur *before* one listens, *as* one listens, or *after* one listens.

Listeners should study their listening habits.

The Listening Inventory in Figure 4–1 is useful in identifying weak listening habits and indicating when those habits occur in the listening process. Ratings of 5 and 4 indicate that one's listening habits are above average to excellent. Ratings of 4 and 3 denote average to above average listening tendencies. A majority of 3 ratings indicates substandard listening. Ratings of 2 and 1 reveal a serious need for listening improvement.

The *listening process* involves three stages of listening activity: prelistening, actual listening, and postlistening. Some of the habits listed in the Listening Inventory occur in more than one stage of the listening process.

The listening process involves three stages: prelistening, actual listening, and postlistening.

LISTENING INVENTORY

Listening Habits	Always	Frequently	Sometimes	Infrequently	Never
Establishing an Appropriate Mind-Set Before Listening Begins					
1. Stop talking.	5	4	3	2	1
2. Concentrate.	5	4	3	2	1
3. Resist distractions.	5	4	3	2	1
4. Exercise mind—think.	5	4	3	2	1
5. Become interested.	5	4	3	2	1
6. Put the speaker at ease.	5	4	3	2	1
7. Avoid jumping to conclusions.	5	4	3	2	1
8. Control your emotions.	5	4	3	2	1
9. Understand yourself.	5	4	3	2	1
10. Build an awareness of factors that affect listening.	5	4	3	2	1
11. Decide the purpose for listening.	5	4	3	2	1
As Listening Occurs					
1. Maintain appropriate mind-set.	5	4	3	2	1
2. Concentrate.	5	4	3	2	1
3. Exercise mind—think.	5	4	3	2	1
4. Listen for purpose.	5	4	3	2	1
5. Listen to understand rather than to refute.	5	4	3	2	1
6. Listen for main ideas (if appropriate).	5	4	3	2	1
7. Listen for details (if appropriate).	5	4	3	2	1

FIGURE 4–1   Page 1 of Listening Inventory

LISTENING INVENTORY (Continued)

Listening Habits	Always	Frequently	Sometimes	Infrequently	Never
8. Listen for gist (if appropriate).	5	4	3	2	1
9. Limit talking to asking questions.	5	4	3	2	1
10. Judge content, not delivery.	5	4	3	2	1
11. Listen for ideas, not facts.	5	4	3	2	1
12. Control your emotions.	5	4	3	2	1
13. Take notes sparingly.	5	4	3	2	1
14. Resist internal and external distractions.	5	4	3	2	1
15. Take advantage of thinking speed.	5	4	3	2	1
16. Anticipate what will be said next.	5	4	3	2	1
17. Mentally summarize what has been said.	5	4	3	2	1
18. Watch for nonverbal communication.	5	4	3	2	1
19. Listen between the lines.	5	4	3	2	1
20. Weigh the evidence.	5	4	3	2	1
21. Avoid jumping to conclusions.	5	4	3	2	1
22. Respect others' ideas.	5	4	3	2	1
23. Acknowledge your feelings.	5	4	3	2	1
24. Empathize with the speaker.	5	4	3	2	1
25. Group large amounts of information.	5	4	3	2	1
26. Sort ideas to determine patterns of organization.	5	4	3	2	1
27. Review what should be remembered.	5	4	3	2	1
28. Listen inwardly—monitor your reactions.	5	4	3	2	1

FIGURE 4–1   Page 2 of Listening Inventory

LISTENING INVENTORY (Continued)

Listening Habits	Always	Frequently	Sometimes	Infrequently	Never
29. Avoid violating the speaker's personal space.	5	4	3	2	1
30. Stay on the appropriate listening level.	5	4	3	2	1
31. Maintain good eye contact.	5	4	3	2	1
32. Curb the impulse to interrupt.	5	4	3	2	1
33. Demonstrate patience with the speaker.	5	4	3	2	1
After Listening Occurs					
1. Concentrate.	5	4	3	2	1
2. Exercise mind—think.	5	4	3	2	1
3. Ask additional questions if necessary.	5	4	3	2	1
4. Weigh the evidence.	5	4	3	2	1
5. Mentally summarize what has been said.	5	4	3	2	1
6. Avoid jumping to conclusions.	5	4	3	2	1
7. Respect others' ideas.	5	4	3	2	1
8. Control your emotions.	5	4	3	2	1
9. Acknowledge your feelings.	5	4	3	2	1
10. Group large amounts of information.	5	4	3	2	1
11. Sort ideas to determine patterns of organization.	5	4	3	2	1
12. Review what should be remembered.	5	4	3	2	1
13. Accentuate the positive.	5	4	3	2	1

FIGURE 4–1   Page 3 of Listening Inventory

For example, "Exercise mind—think" is a listening habit that should occur before listening begins, as listening occurs, and after listening occurs. The entire listening process involves thinking intensively. Good listeners establish an appropriate mind-set for listening, listen, and then engage in listening follow-up activities.

Listening awareness starts with an analysis and assessment of personal listening habits; it proceeds to the study of those habits that can lead to listening barriers.

Listening requires thinking intensively.

▲ POTENTIAL BARRIERS TO EFFECTIVE LISTENING

A number of factors have a negative impact on listening. Some of these factors stem from the nature of the communication process. Some are related to the environment in which listening takes place. Some are within the listener.

Speaking Rate Versus Thinking Rate

One of the most important barriers to effective listening results from the fact that people think much faster than they talk. People speak at rates of around 125 words per minute.[1] No one knows for sure how the brain functions during the listening process, but most people think at speeds much higher than 125 words per minute.

People think faster than they talk.

People often read and understand at rates above 500 words per minute.[2] Also, research in the field of speech shows that people can comprehend and retain words spoken at speeds up to 350 words per minute.[3] If reading and speaking comprehension is used as a gauge for how fast thinking takes place, then it is clear that the mind is capable of dealing with words at extremely fast rates, perhaps at speeds measured in thousands of words per minute.

This difference between the low-speed speaking rate and the high-speed thinking rate tends to get the unskilled listener into trouble. While the speaker plods along, the listener's mind may go in different directions. Rather than paying attention to the speaker's message, the unskilled listener may begin to think about Saturday's football game, family and close friends, personal problems, and so on.

Bad listeners tend to daydream during a speaker's message.

How wisely one uses that spare thinking time which is available during the listening process is the key to better listening. Alert listeners use spare time to sort and summarize information that is received. They anticipate what will be shared next and prepare feedback such as clarification questions or statements of agreement.

Distractions

Distractions may be internal or external. Once in a while a listener may encounter only internal distractions or only external distractions, but usually the listener encounters both distractions at the same time.

Internal Factors

When the listener is preoccupied with inner psychological stresses caused by job-related or personal problems, effective listening seldom takes place. The mental gap that exists because people think faster than they talk works against the listener. As the mind begins to wander during a lecture, meeting, or conversation, the listener's thoughts may turn to an unfinished report or a friend in the hospital.

Poor management of stress and time have a negative impact on listening.

A listener's internal competition for attention is affected by poor time management. Failure to achieve greater control of time leads to procrastination and daydreaming. Tension and anxiety caused by procrastination and daydreaming quickly build up; then effective listening becomes almost impossible.

Internal distractions vary according to one's location, feelings, and condition. What is distracting to one person may not bother another person. While internal distractions do not lend themselves to simple solutions, they can be controlled or at least reduced through listener awareness and training.

External Factors

The home and the office are full of distractions that interfere with listening. Some of the external factors that have the potential for blocking effective listening are

Listening ability is affected by many external factors.

▲ Loud noises.
▲ Telephone interruptions.
▲ Drop-in visitors.
▲ Physical environment.
▲ Visual stimuli.

▲ Speaker's mannerisms and/or appearance.
▲ Speaker's vocal characteristics.

External interferences are a continuing problem to the listener. The first step in combating external distractions is to identify the potential factors for distraction in the listening situation. External distractions cannot be entirely eliminated; but like internal distractions, they can be managed through listener awareness and training.

Faking Attention _____

At one time or another, most people have pretended to listen to a speaker, when in fact their thoughts were miles away. Faking attention may happen in church, in the classroom, in business meetings, in face-to-face conversations, and so on. With eyes fixed on the speaker, a smile on the face, and an occasional nod of approval, the listener gives the impression of listening.

Faking attention is a common listening problem.

Problems arise when faking attention becomes a habit. The faker is always polite and usually hears what is being said, but seldom listens. While the speaker is talking, the faker tunes out, switches channels, and takes off on a mental trip.

The listener who fakes attention puts little energy into the communication process and receives nothing of value in return. Faking attention is a bad habit and a waste of time. The habit can be corrected, however, with hard work on the part of the listener.

Word Choice _____

Words are the tools of communication and thought. Although there are over 3 million words in the English language, the average person uses only about 500 words on a regular basis. Words that have multiple meanings are potential barriers to effective listening. A word can mean one thing to the speaker and something different to the listener. For example, jargon or special trade words are clear to members of the trade but may not be understood by others. Most listeners find it difficult to focus their attention on the main points of a message when the speaker uses words that are difficult to understand.

Word meanings can stand in the way of effective listening.

Listeners avoid messages that are difficult to understand.

Perhaps the most serious semantic problem associated with listening is when the speaker uses words that arouse fear or anger within the listener. Emotion-laden words such as redneck, abortion, nuclear bomb, Com-

Many people react to emotion-laden words and fail to listen to the message.

munist, Democrat, and Republican are just a few words that may stand in the way of effective listening. Because of deeply rooted stereotypes, prejudices, convictions, and experiences, a poor listener reacts to the words of the speaker, not the broader message. This listener's mind is busy planning a rebuttal to what is being said, devising a question for the speaker, or thinking about something not related to the speaker's message. Good listeners keep their minds open. They avoid evaluating a message until they have heard it completely.

Physical Factors

Physical barriers such as fatigue, illness, and hearing ability influence listening success.

Fatigue inhibits good listening.

During a normal day, all people have low and high periods of energy. Figure 4–2 shows the peaks and valleys of energy for a typical listener. During the low-energy periods, fatigue takes over and inhibits good listening.

Illness and pain inhibit good listening.

Illness can weaken one's ability to listen. It is difficult to be an attentive listener when one has a sore throat or toothache. In a sense, any type of illness or physical pain is classified as an internal distraction.

Hearing ability influences effective listening.

A person's ability to hear sounds accurately in daily communication situations is basic for listening effectiveness. Before listening can take place, speech sounds must be received and modified by the ear. Exposure to loud noises for long periods of time can result in a hearing loss. Even repeated exposure to sounds in the same frequency range can induce a temporary loss of hearing.

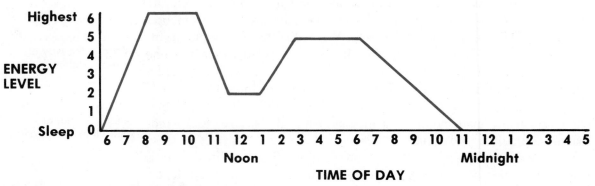

FIGURE 4–2   A Typical Listener's Energy Cycle

▲ AIDS FOR LISTENING IMPROVEMENT

Everyone likes a good listener. A good listener exemplifies the *"Three D's" of good listening:*

1. *Desire* to be a good listener.
2. *Discipline* to eliminate bad listening habits.
3. *Daily practice* of positive listening habits.

A good listener employs aids that eliminate or minimize potential listening barriers. The listening habits in Figure 4–1, Listening Inventory (pages 54–56), serve as listening aids in that they represent habits worth emulating. *Failure* to establish an appropriate mind-set, to listen at the appropriate level, to eliminate distractions, or to engage in listening follow-up can result in the development of bad listening habits.

The "Three *D's*" of good listening are desire, discipline, and daily practice.

Appropriate Listening Mind-Set

To be an effective listener, a specific mind-set must be developed prior to listening. *Listening mind-set* refers to one's mental attitude or disposition to listening. A good listener prepares to listen. Mental cobwebs are cleared, and the listener focuses on the sender and the purpose(s) for the sender's message. Although good listeners avoid prejudging the potential value of communication, they try to decide in advance the type of information they wish to get from the communication. Whenever possible, they determine the purpose(s) for listening, and they decide the type of listening that will be required.

Good listening requires preparation. A proper attitude toward listening is essential.

When possible, one's purpose(s) for listening should be determined prior to actual listening.

Source: © 1985 United Feature Syndicate, Inc. Charles Schulz.

Aids for developing an appropriate mind-set are as follows:

1. *Momentarily closing one's eyes* to symbolize the listener's desire to dispel thoughts or attitudes that might impair objective listening.
2. *Taking a deep breath* to relax and to prepare for listening.
3. *Deciding purpose(s) for listening when possible* to be ready to receive information that is important to the listener and to employ the proper type of listening.
4. *Smiling* to signal the sender that the listener is ready to receive information; to put the sender at ease.

Once an appropriate mind-set is developed, the listener is ready to listen.

Elimination of Distractions

The proper mind-set for listening can be impaired by internal and external factors.

Distractions affect the listening process. The development of an appropriate mind-set can be impaired by both internal and external factors.

Internal Factors

Internal factors vary among people. An internal factor that distracts one listener may not distract another. An example is one's ability to concentrate on a message and to block out personal problems. Personal problems affect people differently. One listener may be successful in blocking out personal problems, while another listener with a similar problem may be distracted. Some internal factors have greater distraction potential than others. Examples of internal factors that have a high distraction potential are prejudice, close-mindedness, lack of trust, physical impairments, and age. Aids for minimizing potential internal distractions include the following:

1. *Understanding one's own position* to control identified personal prejudices.
2. *Concentrating on the speaker's point of view* to expand one's insights and knowledge; to reinforce interest in information that is shared.

External Factors

Most external factors are easier to control than are internal factors. External factors exist outside the sender and receiver. Aids for controlling external factors include the following:

1. *Limiting background noise* to create a positive setting for communication.
2. *Positioning one's self close to the speaker* to improve verbal and nonverbal message reception (but far enough away to avoid violating the speaker's personal space).

3. *Looking only at the speaker* to maintain concentration and to demonstrate continued interest.

Listening Follow-Up

Generally communication is at least a two-person process. The speaker is responsible for organizing and sending messages that are understandable; the listener is responsible for receiving and organizing messages so that they are understood. The communication process should not end until the listener clearly understands the message(s). The organization of received messages occurs *while* the receiver listens and *after* listening occurs. Thus, listening follow-up is needed to complete the listening process. **Listening follow-up** relates to the component of the communication system in which information is processed, filtered, and interpreted. The most important aid to successful listening follow-up is *recognizing* that listening follow-up is an important part of the listening process.

Follow-up completes the listening process; it involves filtering and interpretation.

SUMMARY

Awareness is an important part of listening improvement. Analyzing and assessing one's listening habits can yield insights to where the listener needs improvement. A listening inventory or other valid evaluation device should be used periodically to identify weak listening habits.

Numerous factors have a negative effect on listening. Major factors that could impair listening effectiveness include failure to take advantage of one's thinking rate, distractions, faking attention, word choice, and physical factors. Alert listeners recognize their ability to think faster than a speaker can speak. They understand that spare thinking time can be used to sort and summarize information that is received. They also anticipate what will be shared next and prepare feedback such as clarification questions or statements of agreement.

Good listeners understand how internal and external distractions can be monitored and controlled. They recognize that faking attention is easy and potentially habit forming and that it inhibits effective listening. They understand that words are the tools of communication and thought and that some words evoke emotional reactions.

Physical barriers such as fatigue, illness, and hearing ability influence listening. Effective listeners strive to understand and work around these barriers.

Successful listeners practice the "Three D's" of good listening. First, they *desire* to listen effectively. Second, they *discipline* themselves to eliminate bad listening habits. Third, they *daily practice* positive listening habits.

Successful listeners establish an appropriate listening mind-set by cancelling thoughts or attitudes that impair listening. They ready themselves for listening by relaxing and deciding their purpose(s) for listening. Although they avoid prejudging the potential value of communication, they do predetermine the proper type of listening to be employed. Good listeners put the sender at ease and signal their readiness to listen by smiling.

Actual listening is made easier by eliminating distractions. Good listeners minimize potential internal distractions by understanding their own position and personal prejudices and by concentrating on the speaker's point of view. Limiting background noise, standing or sitting near the speaker, and maintaining good eye contact allow good listeners to reduce external distractions.

Effective listeners not only recognize the importance of developing a proper listening mind-set and practicing positive habits during actual listening, but they also appreciate the importance of listening follow-up. They use follow-up time to filter and interpret communication.

QUESTIONS

1. Define *listening habit*.
2. Describe the two parts of listening awareness.
3. What are the three stages of listening activity?
4. What is the most important aid to successful listening follow-up?
5. Why is it important for listeners to decide in advance their purpose for listening?
6. How does the failure to use time wisely contribute to poor listening?
7. Explain this statement: "Not all hearing involves listening."

8. People think several times faster than they speak. How does the speed differential between thinking and speaking create problems for the unskilled listener?

9. How does one's energy cycle relate to improved listening?

10. Explain this statement: "Poor listeners react to the words of a speaker rather than to the intended message."

PROBLEM-SOLVING EXPERIENCES

1. Prepare a chart similar to the one in Figure 4–2 showing your energy level during a typical day.

   a. At the specific hour along the curve, write the major activities that require your concentrated listening.

   b. Compare your energy level chart with your major listening activities. How might you arrange your daily schedule so that you are using your peak energy times for your most important listening activities?

2. For an entire day make a conscious effort to determine the purpose(s) for listening prior to actually listening. Prepare a brief summary of your listening purpose(s).

CASE 4–1

Brandon is a receptionist for Southeastern Steel. His office is in the lobby of the main plant. His office has a glass wall with a splendid view of the grounds. Unfortunately this wall admits noise from the heavy cranes outside.

In addition to greeting visitors, handling inquiries, locating people, and giving directions, Brandon also collects information and writes articles for the plant newspaper. People often call him or stop by his office to tell him their stories. Occasionally they bring written notes for an article, but almost never a completed story. Brandon enjoys his newspaper, both writing articles and talking with co-workers. However, it gets hectic when there are lots of visitors, particularly as the deadline for the newspaper approaches. Recently Brandon has been working a lot of overtime because one of the other receptionists has been on maternity leave.

Department heads have started complaining about inaccuracies in some of the newspaper articles, particularly in the descriptions of plant modernization and new equipment purchases. One manager has complained that Brandon "couldn't have been listening" when she "clearly explained" the performance capabilities of the new computer system. According to the manager, the facts were reported correctly, but some terms were confused and the article totally missed the point on the implications for smoother plant operation.

As manager of employee relations, you are responsible for the company newspaper.

1. How can you help Brandon improve his listening skills?
2. What are the possible barriers to his listening?
3. Which barriers to listening can you or the company help control?
4. How can you help Brandon control these barriers to listening?

ENDNOTES

[1]Ralph G. Nichols and Leonard A. Stevens, "Listening to People," *Harvard Business Review*, Vol. 35, No. 5 (September–October, 1957), p. 87.

[2]Stanford E. Taylor, "Listening," What Research Says to the Teacher Series, (Association of Classroom Teachers of the National Education Association, 1964), p. 13.

[3]Sara W. Lundsteen, *Listening: Its Impact at All Levels on Reading and the Other Language Arts* (Urbana, IL: National Council of Teachers of English and ERIC-Clearinghouse on Reading and Communications Skills, 1979), p. 33.

CHAPTER

THE
IMPORTANCE
OF
SPEAKING

When you complete this chapter, you should be able to:

▲ Describe the speaking process and the relationship of speaking with other managerial communication skills.

▲ Discuss the crucial role of speaking in the advancement or promotion of managers.

▲ Compare and contrast the major types of and approaches to speaking.

▲ Discuss the impact of nonverbal cues on the spoken message.

▲ Identify the potential barriers inherent in every speaker-receiver situation.

Managers spend a large part of each workday speaking and listening to individuals and groups. Skill in using the spoken word helps managers cope with personal problems, convey information, change a listener's attitude or behavior, and otherwise interact with people. Effective oral communication, however, does not happen by chance. Every speaking situation has built-in barriers that may produce a communication breakdown. The key to successful oral communication may be the manager's ability to control these potential barriers.

▲ WHAT IS SPEAKING?

Speaking involves the exchange of thoughts, opinions, or information from one person to another through the use of spoken words and nonverbal signals. Speaking implies gaining understanding and building motivational appeals among listeners. In the broadest sense, speakers inform, persuade, or entertain.

Speakers inform, persuade, or entertain.

Speaking as a Managerial Tool

The success of athletic coaches is measured in large part by the success of their teams. Likewise, the success of managers is based upon their ability to obtain a high level of output from workers. Effective managers are able to stimulate action and to gain understanding and cooperation from workers. They are aware that speaking plays a vital role in their day-to-day success as managers.

Speaking is an important managerial tool.

Speaking effectiveness begins with a knowledge of the speaking process and an understanding of the relationship of speaking with other communication skills.

The Speaking Process

Speaking is a subsystem of the input-process-output communication system described in Chapter 2. Figure 5–1 shows a general model of the speaking process. The model highlights the five main components of speaking: sender, message, channel, receiver, and feedback.

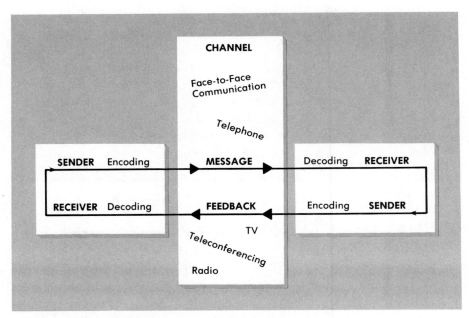

FIGURE 5–1   General Model of the Speaking Process

Relationship with Other Communication Skills

Business managers spend the major part of each workday in communication activities: listening, speaking, reading, and writing. A joint study of 20 job functions conducted by the Administrative Management Society and Drexel University revealed that managers ranked oral communication—speaking and listening—as both their most important and most enjoyable job function.[1]

Most managers prefer oral communication.

The actual amount of time spent in oral communication varies depending upon the manager's job and level in the firm. In general, top-level managers devote a greater portion of their time to oral communication than do lower-level managers.

Top-level managers spend more time in oral communication activities than do lower-level managers.

Speech communication is most often equated with public speaking. Despite the public relations value of speaking outside the organization, managers must not overlook the vital role of speaking within the firm. Speaking in a business context is not limited to presenting an oral message to an audience; it also includes interacting formally and informally in face-to-face and small group situations.

▲ SPEAKING REWARDS AND CONSEQUENCES

In the business world, managers quickly learn that the effective use of oral communication will enhance career opportunities. Research shows that speaking and listening skills play a crucial role in the advancement or promotion of managers.[2]

A successful manager will structure spoken messages to encourage certain responses from receivers. The manager who is a skilled oral communicator will obtain various rewards. A promotion, for example, usually results in increased job responsibility, higher salary, and increased status and self-esteem. These rewards provide the manager with a higher degree of career and job satisfaction. Job success at one level in the chain of command may also increase the manager's promotional opportunities.

> Speaking skills provide a major means of attaining rewards in a firm.

Since good speaking skills are essential to managerial success, the manager with poor speaking skills will probably not receive promotions to higher-level jobs in the firm. A loss of promotional opportunity more than likely means a loss of financial gain. More important, the manager's power and status within the firm may diminish. Any perceived loss of prestige will probably affect the manager's self-confidence and self-respect. Also, many firms will replace a manager who is considered not promotable.

▲ TYPES OF SPEAKING

Spoken communication is classified by the number of people involved in the communication process. The two types of spoken communication are speaking to one person and speaking to a group. The number of people involved and their relationship affect how and what people communicate.

In business and industry, people use spoken communication for a variety of reasons. Examples include

- ▲ Giving instructions.
- ▲ Motivating workers.
- ▲ Handling complaints, grievances, negotiations, and conflicts.
- ▲ Disciplining workers through verbal reminders and reprimands.
- ▲ Informing people of new data or the current status of a situation.
- ▲ Demonstrating procedures.
- ▲ Discussing plausible plans or alternatives and solutions to problems.
- ▲ Deciding a course of action.

Managers may engage in both types of spoken communication during the course of a workday; they may speak with others face-to-face or through an intermediary device such as a telephone.

Person-to-Person Speaking

The bulk of a manager's on-the-job speaking is done with one person at a time and is referred to as *person-to-person speaking.* On the surface, person-to-person speaking may seem easy, but it requires just as much planning and attention as speaking to a group. Often people are more comfortable or less nervous when talking one-on-one because they have fewer eyes and ears focused on them. Person-to-person speaking offers an opportunity for quick feedback.

Person-to-person speaking can offer quick feedback.

Person-to-Group Speaking

Managers frequently communicate in group situations. This type of speaking is referred to as *person-to-group speaking.* The size of a group may range from small to large. Committees, departments, divisions, and task forces are examples of work groups that exist for the purpose of achieving common goals. Person-to-group speaking becomes more one-sided as the size of the group increases. Speaking to large groups or audiences generally provides fewer chances for interaction than does speaking to one person or a small group. Speaking to a massive audience is commonly called *public speaking.* As with person-to-person speaking, the major purposes of speaking to groups are to inform, persuade, or entertain.

Person-to-group speaking may involve either a small or a large group.

▲ APPROACHES TO SPEAKING

The basic theme of a message affects how the message should be conveyed. Speakers may use either a direct or an indirect approach to share a message. The approach used is based on anticipated listener reaction to the message. If a speaker anticipates a listener's reaction to be favorable or neutral, a direct speaking approach is used. An indirect speaking approach is used to share a message for which the anticipated listener reaction is unfavorable.

Direct Approach

A *direct approach* to speaking is used when sharing a positive or routine message. The main theme or idea of the message is in the opening statement. Essential details follow the main idea; the main idea may be restated at the end of a message.

The direct approach is used to convey positive messages.

Indirect Approach

An unpleasant or negative message can displease a listener. If an unpleasant idea is in the opening statement, a listener might stop listening before the complete message is given. Therefore, the *indirect approach* is used whenever unpleasant news must be given. The message begins with a neutral opening, or buffer. Reasons for the unpleasant news are given before the unpleasant idea or theme. The unpleasant idea is sandwiched between a buffer and a positive closing that provides even more cushioning.

The indirect approach is used to convey negative or unpleasant messages.

▲ THE INFLUENCE OF NONVERBAL COMMUNICATION

Nonverbal cues are an important aspect of all spoken communication; they may clarify, confirm, confuse, cloud, or contradict spoken messages. They may also positively or negatively affect the speaker's credibility in the eyes of the audience. In some cases, the nonverbal communication may have a stronger impact than the content of the spoken message.

As mentioned in Chapter 3, messages can be clarified nonverbally in several ways. The speaker's hands can draw a picture to show the size, shape, or relative position of the objects being discussed; the speaker's hands can also clarify the sequence of events. Whole body movements can be used to act out the sequence being discussed. Descriptions can be made more vivid by nonverbal cues; for example, a speaker's swaying could enhance the description of a roller coaster ride. Facial expressions and vocal tones clarify and confirm by adding emphasis to important points; these cues help listeners grasp the organization and relative importance of different parts of a message.

A speaker must control nonverbal cues to avoid confusing a message. Jittery, uncoordinated motions divert a listener's attention from a message.

Nonverbal cues must be controlled.

Body movements that are out of sync with the speaker's prose may cloud a topic. Monotones and poker faces deprive the listener of nonverbal cues that indicate the importance of ideas, thus making listening more work.

Similarly, nonverbal cues can contradict a spoken message. An example of this is the employee who frowns when congratulating a co-worker for receiving an award.

Nonverbal cues help shape the speaker's credibility, particularly when the speaker is not well known by the listener(s). Society has many role/appearance expectations. The concept of stereotypes is not in vogue, but expectations exist. People do not expect an international banker to wear a sweatshirt and faded jeans. A scowl or gruff demeanor looks out of place on a public relations expert. One might question whether a mechanic with clean fingernails really does engine work.

The speaker's level of conformity to the audience's expectations either enhances or damages credibility. Some thought should be given to the audience's expectations and to the image the speaker wants to project.

Eye contact helps establish a bond between speaker and listener. Without it, listeners may decide that they are not the intended audience and stop listening. Eye contact should be natural; stares make people uncomfortable. Darting or diverted eyes are seen by many as a sign of dishonesty. Focusing on the floor or reading notes leaves listeners out of the conversation.

▲ POTENTIAL BARRIERS TO SPOKEN COMMUNICATION ━━━━━━━

Numerous factors can become barriers to spoken communication. Table 5–1 depicts common potential barriers. Potential barriers to spoken communication include internal factors within the speaker and/or listener, external factors outside the communicators, and factors which are both internal and external in nature.

Controllable Internal Barriers ━━━━━━━━━━━━

Some internal barriers can be controlled.

The speaker can control several internal factors which can become barriers to spoken communication. These are inappropriate use of buzz words, jargon, or acronyms; unclear purpose; lack of preparation; ineffective delivery style; too much time used to communicate a message; insufficient

Table 5–1   *Speaker's Control of Potential Barriers
to Spoken Communication*

Potential Barrier	Type of Barrier	Controllable (by speaker)
Inappropriate use of buzz words, jargon, or acronyms	Internal	Yes
Unclear purpose	Internal	Yes
Lack of preparation	Internal	Yes
Ineffective delivery style	Internal	Yes
Too much time used to communicate message	Internal	Yes
Insufficient similarity or background between/among communicators	Internal	Limited
Weak speaker credibility	Internal	Limited
Poor eye contact	Internal/ External	Yes
Inappropriate physical distance between communicators	External	Yes
Poor timing in communicating message	External	Yes
Improper approach used to convey message	External	Yes
Too little time used to communicate message	External/ Internal	Limited

similarity or background between or among communicators; and weak speaker credibility.

Buzz words or **jargon** refers to the specialized language of a trade or professional group. **Acronyms** refer to a word formed from the first letters of a name such as AMA for American Management Association. Appropriate use of acronyms occurs when both the speaker and the listener understand the meaning of a particular word. However, the use of buzz words and acronyms can become a barrier to spoken communication if the listener does not understand the words the speaker has used. Speakers should avoid using buzz words or acronyms to impress listeners. Excessive use of such words can alienate speakers from their audiences.

Source: © 1984 Newspaper Enterprise Association, Inc. Bob Thaves.

Speakers who start talking without a clear purpose can waste their time and the time of others. Wise speakers identify their purpose for speaking, organize their messages, and determine an appropriate style of delivery. Wise speakers also safeguard against taking too much time to convey a message. They realize that listeners grow weary when message delivery takes too long.

Parallel perceptions or similar backgrounds aid oral communication because they enable speakers and listeners to communicate more effectively. Likewise, insufficient similarity between communicators may impair communication. Speakers can exert little control over speaker/listener similarity. Limited control is possible, however, if speakers choose to communicate with people of similar backgrounds, experiences, interests, and attitudes.

Limited control can also be exerted with the barrier of weak speaker credibility. Speakers can identify their purpose, prepare and deliver their messages well, and still experience weak credibility if major differences exist between the speakers and the listeners. Speaker preparation can facilitate credibility, but it cannot ensure credibility. Whenever possible, speakers should try to use differences to their advantage. Explaining how varied opinions provide diversity is an example of how a speaker can benefit by using differences.

Controllable External Barriers

Several external barriers are controllable.

Inappropriate physical distance between communicators, poor timing in communicating a message, and use of an improper approach to convey a message are external barriers that can be controlled by speakers.

The physical distance between communicators can be adjusted so that speakers and listeners feel comfortable. The timing of a message is another controllable barrier that can be critical. Speakers should control timing to enhance listener reception. A manager who gives instructions for an assignment at the beginning of a workday rather than just before lunch or just before closing time is using controlled timing. The approach used to convey a message is an external factor since it is based upon the nature of the message. Speakers should shape messages based upon anticipated listener reaction.

Mixed Barriers

Speaker and listener eye contact is important to spoken communication. Eye contact allows the speaker to project sincerity in delivery; it enables the speaker to determine whether the listener understands the message. Poor speaker eye contact is an internal barrier; however, poor listener eye contact is an external barrier. Speakers cannot control listener eye contact, but they can encourage listener eye contact by practicing it themselves.

Spending too little time to share a message does not fit neatly as an internal or an external barrier, but it can be both. The speaker has limited control over too little time used to communicate a message. A rushed speaker, however, can slow down to avoid rushing message delivery or glossing over information.

At times, speakers are confronted with situations in which only small amounts of time can be spent on communication. Consequently, message format and delivery may be less than desirable. An example of this is a manager who has only one hour in which to proofread, edit, and mail a document. In his or her haste, the manager may be gruff in giving correction instructions because of the limited time factor.

SUMMARY

Speaking is an important managerial tool. It is a quick and effective method for communicating ideas. Speakers inform, persuade, or entertain. Managers spend much of their time in oral communication, either speaking or listening. Speaking skills are critical in determining a manager's effectiveness and personal success.

Much of a manager's oral communication is person-to-person. Person-to-group speaking is also an important part of a manager's job. The direct approach—the main idea appears early in the message—is used to convey a positive message. The indirect approach—the main idea is buffered by preliminary comments and supporting data that appear before the main idea—is used to send unpleasant messages.

Nonverbal cues are an integral part of the communication process. They should be planned and controlled to enhance communication. Nonverbal cues result from body position and movements, facial expressions, overall appearance, and voice tone. Good eye contact is critical to holding an audience's attention.

Several barriers to effective communication can occur. Some are beyond the speaker's control, but others are controllable. Speakers should plan ahead when possible. They should identify their audience and consider their audience's interests when planning a delivery style. Messages should be organized so that the purpose is clear and the major points are in logical order. Good eye contact, appropriate physical distance between communicators, and the limited use of jargon, buzz words, and acronyms will encourage receivers to listen. Speakers should be sensitive to the effect that timing has on message reception. They should consider the amount of time available or desired for communication. It is possible to spend too little time as well as too much time conveying a message.

QUESTIONS

1. What is meant by this statement: "Speaking is a powerful tool for action"?

2. At what point in Figure 5–1 would the last speaking problem occur? Explain.

3. Why should speakers avoid using buzz words in a message?

4. What types of rewards can a manager who possesses good speaking skills expect to obtain in an organization?

5. What are the possible consequences associated with a manager who has poor speaking skills?

6. Contrast the two types of speaking.

7. Identify three reasons for spoken communication in business and industry.

8. Why are some people more comfortable speaking one-on-one?

9. When is a direct speaking approach used?

10. When is an indirect speaking approach used?

PROBLEM-SOLVING EXPERIENCES

1. During your next meal with someone, analyze the speaking approaches used. Be prepared to share your findings with the class.

2. After being assigned to a group of eight to ten students, have one person in the group write a two- or three-sentence message. Ask that person to whisper the message to a member of the group; then pass the message along from one person to the other. Have the last student in the group repeat the message aloud. Compare this message to the original message. Discuss the results.

CASE 5–1

Mary Nell Meadows is orientation director for all new personnel at Southern Logo. She has been with the company for 12 years and knows her job. Mary Nell's primary responsibilities involve acquainting new employees with the physical layout of the plant, the fringe benefit package, and personnel policies.

The job of orientation director has become "old hat" for Mary Nell; therefore, she uses buzz words and acronyms during orientation sessions. Few new employees ask for clarification of the terms Mary Nell uses for fear of appearing uninformed or ignorant in front of Mary Nell and the other new employees. Instead, new employees tend to call and ask questions of Jim Snyder, the personnel director. Jim does not mind responding to occasional questions. Lately, however, he has received several calls asking for clarification of the R & D Comp-Time Program. When Jim discussed the matter with Mary Nell, she was at a loss as to why the employees failed to pick up the information in their orientation session. She concluded that new employees are not as sharp as they used to be.

1. What is the apparent cause(s) for Jim receiving calls concerning the R & D Comp-Time Program? What other aspects of Mary's presentation may be causing a communication breakdown?

2. How can the situation be improved?

3. When, if ever, is it appropriate for Mary Nell to use buzz words and acronyms?

ENDNOTES

[1]Donald W. Jarrell, "Administrative Managers Profiled in Study," *Management World*, Vol. 11, No. 10 (October, 1982), p. 19.

[2]G. W. Bowman, "What Helps or Harms Promotability," *Harvard Business Review*, Vol. 42, No. 1 (January–February, 1964), pp. 6–26; also see J. C. Bennett, "The Communication Needs of Business Executives," *Journal of Business Communication*, Vol. 8, No. 3 (Spring, 1971), pp. 3–11.

6

PERSON-TO-PERSON SPEAKING

When you complete this chapter, you should be able to:

▲ Discuss the major purposes of person-to-person speaking and the types of messages that are sent.

▲ Describe the positive features, potential limitations, and strategies for the improvement of face-to-face speaking.

▲ List the techniques designed to increase the effectiveness of telephone speaking.

▲ List the practices designed to increase the effectiveness of machine dictation.

Spoken communication is powerful. The masterful use of language has changed the course of history. Through the spoken word, images are created, emotions are touched, and listeners are stimulated to action.[1] Conversely, the careless or improper use of language can impair or misdirect listener action.

▲ NATURE OF PERSON-TO-PERSON SPEAKING

Person-to-person speaking is a two-way process.

Face-to-face speaking involves two people in one another's presence.

An electronic device joins communicators in intermediary speaking.

Channel selection can affect the power or impact of a message. Rather than choose a channel that makes delivery easy, managers should choose the route and medium which best suit message reception. Person-to-person channels are the best means for conveying most messages. These channels are superior to other channels because the intended receiver gets the message firsthand from the sender; the message does not pass through any middle people. Person-to-person speaking refers to two people communicating with one another by speaking.

There are two kinds of person-to-person speaking: face-to-face speaking and intermediary speaking. *Face-to-face speaking* refers to two people conversing while in one another's presence. *Intermediary speaking* refers to two people separated by distance conversing through an electronic device. The device serves as a means (or intermediary) for joining the communicators so that they can speak person-to-person. An example of intermediary speaking is an employee in Cincinnati talking on the telephone with a superior in Atlanta.

Purposes for Person-to-Person Speaking

The initial speaker starts a conversation.
The feedback speaker responds to the initial speaker.

Managers may use person-to-person channels when speaking with superiors, peers, and subordinates. These channels are conducive to the fulfillment of the three major purposes of communication: to inform, to persuade, and to entertain. While fulfilling these purposes, speakers may assume one of two roles. They may serve as the *initial speaker,* the person who initiates conversation, or as the *feedback speaker,* the person who responds or reacts to a message. Regardless of how communication is directed in an organization—vertically or horizontally—the initial speaker tends to control the conversation and assumes responsibility for ending the conversation.

Speaking to Inform

People may assume the role of an initial speaker or a feedback speaker when speaking to inform. Person-to-person *speaking to inform* pertains to sharing information with or obtaining information from another. For example, a manager who visits employees in their respective offices and describes what is expected of them is acting as an initial speaker who initiates conversations to inform. Another example of a manager sharing information with an employee occurs when the employee calls the manager and asks for a clarification of job expectations. In this instance, however, the manager assumes the role of feedback speaker. A job applicant and an employer conversing about a job opening could each assume the roles of initial speaker and feedback speaker; they both give and obtain information.

People either give or obtain information when speaking to inform.

Speaking to Persuade

Person-to-person *speaking to persuade* involves selling an idea, goods, or services. When speaking to persuade, a speaker attempts to influence the listener's thinking. The power of a persuasive message is dependent upon proper message construction and delivery. Persuasion is achieved when the speaker methodically constructs and delivers the message. The word *persuasion* denotes possible resistance. Thus, the indirect approach should be used to gradually shape the listener's thinking. A listener is less inclined to being persuaded if the speaker rushes the message or if the speaker delivers the message in an arrogant, overly confident way. To persuade a superior to accept an innovative marketing strategy, a speaker should prepare and deliver the message using the indirect approach. First, the speaker should introduce the topic in an interesting way. Second, the speaker should present evidence showing the inadequacies of the current strategy and the benefits of another strategy. Third, the speaker should recommend the acceptance of a new strategy.

Speaking to persuade involves selling an idea, goods, or services.

Speaking to Entertain

Successful *speaking to entertain* amuses the listener. Some of the underlying or hidden motives for person-to-person speaking to entertain include improving self-concept, deprecating one's self, gaining acceptance or approval, being polite, covering up inadequacies or incompetence, diverting attention, easing tension, and filling time. An example of speaking to entertain is a subordinate and manager swapping jokes while waiting for a meeting to start. Although managers occasionally speak to entertain,

Speaking to entertain may involve underlying speaker motives.

much of their person-to-person speaking time is spent informing or being informed and persuading or being persuaded.

Types of Messages

While speaking to inform, to persuade, or to entertain, managers and employees send two types of messages. These messages may be either business related or social.

Business-Related Messages

Business-related messages may be shared vertically between a manager and a superior or between a manager and a subordinate. These messages may also be shared horizontally between peers. Business-related messages focus on topics related to the attainment of organization and employee goals within an organization. Examples of business-related messages include employees discussing a project, an employer counseling an employee about absenteeism, or an employee questioning a manager about preferred operating procedures.

Business-related messages focus on organization and employee goals.

Social Messages

Social messages focus on topics other than the attainment of organization or employee goals. These messages cover a broad range of topics including the weather, politics, religion, family, and avocational interests. Social messages are generally delivered before a business-related message, but they also can be interwoven with business-related messages. Although an excessive amount of work time should not be spent on social messages, managers and employees should make time and create opportunities to share social messages person-to-person. Sharing these messages in a person-to-person setting can imply that the speaker enjoys the listener's company. People enjoy being liked for themselves as well as for their work. Lines of communication are strengthened and the communicator's credibility may be improved through the occasional sharing of social messages. Managers who seldom or never share social messages with peers and subordinates may be perceived as distant, cold, or impersonal.

Social messages, when shared periodically, can strengthen communication lines.

▲ FACE-TO-FACE SPEAKING

Face-to-face speaking is an effective channel for communicating with another person. Occasionally factors such as time constraints, pressing commitments, geographic separation, and expense prohibit communicators from speaking face-to-face. Whenever possible, however, communicators should use this channel for conveying messages. Like any other communication channel, face-to-face speaking has its strengths and limitations. A manager can employ specific strategies to manage or minimize the limitations associated with face-to-face speaking.

Strengths

Face-to-face speaking has three strengths which set it apart from other communication channels. These strengths make face-to-face communication the preferred communication channel in many situations.

Communicators should maximize the positive features of face-to-face speaking.

1. *Face-to-face speaking is personal.* It surpasses all other channels, including intermediary person-to-person speaking, by allowing communicators to feel that they are important and that what they wish to communicate is important.
2. *Face-to-face speaking provides numerous avenues for communicating.* Communicators can draw upon a wide variety of visual nonverbal cues. Both people involved in face-to-face speaking can be graphic with nonverbal cues, such as eye contact and hand motions.
3. *Communicators can adjust their messages as needed during a conversation.* This provides immediate feedback which enables speakers to adjust their messages or to vary message delivery as needed.

Potential Limitations

Although face-to-face speaking is the preferred communication channel, it has four potential limitations:

Communicators should minimize the potential limitations of face-to-face speaking.

1. *No documentation of communication is available* with face-to-face speaking unless the conversation is recorded. The face-to-face channel cannot be "read" later like written communication.
2. *There is limited preparation time in some instances.* Speakers may make time to prepare for the delivery of messages; however, daily face-to-face speaking seldom receives the preparation time given to written communication channels.
3. *The evaluation of messages received through face-to-face speaking can be complex or confusing* if nonverbal cues conflict or contradict verbal messages.
4. *Closure may be more difficult to attain* with face-to-face speaking than with some other channels. Some people tend to ramble or go off on tangents. Thus, many people feel more in control when they

speak using a telephone; they know that either party can end the conversation if a situation gets unmanageable.

Strategies for Improvement _____

Managers can maximize the strengths and minimize the potential limitations of face-to-face speaking if specific strategies for improvement are used on a daily basis. Managers should develop subconscious competence in employing these strategies for improving face-to-face speaking. Recommended strategies for improvement include the following:

Managers should develop subconscious competence in using strategies to improve face-to-face speaking.

1. *Know the purpose or reason for communicating.* A speaker communicates to inform, to persuade, or to entertain.
2. *Limit the subject.* A speaker should not overload the listener with multiple subjects.
3. *Know the audience.* The listener is an influential factor in determining the nature, scope, and delivery of a message. Assess the audience before and during message delivery so that needed adjustments can be made.
4. *Arrange or sequence parts of a message based on desired goal and audience assessment.* Messages which are arranged orderly and delivered well are easier to understand and retain.
5. *Show the importance of message content.* The listener needs to know where the conversation is headed.[2] If the message requires lengthy delivery time, the conversation might be postponed until a more convenient time.
6. *Talk in terms of listener interest.* Speakers should avoid showing off or drawing attention to themselves. Be listener-oriented in order to maintain listener interest.
7. *Be yourself.* Speakers should not try to project a false image or use an unnatural delivery style. Awkward message delivery clouds or confuses message reception.
8. *Be a good listener.* Effective face-to-face speakers demonstrate good listening skills so that they can obtain feedback about their messages.
9. *Use nonverbal communication.* Use appropriate nonverbal communication with a spoken message to clarify or confirm the message's meaning.
10. *Adjust message delivery as required.* Speakers should learn different ways to say the same thing to meet the comprehension level of the listener.

▲ TELEPHONE SPEAKING ▬▬▬▬▬▬▬

After face-to-face speaking, telephone communication is the most common means of exchanging information. Today's manager is expected to meet the challenge of exploding telephone technology and to use the telephone efficiently and effectively.

Telephone Technology ▬▬▬▬▬▬▬

Stimulated by the breakup of the Bell system in 1984 and by rapid technological advances in the telecommunications industry, new generations of telephones are being paraded before the confused user even before the last telephone systems have gone by.[3] The 1980s will long be remembered as a period when telephone technology ran wild. People can purchase many types of telephones, including those that are shaped like Mickey Mouse, those that automatically redial a busy number every 45 seconds, and those that quack rather than ring.

> Today's telephone technology is revolutionary.

A sampling of telephone technology includes the following instruments:

1. *Telephone-answering machines* permit a person to receive voice messages while attending to other matters. These units automatically answer every call, ask the caller to leave a message, and then record the caller's message. Some advanced answering machines are designed so that a person can play back messages from remote areas or have calls automatically transferred to another telephone number.

2. The *cordless telephone* consists of a radio-operated base unit (which plugs into the telephone line) and a portable battery-powered handset. A person can place calls on the handset anywhere within a few hundred feet of the base unit. Newer models of the cordless telephone will use channel frequencies less susceptible to interference from fluorescent lights, electric motors, and ham radio broadcasts.[4]

3. A *computer telephone* is both a computer and a telephone housed in a single desktop unit. It permits the simultaneous transmission of both computer data and voice data. These units have features that combine several high-powered telephone operations, such as one-touch dialing and automatic dialing from personal listings or from a mainframe data base. Industry analysts predict a billion-dollar computer-telephone market by 1990; they believe that this technology will have a profound effect on how information is processed and disseminated worldwide.[5] For example, Zaisan Corporation's ES.3 is the first stand-alone unit to combine multiple phone options with

the computing power of an IBM personal computer. Also, several United States and European countries are constructing the world's first fiber optic undersea telephone cable linking the United States with Britain and France. The cable, expected to be operational by mid-1988, will carry computer-telephone data at high speeds.

4. *Cellular radio telephone systems* are small hand-held mobile telephones that will overshadow the cordless telephones as early as the 1990s. These systems will use scarce radio frequencies that will permit mobile communication from anywhere in the world. Telephone numbers will not be attached to a particular telephone; but numbers will be assigned to the owners, which may stay the same for life. These systems will be able to keep track of a person at all times. When a person's number is dialed, the telephone closest and most accessible to the person will ring.[6]

Telephone Techniques

The telephone is a convenient and personal method for person-to-person communication. Yet, the ring of the telephone can be very demanding; it often becomes a signal of rudeness. Unless the manager gains control of the use of the telephone, it will break up creative thinking, work, and private conversations. When the manager does not want to be disturbed, telephone calls should be screened by the secretary or recorded on an answering device.

Effective use of the telephone is critical in the business world.

Incoming Calls

Managers should follow these telephone practices in handling incoming calls:

Managers should follow good telephone practices in handling incoming calls.

1. Answer the telephone promptly. Incoming calls should be answered as soon as possible after the first ring.
2. Identify yourself immediately. When answering an outside line, also give the company name.

Poor	Good
"Hello!"	"General Insurance, Jim Wilson speaking."

3. Speak in a relaxed, low-pitched tone of voice and hold the transmitter about one inch from your mouth.
4. Explain any time constraints at the beginning of the conversation. It will be easier to end the call when the caller knows at the outset that time is limited.
5. Promptly and accurately record all messages for others on a pad or message form, which is kept next to the telephone. All written mes-

sages should include the date, time of call, the caller's correctly spelled name, and the caller's correct telephone number.

6. Allow the caller to end the call. Before hanging up the telephone, thank the caller in a courteous, unhurried manner.

Poor   *Good*

"Bye."   "Thank you for calling, Mr. Jones."

Outgoing Calls

Managers should follow these techniques for placing outgoing calls:

Here are seven techniques for placing calls.

1. Keep a list of frequently called numbers by the telephone. Some managers have a telephone that stores frequently called numbers.
2. Group calls during set times each day. If brief calls are made before lunch or toward the end of the workday, receivers may be less inclined to engage in idle conversation.
3. Place calls in priority order. If all calls cannot be made, at least the most important ones will have been completed.
4. Introduce yourself immediately to the person who answers the telephone. Avoid "Guess-who-I-am?" games.
5. On a first-time call, ask for the name and number of the person who answers the telephone if that person does not provide identification. Outgoing calls are occasionally cut off, particularly those in which the caller is about to be placed on hold.

THE WALL STREET JOURNAL

"You have reached a live operator. All our recorded messages are busy at the moment. If you will wait we will connect you with our next available recorded message."

Source: From THE WALL STREET JOURNAL—Permission, Cartoon Features Syndicate.

6. Make an appointment to call at a specific time or leave a message when returning a call to someone who is out. Avoid *telephone tag,* the time-wasting activity of making repeated, unsuccessful attempts to reach another person by phone.
7. Carefully plan each call by listing important points to be discussed and by having all appropriate reference materials nearby.

Telephone Management

Telephone effectiveness can be increased by an analysis of calls.

To increase the effectiveness of time spent in using the telephone, managers should periodically analyze their incoming and outgoing calls. A simple form like the one shown in Figure 6–1 can be used to record pertinent information for study. All calls should be logged in on the forms, one call per form, for a period of at least two weeks.

The analysis of calls may show, for example, that many incoming calls have to be transferred to someone else in the organization. A study of this

---

TELEPHONE MANAGEMENT FORM

Call made by: Date_____

  Self _____

  Other party_____

Name and firm of person talked to: _____

_____

Subject of call: _____

_____

Was call transferred to someone else? _____

If yes, who?_____

Was call a follow-up of a previous call? _____

Was call a follow-up of correspondence? _____

Was call really necessary? _____

Total time of call in minutes: _____

Comments: _____

_____

_____

FIGURE 6–1 Telephone Management Form

problem may reveal that the company telephone directory contains wrong numbers, similar names, or confusing organization titles. Further study of the problem may reveal that the company switchboard operator does not know the difference between the Administrative Services Division and the Business Services Division or that the operator often rings the first name on a list of similar names. Too many follow-up calls usually mean poor planning of the initial call. A large number of follow-up calls pertaining to written correspondence may suggest a need for improving written messages.

▲ MACHINE DICTATION ▬▬▬▬▬▬▬▬▬

Recent technological improvements have increased the capabilities and popularity of dictation equipment; now many managers find the use of machine dictation to be more convenient and economical than dictating to a secretary. In the strictest sense, machine dictation is not an interactive speaking process; it is one-way communication with a time lag between sending and receiving a message. Machine dictation, however, does involve two people—one person to send information and one person to receive information.

Machine dictation is a form of speaking person-to-person.

Dictation Technology ▬▬▬▬▬▬▬▬▬▬▬▬

Many managers have been reluctant to switch from the traditional mode of secretarial dictation to machine dictation. Several studies show, however, that machine dictation saves time for both the manager and the transcriptionist.[7] The use of machine dictation is expected to increase as more and more companies strive to boost managerial and office productivity with new technologies.

The use of machine dictation is expected to increase in the years ahead.

The major components of a dictation system are input or recording units, media or storage devices, and output or transcription units.

Input Units

The three basic types of input units are portable models, desktop models, and central recording systems.

Portable models are hand-held, battery-powered units that are available in sizes small enough to fit into a shirt or coat pocket. Most units have built-in microphones and use cassettes for recording. Portable models are very popular among managers who must dictate material while on business trips, and the small size of the cassettes allows managers to mail their

Portable models provide great flexibility in dictation.

dictation to the office for transcription. By using any telephone, these special portable units retrieve messages from one's office or home-answering device.

Desktop models are designed for managers who spend a large amount of time dictating. Most units have microphones which are directly wired into the desktop unit; however, some models can be used for both dictating and transcribing. Like the portable units, desktop units often use cassettes for recording. Many units use **electronic cueing** to mark the beginning and end of dictated material. This feature permits the transcriptionist to scan the cassette to determine the length of a document or to listen for special dictation instructions or comments.

Central recording systems enable several people to dictate simultaneously from different locations to a central transcription area. Central systems are accessed by dictation units wired to a central recorder or by telephones through a line that ties into the system. Some systems are designed to record dictation at any time during the day or week through an outside telephone line. These systems commonly record dictation on cassettes that are automatically fed one at a time into a recording position. Although advances in machine dictation technology have slowly evolved over the past few years, one important technological trend is away from central systems and toward the use of individual units.[8]

Many central systems are accessed by telephone.

Media

The recording media used in today's dictation equipment are classified as either discrete or endless-loop.

Discrete medium refers to any type of magnetic tape, disk, or belt that can be removed from an input unit. Common types of discrete media are standard cassettes, minicassettes, and microcassettes. **Standard cassettes** are available in tape lengths ranging from 30 to 180 minutes. **Minicassettes** are smaller than a standard-size cassette and provide 30 to 60 minutes of recording time. **Microcassettes** are the smallest cassettes available and hold up to 60 minutes of recorded material. Discrete media can be recorded on an input unit at one location and transcribed on an output unit at another location, or it can be used with a variety of input/output devices. Discrete media can also be mailed or filed.

Cassette tapes are a popular recording medium.

Endless-loop medium refers to a continuous-loop magnetic tape housed in a central tanklike device that cannot be handled or removed from the machine. Dictation is transmitted to the endless-loop tape through special wires that connect the dictator's microphone to the central device. Dictation flows from the tape to a transcribing machine located at the transcriptionist's desk. Endless-loop media do not have to be loaded, reloaded, or replaced.

Output Units

Output or transcription units are used by transcriptionists to listen to recorded dictation for processing. Transcription units are of two basic types—individual and centralized.

An *individual transcription station* is equipped with a machine that holds the magnetic medium, a headset for listening to the dictation, and foot or thumb controls to regulate the playback speed. Many individual stations are combination input/output units; however, since they must be carried back and forth between the dictation source and the transcription source, these units are recommended only for managers who spend relatively little time dictating.

A *centralized station* features several transcription stations attached to a single storage unit. These stations are located in a central place and service a large number of dictators.

Dictation Techniques _____

Speaking into a machine that doesn't respond can be an uneasy experience for some managers. Learning to use effective machine dictation techniques requires proper training, frequent practice, and a great deal of patience.[9]

Managers should follow these predictation steps to become an effective dictator:

Here are several steps
to take before dictating.

1. Organize incoming mail based on the importance of replies. If the volume of dictation for a given day is heavy, shift low-priority items to the next day.
2. Outline important points that should be answered. Some managers prefer to make marginal notations on incoming letters and memos.
3. Gather all needed materials before beginning dictation; for example, names, addresses, telephone numbers, and other reference items. If the dictation is a reply to a message, attach all reference materials to the message.
4. Select a time for dictation when interruptions will be minimal. For many managers, the first thing in the morning or after work hours are the quietest times in the office.

Many managers have followed these guidelines to improve their machine dictation skills:

Good dictators use
these techniques.

1. Identify yourself.
2. Dictate special instructions, including
   a. The type of document to keyboard—letter, memo, report, table, etc.

b. The type of paper to use—company letterhead, memo, plain paper, envelopes, etc.

c. The number of copies needed.

3. Dictate the name and address of each receiver unless the transcriber already has this information on file.

4. Speak clearly using a relaxed, natural tone. Keep in mind that dictation voice speed is much slower than normal conversational speaking.

5. Spell out words that might be misunderstood. Use a phonetic alphabet such as the following:

A	Alice	H	Henry	O	Oliver	U	Utah
B	Bertha	I	Ida	P	Peter	V	Victor
C	Charles	J	James	Q	Quaker	W	William
D	David	K	Kate	R	Robert	X	X-ray
E	Edward	L	Lewis	S	Samuel	Y	Young
F	Frank	M	Mary	T	Thomas	Z	Zebra
G	George	N	Nellie				

For example, the word *apted* is spelled "A as in Alice, P as in Peter, T as in Thomas, E as in Edward, and D as in David."

6. Dictate all punctuation.

7. Dictate end of paragraphs by saying, "Paragraph."

8. Dictate first-letter capitalization for a word within a sentence by saying, ". . . initial cap, Plan . . . ." For a word entirely in capital letters, say, ". . . all caps, MBO . . . ."

9. Dictate all mechanical instructions—special indentions, quotes, columns of figures, numbered entries, underscoring, special spacing, and the like.

Dictation Management _____

Monitoring devices help control dictation and transcription activity in central systems.

The complex nature of large central recording systems created a need to monitor the activities of the many recorders connected to the systems. Monitoring devices log and track all dictation and transcription activity. Some monitoring devices provide detailed productivity information by dictator, department, type of work, transcriptionist, and type of media. Advanced monitoring systems feature microprocessor-controlled visual display terminals which provide status information on thousands of jobs in the system.

SUMMARY

Person-to-person speaking implies interaction between two people. It is a two-way process in which two people communicate with one another by speaking. The two kinds of person-to-person speaking are face-to-face speaking and intermediary speaking. Face-to-face speaking involves two people conversing while in one another's presence; intermediary speaking refers to two people separated by distance but joined by an electronic intermediary device.

The person-to-person channels for speaking fulfill the three purposes of communication: to inform, to persuade, and to entertain. Speaking to inform involves giving or obtaining information. Speaking to persuade influences the listener's thinking. Speaking to entertain amuses the listener.

People send two types of messages while speaking: business-related messages and social messages. A business-related message focuses on the attainment of organization and employee goals within an organization. A social message focuses on topics other than the attainment of organization or employee goals. Managers should avoid spending an excessive amount of work time on social messages, but occasionally managers should make time to share social messages with employees. Sharing social messages can strengthen interpersonal relationships and, therefore, strengthen communication lines.

Face-to-face speaking has its strengths and potential limitations. Communicators should employ strategies to maximize the strengths and to minimize the potential limitations.

Next to face-to-face speaking, telephone communication (an intermediary type of speaking) is the most common means of exchanging information. New types of telephones appear frequently. Telephone-answering machines allow a person to receive voice messages while attending to other matters. Cordless telephones enable people to place calls on handsets anywhere within a few hundred feet of a base unit. Computer-telephones combine computer and telephone technology. As early as the 1990s, cellular radio telephone systems will use scarce radio frequencies so that mobile communication will be possible from anywhere in the world.

Managers should routinely use effective techniques for handling incoming and outgoing calls. Periodically, managers should analyze their telephone use to identify areas which need improvement.

Face-to-face speaking can include dictation, particularly if a secretary provides feedback to a manager's dictation. However, many managers use machine dictation equipment rather than dictating face-to-face. Machine dictation is not an interactive speaking process; it is one-way communication. The major components of a dictation system are input units, media devices, and output units. The basic types of input units include portable models, desktop models, and central recording systems. The media devices used in today's dictation equipment are either discrete or endless-loop. Common output systems use either individual stations or centralized stations. Managers can improve dictation effectiveness through proper training, frequent practice, and patience.

QUESTIONS

1. Why is message reception more important than message delivery when choosing a communication channel?

2. What are the two roles that speakers may assume?

3. What are the three purposes for speaking person-to-person?

4. Give an example in which a subordinate assumes the role of initial speaker. Give an example in which a manager assumes the role of feedback speaker.

5. Contrast person-to-person speaking to persuade with person-to-person speaking to inform.

6. Define *telephone-answering machine*.

7. How can uncontrolled telephone use break up a manager's creative thinking?

8. What can be gained as a result of periodically analyzing telephone use?

9. How do individual output units and centralized output units differ?

10. Why isn't machine dictation considered an interactive process?

PROBLEM-SOLVING EXPERIENCES

1. With a partner, role-play three different scenes involving person-to-person speaking to inform. Afterwards, analyze how much time was de-

voted to social messages and to business-related messages. In what sequence were the messages shared?

2. Prepare a form for analyzing telephone use.

CASE 6–1

Until the current fiscal year, most of Montgomery Mutual's whole-life and term insurance policies were generated by company agents who personally visited people in their homes. At the beginning of this fiscal year, Mo Chang, company president, established a new and somewhat controversial recruiting policy. New clients are now recruited over the telephone rather than by personal visits. Chang viewed the home visits as too time-consuming because agents and prospective clients tended to discuss social matters in addition to business-related matters.

New policy sales were off 27 percent during the first quarter of this fiscal year. Chang attributes the decline in sales to the agents not giving the new recruiting policy a fair chance. In an attempt to get to the bottom of this issue, Chang has called a meeting of all district managers.

Now is your chance to air your feelings as to the real reasons for the drastic drop in policy sales.

1. List (in order of priority) what you consider the true reasons for the decrease in policy sales.

2. Describe the advantages of face-to-face visits with prospective clients.

3. Of what value is incorporating social messages as well as business-related messages in conversations with prospective clients?

4. Can agents effectively recruit new clients using the telephone? Support your response.

ENDNOTES

[1] J. Thomas Miller, "Communication . . . or Getting Ideas Across," *S.A.M. Advanced Management Journal*, Vol. 45, No. 2 (Summer, 1980), p. 32.

[2] Philip Lesly, "Mastering the Techniques of Two-Way Communication," *Supervisory Management*, Vol. 24, No. 11 (November, 1979), pp. 2–5.

[3]International Data Corporation, "The Revolution in Business Communications: How Businesses Can Cope," *Fortune*, Vol. 109, No. 6 (March 19, 1984), p. 152.

[4]Herb Brody, "Remember This?" *Technology Illustrated*, Vol. 3, No. 10 (October, 1983), p. 23.

[5]John Naisbitt, "High-Tech Trends Lead Way on Fast Road to Tomorrow," *The Atlanta Journal-Constitution*, January 6, 1985, p. 6D.

[6]Ronald R. Thomas, "The Telecom Web," *Management World*, Vol. 13, No. 6 (July, 1984), p. 15; also see The University of Georgia, "People Phones to Replace Telephones," *Continuing Education*, Vol. 2, No. 3 (March, 1983), p. 2.

[7]Nonie Steinmetz, "What's New in Dictation Equipment," *Management World*, Vol. 9, No. 12 (December, 1980), p. 10.

[8]Lawrence Feidelman, "Dynamic Dictation," *Management World*, Vol. 13, No. 2 (February, 1984), p. 17.

[9]H. Lon Addams, "How to Overcome 'Mike Fright,'" *Management World*, Vol. 9, No. 12 (December, 1980), p. 16.

CHAPTER

7

SPEAKING IN GROUP SITUATIONS

When you complete this chapter, you should be able to:

▲ Describe the general nature and purposes of group communication.

▲ Identify the primary responsibilities that both group leaders and group members must assume to ensure successful group communication.

▲ Explain the effects that room layout and distance between group members have on group communication.

▲ Contrast the five common forms of teleconferencing systems.

▲ Discuss the potential impact of teleconferencing on group communication.

Managers interact formally and informally in countless types of small group meetings during the course of a work year. Most of these meetings are held for specific purposes; indeed, important business decisions are often made by groups rather than by individuals. In order to maximize face-to-face participation in group meetings, managers must have a clear understanding of their responsibilities both as group leaders and as group members. To overcome the barriers of time and distance, many managers are using, or are likely to use, some form of technology to create communication links between people at different locations across the country.

▲ NATURE OF GROUP COMMUNICATION

Group communication helps fulfill the human need of belonging to a team or being part of a human cluster. Listening and speaking are the most common forms of group communication. The term *meeting* refers to people gathering together for a purpose. A meeting is the common forum through which groups of people communicate. People are social creatures. "In every organization and every human culture of which we have record, people come together in small groups at regular and frequent intervals and in larger 'tribal' gatherings from time to time."[1]

Examples of groups which communicate through meetings are staff, division, or functional work groups; professional, civic, or religious associations; and avocational or special interest groups. The purposes for speaking in groups are the same as the purposes for speaking person-to-person. However, these purposes—to inform, to persuade, and to entertain—vary among groups based on the nature of the group, its size, and its reason for being.

Group size may range from small to large, with a small group having 3 members and a large group having more than 100 members. A group of 12 or fewer people is called a *committee.* A group of 13 to 50 people is called a *council.* A group of 51 or more people is called an *assembly.*[2]

According to Jay, group communication has several functions:[3]

1. Group communication helps group members define the group; members discuss similarities and differences. Thus, group members

Meeting refers to people gathering together for a purpose.

A committee consists of 12 or fewer people. A council is a group of 13 to 50 people. An assembly is comprised of more than 50 people.

are able to better understand the collective aims and objectives of the group and how group members interrelate.

2. Group members revise, update, and add to what they know as a group. They receive progress or status reports or announcements.
3. Members have the opportunity to exist and work as a group. Participation in group decision making enhances the acceptance of and commitment to group decisions; participation also promotes group unity.
4. Group communication provides a status arena, a situation in which people emerge as leaders or followers. There is an opportunity for people to be noticed.

Improved decision making and problem solving are possible through group communication. Usually the innovativeness and creativity of group thinking surpass that of an individual's.

Well-planned and -conducted meetings can provide an opportunity for group members to grow as individuals and as part of a group. Poorly planned meetings, however, can waste time, frustrate or confuse group participants, and decrease productivity and morale. Five major stumbling blocks to effective group communication are

▲ Vague or mixed objectives for a group meeting.
▲ Chairpersons who unwittingly discourage creativity and free speculation.
▲ Chairpersons who use power unwisely.
▲ Group members who express antagonism toward ideas.[4]
▲ Poor room environment such as improper size, noise, light, or temperature.

Awareness of the roles and responsibilities of group participants can help prevent the occurrence of such stumbling blocks.

▲ ROLES ASSUMED WITHIN A GROUP

Group communicators assume the roles of group leader and/or group member. A **group leader** guides the group in performing its responsibilities; the group leader may also provide or obtain information during a meeting. A **group member** provides and obtains information in a meeting.

How well people communicate in groups influences how well they communicate in other relationships within the organization. Group com-

The person who guides a group in accomplishing its responsibilities is called a group leader. Group members provide and obtain information in a meeting.

munication can affect chances for advancement; during meetings, people observe and are observed by others.

Group Leader

Group leaders are called chairpersons, presiders, group facilitators, or group discussion leaders. Usually the leadership of a group is defined by the person who calls or arranges the meeting. However, group leaders may lose control if they are ill prepared to conduct the meeting. In some small group meetings where there is no designated leader, the member with leadership qualities emerges as group leader.

Premeeting Responsibilities

Prior to calling a meeting, group leaders should complete a premeeting checklist.

The managerial function of planning is critical to a group leader's success. Through proper planning, the group leader sets the stage for effective group communication. Figure 7–1 includes key questions group leaders should ask themselves prior to scheduling and conducting a meeting. Thinking through these questions helps the group leader prepare for a successful meeting.

▲ Should a meeting be held?

▲ What are the true purposes and objectives of the meeting?

▲ Who should attend the meeting?

▲ Does the proposed meeting date allow ample time for group members and the group leader to prepare for the meeting?

▲ Is a properly equipped and furnished meeting room available?

▲ What items should be included in the meeting agenda?

▲ What materials, other than the agenda, do group members need to review prior to the meeting?

▲ What meeting procedures should be followed?

▲ What questions should be asked to maximize group member participation?

▲ How can discussion be kept on target?

▲ How can group member similarities and points of agreement be emphasized?

▲ How can a group decision be reached without forcing conformity?

FIGURE 7–1   Group Leader's Premeeting Checklist

Meeting Responsibilities

The group leader calls the meeting to order and serves as the communication role model during the meeting. During a meeting, the group leader's primary responsibilities are (1) to maintain order, (2) to encourage participation among group members, (3) to emphasize elements of agreement, and (4) to reach a decision at the end of discussion. The group leader's secondary responsibilities are to provide and obtain information.

Group leaders are responsible for four major activities during a meeting.

Maintaining Order.   The group leader can maintain order during a meeting by effectively using parliamentary procedure as prescribed in *Robert's Rules of Order*.[5] Consistent use of standard procedures helps group members distinguish between acceptable and unacceptable meeting behavior. Excessive talking and rambling are not permitted. Parliamentary procedure also facilitates ending a meeting on time or early.

Encouraging Participation.   Generally group leaders delegate responsibility for recording the transactions conducted during meetings. Having group members participate in documenting meeting transactions frees the group leader to fulfill other meeting responsibilities. Group leaders encourage good listening and the proper use of grammar by practicing good communication skills and courteous behavior during meetings. Group leaders who speak concisely, accurately, and enthusiastically encourage group members to do the same. However, group leaders should avoid telling group members what to do or how to participate.

THE WALL STREET JOURNAL

"We need two hundred million bucks by Friday
— any ideas?"

Source: From THE WALL STREET JOURNAL—Permission, Cartoon Features Syndicate.

Emphasizing Elements of Agreement.   Group leaders should make a concerted effort to emphasize common or complementary discussion items. Productive groups agree to disagree. They welcome diversity of thought because their collective thinking is more powerful and dynamic than individual thinking. Skilled group leaders steer group discussion to emphasize elements of agreement and to complement or broaden group discussion through differences of opinion. Certain remarks accentuate common or complementary discussion items. For example, the group leader might say, "Bob, your remarks concerning budget amendments support Bill's departmental projections." Group leaders can pack power in their speech. They should avoid phrases such as "I think," "I guess," "you know," and the like. Group leaders should also avoid hedges like "kinda," "sorta," and "maybe," which diminish commitment.[6]

Reaching a Decision.   Prior to adjourning a meeting, group leaders should recap major discussion points and assist the group in reaching a decision on debated issues. A decision can be accomplished by having group members vote or reach a consensus. A ***consensus*** refers to the collective agreement or acceptance of a general opinion; it does *not* denote compliance. Group leaders must guard against forcing conformity.

A consensus refers to the collective agreement of a general opinion.

Postmeeting Responsibilities
Once a meeting has ended, the group leader should evaluate the meeting's effectiveness and his or her performance as a group leader. The group leader should maintain a log of the meeting's strengths and weaknesses. Minutes or a summary of the meeting should be shared with group members.

Group Member

Group members are frequently referred to as ***discussants.*** They are invited to a meeting based on their need to know information or their ability to share information on a particular topic. While group members are not responsible for calling or conducting a meeting, they are expected to prepare for participation in the meeting.

Premeeting Responsibilities
Figure 7–2 supplies key questions that group members should ask themselves prior to attending a meeting.

Group members should prepare for a meeting by reading material shared by the group leader and by researching information included in the agenda. Meetings should be approached with an open mind.

▲ What are the purposes and objectives of this meeting?

▲ What can I learn from this meeting?

▲ What questions should I ask during the meeting?

▲ What can I contribute to this meeting?

▲ What do I need to do to prepare for this meeting?

FIGURE 7–2   Group Member's Premeeting Checklist

Meeting Responsibilities

Group members are responsible for sharing and obtaining information. Questions are critical to group discussion. Group members are expected to ask clear, concise questions and to provide intelligent and understandable information in the form of answers or comments. They also give formal and informal presentations upon request. (Making presentations and speeches is addressed in Chapter 8.) Otherwise group members should speak only when speaking contributes to the meeting's objectives.

Auger recommends that group members listen carefully to what others say, take notes, avoid provoking controversy, prepare in depth when responsible for a presentation, avoid bluffing in response to a question, and ask questions for clarification.[7]

Group members should demonstrate respect for other people at meetings. Group members should not shuffle papers or engage in side conversations.

Postmeeting Responsibilities

After a meeting has ended, group members should complete any meeting-related assignments. They should also evaluate their performance as group members.

▲ THE IMPORTANCE OF PROXEMICS

Proxemics, the physical distance between communicators, is important to group leaders *and* members. An awareness of proxemics can increase the likelihood of successful group communication.

Everyone has his or her own personal space, even when away from familiar surroundings. *Personal space* refers to the invisible boundaries of a person's private domain. Personal space in a meeting is the space in

Proxemics is the physical distance between communicators.

Personal space involves invisible boundaries.

which the group leader or group member sits or stands. Violation of personal space inhibits communication by drawing attention away from the discussion and toward the invasion of personal space. Respect for personal space helps to build trust and rapport among group members and enhances open, productive communication.

The boundaries of one's office or work area are easily defined, but the boundaries of personal space are not. People do not draw lines to define their space; in fact, most people are not consciously aware of their personal space. When someone gets too close, a person often gets uncomfortable or even tense and defensive without consciously understanding that a territorial violation has occurred. Discomfort results when personal space is trespassed. Territorial violations can occur by standing too close to someone, sitting where someone else usually sits, or entering someone's office without knocking.

Four proxemic zones have been identified.[8] The ***intimate zone*** refers to personal space of zero up to two feet from an individual; this zone is reserved for family and close friends. The ***personal zone*** is personal space ranging from two to four feet from an individual; friends and trusted associates are welcomed in this zone. The ***social zone*** involves personal space of four to twelve feet between communicators; this is the space within which most business relationships start. The ***public zone*** is personal space of twelve or more feet between communicators; generally anyone is permitted to communicate in this zone. The boundaries of an individual's personal space vary depending on the situation, the culture, and the people involved.

In considering proxemics, people are labeled as either touchers or nontouchers. Touchers are more willing to be close and to have others close to them than are nontouchers. Personality differences can lead to tension when touchers and nontouchers interact. Touchers sometimes feel that nontouchers are cold; nontouchers sometimes feel that touchers are pushy or aggressive.

Personality differences should be considered when planning or attending a meeting. The meeting area should be small enough for the participants to feel part of a group but large enough for each person to have ample space. Round-table seating allows everyone equal access to the discussion and nonverbal cues, but it increases the distance between members, particularly across the circle. Seating group members in rows may keep people close but may restrict nonverbal cues among group members who are seated in different rows. Seating along both sides of a table is common. In such an arrangement, everyone has fair access to the person at the head of the table; but competitiveness sometimes develops between the two

One's intimate zone refers to personal space up to two feet from an individual.
The personal zone ranges from two to four feet from an individual.
People communicate socially in a zone of four to twelve feet.
One's public zone refers to personal space greater than 12 feet.

"sides." Multisided tables that have sides of equal length, such as square- or pentagon-shaped tables, can alleviate group members from teaming up on sides. On an individual level, people should avoid sitting where they know someone else usually sits or is planning to sit.

Technology has affected group communication a great deal in recent years. Proxemics are less manageable as groups communicate long-distance.

▲ TELECONFERENCING

Teleconferencing is an electronic method of communication between two or more people at two or more locations. Teleconferencing, as well as the technology that supports it, is still maturing. In today's business world, several well-defined teleconferencing systems are beginning to emerge. Despite a growing awareness of teleconferencing technology, many business managers do not clearly understand how teleconferencing systems should be used or integrated in the future. Teleconferencing is often perceived as a rather simple alternative to face-to-face group meetings, yet its potential impact on management and business communication may be profound.

The field of teleconferencing is in its infancy.

Teleconferencing Systems

The five common forms of teleconferencing systems are (1) audio conferencing, (2) audiographics, (3) slow scan television (SSTV), (4) video conferencing, and (5) computer conferencing.

Audio Conferencing
Audio conferencing refers to a voice-only meeting between people at two or more locations linked via telephones or microphones and loud speakers. Audio conferencing is the most common form of teleconferencing. In 1983, experts projected that audio conferences would comprise 90 percent, or 2.25 million, of the teleconferences conducted during 1983–1984. Projections for the late 1980s are similar.[9]

Devices that can be attached to the telephone to improve audio conferencing include

Many teleconferences today are voice-only meetings.

▲ Telephone headsets that allow the user to have both hands free to take notes or hold reading material. The units are lightweight, portable, and easily plugged into the telephone.

▲ Speakerphones that allow several people in a room to hear and to be heard. The speakerphone consists of a microphone and a loud-speaker. Lower-cost systems use a device for switching from a talking mode to a listening mode. The more sophisticated systems use push-to-talk buttons on separate microphones located around the conference table.

A system known as a **bridge** interconnects telephone lines from more than two locations. Whenever more than two telephones are connected to the same line at one time, a bridge is necessary to maintain high-level audio.

Since audio conferencing is a voice-only medium, the nonverbal cues of face-to-face meetings are missing. To guard against the potential for misunderstanding, the following guidelines are suggested:[10]

1. Plan the audio conference with great care. Prepare a clear agenda and distribute premeeting reading materials to the participants well in advance of the meeting.

A successful audio conference must be well planned.

2. Limit audio conferences to one hour since such meetings are more tiring than face-to-face meetings. If a conference must exceed one hour, schedule a short break.
3. Introduce the participants at the start of the meeting. If the conference exceeds five people, speakers should introduce themselves each time they speak. Introduce late arrivals, and avoid side conversations and unannounced departures.
4. Select an effective chairperson for the audio conference.
5. If translators are required, locate them next to the person or persons for whom they are translating.
6. Select a conference room that is located in a convenient place for all user departments.
7. Speakers should pause occasionally to allow questions or comments from other conference participants. If a speaker goes on for too long, the chairperson should intervene.
8. Speakers should be close to the microphone to ensure the highest level of audio quality.

Audiographics

Audiographics are graphic devices added to an audio conference when participants find it necessary to illustrate information with slides, drawings, or writing. The basic types of audiographic devices are remote control slide projectors, facsimile devices, and electronic blackboards.

Slides can enrich an audio presentation.

Remote Control Slide Projectors.   Slide presentations are a popular form of enhancing business and educational meetings. In an audiographic conference, the presenter sends to each conference site duplicate 35mm slides equipped with a remote control slide projector. The control signal is carried over a standard telephone line, the same line used for the audio portion of the conference. During the conference, the presenter presses a button when a new slide is to be seen; all projectors then advance at the same time. If the presenter wishes to present slides in a random sequence, such as going back to a slide presented earlier in the meeting, a random-access remote control projector is required.

Facsimile (FAX) Devices.   A *facsimile device* (also called FAX) is a machine used to relay printed material, pictures, or figures to distant sites. Two telephone lines are required—one for the FAX machine and one for the audio. A page of material is placed on a FAX machine at one conference site and sent to compatible FAX machines at the other sites. There the material is converted into hard copy. FAX documents may be sent either prior to or during a conference. One popular method for using FAX is sending a document just prior to the conference, changing the document during the conference, and sending the revised document back for review before the conference ends.

The use of FAX machines allows participants to share key documents during a conference.

Electronic Blackboards.   When "chalk talk" presentations are needed for a meeting, the electronic blackboard provides a means for turning an audio conference into a lively session. The **electronic blackboard** is a device that displays on a TV screen at one site whatever is being written on the electronic blackboard at another site. The electronic blackboard is equipped with sensors behind the blackboard that detect the exact location of the chalk while the user is writing. The chalk location is converted into tones that are sent over telephone lines to all conference sites. The participants see the user's writing or drawings on a TV monitor. Two telephone lines are required—one for the blackboard tones and one for the audio. For group participation, a number of blackboards can be linked so that the TV monitors will show the participants' writings; or a TV camera can show the blackboard to all viewers.

How might the electronic blackboard be used during an audiographics conference?

Slow Scan Television (SSTV)

Slow scan television (SSTV) consists of equipment designed to store images at one site and to transmit the images over telephone lines to SSTV units at other sites. When a teleconference requires still images of a higher quality than FAX machines can provide, SSTV fills that need. The unique feature of SSTV is that transmitted images slowly develop or unfold on the TV viewing screen. As in the case of electronic blackboards, SSTV requires two telephone lines for transmitting the visual and audio information.

Using an electronic pencil with SSTV works well for conference members who work together in developing or revising graphic material.

Several devices on the market today permit users to write on an SSTV image with an electronic pencil. When a user writes, circles, underlines, or draws on the face of an SSTV graphic, the notations on the TV screen appear at the same time on all other conference TV screens. This type of system is of great value for participants who must work together in developing or revising graphic material.

Video Conferencing

Video conferencing refers to systems that combine TV-quality images and high-quality audio in specially constructed rooms. The more sophisticated rooms are equipped with full color TV screens and several cameras for self-view, overview, and close-ups. Cameras are switched automatically by the voices of the speakers so that the appropriate camera is always directed at the person speaking. A special graphics camera permits close-up views of charts, papers, photos, and transparencies; another camera is pointed at a chalkless board or screen. The room may also be equipped with film and slide projectors, a tape recorder, and a copy machine. Figure 7–3 shows a basic layout for a well-equipped video conference room.

Video conferencing is the first-class system of teleconferencing.

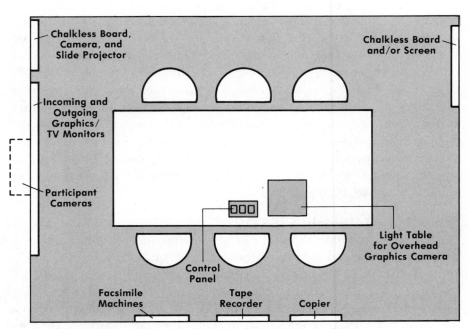

FIGURE 7–3   Layout of a Video Conference Room

During a video conference, the TV signal travels from the originating site to an **uplink device** that transmits the signal to a satellite. The satellite then transmits the signal to the receiver site.

A well-equipped video conference room costs several thousand dollars, not to mention the extremely high transmission fees. As more firms enter the video teleconferencing equipment market, however, competition among the manufacturers will more than likely lower start-up costs. Also, competition among long-distance telecommunication carriers and the use of new technologies will reduce future transmission costs.

Most of the guidelines suggested for audio conferencing also apply to video conferencing. Some other guidelines are as follows:[11]

1. Good lighting is essential to ensure quality TV images.
2. Color TV is preferred over black and white.
3. A separate telephone line should be used for side conversations or as a backup system if TV transmission problems arise during the conference.
4. Participants should avoid talking to people who are off camera.
5. Speakers should avoid gesturing with their hands since TV cameras distort perspectives.

Although all forms of teleconferencing have strengths and weaknesses, video conferencing is particularly useful for business meetings, problem-solving sessions, and training.[12]

Computer Conferencing

Computer conferencing is a form of conference based entirely on transmitting data through terminals or personal computers connected by telephone lines to a central store-and-forward computer. A computer conference is the most unique form of electronic meetings because it does not include images or voices.

In a computer conference, the central computer stores a message entered by a participant and forwards the message to other participants when they call the computer. A conference member may send a message at any time, day or night, and others may read the message whenever they have time.

Computer conferencing eliminates the communication barriers of time and distance.

Participants who wish to share facts and ideas about a common problem may be located in any geographical area or time zone. Since the central computer retains all input from all participants, conference members may drop in and out of the "meeting" whenever they wish and still not miss what others are saying. Between input/output sessions at their terminals, participants can check references, do research, draft responses, or confer with colleagues without disrupting the conference. Also, a computer conference can be carried on by any number of people over periods of hours, weeks, or months.

Potential of Teleconferencing

New technology brings with it new human behavior. Managers who are convinced that teleconferencing is a productive and cost-effective way of conducting a meeting between groups of people at distant sites use the system to maintain a competitive edge for their firms. When managers install in-house systems, the nature of group communication changes. Face-to-face meetings are enhanced, and new opportunities for group communication are created.

Most likely, the forward progress of technology will gradually integrate audio, video, and computer systems in ways that will require new thinking about how groups of people communicate with one another; it will certainly make new demands on managers.

A number of organizations have successfully used various forms of teleconferencing for group meetings, and the idea of linking corporate offices around the country or world has sparked the interest of many managers. A few examples of the use of teleconferencing in the business world are offered by Johansen and Bullen.[13]

1. Since 1968, the executives of the Bank of America have held regular audio conferences linking the corporate offices in San Francisco and Los Angeles.
2. Since 1975, IBM has used slow scan television for solving technical problems. This system works well for such problems, and it allows groups of technical people from several sites to work together.
3. Since 1978, Procter & Gamble's division managers have used computer conferencing to share thoughts and timely information with one another.
4. Since 1981, Aetna Life and Casualty Company has used full color video conferencing to link its offices in Connecticut and in other parts of the country. The system is used on a regular basis.
5. Since 1981, Hewlett-Packard has used live video presentations to introduce new products to its national sales force. This system allows the sales staff to ask questions about the new products from the people who developed them.

Teleconferences should not be used merely to replace face-to-face meetings; they should be used to assist users to be more productive in their work, to reduce costs, and to improve the competitive advantage of the firm. As with other forms of office technology, teleconferencing must support the goals of the firm.

Presented here are some of the potential benefits of teleconferencing:

1. Reduces travel costs, travel time, and travel fatigue.
2. Increases the opportunities for training and developing a company's staff.
3. Provides new opportunities for marketing new products.
4. Encourages new forms of communication channels both within a firm and between different firms.
5. Increases the ability to communicate one message to many people at the same time.
6. Increases the opportunities to identify, formulate, and solve problems.
7. Improves managerial control over remote field sites.

Despite the large number of polished ads, speeches, and demonstrations on the types of teleconferencing, relatively few organizations have in-house systems today. In the mid-1980s, there were "about 75 organizations with permanently installed audio systems in North America, 20 full video, and perhaps 100 still video or audiographic systems."[14] These figures suggest that many managers are taking a cautious approach to the use of teleconferencing as a method of communicating with others.

Choosing the best teleconferencing system requires managers to understand the firm's current and long-range objectives, the nature of the various technologies, and the needs of the potential users. The following suggestions are offered for planning and implementing a teleconferencing system:

1. Read the literature available. One of the most objective publications is *Telespan Newsletter*, which is published monthly by the Telespan Publishing Corporation, 50 West Palm Street, Altadena, CA 91001.
2. Attend national conferences, seminars, and equipment shows.
3. Examine what other firms have already done. Try to identify the specific reasons for their successes or failures.
4. Talk to other managers, both within and outside the firm, who are familiar with one or more systems.
5. Talk to one or more consultants.
6. Experiment with the different systems by renting equipment for in-house use or by contracting to use outside facilities.
7. Seek input from the potential users of the system.

Will teleconferencing eventually eliminate the need for face-to-face meetings?

Before selecting a teleconferencing system, managers must thoroughly analyze each system.

8. Start with a system designed for people in an area of the firm where the probability for success is high; for example, engineers, data processors, and other people who do not fear new technology and who will take in stride the unforeseen problems of implementing a new system.

9. Develop an in-house training program for users and potential users of the system. The initial focus of the training should be on basic communication skills, such as setting conference objectives, preparing graphics and materials needed during a conference, and planning how to get people to interact with one another.

10. Develop instruments to evaluate how well the system matches the firm's objectives. The users of the system should also have an opportunity to evaluate it.

SUMMARY

Group communication accounts for a substantial portion of the total information interchange in an organization. Depending on the size of the group, group members may meet as part of a committee, a council, or an assembly.

Group communication has several functions; it helps the group build identity as a group, and it helps the development of collective aims. Group communication also helps group members stay up-to-date through status reports and announcements. Additional functions of group communication are improved decision making, a commitment to group decisions, and the opportunity for group members to emerge as leaders and followers.

The major responsibility for setting the stage for or planning a successful meeting rests with the group leader. Meetings should be well planned with well-defined agendas. The group leader is responsible for maintaining order and generating participation in meetings. Input and creative suggestions should be encouraged rather than suppressed. Group members are responsible for being well prepared and coming to meetings with open minds.

Proxemics plays an important role in group meetings. Proper distance between group members can help build trust and unity in the group. Getting too close can detract attention from the communication and focus it instead on the violation of personal space. Personal space or territory is divided into four zones: intimate, personal, social, and public. The boundaries of these zones vary depending upon the situation and people involved.

Technology now permits group meetings to occur with the discussants at widely separated points. Teleconferencing is a broad term that applies to several people participating in a single meeting from different locations.

Current forms of teleconferencing include audio conferencing, audiographics, slow scan television, video conferencing, and computer conferencing.

Special preparation is needed for teleconferences because of the restrictions on visual and other nonverbal communication. Speakers must stay close to the microphone. Visuals are generally limited to one camera at a time. Video resolution is sometimes limited.

The new technology has potential for improving the speed and clarity of communication. Currently, teleconferencing technology is relatively expensive. Its potential benefits and limitations are still being explored primarily by large corporations.

QUESTIONS

1. Cite examples of groups that communicate through meetings.
2. Define *committee, council,* and *assembly.*
3. What is meant by this statement: "Group communication generates commitment to the decisions made by the group"?
4. What are the primary responsibilities of a group leader?
5. Why are group members referred to as *discussants?*
6. What do facsimile machines, remote control slide projectors, and electronic blackboards have in common?
7. How does a computer conference differ from the other forms of teleconferencing?
8. What is meant by this statement: "Teleconferencing is more than technology"?
9. If you were assigned the task of selecting a teleconferencing system for an organization, what would you do during the planning stage?
10. Should the initial emphasis of an in-house teleconferencing training program be on operating the system or on improving basic communication skills? Why?

PROBLEM-SOLVING EXPERIENCES

1. Role-play group communication in which group members are seated within one another's (1) intimate zone, (2) personal zone, (3) social zone, and (4) public zone.

2. Obtain a copy of *Robert's Rules of Order*, New York: The Berkley Publishing Group, 1984. Simulate a brief meeting using proper parliamentary procedure.

CASE 7–1

Quintess Corporation's Information Technology Committee meets for one hour on a bimonthly basis. Reba Nix, systems manager for Quintess's plant in Dayton, Ohio, is the committee's chairperson. The committee is responsible for reviewing hardware and software purchase requests.

The Quintess Corporation recently opened a facility in Columbus, Ohio. Until the Columbus plant is fully staffed, Reba's committee is responsible for reviewing purchase requests for both Columbus and Dayton. Two members have been added to the Information Technology Committee to represent the Columbus plant. Thus far, committee meetings have been held in Dayton, which means that the committee members from Columbus must drive 160 miles round trip to attend committee meetings.

Reba's schedule has been so hectic during the last six months that she has given only a few days' notice prior to each of the last three meetings. With such short notice of meeting dates and times, some divisions within the two plants have not had adequate time to prepare written purchase requests. Bill Norman, a member of the Information Technology Committee, is one of Reba's closest friends. Reba allows Bill to dominate many of the committee meetings with discussion of purchase requests for his division. Lori Johnson from the Columbus plant has confronted Reba about scheduling meetings on short notice and showing favoritism to Bill.

1. Critique Reba's performance as a group leader.

2. What can committee members do to improve group communication?

3. Could the Information Technology Committee conduct its meetings using teleconferencing? Defend your response.

ENDNOTES

[1]Antony Jay, "How to Run a Meeting," *Harvard Business Review*, Vol. 54, No. 2 (March–April, 1976), p. 43.

[2]Ibid., p. 46.

[3]Ibid., pp. 44–45.

[4]George M. Prince, "How to Be a Better Meeting Chairman," *Harvard Business Review*, Vol. 47, No. 1 (January–February, 1969), p. 99.

[5]*Robert's Rules of Order* (New York: The Berkley Publishing Group, 1984).

[6]Janet Falon, "How to Be a Meeting 'Manager,'" *Successful Meetings*, Vol. 31, No. 5 (May, 1982), pp. 63–66.

[7]B. Y. Auger, *How to Run Better Business Meetings; An Executive's Guide to Meetings That Get Things Done* (Minneapolis: Minnesota Mining and Manufacturing Company, 1979), pp. 82–84.

[8]Philip L. Hunsaker, "Communicating Better: There's No Proxy for Proxemics," *Business*, Vol. 30, No. 2 (March–April, 1980), pp. 41–48.

[9]"Survey for Public Television Stations Predicts Growth in Teleconferencing," *Telespan Newsletter*, Vol. 3 (June 15, 1983), p. 3.

[10]Martin C. J. Elton, *Teleconferencing: New Media for Business Meetings*, AMA Management Briefings (New York: American Management Associations, 1982), pp. 24–26.

[11]Ibid., p. 38.

[12]John Penrose, "Telecommunications, Teleconferencing, and Business Communications," *The Journal of Business Communication*, Vol. 21, No. 1 (Winter, 1984), p. 102.

[13]Robert Johansen and Christine Bullen, "What to Expect from Teleconferencing," *Harvard Business Review*, Vol. 62, No. 2 (March–April, 1984), p. 164.

[14]Ibid., p. 165.

8

GROUP COMMUNICATION: MAKING SPEECHES

When you complete this chapter, you should be able to:

▲ List and briefly explain the variables associated with the formality or degree of structure of a speech.

▲ List and describe the eight phases that comprise the speech-making process.

▲ Discuss the distinguishing characteristics and limitations of the four basic delivery styles for presenting a speech.

▲ Describe the characteristics (advantages and disadvantages) of the seven visual aids used to enhance a speech.

Today's up-and-coming leaders and managers often find it necessary to give speeches to large and small groups within or outside their organizations. Thus, managers need to develop the ability to make formal and informal speeches. They also need to understand how to select and use visual aids to enhance their speeches. In short, managers need to strive constantly to perfect their speaking skills and to become speakers that others admire—speakers who can get the job done in any speaking situation.

▲ SPEAKER'S ROLE

Periodically, managers are asked to speak or to give a speech at a meeting. A *speech* is a requested address or talk given before a group. Upon request, speakers deliver a speech or presentation that informs, persuades, or entertains. A speaker's purpose for giving a speech varies based on the nature of the group, the size of the group, and the reason for the group's meeting. The *formality* or degree of structure of a speech depends on the following variables:

A speech is a requested address or talk.

Several variables influence the formality of a speech.

1. Speaker's personality — Shy, introverted speakers tend to give more formal speeches; gregarious, extroverted speakers tend to be more relaxed and give less formal or informal speeches.
2. Speaker's purpose — Generally speeches to inform and persuade tend to be more formal than speeches to motivate or entertain.
3. Speaker's relationship with the group — Speeches tend to be less formal when given before internal groups — groups to which the speaker belongs as either group leader or group member. Speeches tend to be more formal when given before external groups — groups to which the speaker does not belong.
4. Size of the group — Speeches given to small groups tend to be less formal than speeches given to large groups.
5. Membership of the group — The formality of a speech tends to increase in direct proportion to the number of group members who outrank the speaker.
6. Meeting atmosphere — A relaxed atmosphere is conducive to informal speeches.
7. Amount of time allotted for the speech — Generally short speeches tend to be less formal than long speeches.

As with any form of communication, speech making requires planning. Whenever possible, speakers should plan their speeches. Proper planning enables speakers to control their performance in delivering speeches. Exercising control over performance involves controlling one's body movements, one's eye contact, the time allotment, and the speech itself.[1]

▲ SPEECH DEVELOPMENT

Speakers should plan speeches based on the eight phases of speech development.

The eight phases that comprise the speech-making process are (1) analyzing the audience, (2) researching the topic, (3) preparing an outline, (4) choosing a delivery style, (5) practicing delivery, (6) delivering the speech, (7) entertaining questions, and (8) evaluating the performance. Each of these eight phases should be planned carefully.

Analyzing the Audience

Speakers need to know their audience. Audience analysis is important if a speaker wishes to deliver a speech that is informative and timely. Speakers should ask and answer these questions prior to preparing their speeches: Who is the audience? Why are these people assembling? What is the age range of the audience? What interests, abilities, and knowledge does the audience possess? Answers to these questions affect the topic selected and the kinds of information to be included.

Researching the Topic

Speakers should express complex concepts in clear, concise terms.

After analyzing the audience, speakers should research the assigned topic of the speech; if a specific topic is not assigned, speakers should choose and research a topic based on audience analysis. Speakers should determine the purpose for making a speech. Is the purpose to inform, to persuade, or to entertain? Researching a topic requires identifying what the audience knows and what the audience wants or needs to know. Speakers should express complex concepts in clear, concise terms.

Preparing an Outline

Researching the topic helps speakers generate ideas for the speech's content. The outline of a speech should be simple and should contain only a few main points. A lengthy, complicated outline yields a lengthy, complicated speech. When such a speech is given, the audience may have difficulty comprehending and retaining the speech's message. A speaker should develop an interest-arousing introduction, logically organize the main points, integrate appropriate visuals, and develop a positive summary statement.

Choosing a Delivery Style

Much of a speaker's success in making a speech depends on delivery style. How a speech is delivered is as important as the speech's content. The selection of an appropriate delivery style is so significant that a major part of this chapter (pages 123–127) pertains to commonly used delivery styles and the variables to consider when choosing a delivery style.

Practicing Delivery

If possible, speakers should practice their speeches prior to delivery. Practicing a speech helps speakers identify strengths and weaknesses in content and delivery. It also allows speakers to approximate the amount of time needed. Rehearsals have a calming effect on some nervous speakers. During the rehearsal, speakers should be sensitive to how their nonverbal and verbal messages blend in the speech. Speakers should check nonverbal messages such as posture, poise, hand gestures, and eye contact.

Speakers should practice blending nonverbal and verbal messages in their speeches.

Good posture helps speakers project competence and professionalism. Poor posture and lack of composure or confidence can distract the audience's attention and can negatively influence the audience's perceptions of the speaker's credibility. Hand gestures may complement verbal messages, but excessive hand gestures may distract. Speakers should maintain good eye contact with the audience. Eye contact is helpful to both the speaker *and* the audience. The audience can use eye contact to verify the meaning of spoken messages, and speakers can adjust their speeches based on nonverbal messages received from eye contact with the audience. Good eye contact is essential if a speaker and an audience are to communicate effectively.

Speakers should monitor their voice pitch, speaking rate, volume, pronunciation, transitions, and English usage. Speakers should regulate their voice pitch so that they speak within a moderate to low range; high-pitched voices can be abrasive and can make listening difficult. Speakers should speak quickly enough to maintain the audience's interest but slowly enough to be understood. Speaker volume should fluctuate, raising when main points are emphasized and when audience interest appears to wane. Speakers should pronounce words properly, use smooth transitions to join the parts of a speech, and use correct grammar.

Speakers should practice greeting the audience, introducing the topic in an interesting manner, sharing the main points, using visuals, summarizing the main points, and entertaining any questions.

Delivering the Speech

Speech delivery should be an enjoyable experience for the audience and for the speaker. It represents the culmination of time and effort spent in earlier phases of the speech-making process. In all likelihood, speech delivery will closely resemble rehearsals. Speakers should dress appropriately when delivering a speech; appearance affects how speakers feel about themselves and how audiences react to them.

A good speech has a strong opening. Speakers may wish to capture audience attention immediately by starting speeches with a quote, an anecdote, a statistic, or a question. "One year from now more than 30 percent of this audience will have changed jobs" is an example of how a statistic is used to open a speech. Speakers can gradually move into their speeches by first thanking the audience and/or their introducers for the opportunity to speak. Speakers should avoid starting speeches with a joke unless the joke is directly related to the speech. Suggestive or rude remarks are inappropriate when giving a speech.

During delivery, speakers should speak at a comfortable pace so that breathing is natural; speech content should be sequenced so that transitions are smooth. Speakers should use examples and visuals to make main ideas easy to understand. Often speakers use literary devices such as analogies, metaphors, and similes to simplify complex concepts. Positive closing statements should be used to tie together the main ideas of a speech.

Entertaining Questions

Speakers should offer to entertain questions regarding the content of their speeches. If a speaker prefers to entertain questions during a speech, the speaker should tell the audience to ask questions accordingly.

Entertaining questions at the end of a speech prevents disruptions in speech delivery and allows better control of delivery time. However, delayed audience interaction can be a major disadvantage of entertaining questions at the end of a speech.

Some speakers let questions intimidate them. However, remember that ". . . as the person at the podium, you are in charge and cannot be pushed into a corner unless you permit it."[2] Speakers are considered experts on their topics; listeners want to know what speakers think. Thus, questions should flatter rather than intimidate speakers.

Speakers are considered experts on their topics.

Evaluating the Performance

Many speakers provide formal evaluation instruments for group members to use in evaluating the effectiveness of a speech. Formal evaluations can prove beneficial to the speaker and the audience. The speaker benefits by learning how the audience perceived the speech's content and delivery. Formal evaluation helps the speaker assess whether a speech served its intended purpose or met the audience's expectations. An example of a general speech evaluation instrument is shown in Figure 8–1 on page 124. This type of instrument may be used by an audience as a formal evaluation or by the speaker as an informal self-evaluation. Speakers should use formal evaluation feedback to improve content and delivery. Speakers should give special attention to content areas rated "Disagree" or "Strongly Disagree," indicating weaknesses in audience analysis, topic research, and speech outline preparation. Speakers should also seek to improve delivery areas rated "Fair" or "Poor," which denote an inappropriate choice of delivery style, inadequate practice, improper speech delivery, or inappropriate handling of questions. In addition to having the audience complete evaluation instruments, some groups formally evaluate a speech by having a reactor comment on the speech's strengths, weaknesses, and implications immediately following delivery.

Both the audience and the speaker may evaluate a speech.

Speakers can evaluate a speech informally by observing audience verbal and nonverbal feedback during and after a speech or by taping the speech and critiquing it at a later date. Evaluation criteria varies depending on the type of speech. Including timely, accurate, and research-based content is more important when speaking to inform than when speaking to entertain. The evaluation of a speech to persuade should determine whether the speaker has moved the audience to take the desired course of action.

▲ SPEECH DELIVERY STYLES

Managers and other professionals use four basic delivery styles for presenting a speech: written, memorized, extemporaneous, and impromptu.

SPEECH EVALUATION FORM

CONTENT				
	Strongly Agree	Agree	Disagree	Strongly Disagree
Timely				
Accurate				
Research Based				
Logically Organized				
Interesting				
Provocative				

Comments: _____
_____

STRUCTURE				
	Strongly Agree	Agree	Disagree	Strongly Disagree
Effective Opening				
Smooth Transitions Between Speech Parts				
Effective Closing				
Adequate Question/ Answer Period				

Comments: _____
_____

DELIVERY				
	Excellent	Good	Fair	Poor
Nonverbal Skills:				
Eye Contact				
Facial Expressions				
Gestures				
Voice:				
Quality				
Volume				
Pitch				
Rate				
English Usage:				
Grammar				
Word Choice				
Visuals:				
Relevance				
Appearance				
Readability				
Coordination				

Comments: _____
_____

FIGURE 8–1   Evaluation Instrument for Speeches

The style or combination of styles used depends largely upon the subject matter of the speech, the type of audience, and the speaking occasion or situation.

Written Speech

A *written speech* occurs when the speaker presents a subject to an audience by reading word for word from a written manuscript. Actually, this delivery style is more accurately described as a reading skill rather than a speaking skill.

On most speaking occasions, managers should avoid the written speech. When viewed as a specialized delivery style, however, many managers find the written speech to be appropriate, perhaps even necessary. The presentation of certain types of technical, legal, or complex material that demands absolute accuracy may call for the written speech. Also, time limits imposed on managers in certain speaking situations, such as preparing a cassette tape or making a presentation on radio or television, may require reading from a manuscript.

> Use the written speech when careful wording is required.

Three basic problems are often associated with reading a speech. First, the speaker's eyes are typically glued to the manuscript, which severely restricts adjusting the message to the audience's feedback. Second, the presentation often becomes flat and somewhat mechanical unless it has been thoroughly prepared and rehearsed. Third, several sheets of manuscript paper on the podium or in the speaker's hands may cause unrest among members of the audience who fear that the speech will run too long.

THE SATURDAY EVENING POST

"Well, I see my time is up . . ."

Source: © 1959 The Curtis Publishing Company.

If a speech must be read from a manuscript, the following guidelines are suggested:

1. Use simpler words and shorter, less complex sentences than might be used for a written essay.
2. Use short paragraphs.
3. Repeat main ideas and key words.
4. Provide many definitions, illustrations, examples, and comparisons.
5. Use personal pronouns such as *I*, *we*, *our*, *us*, or *you* rather than *they*, *people*, or *the speaker*.
6. Use large type to enhance visibility.
7. Triple-space the typed manuscript and use wide margins to reduce the chances of misreading the text.
8. Type on only one side of the paper.
9. Mark the manuscript for pauses; underscore words to be emphasized.
10. Mark the places where visual aids are to be used.
11. Practice reading the speech aloud, perhaps once a day for several days prior to the presentation. Record the speech on a cassette recorder and listen to the cassette to discover where the text can be improved.
12. Practice in front of a mirror while reading as the manuscript becomes more familiar.

Memorized Speech

A *memorized speech* occurs when the speaker commits to memory every word of a written speech. Of all the delivery styles, the memorized speech has the potential for the greatest number of problems.

Avoid memorizing an entire speech.

Managers will find little justification in devoting large amounts of time to memorizing entire speeches. The danger of forgetting part of a speech, perhaps a crucial point or important data, is very real. If one's memory fails during the presentation, panic may set in and cause the speaker to forget the rest of the speech. Also, the actual delivery of a memorized speech often sounds too formal or impersonal. Moreover, managers find it almost impossible to adapt memorized material to audience feedback.

However, to dramatize the opening, closing, or key points of a speech, a speaker may memorize a quotation, joke, poem, or statistic. When used at just the right place in a speech, a memorized passage can be most effective in gaining and holding the attention of the audience.

Extemporaneous Speech

The *extemporaneous speech* is a carefully planned, thoroughly researched and rehearsed presentation. Generally the speaker prepares a detailed plan or outline of the speech and then practices it several times prior to the presentation. The extemporaneous delivery style is preferred for most speech-making occasions.

Strive to use the extemporaneous speech in most speaking situations.

Managers who use this mode of presentation can prepare by drawing upon their past experiences as well as collecting current material from newspapers, magazines, and professional journals. The key to successful extemporaneous speaking is to organize main ideas as clearly as possible. Many managers prefer to prepare a simple outline of key points on 3"-by-5" index cards.

Establishing and maintaining constant eye contact with the group or audience during the delivery permits the speaker to adapt the language and content of the speech to the audience's feedback. As the need arises, a speaker may repeat or expand any ideas not understood by the listeners. The delivery should be casual and conversational.

Impromptu Speech

An *impromptu speech* occurs when the speaker is called upon to deliver a few words on the spur of the moment with little or no time for preparation. Impromptu speaking may be a stressful experience for the speaker, and the response may be a fumbling, disorganized presentation.

Managers who are well known for their expertise in a field or subject or who have made significant contributions to their profession are prime targets for impromptu speaking requests. Managers can avoid being caught off guard by anticipating situations in which they may be called upon to speak. They should be prepared at all times to share an idea or two with the group or audience. These ideas should be clearly presented in a natural order, such as periods of time or pros and cons. With experience, managers will be able to make short mental outlines of their main ideas, say what needs to be said as briefly as possible, and end the speech.

Always be prepared to say a few words.

▲ VISUAL AIDS

Visual aids are graphic or written materials used to convey a message or to reinforce a spoken message. Speakers often use visual aids to enhance a

Visual aids enhance a presentation.

presentation. Visual aids allow listeners to supplement sound messages with sight messages. Effective visual aids make spoken presentations clearer to the audience.

Visual aids represent a form of security for many speakers; using visual aids gives speakers something to do with their hands during a presentation. A speaker should use visual aids to support the presentation. For example, the use of a handout showing tuition reimbursement policy in a personnel director's speech on training opportunities is an appropriate visual aid. Nevertheless, "Visuals can be misused . . . . If a visual can be dropped with no loss, it probably should be."[3] Unnecessary visual aids detract from the effectiveness of a presentation. For example, the use of a transparency listing budget department personnel in a plant manager's speech on retirement benefits is unnecessary.

Source: © 1979 King Features Syndicate, Inc. World rights reserved.

If possible, a speaker should prepare visual aids in advance. Advance preparation saves presentation time and reduces interruptions in presentation flow. During a presentation, a speaker may need to add points or prepare additional visual aids to enhance the group communication process.

The graphic or written content of visual aids should be large enough or project large enough for group members to read. Type or print all written information included in a visual aid; cursive writing is not always legible. Figure 8–2 shows the recommended placement of visual aids in a meeting room.

Visual aids should be brief and to the point. Use active verbs whenever possible. Lengthy statements should be included in handout material. When listeners must strain to read lengthy passages from a distance, the visual aid is weakened.

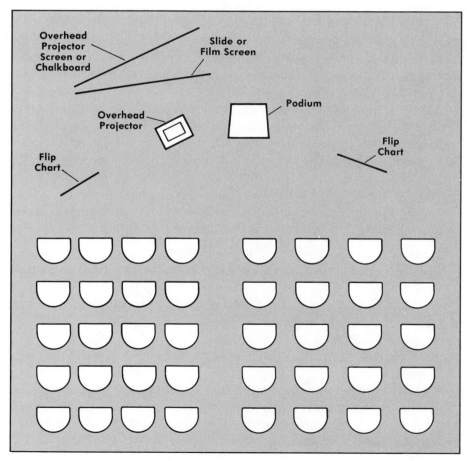

FIGURE 8–2   Recommended Placement of Visual Aids

Presenters should limit the number of points included in a visual aid. Auger recommends only one point be shown in a visual, and he suggests that a visual be limited to six or seven lines containing no more than six or seven words per line.[4] The specific content of visual aids for speeches and written reports is described in Chapter 15.

Commonly used visual aids include the chalkboard, the flip chart, transparencies, handout material, slides, films, and videocassettes.

Chalkboard or Multipurpose Board

Use the chalkboard only before small groups.

The chalkboard is a low-cost, flexible vehicle for displaying nonprojected visuals to small groups. During a speech, the chalkboard is an ideal medium for developing an idea step-by-step or for illustrating an idea or process that was not clearly understood by the audience through words. Although extensive printing and drawing can be placed on the chalkboard prior to a speech, many managers prefer to use the board at an appropriate time during the speech. This allows for quick reference to new words, outlines, classifications, drawings, sketches, and other forms of impromptu support.

Many meeting rooms are now equipped with multipurpose boards rather than chalkboards. These boards have a smooth, nonglare white plastic surface. Special marking pens are used, and marks can be erased easily with a damp cloth. The newer boards with steel backings also serve as magnetic boards for displaying visuals and as screens for projecting transparencies, slides, and films.

Follow these suggestions for using a chalkboard or multipurpose board when delivering a speech before a small group:

1. Have spare pieces of chalk or extra marking pens ready for use.
2. Make words and drawings large enough to be seen from all parts of the room.
3. Avoid using the bottom half of the board if speaking from the same floor level as the audience.
4. Avoid putting too much material on the board at one time.
5. Avoid talking to the board or standing in front of what has been written.
6. Place complex material on the board prior to delivering the speech.
7. Initially cover prepared displays with paper, held in place by scotch tape, so the audience won't see the material until the proper time.
8. Keep the board clean.

Flip Chart

Flip charts are large pads of paper mounted on easels. Presenters use grease pencils, felt-tipped markers, or colored chalk to mark on flip charts. Flip charts are best used with small groups. Large audiences, such as assemblies, experience difficulty in reading flip charts from a distance.

> Flip charts are best used with small groups.

Flip charts are portable; they can be prepared in advance, carried to a meeting, and mounted on most easel-like stands. Their use can appear spontaneous, such as when a presenter lists a group of ideas during a meeting. Ideas on a flip chart should be bulleted or enumerated and should be written using large print.

Transparencies

Use of transparencies projected on a screen by an overhead projector has become very popular. Transparencies are easy and inexpensive to prepare using felt-tipped markers or thermal processing equipment. Transparencies may be used to display graphic material, printed or typed material, or a combination of the two. This medium is convenient to use because it is less susceptible to equipment malfunction than other media and it can be used with any size audience. Transparencies are easy to transport. They can be prepared ahead of time and marked for emphasis during speeches, or they can be prepared and used during a speech. Transparencies can be used effectively when preparation time is limited, such as when a committee brainstorms annual objectives and then wishes to share brainstorming results in a committee report to a larger audience. Colored overlays or multiple transparencies may be used to show the development or progression of variables throughout designated time periods. Points projected on a screen may be revealed one at a time or all at once. Speakers who use transparencies as visual aids should use good quality film and markers. Transparencies should be stored in a dry, cool place when not in use.

> Transparencies are easy to transport.

Handout Material

Speakers may effectively use handout material, such as brochures or copied material, as visual aids when they want audience members to read lengthy quotes or passages. A speaker may use handout material effectively with any size audience. A major advantage of handout material is that audience members get to keep handouts for future reference. A major disadvantage of handout material is that audience members may become

> Handout material may be used with any size audience.

so involved in reading the handouts that they forget to listen to the speaker. Thus, save handouts until the end of the presentation.

Copied materials are easy to prepare, but they can be expensive when used with large audiences. Copied handouts should be of good quality, readable, and in a size that can be filed and retrieved easily by audience members.

Slides

A speaker may build a very effective extemporaneous presentation for both small and large groups by using 35mm slides. These have become the standard for most still picture projection. When a roll of 35mm slide film is sent for processing, the slides are usually returned in 2"-by-2" cardboard or plastic mounts. Anyone with a limited knowledge of a 35mm camera can take high-quality color slides of people, buildings, scenery, and objects. Also, making slides of flat artwork—maps, charts, photographs, magazine illustrations, business forms, and the like—is a rather simple technique when using a copystand such as the Kodak Visualmaker.® The speaker can arrange and rearrange slides in a variety of sequences. In addition, the speaker can place slides in clear plastic slide holders for easy sorting and selection and then store the slide holders in three-ring binders.

Today's slide projectors are designed to give hours of trouble-free performance. Most projectors are tray-loaded and hold up to several dozen slides. The speaker can control the pace of the slide presentation from the front of the room by manually operating the projector or off to the side of the room by using a remote control switch which changes slides, reverses them, and adjusts the focus. The speaker can achieve the dramatic impact of a smooth flow of slides by adding a second slide projector and a dissolve unit. As shown in Figure 8–3, two projectors are pointed at one screen. The slides are then alternated between the two trays, odd numbers in one tray and even numbers in the other. The major drawback to a slide presentation is that the room must be dark, which prevents the speaker from observing the audience's reaction to the presentation and from referencing any notes.

Here are several suggestions that can add a touch of professionalism to a slide presentation:

1. Make certain that the equipment is set up and ready to go.
2. Preview the slides to make sure that they are in the proper sequence and position.

Slides will add color and visual impact to a speech.

A dissolve unit provides smooth transitions between slide images.

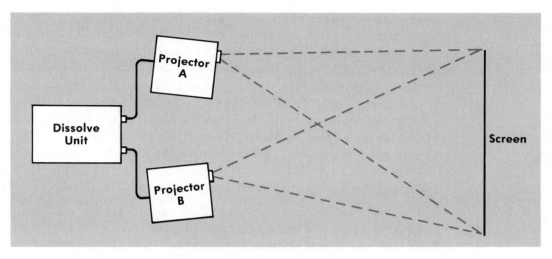

FIGURE 8–3   Two Slide Projectors Connected to a Dissolve Unit

3. Position the screen so that each member of the audience has a clear, unobstructed view. Placing the screen in the corner of a square or rectangular room creates a good viewing area.
4. Know your speech since the darkened room will make notes or scripts extremely difficult to read.
5. Use a conventional stick pointer to focus the audience's attention to specific points of interest in a slide. If the screen is very large or too high for a conventional pointer, use a light pointer.
6. Begin and end the presentation with a solid-colored slide to avoid a large splash of projector light on the screen.

Films

Although a film is an acceptable instructional medium for training situations, a full-length film is seldom used with speeches. Yet, no other audiovisual device has the power to hold the attention of both large and small audiences and to contribute to effective learning as can a film. A speech on time management, for example, would gain considerable impact if presented with the opening segment of the film *The Time of Your Life*.[5]

Use a film segment to reinforce a major point in a speech.

Three major problems confront the manager who plans to use a film to illustrate a main point in a speech. First, locating available films is difficult for most managers. The most comprehensive information sources for films are the *Index to 16mm Educational Film* and *Index to 8mm Motion Cartridges.*[6] Second, a film is exceedingly expensive to purchase. For most managers, film rental is more economical for a single presentation. Third, the technical aspects of setting up the projector and sound system strike fear in many people. Managers would be well advised to hire the services of a skilled operator to set up the equipment and run the projector during the speech.

The key points for using a film in a presentation are as follows:

1. Preview a film before deciding to use all or part of it.
2. Order the film well in advance of its planned use.
3. Position the screen wherever the audience has the best view.
4. If lighting is a problem, move the projector closer to the screen to get a brighter (but smaller) image.
5. Place a single audio speaker as close as possible to the screen and aimed toward the audience. If stereo speakers are used, place them far enough apart to balance the sound.
6. Before the presentation, run the film through the projector to the opening scene of the segment or film.

Videocassettes

Videocassettes are one of the most widely used visual aids today and may soon become the standard for recorded images. The *videocassette* is a videotape completely enclosed in a plastic container. Videocassettes are used with a *videocassette recorder (VCR),* a playback device designed for use by the nontechnical person.

The VCR is extremely easy to use. A videocassette is placed into an opening in the front or on top of the VCR, and the machine automatically threads the tape. The VCR will play back into an ordinary TV set. The user can easily start, stop, restart, rewind, fast forward, and repeat a videocassette by operating the appropriate knob, lever, or button on the VCR.

Since many popular films and training films have been copied onto videocassettes, the VCR is ideal for enhancing a speech to a small audience. The VCR can be preset to the beginning of a segment on the videocassette and turned off at the end of the segment. Furthermore, the TV screen does not need a darkened room, which means that a videocassette can be used in conjunction with other visual aids.

SUMMARY

Occasionally managers and other leaders are asked to give speeches before groups within or outside their organizations. The major purposes for giving a speech are to inform, persuade, or entertain. The formality of a speech depends on the speaker's personality, the speaker's purpose, the speaker's relationship with the group, the size of the group, the membership of the group, the meeting atmosphere, and the amount of time allotted for the speech.

Proper planning enables speakers to control their speech performance. Speakers should carefully plan each of the eight phases which comprise the speech-making process: analyzing the audience, researching the topic, preparing an outline, choosing a delivery style, practicing delivery, delivering the speech, entertaining questions, and evaluating the performance.

Speakers use four basic delivery styles for presenting speeches. A speaker uses a written speech to present a subject by reading word for word from a written manuscript. A written speech can be used effectively when technical, legal, or complex material is shared with an audience. A speaker uses the memorized speech by committing to memory every word of a written speech. This delivery style has numerous disadvantages; speakers who use this delivery style run the risk of forgetting part of a speech. Yet, memorizing parts of a speech may effectively gain and hold the audience's attention. Memorizing passages is preferred to memorizing an entire speech. An extemporaneous speech is casual and conversational; it is carefully planned and rehearsed so that it appears natural. The extemporaneous delivery style is preferred for most speaking occasions. The impromptu speech occurs when the speaker is asked to speak but has little or no time to prepare. Speakers can avoid being caught off guard if they learn to anticipate situations in which they might be called upon to speak.

Speakers often use visual aids to enhance speeches. Visual aids are graphic or written materials used to convey a message or to reinforce a spoken message. If possible, speakers should prepare visual aids in advance. Speakers should make sure that the content of visual aids is large enough for an audience to read. All visual aids should be clear and concise, and presenters should limit the number of points included in a visual aid. Commonly used visual aids include the chalkboard, the flip chart, transparencies, handout material, slides, films, and videocassettes.

QUESTIONS

1. What variables influence the formality of a speech?
2. Name and describe the eight phases of the speech-making process.
3. Why is audience analysis important?
4. How can a speaker evaluate speech content and delivery?
5. Is it possible to be prepared to deliver an impromptu speech? Explain.
6. Which of the four speech delivery styles is preferred for most speaking occasions? Why?
7. Can speakers overuse or misuse visual aids? Defend your response.
8. When would it be appropriate to use a chalkboard as a visual aid for an oral presentation?
9. What accounts for the popularity of a 35mm slide presentation?
10. Why are films seldom used by speakers to increase the effectiveness of oral presentations?

PROBLEM-SOLVING EXPERIENCES

1. You have been asked to speak to your class on the topic of "Time Management." Complete an audience analysis of your class.

2. Prepare a three- to four-minute extemporaneous speech to inform on the topic "I Am a Winner." Use at least one visual aid with the speech.

CASE 8–1

While having their coffee break this morning, Jerold Filbert and Rick Doane compared notes on their professional meeting obligations for the remainder of the month. Jerold remarked that he is scheduled to speak at the Office Systems Society's (OSS) August dinner meeting. His assigned topic is "Motivating Employees through Example." Rick heard Jerold give a similar speech to the Chamber of Commerce earlier in the year. To the best of Rick's recollection, Jerold's speech had been little more than a series of jokes and anecdotes that were read from notes and shown on overhead projector transparencies.

Later, Jerold said, "Rick, weren't you at the Chamber of Commerce meeting when I gave the same speech? Why don't you give me some ideas on how I can improve the speech for the OSS meeting?" Cringing at the thought of having to react to Jerold's questions, Rick responded, "Let me think about this for a couple of days, and I'll get back to you."

1. Give suggestions for improvement that Rick should share with Jerold.

ENDNOTES

[1] Jim Biundo, "The Best Way to Speak; Four Steps to Becoming a Confident Public Speaker," *Management World*, Vol. 11, No. 9 (September, 1982), pp. 34–35.

[2] Richard N. Smith, "Public Speaking, How to Feel at Home on the Podium," *Association Management*, Vol. 32, No. 8 (August, 1980), p. 126.

[3] Ibid., p. 125.

[4] B. Y. Auger, *How to Run Better Business Meetings; An Executive's Guide to Meetings That Get Things Done* (Minneapolis: Minnesota Mining and Manufacturing Company, 1979), p. 90.

[5]The film *The Time of Your Life* is produced and distributed by The Cally Curtis Company, 1111 North Las Palmas Avenue, Hollywood, CA 90038.

[6]The film indexes *Index to 16mm Educational Film* and *Index to 8mm Motion Cartridges* are published by the National Information Center for Educational Media, University of Southern California, University Park, Los Angeles, CA 90007.

9

THE IMPORTANCE OF READING

Reading is defined as the process of extracting information and meaning from text copy, including printed, keyboarded, or handwritten pages; figures; and tables.

Thousands of potential managers graduate from college each year with marginal reading skills. Learning, of course, does not begin with college, and it certainly should not end there. Today's managers must make a serious effort to understand and improve their reading skills in order to meet the job-related and self-improvement reading demands placed on them.

Reading is extracting information and meaning from text copy.

▲ WHAT READING MEANS FOR TODAY'S MANAGERS

Today's managers are responsible for continually increasing and expanding their abilities and for contributing to the improvement of their organizations. To do these well, managers should undertake a reading-based program for professional development.

Professional Development

The professional development of today's managers takes place in several ways—by talking with other people; by attending conferences, seminars, workshops, and classes; by listening to the radio and cassette tapes; by watching television, videotapes, and videodisks; and by reading newspapers, periodicals, and books. Clearly the development of a greatly heightened level of professional thought and behavior can never be accomplished solely through contact with others or the formal systems of education. In fact, reading is the principal means by which managers continue their self-education in life.

Reading is an essential factor of professional development.

Four compelling reasons for managers to develop a sound reading program include the following:

1. Managers need to be informed about what goes on in the business world, in their respective professions, and in related professions. As business becomes more complex, the managers' search for relevant information that will permit them to keep pace becomes an extremely important activity.
2. Managers need to improve their abilities to judge ideas and to solve problems. Continual practice is needed to evaluate ideas effectively

and to deal with problems creatively. Comprehensive reading that focuses on a broad spectrum of general and factual knowledge provides managers with a basis for just that kind of practice.

3. Managers need to seek new personal dimensions of knowledge and skill that can contribute to their career development and self-enhancement. Most managers will discover that what they learn through their professional reading will give them valuable new insights into the work they do.

4. Managers need to improve their reading ability in order to cope with on-the-job reading requirements. Most managers are faced with a large number of letters, memos, and reports to read in their daily work. Efforts to increase reading efficiency for self-development should have a positive effect on the required reading for the job. One researcher has suggested that managers form working teams for the purpose of understanding what helps or hinders the reading of job-related materials.[1]

The reading demands of business require the ability to understand the message the writer is trying to convey. Understanding is the most important factor in the reading process.

Comprehension

The goal of reading is better comprehension.

Although a precise definition of reading comprehension cannot be supported by research, it is clear that **comprehension,** generally referred to as understanding, is the heart of reading; it is a complex, dynamic activity. Despite the lack of solid research, the following general comments about comprehension can be given:[2]

1. Though the end result sought in reading is comprehension, being able to identify words is a necessary means to that end.

2. Materials used to teach comprehension must match the reader's reading level.

Reading comprehension is made up of a number of related and overlapping skills.

3. Comprehension is made up of a number of related and overlapping skills and abilities.

4. Once comprehension skill has been mastered, enough practice must be scheduled to keep the skill at the desired level of competence.

Reading Comprehension Skills

Even though a debate among reading experts has been going on for years about the factors that make up reading comprehension, there is considerable agreement that several comprehension skills are needed for effective reading. These comprehension skills include (1) distinguishing between fact and opinion, (2) interpreting semantic relationships, (3) recognizing main ideas, (4) recognizing details, (5) recognizing sequences of events, (6) recognizing cause-and-effect relationships, (7) following directions, (8) interpreting figurative language, and (9) recognizing propaganda techniques.[3]

Good readers use a variety of comprehension skills.

Distinguishing Between Fact and Opinion

The reader recognizes the difference between a statement that can be proved (fact) and a generally held view (opinion). *Example*: In the following paragraph, identify the sentences that state facts:

> Jill Carter received the outstanding employee award in her division. She received the award because she is friendly and energetic. Stan Worth should have gotten the award; but Stan's boss, Mack Pemberton, does not like Stan. Jess Grogan received the outstanding employee award last year.

Answer: The first and last sentences are facts.

Interpreting Semantic Relationships

The reader uses context clues to derive the meaning of a word. *Example*: Use context clues to determine the meaning of the underlined word in each of these sentences:

How can a reader determine the meaning of an unfamiliar word?

1. The <u>assertive</u> secretary insisted that the clerk-typist work overtime.
   Answer: bold
2. As soon as these pages are <u>collated</u>, I will turn in my monthly report.
   Answer: assembled in order
3. The <u>obstinate</u> employee received a written reprimand.
   Answer: stubborn

Recognizing Main Ideas

The reader recognizes the major point or purpose of the passage. *Example*: After reading the following paragraph, select the best title:

> Jetco Industries was founded at the turn of the century in Columbus, Ohio. Robert Sloan was the company's founder. The company grew to six times its original size under Sloan's leadership. Years later, Sloan's influence still permeates the company.

1. The Growth of Jetco Industries
2. Robert Sloan's Leadership
3. An Enduring Old Company
4. Timeless Leadership

Answer: 2.

Recognizing Details

Readers should recognize facts that support a main idea.

The reader recognizes facts in a passage that support a main idea. *Example*: Read the following passage and answer the questions that follow:

Shortly before 10 a.m. on May 20, Jim stumbled into the office. He said that car trouble had caused him to be late again. Jim's reason may be legitimate, but Alice King, Jim's boss, is starting to wonder whether Jim is truthful. It seems that Jim is *always* having car trouble. He was late three days the week of May 11 and four days the week of May 4.

1. What was the approximate time when Jim arrived at work on May 20?
   Answer: 10 a.m.
2. What reason did Jim give for being late?
   Answer: car trouble
3. How many times has Jim been late?
   Answer: 8
4. How many days was he late the week of May 4?
   Answer: 4
5. How many days was he late the week of May 11?
   Answer: 3

Recognizing Sequences of Events

The reader recognizes the order in which events occur. *Example*: Read the following paragraph and answer the questions that follow:

Of the nine presidents of M & M Construction Corporation, four were born in Michigan. In fact, four of the first five presidents were born in Michigan. Thomas Bryan, the first president, was born in Michigan. The second president, John Hannon, was from Massachusetts, as was the sixth president, Annette Roswell. The third through fifth presidents, all from Michigan, were Janice Butler, Charles Hanes, and Robert Broder, respectively. The seventh and eighth presidents, Donald Pickens, Jr. and David Baker, were born in California and Kansas, respectively. The current president, Michelle Cooke, was born in Texas.

1. Who was the first president of M & M Construction Corporation?
   Answer: Thomas Bryan
2. Which president came before Annette Roswell?
   Answer: Robert Broder

3. List the nine presidents of M & M Construction Corporation in order of their service.
   Answer: Thomas Bryan, John Hannon, Janice Butler, Charles Hanes, Robert Broder, Annette Roswell, Donald Pickens, Jr., David Baker, and Michelle Cooke

Recognizing Cause-and-Effect Relationships

The reader recognizes the connection between an effect (consequence) and its cause or causes. The relationship is sometimes directly stated, sometimes implied. When the relationship is directly stated, signal words or phrases such as *because, caused by, since,* and *due to* may be used. *Example:* Identify the word or phrase in each sentence that signals a cause-and-effect relationship. Tell what the cause and effect are.

The relationship between a cause and effect is sometimes implied.

1. Due to higher interest rates, stock prices sagged today.
   Answer: due to; cause—higher interest rates; effect—lower stock prices
2. Sales Manager Lois Foster was late for work because her car had a flat tire.
   Answer: because; cause—flat tire; effect—late for work
3. Since financier Carl Richards had a headache, he went to bed early.
   Answer: since; cause—headache; effect—went to bed early
4. The Air Atlantic accident was caused by an icy runway.
   Answer: caused by; cause—icy runway; effect—accident

Following Directions

The reader understands written instructions well enough to carry them out. *Example:* Read the following instructions and answer the questions that follow:

Understanding is needed to carry out written instructions.

Instructions for Ribbon Cartridge Installation for
the IBM Personal Computer Graphics Printer

1. Set the printer power switch to OFF.
2. Raise the printer cover and lift it from the printer base.
3. Check the print scale to be sure it is in the rear position.
4. Remove the ribbon cartridge from the packing material.
5. Grasp the ribbon cartridge fin in the center.
6. Guide the two tabs on the left side of the ribbon cartridge into the two slots on the left side of the printer frame.
7. Guide the two tabs on the right side of the ribbon cartridge into the two slots on the right side of the printer frame. Press the ribbon cartridge firmly into place and turn the knob in the direction of the arrow to remove any slack in the ribbon.

8. Using a pencil or your finger, guide the ribbon into the slot between the nose of the print head and the ribbon shield.

9. Carefully move the print head to be sure the ribbon is free to move between the nose of the print head and the ribbon shield.

10. Replace the printer cover by reversing the procedure in Step 2.

a. Before installing the ribbon cartridge, what must be done with the printer cover?
Answer: It must be raised and removed from the printer base.

b. What part of the ribbon cartridge must be grasped during installation?
Answer: the fin

c. What must be done immediately after the ribbon cartridge has been pressed firmly into place on the printer frame?
Answer: Turn the knob in the direction of the arrow to remove any slack in the ribbon.

d. The ribbon must be guided into the slot between what two parts of the printer?
Answer: the nose of the print head and the ribbon shield

Interpreting Figurative Language

The reader interprets figures of speech designed to get points across to the reader or to make the statement more effective. *Example:* For each of the following sentences, explain the meaning of the underlined words or phrases:

1. The chairman of the board is a <u>prince of a guy</u>.
Answer: The chairman is a nice person.

2. <u>Make your pitch</u> directly to the line manager.
Answer: Speak to the line manager.

3. The manager was <u>all ears</u>.
Answer: The manager listened carefully.

4. The petty cash account is <u>in the hole about five bucks</u>.
Answer: The petty cash account is overdrawn by about $5.

5. What the vice-president said <u>got my goat</u>.
Answer: The vice-president's comments made me angry.

Recognizing Propaganda Techniques

Propaganda techniques can influence people to believe a certain way.

The reader recognizes that writers sometimes use words to influence others to believe a certain way. The standard propaganda techniques are

▲ Name-calling—Giving a person, place, thing, or idea a bad label. *Example:* The budget director is the Scrooge type.

▲ Glittering generality—Giving a person, place, thing, or idea a good name. *Example:* Robert's restaurant is the best in the city.

▲ Transfer—The imagine-yourself-in-a-desirable-position technique. *Example*: Picture yourself driving a Jaguar.

▲ Testimonial—A statement from either a well-known person or an unknown person testifying to benefits received. *Example*: Texas oilman Buck Kelly eats Skipper's peanut butter.

▲ Plain folks—Being a part of the plain, folksy people. *Example*: CEO Robert Fox is a good old boy.

▲ Card stacking—Selecting only those facts or falsehoods or logical or illogical statements which present the best or worst possible case for an idea, a person, or a product. *Example*: The sales representatives failed because their supervisors did not motivate them enough.

▲ Band wagon—Everybody does it. *Example*: Young people prefer Koala Cola.

For each of the following statements, identify the particular propaganda technique used:

1. Picture yourself in this beautiful swimming pool.
   Answer: transfer
2. Jim Hamilton, president of the Harper Company, is well known for his country fiddlin' skills.
   Answer: plain folks
3. Everybody shops at Arden's.
   Answer: band wagon
4. The shifty-eyed executive glared at the hostile audience.
   Answer: name-calling
5. I lost 40 pounds by switching to Diet Pop.
   Answer: testimonial
6. There is only *one* way to save money, and that is to open an account at City Bank.
   Answer: card stacking
7. The Sales Department has the greatest managers in the company.
   Answer: glittering generality
8. Our executives live in the most prestigious neighborhood in Seattle.
   Answer: glittering generality
9. Clint Westwood drinks Burpsi.
   Answer: testimonial
10. Joe's Fish Market is the best in the West.
    Answer: glittering generality

▲ THE READING PROCESS

Three theories attempt to explain the reading process: the reader-centered theory, the text-centered theory, and the interactive theory.[4]

Reading experts do not agree on how the reading process takes place.

According to the **reader-centered theory of reading,** readers use their existing knowledge and expectations to make sense out of what they read. For example, suppose several people were asked to read the following passage from *Gone with the Wind* by Margaret Mitchell:

F-r - t-m-l-ss t-m-, sh- l-y st-ll, h-r f-c- -n th- d-rt, th- s-n b--t-ng h-tly -p-n h-r, r-m-mb-r-ng th-ngs -nd p--pl- wh- w-r- d--d, r-m-mb-r-ng - w-y -f l-v-ng th-t w-s g-n- f-r-v-r, -nd l--k-ng -p-n th- h-rsh v-st- -f th- d-rk f-t-r-.[5]

Although the omission of vowels from the passage may have slowed down the rate of reading, chances are the readers were still able to interact with the material and derive meaning from it. Part of the ability to read the material depended on the readers making letter-sound associations of some of the consonants or consonant combinations. In order to comprehend the passage, however, the readers had to draw upon their knowledge of how language works as well as anticipate the meaning of unknown words or strings of unknown words.

The **text-centered theory of reading** emphasizes that a reader's ability to understand the meaning of text material is directly related to the structure or organization of the text itself. For example, scrambling the word order in the following passage provides some reading difficulty:

There a is tide the in affairs men
  of
Which, at taken the leads, flood
  on fortune to.[6]

Even though the passage contains familiar words, the unusual grammatical structure influences reading comprehension. Every third word in the passage has been transposed with the preceding word. In addition to sentence structure, other text-centered factors affecting the reader's ability to understand a text include organizational patterns, complex or abstract concepts, technical vocabulary, readability, and the general quality of writing. While every reader encounters difficult or poorly written text material from time to time, the reader should not be accountable for the text's failure to fulfill its part of the communication process.

The **interactive theory of reading** maintains that comprehension depends upon an interaction between the text and the reader. In brief, all the individualities of the reader—intelligence, interests, background experiences, prior success or failure with reading, knowledge of language, and so on—interact with the content and style of the text to yield a given reading speed and level of comprehension.

While mature readers may have large sight vocabularies—that is, a stock of instantly recognized words—many do not have adequate comprehension skills. They have not been taught to critically evaluate the writer's logic or the meaning behind the words. Such reading deficiencies may develop in childhood and carry over to adulthood and to the professional lives of individuals. People do not become better readers by simply growing up.

▲ TYPES OF READING

Managers use different reading skills depending on the complexity of the reading material, the level of detail they wish to understand, and the length of time they must remember the material. Noe suggests that working adults adjust their reading skills to the materials which they read.[7] Results of research conducted by Seifert[8] in 1979 and Auten[9] indicate that reading requirements at work vary. Consequently, employees should exercise flexibility in job-related reading. The basic types of reading are careful reading, skim reading, and scan reading.

Careful Reading

Careful reading involves the comprehension and retention of main ideas and significant details for either short or long periods of time. For example, a company's operating procedures manual warrants careful reading for long-term retention. Written instructions for completing income tax forms require careful reading for short-term retention.

Some people view careful reading as *slow* reading; however, the two are not synonymous. Careful reading requires concentration; in fact, it is sometimes called concentrated reading. It requires more time than other types of reading because every word is read, but it is not necessarily "slow reading." To achieve comprehension, the mind must be committed to the reading material. If managers read too slowly, they may daydream and break concentration on the main topic.

Adult readers generally engage in careful reading at rates ranging from 225 to 275 words per minute; they comprehend approximately 70 to 80 percent of what they read. They may read more slowly if the material is of a contractual nature, if unfamiliar words are used, or if the author has used words with multiple meanings. Faster careful reading is possible if the material contains direct language and/or if the reader is familiar with the terms and subject. Reading rates of 350 to 800 words per minute can be achieved under these conditions. The complexity of the material may slow down or speed up the reading process—material read for leisure may be consumed at a more rapid pace.

Careful reading involves the comprehension and retention of details.

THE FAMILY CIRCUS ®   **By Bil Keane**

"She's readin' the instructions for dinner."

Source: Copyright 1985 Cowles Syndicate, Inc. Reprinted with permission. All rights reserved.

Skim Reading

Only the main ideas are retained in skim reading.

Skim reading consists of finding information known to be in the material or quickly finding important information without reading irrelevant material. When skim reading, readers may not be sure of what they want to find, but they recognize what they want when they see it. Only the main ideas or general theme is comprehended and retained in skim reading; unimportant material is skimmed over. Information obtained from skim reading may be retained for long or short periods of time, and a reading speed of approximately 1,500 words per minute can be attained. The table of contents in a trade journal is an example of material suitable for skim reading.

Punctuation, spacing, type size, and type style are used as reading clues to show what parts of a document contain the main ideas. Readers should also read topic sentences, key words, and the opening and closing sentences of paragraphs.

Scan Reading

Scan reading involves searching for specific information.

Scan reading requires readers to search for specific information which is to be retained for a short period. Information acquired through scan reading is usually forgotten after immediate use. Scan reading speeds approach

3,000 words per minute with the reader scanning over all material except information specifically sought after. Searching for and locating the balance on a bank statement is an example of scan reading.

Some reading experts question whether scan reading constitutes reading. Scanning through material at the rate of 3,000 words per minute does not mean that a reader reads 3,000 words in a minute's time. However, scan reading is recognized as a means for minimizing reading time when specific information is needed.

▲ KINDS OF MATERIALS THAT MANAGERS READ

Reading is critical for managers. Managers not only read the daily load of materials related to their immediate responsibilities, but they also strive to remain current on business trends, technological developments, competitor activity, and new management techniques. Managers are interested in materials that give a historical perspective to present conditions and materials about plans, policies, and strategies for the future.

Some organizations employ professional readers. These readers are responsible for reading the vast volume of incoming materials, extracting and condensing the main ideas, and transmitting synthesized information to the appropriate managers. Some executives may even have personal readers assigned to them, and secretaries often act as readers of some materials. However, some executives feel that readers lack the proper background to screen material due to an inadequate knowledge of what is important. As a result, many managers, particularly young managers, are responsible for their own reading.

Some organizations employ professional readers.

Managers receive materials to read from many sources. Managers mainly read information generated within their respective companies.[10] Internal written communications may include memorandums, notes, procedural and operations manuals, reports, and the like. External written communications consist of documents such as letters, reports, proposals, advertisements, brochures, and contracts. Most of these materials deal with the status of daily operations. Future plans, schedules, and budgets are also addressed in both internal and external communications.

Managers read internal and external written communications.

A broad range of published materials is important for background reading or reference information. Published materials may include instructional materials (particularly those that accompany equipment and software), magazines, newspapers, trade journals, newsletters, books, monographs, and special reports.

Even leisure reading can have an impact on a manager's work. Biographies, historical works, and even historical fiction can spark insight into current conditions, challenge established patterns, and broaden awareness of the business environment.

Faced with a vast volume of reading materials, managers must decide which items require careful reading, skim reading, scan reading, or a combination of these reading types. Time pressures force managers to do a lot of skim reading and scan reading, but managers should make time for the careful reading of critical information.

The time spent reading a particular document is a personal decision. The reader's experiences, background, and interest in the topic affect the time allocated for reading materials. The topic's relevance to current responsibilities, the source of the document, the complexity or readability of the text, the inclusion of graphics, and time pressures from other tasks influence reading time. Table 9–1 depicts characteristics of materials commonly read by a sample of managerial and technical personnel employed by Sperry Univac.

Table 9–1   Content Analysis of Reading Materials

Type of Material	Content Features	Format Features	Readability Features
Technical piece (22-page research report)	Included review of project, technical concepts, performance models, and changes in production, facility, and equipment listing. Referred to physics procedures and methods without explanation or definition.	Boldface type in two sizes for subtopics. Descriptions before diagrams. No table of contents. 40% prose, 40% diagrams, 20% listings.	Border of college and professional level (Raygor, 1970). Typeset and printed.

Table 9–1   Continued

Type of Material	Content Features	Format Features	Readability Features
Proposal (51-page form request for proposal)	General instructions (what to include, length, how to proceed). Used many helping verbs without definitions (shall, will). Mentioned but did not explain criteria and evaluators for past decisions.	Outline form. Some underlining. No table of contents. 80% prose, 20% listings.	Professional level (Raygor, 1979). Typewritten. Small print for 10%. Wide columns, narrow margins. Many acronyms.
Manual/code (160-page computer handbook)	FORTRAN library routines. Computer and math terminology used but not explained. No prose, some brief phrases, formulas.	Table of contents very detailed. Each page organized by purpose, inputs, etc.	Readability estimate not applicable. Printed material.
Data sheet (4-page work statement)	Requirements on product operations. Some terms used are not explained.	Forms and lists. No prose. Listings using many 1-, 2-, or 3-word items.	Readability estimate not applicable. Printed material, part typewritten.

Table 9–1   Continued

Type of Material	Content Features	Format Features	Readability Features
Memo plus attachments (2-page trip report)	Subjects by item. Action requests. Reference items used but not explained.	Standard format. Information throughout, action at end. 100% prose.	College level (Raygor, 1979). Typewritten. Included nine acronyms.
Nontechnical piece (200-page government report)	Initiatives on software, description of candidates, problem areas, study reviews, evaluation criteria. Terms used but not explained.	Table of contents. List of illustrations. Headings, numbered subheadings. References after sections. 95% prose, 5% tables.	Professional level (Raygor, 1979). Faint typewritten copy.

Source: Reprinted with permission of the International Reading Association and Phyllis A. Miller, "Reading Demands in a High-Technology Industry," *Journal of Reading,* Vol. 26, No. 2 (November, 1982), pp. 112–113.

Solicited documents are generally easier to read than unsolicited documents.

Whether documents are solicited or unsolicited can affect how documents are read. Usually solicited documents are easier to read than unsolicited documents because the reader is also the solicitor. Therefore, the reader has a feel for the purpose of the document and how and when the document should be read. Unsolicited material is generally skimmed over first to determine the relevance of the material to the reader.

What a reader intends to do with information influences how the information is read. Items of general interest do not warrant as much attention as important or urgent materials. The writer's identity is another factor that influences how material is read. Documents written by superiors and customers generally demand more attention than documents from staff members and vendors. Usually managers read documents that were prepared to fulfill a specific purpose.

Keyboarded pages with black-and-white graphics on separate pages are still common, but technological advances have created new forms for reading materials. Word processing facilitates the integration of text and graphics on the same page. Reprographics, such as color photocopies, and microforms, such as microfilm and microfiche, have also brought about changes in business reading materials. Electronic mail documents can be read from a video screen or hard copy.

Most of the new technology is focused on improving writer productivity and reducing the physical volume of paperwork. However, proficient readers use technology to improve reading productivity. The search function of many word processing programs can be used for scan reading. Also, managers can search for boldface type, underlined words, and paragraph-start characters or key words.

While new technology offers some advantages, there are also drawbacks. Microfiche is harder to read than standard-size pages of hard copy. Readers who read electronic mail from a video screen soon discover that it is difficult to skim material rapidly, particularly if a dial-up line and modem are used to obtain the mail.

SUMMARY

Reading skills are essential in a manager's daily activities and future professional growth. Managers must read to stay up-to-date. Reading helps improve a manager's creativity and judgment. Insights gained from reading strengthen personal and professional development. Just handling routine, daily affairs requires a lot of reading. Also, writing skills benefit if reading skills are strong.

Comprehension is a complex, dynamic activity. Comprehension requires a number of related skills other than just knowing the meaning of the words. These skills include distinguishing between fact and opinion; interpreting semantic relationships; recognizing main ideas, details, sequences of events, and cause-and-effect relationships; following directions; interpreting figurative language; and recognizing propaganda techniques. What's more, just reaching a certain comprehension skill level is not enough. Reading comprehension skills must be used regularly in order to maintain the desired skill level.

Comprehension is a critical element in reading. According to the reader-centered theory of reading, comprehension depends on the reader's existing knowledge and expectations of the material. The text-centered theory of reading emphasizes the structure or organization of the text as the key element in attaining comprehension. In the interactive theory of reading, the reader's background interacts with the content and style of the text to yield the level of comprehension.

Reading is classified into three main types. Careful reading is required if comprehension and retention of main ideas and details are important. Slow reading is not necessarily careful reading; concentration is the key to effective careful reading. Skim reading is practiced if only the main ideas must be comprehended and remembered. Skim reading is also used to locate information that is known to be in the document or to locate the important information quickly without spending much time on irrelevant information. Scan reading involves searching for information that is to be retained for a short period.

Managers read many documents from inside and outside their own organizations. Letters, reports, memos, proposals, advertisements, trade journals, contracts, and manuals are all on a manger's reading list. Reports on routine business operations, technological developments, competitor activity, and financial trends also demand managerial reading. Sometimes even reading fiction can give a manager important insights.

Some organizations have professional readers to help condense manager reading loads, but most managers do their own reading. Time pressures force managers to plan and to make decisions about what and how they read.

Technology is changing the form of some reading materials. Microforms are reducing the physical volume of paper documents, and word processors and electronic mail also add to the paperless office trend. At the same time, technology is making it easier to produce and store more documents that have to be read.

QUESTIONS

1. Comment on this statement: "Most managers are poor readers."

2. What is the significance of reading in a professional development program?

3. Are the reading comprehension skills listed and illustrated in this chapter independent of one another? Why or why not?

4. Which theory of reading is related to this statement: "Comprehension is building bridges between the known and the unknown"? Explain.

5. Define reading in terms of the interactive theory.

6. Identify at least three examples of materials you read recently for which careful reading was appropriate.

7. Compare and contrast the three basic types of reading.

8. Comment on why reading slowly is not necessarily the same as reading carefully.

9. List ten different types of materials that managers must routinely read.

10. How has technology affected the way managers read?

PROBLEM-SOLVING EXPERIENCES

1. Obtain a copy of the editorial pages of a recent newspaper. As you read each editorial, use an assortment of colored markers to distinguish facts, opinions, main ideas, cause-and-effect relationships, and propaganda techniques.

2. Obtain a copy of a trade journal related to your professional interests but one that you do not regularly read. Time yourself as you scan the journal to find how to obtain a subscription. Make a note of the time it took you to find the information and write down the subscription office address. Skim the journal to find two articles related to trends or current issues. Read one of the articles carefully and outline the main ideas and significant details.

CASE 9–1

James Burdell is the manager of computer equipment at Vennet Industries. James's office is in the computer area, which is rather chilly, and telephone interruptions from computer users are frequent. Sheila, who has some technical background, is James's secretary. All office mail goes directly into James's mail basket; Sheila never opens any mail.

James is having trouble finding time to read all the materials he needs to read. James is in the process of reviewing plans for the computer expansion at Vennet. Memos and reports about current software developments arrive weekly. Vendors keep sending brochures on new options as well as price quotations for materials that James has requested. James is a careful reader; he tries to remember the details of everything he reads. His reading demands have become so great that he stays late each day to read what he terms as "critical material."

1. Identify three reasons why James cannot read as much as he would like.

2. Suggest ways that James can ease his reading load.

3. What types of reading and comprehension skills should James practice?

ENDNOTES

[1]Phyllis A. Miller, "Reading Demands in a High-Technology Industry," *Journal of Reading*, Vol. 26, No. 2 (November, 1982), p. 112.

[2]Adapted from Ira E. Aaron, *Comprehension in the Reading Program* (Bulletin prepared for the Georgia State Department of Education, 1984), pp. 1–1 to 1–12.

[3]Ibid., pp. 2–1 to 2–52.

[4]Jeanne S. Chall and Steven A. Stahl, "Reading," *Encyclopedia of Educational Research*, edited by Harold Mitzel (5h ed; New York: Macmillan Publishing Co., Inc., 1982), III, p. 1536.

[5]Margaret Mitchell, *Gone with the Wind* (New York: The Macmillan Company, 1936), p. 428.

[6]*Julius Caesar*, act 4, sc. 3.

[7]Katherine S. Noe, "Technical Reading Technique: A Briefcase Reading Strategy," *Journal of Reading*, Vol. 27, No. 3 (December, 1983), p. 234.

[8]Mary Seifert, "Research: Reading on the Job," *Journal of Reading*, Vol. 22, No. 4 (January, 1979), p. 367.

[9]Anne Auten, "The Challenge: Job Literacy in the 1980s," *Journal of Reading*, Vol. 23, No. 8 (May, 1980), p. 753.

[10]Miller, op. cit., p. 112.

10

IMPROVING
READING
SKILLS

When you complete this chapter, you should be able to:

▲ Evaluate your reading habits.

▲ List several aids for improving prereading, reading, and postreading activities.

▲ Describe the three levels of comprehension.

▲ Calculate your reading speed.

▲ Determine your reading comprehension.

▲ Explain one formula for computing readability.

Reading skill improvement involves two stages—awareness and action. In the awareness stage, readers identify deficiencies in reading performance. Even though text complexity is controlled by the writer, an understanding of how complexity affects reading performance can help the reader adjust to the material.

The action stage of reading improvement occurs when the reader makes a conscientious effort to select the appropriate improvement techniques and to adjust his or her reading habits to suit the text material.

Continued reading effectiveness requires that managers periodically assess their reading habits. Managers can employ appropriate improvement aids only after they become aware of their reading habits.

Reading skill improvement consists of awareness and action.

▲ READING HABIT ASSESSMENT

Reading habits, or the manner in which a person reads, either broaden or limit communicator effectiveness. Consequently, managers should assess the habits they demonstrate during each phase of the reading process by using the Reading Habit Survey in Figure 10–1. The three phases of the reading process are prereading activity, reading activity, and postreading activity.[1]

Reading habits affect communicator effectiveness.

Figure 10–1 includes a series of yes/no questions which can be used to assess reading habits during each of the three phases. Responses of yes to questions in the survey denote good reading habits. Responses of no indicate inadequate reading habits, which need corrective attention if readers wish to improve their reading ability. This survey provides insight to desirable reading habits and illustrates when those habits should be used during the three phases of the reading process.

The reading process occurs in three phases.

Prereading Phase

During the prereading phase, readers should implement the following reading improvement aids:

Here are some aids for reading improvement.

1. *Decide on a purpose for reading.* Readers should know their purpose for reading. Having a specific purpose helps readers know what type and speed of reading to use.

READING HABIT SURVEY

	Yes	No

Prereading Activity

1. Do I identify my purpose(s) for reading prior to actually reading? _____ _____

2. Do I use the index of a book for locating specific topics about which to read? _____ _____

3. Do I peruse the table of contents of books, journals, manuals, reports, and newspapers to identify articles or chapters of interest? _____ _____

4. Do I reflect on what I already know about a topic prior to reading? _____ _____

5. Do I use titles and headings to predict what specific reading material describes? _____ _____

6. Do I skim documents to get a feel for what the author has to say? _____ _____

7. Do I prepare to read by eliminating or minimizing outside interference(s)? _____ _____

8. Do I select a comfortable, well-lighted place in which to read? _____ _____

9. Do I schedule blocks of time in which to read? _____ _____

10. Do I approach reading with a positive attitude? _____ _____

Reading Activity

1. Do I concentrate as I read? _____ _____

2. Do I analyze the author's organizational structure? _____ _____

3. Do I use visual aids, such as headings, type size, color, figures, and tables, to enhance comprehension of what I read? _____ _____

4. Do I associate existing knowledge with new knowledge as I read? _____ _____

FIGURE 10–1   Page 1 of Reading Habit Survey

READING HABIT SURVEY (Continued)

	Yes	No
5. Do I determine the approximate meaning of unfamiliar words based on the context in which the words appear?	———	———
6. Do I look for relationships among the main ideas of a document?	———	———
7. Do I adjust my reading approach and speed when reading familiar material within a document?	———	———
8. Do I limit underlining or highlighting text?	———	———
9. Do I read groups of words rather than one word at a time?	———	———
10. Do I read silently?	———	———
11. Do I control head and facial movements as I read?	———	———
12. Do I maintain good posture as I read?	———	———
13. Do I block out distractions as I read?	———	———

Postreading Activity

	Yes	No
1. Do I summarize a document based on the relationship of the main ideas and supportive details?	———	———
2. Do I use a dictionary to determine the meaning of unfamiliar words that I wish to add to my vocabulary?	———	———
3. Do I assess what knowledge I have added to what I already knew?	———	———
4. Do I evaluate the strengths of a document?	———	———
5. Do I evaluate the weaknesses of a document?	———	———
6. Do I think about the implications of what I have read?	———	———

FIGURE 10–1   Page 2 of Reading Habit Survey

2. *Control the reading environment.* Reading without environmental control can be frustrating. Readers should set aside ample time to read; they should eliminate interruptions, use proper lighting, and maintain an uncluttered reading space.

3. *Develop a proper reading attitude.* Readers should be positive about potential reading rewards; they should view reading time as an investment. They should make reading an enjoyable activity.

Reading Phase

These aids are specifically applicable to the reading phase:[2]

1. *Concentrate.* Readers should keep their thoughts on what they are reading; daydreaming should be eliminated as much as possible.

2. *Limit pauses in reading.* Readers should pause while reading only to rest their eyes, make essential notes, or look up unfamiliar words.

3. *Rest.* Readers should occasionally take breaks from reading in order to refresh their ability to concentrate.

4. *Limit regression.* Readers should avoid turning to previously read portions of a document. Reading should be done in a forward direction.

5. *Use physical features of the text as reading guides.* Surface features of a document such as headings should be used to minimize having to read the text word for word. Physical features help show how the material is organized—chronologically, spatially, and so forth.

Postreading Phase

The following aids are useful during the postreading phase:

1. *Engage in postreading activity.* Many readers do not engage in postreading activity immediately following reading; consequently, their comprehension and retention of information are negatively affected. Readers should take time for postreading activity.

2. *Synthesize new material with existing knowledge.* The synthesis process allows new knowledge to blend with existing knowledge rather than storing it in a disjointed manner. Relationships are established.[3] Retrieval ability is also enhanced if information is synthesized immediately after being read.

3. *Analyze how the material might be useful in the future if it is not useful today.* Reading material may pay deferred dividends rather than immediate dividends depending on one's purpose for reading

and existing knowledge. Readers should analyze the value of information to determine both its present and future worth.

4. *Check meanings of unfamiliar words to broaden vocabulary.* While reading, readers should use the context in which unfamiliar words are presented to determine their meanings. Readers should look up any unfamiliar words in a dictionary as they read or at the end of a reading session.

▲ COMPREHENSION ASSESSMENT

Reading resembles listening in that it involves intensive thinking. Effective readers prepare to read successfully; they concentrate as they read, and they perform important postreading activities. In addition to assessing their reading habits, readers interested in improving their skills should also assess the speed with which they read and their level of comprehension.

Reading growth can be measured periodically by taking a sample of reading comprehension and speed. Answering questions tailored to the text material is a common form of assessing comprehension. These questions frequently deal with assessing different levels of comprehension.

Levels of Comprehension

The three levels of comprehension are recall, inference, and applied comprehension.

Because reading is a thinking process, it involves a hierarchy of comprehension levels. The three common levels of comprehension are recall, inference, and applied comprehension.

For example, read the next sentence and answer the questions that follow:

By the year 1990, network television will have lost at least 50 percent of its audience due to the competition of cable television and other newer technologies.

1. By what year will network TV lose one-half of its audience?
2. What specific problem is the sentence suggesting?
3. In your opinion, what impact will a 50 percent decrease in the network TV audience have on the advertising industry?

In answering Question 1, the response, "1990," is taken directly from the text. Comprehension at this level is merely the recall of information. *Recall comprehension* involves getting the facts as stated by the writer of the material.

Recall comprehension involves getting the facts.

Question 2 calls for a different type of comprehension than was required in Question 1. The answer is not directly stated by the writer; it is not obvious to the reader. The reader must focus not only on what the writer says but also on what the writer means. Comprehension at this level requires inference and interpretation. ***Inference comprehension*** requires the reader to interpret what a writer means in order to answer a question.

Finally, in Question 3, the reader is engaged in the most difficult level of comprehension. The answer to the question is not derived from the text; it is drawn from the reader's existing knowledge of the television and advertising industries as well as how technology affects human communication. Comprehension at this level is applied. ***Applied comprehension*** involves expressing opinions about and drawing insights and new ideas from text material based on the reader's existing knowledge.

Inference comprehension is based on what a writer says and means.

Applied comprehension involves drawing new insights by combining text material with existing knowledge.

Comprehension Inventory

To establish your present levels and rate of comprehension, follow these steps:

1. Turn to Chapter 9 and reread the entire section entitled "Types of Reading," pages 149–151. Note the total number of minutes and seconds it takes you to read the section.

2. Figure your rate or speed of reading in words per minute. For example:
   Words in section: 578
   Reading time: 2 minutes, 25 seconds
   Convert reading time into seconds: $(2 \times 60) + 25 = 145$ seconds
   Calculate reading speed using this formula:

   $$\text{words per minute (wpm)} = \frac{\text{total number of words read} \times 60}{\text{reading time in seconds}}$$

   $$\text{wpm} = \frac{578 \times 60}{145} = \frac{34,680}{145} = 239 \text{ wpm}$$

3. To check your levels of comprehension, answer Questions 1–9 as either true or false, and answer Question 10 in a brief paragraph.
   Recall
   (1) Careful reading is slow reading.
   (2) Adult readers who engage in careful reading comprehend 70 to 80 percent of what they read.
   (3) Readers are sure of what they want to find when skim reading.
   (4) About 1,500 words per minute can be read when skim reading.
   (5) Information acquired through scan reading is usually forgotten after immediate use.
   (6) Scan reading speeds approach 3,000 words per minute.

Inference

(7) Searching for specific information in an encyclopedia is an example of careful reading.

(8) Reading a newspaper for the main ideas it contains is an example of skim reading.

(9) Looking for a name in a telephone directory is an example of scan reading.

Applied

(10) In your opinion, why don't high school and college teachers teach students how to read?

4. Check your answers with the following key:

Key to Reading Comprehension Test

(1) False

(2) True

(3) False

(4) True

(5) True

(6) True

(7) False

(8) True

(9) True

(10) Responses will vary but will likely range from "Reading instruction is the responsibility of the elementary schools" to "Teachers in certain subject areas do not know how to teach reading."

5. Multiply the number of correct answers by 10. Because the points on the comprehension assessment total 100, this score forms a percentage. Thus, if you had six correct answers, your comprehension score would be 60 percent. Compare your percent score with this evaluation scale:

90%–100%	Excellent comprehension
80%	Above average comprehension
60%–70%	Average comprehension
Below 60%	Below average comprehension

▲ EVALUATION OF READING MATERIALS

Reading ability and the difficulty of text material do not always match.

One of the serious problems associated with improving reading skills is the frequent mismatch between the reading abilities of the reader and the level of difficulty of the reading material itself. Ideally reading materials should be appproximately equal to the reading level of the readers.

Evaluating reading materials requires both personal judgment and quantitative analysis. Checklists are commonly used to help assess reading materials. A quantitative or numerical measurement that indicates the difficulty of a document can be calculated by using a readability formula designed to estimate the grade level of the material.

Reading Material Checklist _____

The checklist in Figure 10–2 is an example of an instrument that readers can use to make decisions regarding the difficulty of most nonfictional reading materials. Knowledge of reading material difficulty enables readers to make better decisions about the type(s) of reading they should use with a particular document. The checklist can be easily adapted to evaluate fictional material.

READING MATERIAL EVALUATION CHECKLIST

	Has None	Poor	Adequate	Good
External Organizational Aids				
1. Does the table of contents provide a clear overview of the material?	___	___	___	___
2. Do headings clearly define the content?	___	___	___	___
3. Do headings clearly emphasize the important concepts?	___	___	___	___
4. Do topic headings provide assistance in breaking the material into relevant parts?	___	___	___	___
5. Are graphs, charts, and figures clear and do they support the text material?	___	___	___	___
6. Are photographs well done and up-to-date?	___	___	___	___
7. Are type size and quality appropriate for the intended reader?	___	___	___	___

FIGURE 10–2   Reading Material Evaluation Checklist

READING MATERIAL EVALUATION CHECKLIST (Continued)

	Has None	Poor	Adequate	Good
8. Is the bibliography or reference section helpful in locating related reading materials?	___	___	___	___
9. Are important terms in italics or boldfaced type for easy identification?	___	___	___	___

Internal Organizational Aids

	Has None	Poor	Adequate	Good
1. Are concepts spaced throughout the material rather than being crowded in too small a space?	___	___	___	___
2. Is adequate context provided to allow the reader to determine meanings of new words and technical terms?	___	___	___	___
3. Are sentence lengths appropriate for the intended reader?	___	___	___	___
4. Is the writer's style (word length, sentence length, sentence complexity, paragraph length, number of examples) appropriate for the intended reader?	___	___	___	___
5. Does the writer use a predominant pattern of organization (compare-contrast, cause-effect, sequential order) within the writing to assist the reader in interpreting the material?	___	___	___	___

Readability

	Has None	Poor	Adequate	Good
1. What is the intended grade level of the text?	___	___	___	___

Source: Adapted from *Evaluating Textbooks and Reading Materials* (Juneau: Alaska Department of Education, 1978), p. 11.

FIGURE 10–2   (Continued)

Readability Assessment

Many different readability formulas have been devised to estimate the level of difficulty of reading materials. Most of the popular formulas involve measuring word and sentence lengths to estimate the grade level of the reading material. The Gunning Fog Index[4] and the Raygor Readability Estimate[5] are two quick, easy-to-use formulas.

Word and sentence lengths are used to estimate the grade level of text material.

Gunning Fog Index

Follow these steps to calculate the Fog Index of a passage:

1. Take several samples of about 100 words each.
2. Divide the number of words in the passage by the number of sentences to get the average sentence length. A compound sentence counts as two sentences.
3. Count the number of "hard" words (words of three or more syllables). Don't count words that are capitalized; combinations of short, easy words (for example, *butterfly* and *grandmother*); or verb forms that become three syllables by adding *-ed* or *-es* (for example, *created* or *possesses*). Divide the number of hard words by the total number of words in the passage and multiply by 100. This number indicates the percentage of hard words in the passage.
4. To obtain the Fog Index, add the results of Steps 2 and 3. Multiply the total by 0.4.

Apply the Gunning Fog Index to the following sample:

Innovation is the specific function of entrepreneurship, whether in an existing business, a public service institution, or a new venture started by a lone individual in the family kitchen. It is the means by which the entrepreneur either creates new wealth-producing resources or endows existing resources with enhanced potential for creating wealth.

Today, much confusion exists about the proper definition of entrepreneurship. Some observers use the term to refer to all small businesses; others, to all new businesses. In practice, however, a great many well-established businesses engage in highly successful entrepreneurship. The term, then, refers not to an enterprise's size or age, but to a certain kind of activity.[6]

Calculations for Sample

1. Total words in sample = 111.
2. Number of sentences in sample = 7 (including one compound sentence).
3. Average sentence length = 111 ÷ 7 = 15.9.

4. Number of hard words = 28.

5. Percentage of hard words in sample = 28 ÷ 111 × 100 = 25.2.

The same steps should be followed for several samples to compute an average readability. Thus, the Fog Index calculations for three samples would follow this form:

Sample	Average Sentence Length	Percentage of Hard Words
A	15.9	25.2
B	11.4	8.7
C	20.8	26.0
Average	16.0	20.0

Fog Index = (average sentence length + percentage of hard words) × 0.4. Fog Index = 16.0 + 20.0 × 0.4 = 36.0 × 0.4 = 14.40 or 14th grade.

Raygor Readability Estimate

The Raygor formula uses a readability graph to identify a grade-level score for materials ranging from third-grade level through professional level. Word difficulty is measured by counting long words (six or more letters). The formula was designed to reduce the human error factor in counting syllables. Follow these steps to determine the Raygor Readability Estimate:

1. Take a sample of exactly 100 words at the beginning, middle, and end of the selection or book. However, do not count numbers.

2. Count the number of sentences in each 100-word passage. When the 100-word mark falls within a sentence, estimate to the nearest tenth the partial last sentence. A compound sentence counts as one sentence.

3. Count the number of long words (words with six or more letters) in each 100-word passage.

4. Determine the average number of sentences and long words for the three samples. The point where the two averages intersect is marked on the graph in Figure 10–3. The grade level nearest the mark on the graph is the best estimate of the level of difficulty of the selection.

Apply the Raygor Readability Estimate to the sample on page 169. The same steps should be followed for at least two additional sample

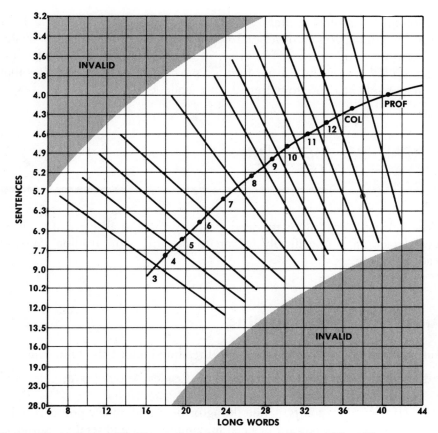

Source: Alton L. Raygor, "The Raygor Readability Estimate: A Quick and Easy Way to Determine Difficulty," *Reading: Theory, Research, and Practice,* Twenty-Sixth Yearbook of the National Reading Conference, edited by P. D. Pearson (St. Paul, MN: Mason Publishing Company, 1977), p. 261.

FIGURE 10–3   Raygor Readability Graph

passages. Thus, the calculations for the average number of sentences and the average number of long words over three samples would follow this form:

Sample	Number of Sentences	Number of Long Words
A	5.4	46
B	7.3	29
C	4.8	39
Average	5.8	38

Plotting 5.8 sentences and 38 long words on the graph in Figure 10–3 gives an estimated grade level of 13 (college). This estimate approximates the Gunning Fog Index of 14. Thus, in addition to being extremely simple and easy to use, the Raygor formula provides readability estimates that are reasonably accurate to within ± one grade level.[7]

▲ READING AIDS FOR SPECIFIC TYPES OF READING

Some reading aids address a specific type of reading.

Although the previously mentioned aids may apply to all types of reading, several aids apply specifically to careful reading, skim reading, or scan reading.

Aids for Careful Reading

Aids particularly appropriate for careful reading include the following:

1. *Preview material by skim reading.* Readers should skim titles and headings to get a feel for content and organization.
2. *Highlight key points.* Underlining or highlighting key points is helpful when readers want or need to comprehend and retain main ideas and significant details. Readers should highlight sparingly; otherwise even careful reading is slowed down.
3. *Skim repetitively.* Readers who need to glean the main ideas and significant details of material but do not have time to read carefully should compensate by repetitively skimming the material.

Aids for Skim Reading

Aids that facilitate skim reading include the following:

1. *Read headings.* Readers should use headings as primary guides in determining the main ideas.
2. *Read first and last sentences.* When a direct writing approach is used, main ideas appear in the opening sentence of a paragraph. When an indirect writing approach is used, main ideas often appear

in the middle of the paragraph or in the last sentence. Readers should skim the opening and closing sentences of paragraphs to glean main ideas.

3. *Watch for variations in type or print*. Physical differences in the document's appearance serve as reading tools. Readers should use variations in type or print to indicate important terms or ideas.

Aids for Scan Reading

The following aids work best when used with scan reading:

1. *Peruse the index*. Readers should first look in the index that accompanies the material to determine where specific pieces of information are located.
2. *Peruse the table of contents*. If an index is not available or if it is limited, readers should search the table of contents to determine where desired information is located.
3. *Peruse headings*. If an index and table of contents are not available, readers should use headings within the reading material to aid in locating information.

SUMMARY

Reading improvement involves awareness and action. Awareness consists of identifying reading deficiencies and understanding how the complexity of reading material affects reading performance.

Poor reading habits can limit communicator effectiveness. Reading is intensive thinking; readers must prepare themselves to read, concentrate as they read, and perform important postreading activities.

Managers should periodically assess their reading habits. Reading aids that should be used during the prereading phase include deciding the purpose for reading, controlling the reading environment, and developing proper reading attitudes. Aids for the reading phase are concentrating, limiting pauses, resting, limiting regression, and using physical text features as reading guides. Postreading aids consist of engaging in postreading activity, synthesizing new material with existing knowledge, analyzing the value of information, and checking the meanings of unfamiliar words. Readers should also use aids that apply to the particular types of reading.

Reading comprehension consists of three levels: recall, inference, and applied comprehension. Reading speed is determined in words read per minute. Comprehension rate is computed by determining the percentage of correct answers obtained on questions pertaining to a sample of reading material.

A document's complexity or readability is measured using formulas that compute the average sentence length and the number of complicated words in a random text sample. The Gunning Fog Index and the Raygor Readability Estimate are commonly used to measure readability. The Fog Index is based on the average sentence length and number of words with three or more syllables; the Raygor Estimate uses the average number of sentences and the average number of words containing six or more letters.

QUESTIONS

1. Name the stages of reading skill improvement.
2. Give examples of desirable prereading habits.
3. Name the three levels of comprehension.
4. Define *inference comprehension*.
5. Explain the value of assessing reading comprehension.
6. Why does the evaluation of reading material require both personal judgment and quantitative analysis?
7. How do the Gunning Fog Index and the Raygor Readability Estimate differ?
8. What reading aids should be used during the three phases of reading?
9. How can readers improve their careful reading?
10. Describe the similarities between reading skill improvement and listening skill improvement.

PROBLEM-SOLVING EXPERIENCES

1. Use the Gunning Fog Index to compute the readability of the first three paragraphs of Chapter 10.
2. Assess your reading habits by taking a reading habit survey.

CASE 10–1

Tindall Enterprises manufactures insulation fiber. Top management of Tindall Enterprises is working on a deal to merge with Wakeforrest, Inc., another insulation manufacturer. A major competitor, Nuranco Inc., is trying to abort the deal. Rumors have circulated throughout the Southeastern Region concerning Nuranco's attempt to intervene.

Bill Flores, a reader at Tindall Enterprises, has been assigned the job of staying up-to-date on all newspaper publicity relating to the rumors involving Nuranco, Tindall, and Wakeforrest. Bill's new reading assignment will remain in effect until Tindall completes the merger with Wakeforrest or until the deal is aborted—whichever happens first. Bill is so overwhelmed with his regular reading that he can allot only 30 minutes a day to his new reading assignment.

1. Advise Bill on how he can fulfill his new reading assignment.

ENDNOTES

[1]Katherine Noe, "Technical Reading Technique: A Briefcase Reading Strategy," *Journal of Reading*, Vol. 27, No. 3 (December, 1983), pp. 235–236.

[2]Holly O'Donnell, "Reading Strategies for the Adult, Nontraditional Student," *Journal of Reading*, Vol. 26, No. 2 (November, 1982), p. 178.

[3]Deanne Milan, *Developing Reading Skills* (New York: Random House, Inc., 1983), pp. 70–74.

[4]Robert Gunning, *The Technique of Clear Writing* (New York: McGraw-Hill Book Company, 1952), pp. 36–38.

[5]Alton L. Raygor, "The Raygor Readability Estimate: A Quick and Easy Way to Determine Difficulty," *Reading: Theory, Research, and Practice*, Twenty-Sixth Yearbook of the National Reading Conference, edited by P. D. Pearson (St. Paul, MN: Mason Publishing Company, 1977), pp. 259–263.

[6]Peter F. Drucker, "The Discipline of Innovation," *Harvard Business Review*, Vol. 63, No. 3 (May–June, 1985), p. 67.

[7]Raygor, op. cit., p. 262.

11

THE IMPORTANCE OF WRITING

When you complete this chapter, you should be able to:

▲ Discuss the importance of clarifying the specific purposes for writing before beginning work on a first draft.

▲ List and explain briefly the four essential steps in the writing process.

▲ Name the four key elements of effective writing.

▲ Contrast internal and external written communications.

Many managers do not write because they want to; they write because their job requires it. The pressure of business deadlines frequently results in hastily written messages that are vague and disorganized.

Managers can improve their writing skills by establishing the primary purpose for a message and then following a logical sequence of steps for writing the message. As with any skill, good business writing comes only with practice.

▲ PURPOSES FOR WRITING

Before managers plan the mechanics and format of a written message, the general and specific purposes for writing it should be clearly defined. The general purpose of all writing is to get the message across to the reader. The specific purposes of writing are the same as the purposes for speaking—to inform, to persuade, and to entertain.

Managers may have more than one specific purpose for a written message. For example, the basic purpose of a business letter may be to persuade the reader to purchase a new product. The emotional appeal to purchase the product may be supported with clear-cut facts and data that inform the reader of the major benefits of the product. Usually, however, a written message has one specific purpose which is more powerful than any other purpose or combination of purposes.

Written messages may have more than one specific purpose.

Here are two questions managers should ask themselves to clarify the primary purpose, and perhaps other purposes, of any written communication:

1. *Who will read it?* A message intended for a single reader may require a different form of writing than the same message intended for several people. Also, a manager would write about a particular subject in a much different way if writing to a senior systems analyst than if writing to a business-minded member of the board of directors. A message should be aimed at the reader's background and vocabulary level.

Always keep the reader in mind.

2. *What reaction or response is expected from the reader?* The answer to this question will strongly affect the organizational pattern, the style, and the amount of detail of the written message.

After a purpose has been established, the writer should assess the reader's identity, needs, and desires.

179

Closely related to clarifying the purposes for writing is determining whether the message should be written or spoken. While face-to-face speaking and using the telephone are very effective forms of message delivery, many business situations require a permanent record in the form of a written message for reference or possible legal purposes.[1] A writer should base the decision to write or to speak on the specific purpose or purposes of the message as well as on company policies. King suggests that communicators should write rather than speak (1) when communicating with more than one person if a meeting is not practical, (2) when message content is complex and requires analysis, and (3) when documentation is needed.[2]

Effective communication requires a decision to speak or to write.

▲ THE WRITING PROCESS

The four steps in the writing process are planning, organizing, drafting, and editing. These steps are essential for effective written communications.

Planning

Proper planning is crucial in achieving the specific purpose or purposes of business writing. Planning forces the manager to think about what is to be written before placing words on paper.

Assemble the materials needed for writing during the planning stage.

First, the manager assembles all relevant business documents, references, and other materials that may be needed for the written message. Routine messages, of course, may require little, if any, reference materials.

List the ideas for the content of a written message as quickly as possible without editing.

Next, the manager lists all ideas that pertain to the purpose of the message. At this point, the ideas do not have to be in logical order. The objective of this step is to generate as many ideas as possible without worrying about their relevance, importance, or order.

Organizing

Once the ideas for a written message have been listed, they must be organized in some logical fashion. The best way for a writer to analyze, group, and relate the various ideas about the message content is to prepare an outline. A writer can arrange and rearrange, expand, and delete ideas in a tentative outline until a polished version emerges.

Organize in outline form the ideas generated in the planning stage.

Some managers avoid organizing ideas in outline form before writing on the pretext that preparing an outline takes too much time. Except for the most routine correspondence, an outline actually saves writing time, since changes and deletions are much easier to make on an outline than on a finished document. Also, an outline guides the manager during the actual writing and rewriting stages. In a very practical sense, preparing an outline demonstrates good time management.

An outline helps the writer organize ideas in a logical order.

Types of Outlines

The two basic types of outlines are topic and sentence outlines. In the *topic outline,* each entry is expressed as a word, a few words, or a short phrase. The advantage to using this popular type of outline is that the writer can express and rearrange ideas with ease. The major disadvantage of the topic outline is that the writer may forget what one or more entries mean after they are written. A partial topic outline follows:

The topic outline consists of a few key words or phrases.

I. THE ECONOMIC SYSTEM

    A. People
    B. Resources
        1. Land
        2. Labor
        3. Capital

II. MEASURING THE ECONOMY

    A. Gross National Product
        1. Real GNP
        2. Services versus products in GNP
        3. Productivity
    B. Economic Stability
        1. Recession
        2. Prosperity and recovery
        3. Inflation

In the *sentence outline,* each entry is written as a complete sentence. The advantage of the sentence outline is that the writer structures ideas more completely than in the topic outline. The disadvantage of this type of outline is that the writer may forget that the outline is only a guide and

The sentence outline can be used on large or complex writing projects.

attempt to convert the outline sentences into a final document. A partial sentence outline follows:

I. COMPUTERS ARE ESSENTIAL TOOLS FOR BUSINESS, INDUSTRY, AND GOVERNMENT.

    A. There are several major advantages of using computers.
       1. They can process data rapidly.
       2. They are accurate when programs are properly written.
       3. They can store a large amount of data in a small space.
    B. Computers also have limitations.
       1. They are expensive.
       2. They cannot think.

II. COMPUTER LANGUAGES TELL COMPUTERS WHAT TO DO.

    A. The BASIC language was designed as an interactive language to be used by persons with little or no experience in programming.
    B. COBOL uses English words and sentences and was designed for business data processing applications.
    C. FORTRAN is the dominant scientific computer language.

Styles of Outlines

An outline should follow a consistent numbering style.

Two common methods of outlining are the numeral-letter style and the decimal style. Note that at least two divisions are needed to subdivide an outline category. These styles are numbered as follows:

Numeral-Letter Style

I. FIRST PARAGRAPH TOPIC

    A. Supporting Data for I.
    B. Supporting Data for I.
       1. Item related to B.
       2. Item related to B.
          a. Item related to 2.
          b. Item related to 2.
             (1) Item related to b.
             (2) Item related to b.
                (a) Item related to (2)
                (b) Item related to (2)

II. SECOND PARAGRAPH TOPIC

    A. Supporting Data for II.
    B. Supporting Data for II.

Decimal Style

1. FIRST PARAGRAPH TOPIC

    1.1 Supporting Data for 1.
    1.2 Supporting Data for 1.
        1.21 Item related to 1.2
        1.22 Item related to 1.2
            1.221 Item related to 1.22
            1.222 Item related to 1.22
                1.2221 Item related to 1.222
                1.2222 Item related to 1.222
                    1.22221 Item related to 1.2222
                    1.22222 Item related to 1.2222

2. SECOND PARAGRAPH TOPIC

    2.1 Supporting Data for 2.
    2.2 Supporting Data for 2.

Approaches to Organizing Ideas

Managers may use either the direct or indirect approach when organizing ideas. Their choice of organization is based on anticipated reader reaction to the written message. The direct and indirect approaches to organizing messages are shown in Figure 11–1. These approaches are described in Chapter 5 for speaking, Chapter 12 for memos, and Chapter 13 for letters.

The choice of organization depends on the expected reader reaction to the message.

Drafting

Once the message has been planned and outlined, the writer is ready for the third step in the writing process—writing a first draft of the message. The draft should follow the outline point by point and should be written as rapidly as possible without editing.[3] The objective of the first draft is to get words on paper without being concerned about sentence structure, word choice, format, and other mechanics of writing.

The first draft should follow the outline and should be written quickly without editing.

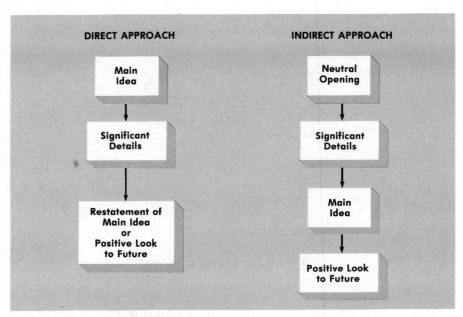

FIGURE 11–1   Direct and Indirect Approaches to Organizing Messages

The draft can be handwritten, typed, or keyboarded with the expectation that revisions will be made. Wide margins and double- or triple-spacing between the lines will provide ample space for revisions.

Editing

After the first draft has been completed, the writer will need to evaluate its content and organization. The key to clear, readable writing is editing and rewriting. One of the advantages of written communications is that a draft can be put aside and then revised and rewritten at a later time.

A writer should edit each draft for communication principles, organization, proper audience identification, basic writing elements, spelling, grammar, and punctuation. *Editing* is the critical thinking phase of the writing process during which the writer analyzes and scrutinizes what has been written.[4] Depending on the writer's communication skills and familiarity with the topic, planning and editing tend to be more time-consuming than organizing and drafting.

Edit and rewrite drafts with a critical eye.

"He throws away his best work."

Source: © SATURDAY REVIEW 1974 Bernard Schoenbaum.

▲ ELEMENTS OF EFFECTIVE WRITING

Generally written documents are tangible and permanent; they are easier to quantify than spoken messages. Consequently, the effectiveness of written communication is often used as a criterion for evaluating the overall effectiveness of a manager.

Written communication requires more time than spoken communication. The interaction or response time between communicators is not as immediate as the interaction in spoken communication. Usually the sender is not with the receiver when the written document is received and decoded. The writer is unable to provide immediate clarification of verbal and nonverbal messages in the written document.

For a variety of reasons, some executives feel uncomfortable with writing. They may not possess strong writing skills, or they may feel awkward or insecure about committing themselves on paper. Some managers *deliberately* avoid documentation; when they must write, their writing is unclear. Brown quotes Marino as saying:

Can unclear writing protect a writer?

> When you write something, you lose power over it. Other people can take over and use it against you. Unclear writing protects you, because when your writing is ambiguous, people can't pin you down.[5]

Although writers may communicate unclearly to protect themselves, they risk damaging relationships with their readers and causing declines in profit and productivity. To avoid being pinned down, writers may choose to communicate orally rather than in writing.

When writing is necessary, communicators should plan, organize, draft, and edit their documents to include the elements of effective writing. These elements are thought, appropriateness, correctness, and readability.[6] Figure 11–2 is a Writing Performance Inventory that can be used to identify good and weak writing behavior. The inventory is designed to assess writing behavior pertaining to the elements of effective writing. Responses of yes to questions in the inventory indicate effective writing behavior. Responses of no denote ineffective writing behavior. If all or most of the responses are yes, then generally one's writing performance is very good. Responses of no indicate writing behavior which needs corrective action if communicators want to improve their writing ability and performance.

What are the elements of effective writing?

Thought

Thought given to writing involves clarifying one's purpose for writing and choosing what information to include or exclude from a message. All four of the writing steps—planning, organizing, drafting, and editing—are involved in the thought process.

Thought affects planning, organizing, drafting, and editing.

Planning and organizing require considerable thinking. Deciding on the purpose for writing, organizing the resources, and outlining the main ideas, assumptions, and supporting details are all thought-centered activities.

Drafting and editing require thought to prevent rambling and to ensure that assumptions are clearly identified. In addition, thought is needed to ensure that information, findings, conclusions, and implications are presented objectively.

Appropriateness

Appropriateness refers to the structure of a message—its emphasis and formality—based on whether the message is an upward, lateral, or downward internal communication or an external communication.

Appropriateness refers to message emphasis and formality.

Internal Written Communications

Internal written communications refer to written documents that are sent and received *within* an organization. Examples include memorandums, notes, meeting minutes, reports, graphic materials, manuals,

WRITING PERFORMANCE INVENTORY

	Yes	No

Thought

1. Do I give adequate thought to the planning of my document? _____ _____

2. Do I organize my writing resources prior to writing? _____ _____

3. Do I possess the needed experience or aptitude in the area about which I write? _____ _____

4. Do I clearly identify my purpose for writing? _____ _____

5. Do I write about my topic without rambling? _____ _____

6. Do I identify necessary assumptions? _____ _____

7. Do I justify necessary assumptions? _____ _____

8. Do I objectively convey information? _____ _____

9. Do I report substantiated findings? _____ _____

10. Do I reach substantiated conclusions? _____ _____

11. Do I report objective implications? _____ _____

12. Would I take action based on the information I communicate? _____ _____

Appropriateness

1. Do I demonstrate tact in upward communications? _____ _____

2. Do I provide a balance between generalization and supportive details in upward communications? _____ _____

3. Do I provide a balance between fact and opinion in upward communications? _____ _____

4. Do I demonstrate tact in lateral communications? _____ _____

FIGURE 11–2   Page 1 of Writing Performance Inventory

WRITING PERFORMANCE INVENTORY (Continued)

	Yes	No
5. Do I provide a balance between fact and opinion in lateral communications?	____	____
6. Do I serve as a communication role model in downward communications?	____	____
7. Do I provide clear information in downward communications?	____	____
8. Do I provide necessary instructions in downward communications?	____	____
9. Do I explain reasons for assigning responsibility and authority in downward communications?	____	____
10. Do I share the benefits of decisions reported in downward communications?	____	____
11. Do I initiate or maintain goodwill in external communications?	____	____

Correctness

	Yes	No
1. Do I include only accurate information in my writing?	____	____
2. Do I use correct grammar?	____	____
3. Do I avoid redundancy except where necessary for emphasis?	____	____
4. Do I use correct spelling?	____	____
5. Do I use correct punctuation?	____	____
6. Do I use the appropriate format so that my document is attractive and conforms to accepted standards?	____	____
7. Do I develop my sentences so that they logically relate to one another?	____	____
8. Do I develop my paragraphs so that they logically relate to one another?	____	____

FIGURE 11–2   Page 2 of Writing Performance Inventory

WRITING PERFORMANCE INVENTORY (Continued)

	Yes	No
9. Does my message lead the reader to the desired conclusion?	___	___

Readability

	Yes	No
1. Do I base my writing style on the receiver's reading ability and interests?	___	___
2. Do I adapt my writing style to the circumstances under which the document is written?	___	___
3. Do I shape the tone of my message so that *how* the message is stated enhances *what* is said?	___	___
4. Do I choose words that project a positive image?	___	___
5. Do I use simple language to describe complex material?	___	___
6. Do I use language that is active, concrete, concise, and objective?	___	___
7. Do I develop my document so that it contains digestible units?	___	___
8. Do I include only one topic sentence in each paragraph?	___	___
9. Do I lead the reader in focusing on the main idea(s) contained in the document?	___	___
10. Do I use parallel structure to enhance the readability of my document?	___	___
11. Do I use jargon and buzz words only when the reader is familiar with such words?	___	___

Source: Adapted from John S. Fielden, "What Do You Mean I Can't Write?" *Harvard Business Review*, Vol. 42, No. 3 (May–June, 1964), p. 147.

FIGURE 11–2 Page 3 of Writing Performance Inventory

bids, contracts, and bulletin board materials. Written documents may be handwritten, keyboarded, or drawn. Written documents may move through the formal and/or informal organization, as described in Chapter 1. When communication flows vertically and horizontally within a company, written messages may be used to link managers and subordinates as they share business-related and social messages. Many written communications are internal; thus, special attention should be given to the direction in which documents are sent. Chapters 12 and 14–17 contain specific information concerning the development of internal written communications.

Internal written communications are sent and received within a company.

Upward Written Communications.   *Upward written communications* are documents sent to superiors. Fielden recommends that upward written communications include fact, adequate opinion, tact, and adequate supportive details.[7] Writers should recognize differences between their position and the receiver's position. Superiors depend upon subordinates to supply facts and personal insights. Writers should construct written messages so that readers have little difficulty in separating fact from opinion. They should give ample supportive details to verify and clarify main points or generalizations. However, subordinates should not include an excessive amount of detail, which wastes the writer and reader's time.

Upward written communications go to superiors.

Lateral Written Communications.   *Lateral written communications* are written messages sent to peers or colleagues. Similar to upward written communications, lateral messages should contain fact, opinion, and tact. Lateral messages tend to be less formal than upward messages because the sender and receiver are on the same level in the formal organization.

Lateral written communications go to peers.

Downward Written Communications.   *Downward written communications* are written messages sent to subordinates. By using diplomacy, managers can avoid communicating in a condescending manner when sending messages downward in the formal organization. Superiors should clarify what the subordinates are expected to do upon receiving a message. Whenever possible, downward written messages should be structured to motivate employees.[8]

Downward written communications go to subordinates.

External Written Communications

External written communications are written documents that a company sends to or receives from its outside environment. An organization's external environment consists of clients and prospective clients, competitors, vendors, government agencies, and media. Writers should strive to initiate or maintain goodwill in all external written communications. External written communications are discussed in Chapters 13–16.

External written communications are sent to or received from the outside environment.

Correctness

Correctness means adhering to the commonly accepted practices of writing. Correctness is based on accuracy, grammar, spelling, punctuation, format, and coherence. First impressions are important; bad impressions caused by incorrectness can negatively affect business, a company's image, and the reader's impression of the writer's capabilities.

Software is being developed to spruce up the correctness of written communication. In 1981, Bell Laboratories Computing Science Research Center reported working on copyediting software which will help managers with weak writing skills. With copyediting programs, poor writing such as incorrect punctuation and spelling and awkward use of phrases will be detected and edited on command. The computer can provide explanations as to why certain grammatical structures are inappropriate, and it can also provide assistance in simplifying those structures.[9]

Correctness involves following accepted writing practices.

Accuracy

The information in a document must be accurate. If the reader detects an error in content, the credibility of the writer and the message is damaged. It is unlikely that a plan of action based on faulty data will be acted upon; in which case, the main purpose for writing is lost.

What factors influence correctness?

Grammar

Good grammar means following the normal conventions of the English language. Effective writers use correct grammar. Writers should use subjects and verbs that agree. They should avoid splitting infinitives and using dangling modifiers. Prepositions should have clear antecedents. Redundancy should be avoided; however, repetition may be necessary for emphasis. The message's content should be parallel.

Spelling

Correct spelling is a must. Incorrect spelling demonstrates an uncaring attitude on the writer's part. It casts doubt on the quality of the thought process underlying the message. Computer programs that check spelling are widely available for word processing systems. However, they typically just check each word for its existence in a long list of "valid" words stored in the program. Errors in word choice or usage or errors that generate another valid word usually go undetected by such programs.

Punctuation

Improper punctuation not only demonstrates an uncaring attitude, but it can also destroy the logical flow of the document and make understanding its message very difficult.

Format

The document's appearance should complement or enhance the written message. A messy memo or letter can detract from the attractiveness of the written message. For a positive impression, the physical format of a document should be correct. Poor-quality copies, unusual margins, and skewed pages reflect a careless approach to document preparation. These errors detract from the impact of a message and also reflect negatively upon the thought processes that went into the preparation of the document.

Coherence

Coherence means linking ideas together in a sensible manner.

Coherence is essential for a readable document. There must be a clear, sensible linking of ideas to lead the reader through the development of the message to the desired conclusion. Normally the desired conclusion is the reader taking action based on the ideas and recommendations made in the message. Incoherence, the jumbled linking of ideas, can cause the reader to miss the point of the message or even quit reading it. In either case, the desired conclusion is not reached.

Readability

What factors affect readability?

Readability refers to the reader's ability to read a message and extract the intended meaning. The factors that influence readability are style, tone, language, organization, and vocabulary.

Style

Writers should adapt their writing style to accommodate the receiver's reading ability and interests. Abilities, interests, and perceptions vary among readers. Consideration should also be given to the circumstances under which a document is written. Circumstances influence whether a direct or an indirect writing approach is used.

Tone

Word choice affects the tone of a message.

In written messages, tone refers to the intensity of a message as projected by the writer and/or perceived by the reader. Tone is shaped by word choice. According to Fielden, ". . . tone comes from what a reader reads into the words and sentences used."[10] Writers should choose their words carefully so that a positive image of the writer and the company is projected. An example of a negative and a positive tone follows:

Negative	*Positive*
Your payment must be made by June 10.	Please make your payment by June 10.

Language

Writers may vary the language they use to express thoughts and feelings. Circumstances affect the language writers use in business documents. Whenever possible, however, writers should use language that is active, concrete, concise, and objective.

Circumstances influence the language used in writing.

Passive Versus Active Voice.   Action is done to the subject when passive voice is used, and the subject performs the action when active voice is used. Passive voice is preferred when the action is more important than the actor or when the writer does not want to point a finger at someone for an error or misjudgment. Messages are less friendly and weaker when passive voice is used; sentences are stronger when active voice is used. The following examples contrast passive and active voice:

Active voice makes sentences stronger.

Passive	*Active*
The job evaluation was completed by the boss.	The boss completed the job evaluation.

Abstract Versus Concrete Language.   Abstract language is general and sometimes vague, whereas concrete language is simple and specific. Writers should use concrete language in constructing messages because concrete language creates clear images in the reader's mind. Special care should be taken to use concrete language to describe complex material. Generally the greater the complexity of the material, the greater the need for simplicity of language. The following examples show the difference between abstract and concrete language:

Concrete language creates clear images.

Abstract	*Concrete*
The quarterly reports must be turned in sometime in the near future.	The quarterly reports are due June 1.

Wordy Versus Concise Language.   Succinct writing makes reading easier. Consequently, writers should eliminate extra words that add nothing to the meaning of a message. Words should convey the message rather than hide or distort the message; the writer's message can get lost in excess words. The following examples contrast wordy and concise language:

Extra words add nothing to a message's meaning.

Wordy	*Concise*
The memo was long in length.	The memo was long.

Wordy	Concise
The management team will hire four consultants, who will serve as experts in strategic planning. The consultants will be expected to help with long-range planning. They will be on board to assist in intermediate-range planning as well. In addition, they will help supervisors with short-range planning endeavors.	The management team will hire four strategic planning experts. The experts will assist in long-, intermediate-, and short-range planning.

Subjective Versus Objective Language.   Written messages convey *denotations* (literal meanings) and *connotations* (suggested meanings) based on *how* the message is stated and interpreted by the reader. Writers can control some of the negative connotations that readers associate with certain words by using objective language rather than subjective language. The following examples show the difference between subjective and objective language:

Connotations are suggested meanings.

Subjective	Objective
Management and labor battled out an agreement.	Management and labor reached an agreement.

Organization

The organization of ideas in a document can add to or detract from readability. Writers should sequence ideas so that they appear in a logical order. Frequently writers, deliberately or unintentionally, omit specific information from a document. A company's strategy is an example of information that may be deliberately omitted from external written communications. When information is omitted on purpose, the writer should structure the message so that the omission is not obvious. Otherwise, the reader may misinterpret or misunderstand the written message, realizing that some information has been deliberately omitted. Writers should take special care to avoid unintentional omissions. Writers should ask themselves this question: "Is my message complete?" Incomplete messages reflect that inadequate time was spent in planning and organizing the main ideas.

Omissions from messages should not be obvious.

Readable documents focus the reader's attention on the main purpose and subject of the message. Opening statements should explain the purpose of the message and provide clues to the structure of the document and its main points. A clearly written opening statement helps the reader know what to expect and how the main points will be tied together. The structure should conform with the message that is presented with smooth transitions between sentences and between paragraphs.

Sentences and paragraphs should be carefully constructed to provide some variety. Yet the structure of a document should direct the reader's attention to the main points in logical order. The following examples illustrate the importance of the logical presentation of ideas:

Illogical	*Logical*
The last sentence provides transition between the end of a paragraph and the beginning of the next paragraph. Succeeding sentences contain additional information about a topic. A topic sentence includes the main idea of a paragraph, and it usually appears as the first sentence.	A topic sentence includes the main idea of a paragraph, and it usually appears as the first sentence. Succeeding sentences contain additional information about a topic. The last sentence provides transition between the end of a paragraph and the beginning of the next paragraph.

Sentence and paragraph construction is important for good readability. A writer should generally avoid long sentences, particularly if the subject is complicated. However, writers should also avoid using a choppy, overly simple style. The normal subject-verb-object structure should be used freely; some variety in structure helps avoid monotony.

Vary sentence and paragraph structure.

Each paragraph should have a clear topic sentence. Supporting ideas should be expressed in the same paragraph. Having only one topic per paragraph will help prevent the paragraph from becoming too long. Some paragraphs are so long that the reader may forget the topic before finishing the paragraph. Average sentence length is about two typewritten lines, and average paragraph length is about four to five sentences.

A paragraph should contain one topic sentence.

Readability formulas such as the Gunning Fog Index and Raygor Readability Estimate may be used to measure the readability of lengthy documents or documents structured for general audiences. Mechanical formulas are little help when developing documents for specialized audiences.

Vocabulary

Readable documents contain a vocabulary that is appropriate for the reader's educational or professional background and interest. When planning a document, writers should consider the receiver's reading ability.

Use jargon and buzz words sparingly.

Writers should limit the use of jargon and buzz words. If the writer is more familiar with the subject matter than the reader, it is very easy to be too specialized and pretentious or to assume too much knowledge on the reader's part. The following examples show the importance of limiting the use of jargon:

Poor	*Good*
VAX/VMS is capable of supporting simultaneous multi-user, multitasking operations with interprocess communication via mailboxes, event-flag clusters, and shared-memory maps.	The company computer operating system can be used concurrently by more than one person to perform more than one task. There are several methods whereby these independent programs can communicate with one another.

SUMMARY

Managers should determine their purposes for writing prior to planning the mechanics and format of their messages. Although writers may have several purposes in a message, a written message usually has one specific purpose. Managers should ask themselves two questions prior to writing a message: Who will read the message? What reaction or response is expected from the reader? The writer should assess the reader's identity, needs, and desires. A writer should base the decision to write or speak on the specific purpose of the message as well as on company policies. Managers should send written messages when communicating with more than one person if a meeting is not practical, when message content is complex and requires analysis, and when documentation is needed.

The writing process includes planning, organizing, drafting, and editing. Proper planning is needed to achieve the purpose of writing. Planning involves assembling all relevant materials needed for the written communications and listing all ideas that pertain to the purpose of the message.

Organizing involves analyzing, grouping, and relating message ideas in outline form. Except for the most routine correspondence, preparing an outline saves writing time and guides writers through the writing and rewriting stages of message development. The two basic types of outlines are topic and sentence outlines. In the topic outline, each entry is expressed as a word, a few words, or a short phrase. In the sentence outline, each entry is written as a complete sentence. Two common methods of outlining are the numeral-letter style and the decimal style. Managers may organize their ideas using either the direct or indirect approach.

Drafting occurs after a message is planned and organized. The objective of developing a first draft is to get words on paper. The draft may be handwritten, typed, or keyboarded with the expectation that revisions will be made. Messages are refined through editing. Writers should edit drafted documents to ensure that the intended message is communicated effectively.

Generally written communications are tangible and permanent. As a result, the effectiveness of written communications is often used as a criterion for evaluating the overall effectiveness of a manager. Some managers feel uncomfortable with writing. Some managers deliberately avoid documentation, or they write unclear messages. Although writers may communicate unclearly to protect themselves, they risk damaging relationships with their readers and causing declines in profit and productivity.

Writers should plan, organize, draft, and edit documents to include the elements of effective writing. These elements are thought, appropriateness, correctness, and readability. Thought involves clarifying one's purpose for writing and choosing what information to include or exclude from a message. Thought is needed to prevent rambling. Thought is also needed to ensure that assumptions are clearly identified and that facts, conclusions, and implications are presented objectively.

Appropriateness refers to structuring a message based on whether the message is an internal or external communication. Internal written communications are sent and received within an organization; these may be upward, lateral, or downward communications. External written communications are documents that a company sends to or receives from its outside environment.

Correctness means adhering to the commonly accepted practices of writing. Correctness is based on accuracy, grammar, spelling, punctuation, format, and coherence. Incorrectness can negatively affect business, a company's image, and the reader's impression of the writer's capabilities.

Readability refers to the reader's ability to read the message and extract the intended meaning. Factors such as style, tone, language, organization, and vocabulary affect readability. Writers should adapt their writing style to accommodate the receiver's reading ability and interests. Abilities, interests, and perceptions vary among readers. Consideration should be given to the circumstances in which a document is written because circumstances influence the approach used in writing. Writers should choose their words so that a positive image of the writer and the company is projected. Whenever possible, writers should use language that is active, concrete, concise, and objective. Writers should sequence ideas so they appear in a logical order and should use vocabulary that is appropriate for the reader's educational or professional background and interest.

QUESTIONS

1. Explain why the content of a written message may vary depending on who will read it.
2. What is the relationship between planning and organizing?
3. What outline style is recommended for assisting writers to express their thoughts in writing?
4. Why should a draft be written as rapidly as possible?
5. What is meant by this statement: "Editing is the critical thinking phase of the writing process"?
6. Name and explain the four key elements of effective writing.
7. Define *readability*.
8. How do internal and external written communications differ?
9. Explain the importance of correctness in writing.
10. Describe how language affects readability.

PROBLEM-SOLVING EXPERIENCES

1. Find a written document you prepared recently. Critique your writing performance using the four key elements of effective writing as your evaluation criteria.

2. Complete the following activities:
    a. Assume you have been asked by top management to write a brief report on effective time management. As quickly as possible, write down all ideas that come into your mind about the subject of time management. Do not worry about the order or importance of the ideas. You do not have to put the material into report form.
    b. In a small group of students assigned by your instructor, prepare a *topic* outline in the *numeral-letter* style for the ideas listed in Problem-Solving Experience 2a. Be prepared to discuss the outline in class.

CASE 11–1

Mark Stone is the production manager for Stepside Inc.; he supervises 53 hourly employees in the company's production shop. Mark's boss, Ned Demorest, has asked Mark to inform the production shop employees of the recent changes in the company's benefit package for hourly employees. Mark has decided to send the employees a written notice of the changes.

1. Substantiate why Mark should prepare a written message rather than a spoken message.
2. What should Mark emphasize in his written message?
3. Prepare the message's content.

ENDNOTES

[1] Charles J. Hamed, "Phone or Write?" *The ABCA Bulletin*, Vol. 45, No. 10 (June, 1982), p. 46.

[2] Patricia King, *Mind to Disk to Paper: Business Writing on a Word Processor* (New York: Franklin Watts, Inc., 1984), pp. 108–109.

[3] Peter Elbow, "Teaching Thinking by Teaching Writing," *Change*, Vol. 15, No. 3 (September, 1983), p. 37.

[4] Marvin H. Swift, "Clear Writing Means Clear Thinking Means . . .," *Harvard Business Review*, Vol. 51, No. 1 (January–February, 1973), p. 62.

[5]Dick Brown, "Why Executives Can't Write," *World Press Review*, Vol. 28, No. 5 (May, 1981), p. 52.

[6]John Fielden, "What Do You Mean I Can't Write?" *Harvard Business Review*, Vol. 42, No. 3 (May–June, 1964), pp. 149–150.

[7]Ibid., p. 149.

[8]Ibid., p. 150.

[9]"At Work, 'On-the-Job Communicating,'" *Changing Times*, Vol. 35, No. 5 (May, 1981), p. 74.

[10]John Fielden, "What Do You Mean You Don't Like My Style?" *Harvard Business Review*, Vol. 60, No. 3 (May–June, 1982), p. 12.

12

MEMORANDUMS, NOTES, AND MESSAGES

When you complete this chapter, you should be able to:

▲ Explain the nature of memos used for internal communication.

▲ Distinguish among formal, semiformal, and informal memos.

▲ Distinguish between the direct and indirect approaches for writing memos.

▲ Describe the essential parts of memos, notes, and messages.

▲ List the benefits of using a computer-based message system to transmit and receive interoffice memos and messages.

Memos. The word has a strong, well-defined sound. It implies a simple, clear, and direct message. Memos are the primary written communication tool used by managers; they are indispensable to business life. Today technology has a great impact on this precise form of writing. Easy-to-use computers are changing the way managers handle office memos and messages.

▲ NATURE OF INTERNAL WRITTEN COMMUNICATIONS

As described in Chapter 11, internal written communications are documents that are sent and received within an organization. Common internal written communications addressed in this chapter are memorandums, notes, and messages.

Memorandums

Memos dominate in-house written communication.

Interoffice and intraoffice memos dominate the written communication of most managers. **Interoffice memorandums** are sent between or among employees of different work units. **Intraoffice memorandums** are sent between or among employees of the same work unit. Contemporary managers spend much of their time communicating with superiors, peers or colleagues, and subordinates. Managers can use memos to serve as documentation for future reference of communication within the firm.

Like all other areas of communication, writing skills improve with practice. A good starting point for writing skill improvement is knowing when a document should be written. Writing should occur *only* when it serves a useful purpose. Unnecessary memos not only cause wasted writing and reading time, but they also cause wasted storage space if the memo is filed.

Writing should occur only when warranted.

Three questions should be asked prior to writing a memo: Is the proposed content important? Is the proposed content important enough to put in writing? Is the proposed content worth keeping?[1] Answering yes to the first two questions indicates that a memo is warranted. A response of yes to the third question indicates that a printed or protected electronic copy of the memo needs to be kept for future reference.

"REMEMBER, STODDARD, AROUND HERE YOU'RE ONLY AS GOOD AS YOUR LAST MEMO."

Source: © 1982 Leo Cullum.

According to James Hayes, a former president of the American Management Association, a memo should be written on a single subject. If multiple subjects are included or discussed, their importance is minimized.[2] Remember these additional points when developing an effective memo:

1. Limit the memo to one page, if possible.
2. Use numbers, letters, or symbols for significant points about the subject if such an enumeration would clarify the information.
3. Generally use active voice.

Memorandum Parts

Although memos tend to be less formal than letters which are sent outside the company, memos and letters are equal in importance. Memos contain six standard parts and may include three optional parts.

Standard Parts.   The parts of a memo may vary based on individual company procedures, but parts commonly included are the *To*, *From*, *Date*, and *Subject* lines, the body of the memo, and reference initials. Interoffice or intraoffice memorandum stationery should be used if the preprinted form is available. The **To** *line* indicates the name of the person to whom the memo is written. If writing to more than one person, list the names in order of importance. Receivers of equal rank or importance are listed alphabetically.[3] The writer's name appears on the **From** *line*. Omit

Memos contain six standard parts.

the official title of the writer unless the memo is written to a person who may not know the writer. The *To* and *From* lines are generally parallel in content.[4] The **Date** *line* documents the timing of the memo. The **Subject** *line* enables the reader to know the theme or topic of the memo prior to reading it. Specific, concise language should be used in the *Subject* line. The *body,* which begins a double space below the *Subject* line, is the message that the sender conveys to the receiver. Allow a right margin for the body that is approximately the same as the left margin. ***Reference initials,*** typed a double space below the body, are used to indicate if someone other than the sender keyboarded the memo.

> Reference initials are not used if the writer keyboards the memo.

Optional Parts.   The *Memorandum* heading, the enclosure notation, and the copy notation are optional memorandum parts. Ordinarily a memo is labeled ***Memorandum*** unless a preprinted form is used. The ***enclosure notation*** indicates that items are enclosed with a memo. The enclosure notation is typed a double space below the reference initials. The ***copy notation*** identifies the individuals who also receive a copy of the memo and is typed a double space below the enclosure notation. Carbon copy—*cc*—used to be the common copy notation. However, due to the increase in photocopying, *pc* is now a more acceptable copy notation.

> If a photocopy of a memo is made, *pc* is used as the copy notation.

Figure 12–1 shows the standard and optional parts of a memo; it also depicts spacing guides for the various parts of a memo. Memorandum format varies based on the procedures preferred within individual companies and whether memos are printed or read from video screens.

Formal, Semiformal, and Informal Memos

Memos may be formal, semiformal, or informal. Memos may vary in formality depending upon the sender, the receiver, and the message's content. For instance, a message may differ based upon the direction it is sent—vertically or horizontally. The formality of a memo is ordinarily denoted by the information provided in the *To* and *From* lines. Regardless of a memo's formality, the tone employed should be conversational and natural.

> The formality of a memo depends on the sender, the receiver, and the message.

A ***formal memo*** is sent to a superior or colleague with whom the sender is unacquainted or not well acquainted. Position or department titles and names are used in formal memos, and the sender generally signs his or her complete name at the right of the *From* line. Figure 12–2 on page 206 depicts a formal memo.

> The sender signs a formal memo.

A ***semiformal memo*** is sent to a superior or colleague with whom the sender is acquainted. The memo is initialed at the right of the *From* line, indicating that the sender saw the printed or final copy of the memo prior to sending it; official department titles are optional. Figure 12–3 on page 206 shows a semiformal memo.

> The sender initials a semiformal memo.

(one-inch top margin)

A MEMORANDUM

(triple-space)

1   TO: Martha Nelms, Ed.D.

(double-space)

2   FROM: Melissa L. Bryan, Ph.D.   *Melissa L. Bryan*

(double-space)

3   DATE: April 20, 19--

(double-space)

4 SUBJECT: Retirement Dinner for Jim Kern

(double-space)

You are invited to attend a retirement dinner for Jim Kern.
The dinner will be held at the History Village Inn on
Friday, June 12, at 7:30 p.m.

(double-space)

5   Jim's retirement present has not yet been purchased. A
gift idea list is enclosed. Please let me know if you have
a preference as to what the gift should be. All gift ideas
should be turned in to me no later than May 25.

(double-space)

Mary Gleason is handling reservations for the dinner.
Please call Mary at extension 132 by May 20 to make your
reservation.

(double-space)

6 wjb

(double-space)

B Enclosure: Gift List

(double-space)

C pc Mark Knoll

Standard Parts

1 *To* Line
2 *From* Line
3 *Date* Line
4 *Subject* Line
5 Body
6 Reference Initials

Optional Parts

A *Memorandum* Heading
B Enclosure Notation
C Copy Notation

FIGURE 12–1   Parts of a Memorandum

SCHURTTER STEEL PRODUCTS INC.   **INTEROFFICE MEMORANDUM**

TO: Bob Johnson, Analytical Chemistry Division

FROM: Vickie Aven, Solid State Division *Vickie Aven*

DATE: March 25, 19--

SUBJECT: Interdepartmental Meeting

A joint meeting of the Analytical Chemistry Division and the Solid State Division will be held on Friday, April 8. Matrix personnel will discuss overlapping projects scheduled for the next fiscal year.

Please let me know if you would like to place an item on the formal agenda. I look forward to meeting the new employees in the Analytical Chemistry Division.

jav

FIGURE 12–2   Formal Memorandum

Gemini International, Inc.   **INTEROFFICE MEMORANDUM**

TO: Tanya Temple

FROM: Mickey Gentry *MG*

DATE: June 23, 19--

SUBJECT: Al Kent's Human Resource File

Please return Al Kent's human resource file. You checked out the file on Friday, June 20, at 11:00 a.m. for a three-hour period. As of 8:15 this morning, you had not returned the file. All human resource records may be checked out for only three hours. I have tried to call you and come by your office, but you were either in a meeting or out of the office. Please return Al Kent's file <u>immediately</u>.

FIGURE 12–3   Semiformal Memorandum

An ***informal memo*** contains the standard memo parts, but generally the sender and receiver communicate on a first-name basis. The sender usually writes an informal memo on a preprinted form. As shown in Figure 12–4, the sender's signature or initials are not necessary in an informal memo.

Memo Organization Based upon Reader Reaction

In developing a memo, a writer should think of how the written message will be received by the reader.

> Because managers are in positions of authority, it is especially important that they recognize the effect they can have on their receivers, just because they are managers. This power can cause people to react to them in ways that have little or nothing to do with the facts of the situation.[5]

Originally memos were used to "remind."[6] Today memos are used to thank, praise, give directions, and describe or clarify situations. They are also used to suggest alternative solutions, motivate, chastise, persuade, transmit data, or establish position. Based upon expected receiver reaction, a writer should prepare a memo using either a direct or an indirect

---

GREELEY
CONSTRUCTION CO., INC.   **INTEROFFICE MEMORANDUM**

TO: Pat

FROM: Jerry

DATE: May 23, 19--

SUBJECT: Previewing Training Films

    You are invited to preview our new telephone communication training films. We just purchased three 15-minute films that are appropriate for training all levels of employees. If you are interested in seeing these films, let me know.

FIGURE 12–4   Informal Memorandum

approach. Because writing is used as input and/or output components of the communication system, the direct and indirect approaches are useful in constructing written messages.

Follow the elements of effective writing when constructing a memo.

Observe the elements of effective writing—thought, appropriateness, correctness, and readability—in both directly and indirectly written memos. Omit *gobbledygook,* commonly used to describe nonsensical wording, and inflated language. The following example illustrates how gobbledygook clouds a message:

> Transmitted herewith is a matrix which should facilitate the incorporation of the accessible arrangement of information in the recently incorporated network structure. In the near future, a policy statement of the expected benefit to be derived and the ensuing adherence to the new procedures will be distributed for inclusion in your primary reference.

This example means:

> Here is your copy of the company procedures manual. You will receive the preface of the manual soon. The preface will describe how you can benefit by following the prescribed procedures.

Direct Approach.   If anticipated reader reaction is positive, a direct writing approach should be used. The direct approach involves placing the main theme or idea of the memo in the opening paragraph, preferably in

"Crampton, would you rewrite this memo using
simple, straightforward buzzwords?"

Source: From THE WALL STREET JOURNAL—Permission, Cartoon Features Syndicate.

the first sentence. Essential details follow the main idea in paragraph or enumerated form. If extra emphasis is desired, a restatement of the main idea appears in the closing lines of the memo. The sharing of good news generally results in positive reader reaction. Likewise, a positive reader reaction occurs when useful or needed information is shared. Figure 12–5 illustrates a memo written in the direct approach.

When anticipated reader reaction is positive, a direct approach should be used.

Indirect Approach.   Placing an unpleasant main idea in the opening sentence or paragraph of a memo might cause a reader to stop reading before the reasons or explanations for the unpleasant news are given. A buffer consisting of a neutral opening and any necessary reasons or explanations should precede the main idea. When the main idea is followed by a positive or neutral closing, more cushion is added. Managers should write memos from an offensive rather than a defensive position. They should avoid negative language. If constructed carefully, the indirect approach camouflages failure, rejection, or refusal and calls attention to positive accomplishments.[7] The memo in Figure 12–6 illustrates the indirect approach. Notice that the unpleasant main idea is sandwiched between a buffer and a positive or neutral closing.

When anticipated reader reaction is negative, an indirect approach should be used.

Continental Industries, Inc.
INTEROFFICE MEMORANDUM

TO: Don Johnson
FROM: Susan Humphrey   *SH*
DATE: November 1, 19--
SUBJECT: Quality Circle Meeting

The Finance Division will have its first quality circle meeting on Tuesday, November 15, in Room 624 at 3:15 p.m.

Topics to be covered include an introduction to quality circles, an overview of the quality circle concept, and the Finance Division's plan for implementing quality circles. We will select circle leaders at the conclusion of the meeting.

Please join us for this important meeting.

mas

FIGURE 12–5   Memo Using the Direct Approach

NW NORTHWEST INDUSTRIES, INC.

INTEROFFICE MEMORANDUM

TO: Julia Price

FROM: Erv McCormick *E McC*

DATE: November 20, 19--

SUBJECT: Travel Reimbursement

Northwest Industries, Inc., is pleased to sponsor employee participation in professional conferences. Employees are encouraged to attend at least one conference a year. As mentioned in the September newsletter, the maximum reimbursement for conference participation is $325 per employee.

Each employee is free to choose which conference he or she attends, but the reimbursement remains at $325 no matter where the meeting is held. A check for $325 is enclosed; your reimbursement is for the AMS conference you attended in Ontario. Receipts for expenses which exceeded $325 are also enclosed. Although the company cannot reimburse you for these expenses, you can deduct them from your income taxes.

Meetings like the one you attended help our employees stay current. Thank you for participating in the AMS conference.

drt

Enclosures

FIGURE 12–6   Memo Using the Indirect Approach

The nature of managerial work often necessitates the use of persuasion. Through persuasion, managers sell ideas, concepts, and strategies. Persuasion can be employed in either oral or written communications. Managers produce written communications to persuade twice as often as do professional or technical personnel.[8] Typically, managers follow a modified version of the indirect approach when trying to persuade a reader. A neutral beginning is recommended, followed by an introduction to the idea, concept, or strategy that the writer wishes to promote. Next, the writer shares any favorable features or characteristics of the idea. As a conclusion, the manager makes action easy for the reader. Figure 12–7 illustrates a memo using the persuasive approach.

Notes and Messages

Typed or handwritten notes and messages are an important part of internal written communications. They are easy to use and usually do not require a permanent copy. Yet, if treated casually or carelessly, they may cause misunderstanding and needless expense.

Notes and messages are easy to use but should not be written thoughtlessly.

Managers frequently attach notes to reports and other business documents rather than take the time to write memos. Occasionally managers must take telephone or face-to-face messages for colleagues or staff members. Notes and messages are generally written under the pressure of time which requires managers to analyze situations quickly and write concise, accurate messages.

Managers frequently write notes and occasionally take messages.

Standard Parts

Notes and messages, although less formal than memos, should include the following information:

1. Name of the person to whom the message is directed.
2. Name of the person sending the message.
3. Current date and time.
4. Action to be taken.
5. Time requirement or desired response time.

Like other forms of business writing, notes and messages are judged by their accuracy and clarity. The reader will use them to make business decisions and to prompt action. Carelessly worded notes and messages run the risk of not being understood by the reader. Misunderstanding leads to wasted time and money. Therefore, writers should strive to make every word clear. Managers should not substitute brevity for effective communication.

Use short, clear, and accurate statements when writing notes and messages.

Office Services, Inc.

INTEROFFICE MEMORANDUM

TO: Pam Hill, Marketing Division

FROM: Lynn Stephens, Personnel Division   *Lynn Stephens*

DATE: April 1, 19--

SUBJECT: Time Management

The most valuable commodity each of us has is time. Successful people and mediocre achievers all have 24 hours in a day. How they manage their time determines their level of success. The Personnel Division is starting a time management campaign to promote success throughout the company.

As part of that campaign, we would like all employees to analyze how they typically spend their time on the job. Conducting a personal time management analysis can assist you in determining the amount of time you spend on various tasks, and it can facilitate in maximizing your accomplishments.

You will receive a time log notebook in the next few days. Please use it in conducting your personal time management analysis. The notebook is yours to keep; consider it a working document. No one but you will review its contents.

bib

FIGURE 12–7   Memo Using the Persuasive Approach

Preprinted Note and Message Forms

Many firms use preprinted note and message forms. These forms vary widely in format; two examples are shown in Figure 12–8.

Interoffice messages and notes often combine oral and written communication and involve an intermediary person. When taking a message for another person, one should follow these basic suggestions:

Follow these steps when taking a message.

1. Complete all blank spaces on the preprinted form with the correct information.
2. Write the message verbatim or in complete sentences.
3. Write legibly.
4. Check the spellings of unusual names, and always verify the telephone number and the caller's name.

Additional information about telephone speaking or face-to-face speaking was addressed in Chapter 6.

▲ ELECTRONIC MEMOS AND MESSAGES ▬▬▬▬▬▬▬▬▬

Technological advances are being introduced in many organizations at an incredible rate. The following scenario is an example of how one person uses communication technology to send and receive messages:

> When I arrive at my office in the morning and begin my work, I flip a switch and press a few keys and an index of incoming messages is displayed on the screen before me. Since I am pressed for time, I read only one relatively urgent message. Moving a pointer, I position an arrow on the screen and press a button. Instantly, the message I have selected is displayed. I read it easily, since messages sent directly from screen to screen tend to be short and direct. After some thought, I send a message to a colleague asking for help in organizing a somewhat lengthy response. Then I set about the principal work of the morning . . . . Meanwhile, my colleague is structuring an answer to the urgent inquiry. He calls to the screen an old, but relevant, report, composes an appropriate "cover letter," and sends it on to me. Later, after I have added some new information to the response, I send it via the network linking . . . parts of our organization. The message is automatically stored for future reference, and if a printed copy is desired, it is available in seconds from the nearby copier-printer.[9]

This scenario describes a system commonly called electronic mail. *Electronic mail* is the transmission of a written message using a computer system which is responsible for routing and delivering the message. It is a technology in which information is delivered at electronic speeds to an

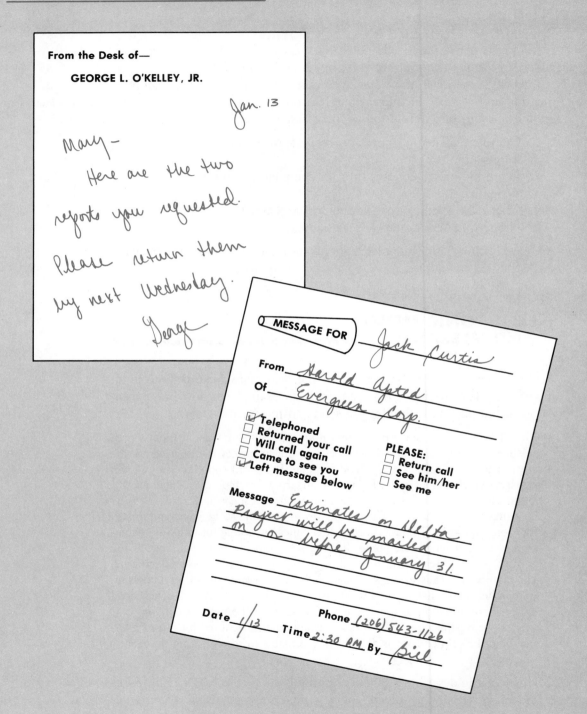

FIGURE 12–8   Note and Message Forms

internal or external location.[10] Computer networks are gaining rapid acceptance in offices. The day is now in sight when networks will link more than half of the personal computers in business.[11] A considerable amount of the traffic over these networks will consist of electronic memos and messages.

A common method used by managers to deliver electronic memos and messages is the ***computer-based message system (CBMS).*** In a CBMS, managers input their memos at their terminals and send the memos over wires or cables to a main computer. As shown in Figure 12–9, memos are held in "electronic mailboxes" in the computer until the recipients want to receive them. Users of a CBMS are assigned a password code to access the memos. They can read the memos on their video display terminal screens and use their terminals to respond. Hard-copy printouts of the memos can be made if needed, as shown in Figure 12–10.

For electronic documents, the writer may be identified on the computer from password information. Another alternative is the use of a special graphics area which allows for a more traditional signature. The methods for providing document control and security in electronic mail are still being developed by software manufacturers.

Technology is changing the way memos are handled.

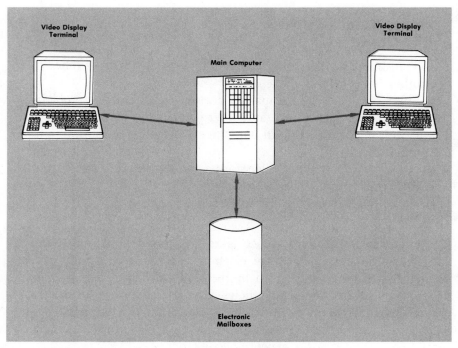

FIGURE 12–9   Computer-Based Message System (CBMS)

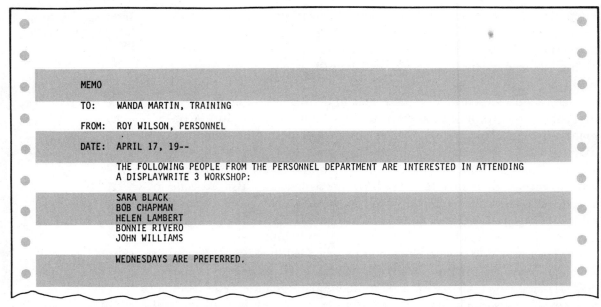

```
MEMO

TO:    WANDA MARTIN, TRAINING

FROM:  ROY WILSON, PERSONNEL

DATE:  APRIL 17, 19--

       THE FOLLOWING PEOPLE FROM THE PERSONNEL DEPARTMENT ARE INTERESTED IN ATTENDING
       A DISPLAYWRITE 3 WORKSHOP:

       SARA BLACK
       BOB CHAPMAN
       HELEN LAMBERT
       BONNIE RIVERO
       JOHN WILLIAMS

       WEDNESDAYS ARE PREFERRED.
```

FIGURE 12–10   Computer Printout of a Memo

Some of the major benefits of using an electronic system to send and receive office memos and messages are[12]

▲ Transmitting information at electronic speeds from one office to another.

▲ Shortening the time for making decisions and resolving problems.

▲ Eliminating delays, cost, and other problems in mail delivery.

▲ Permitting keyboarding in one office and editing and printing in another office.

▲ Providing a central point for storing and transmitting information.

▲ Reducing excess paperwork.

▲ Facilitating informal communication.

Computer-based message systems can save time and money.

The last benefit listed requires a word of caution. Clearly the daily message traffic in an electronic office takes on a less formal, more succinct air. The real danger is that the electronic memo may become so fragmented that it is misunderstood by the reader. When a memo becomes fragmented, efforts to increase efficiency result in ineffectiveness. Managers using an electronic system must continually strive for a balance between efficiency of operation and effectiveness of performance. One factor cannot be sacrificed at the expense of the other.

Electronic memos should not economize on the use of words to the point where the reader does not understand the message.

SUMMARY

Memos are the most common form of written communications in offices. Standard parts of a memo are the *To, From, Date,* and *Subject* lines; the body; and reference initials. Optional memo parts may include the *Memorandum* heading and appropriate enclosure and copy notations. The formality of memos may vary depending upon the relationship that exists between the sender and the receiver. Formal memos are signed; semiformal memos, initialed; and informal memos, unsigned.

The body of the memo is organized according to anticipated reader reaction. If the reader is expected to be pleased or interested, a direct approach is used, and the main idea is stated in the opening. An indirect approach is used if anticipated reader reaction is negative; a neutral beginning and reasons for disappointing the reader are provided before the main idea. A modified indirect approach is used for persuasive memos.

Notes and messages contain much of the same vital information as memos. Standard parts of notes and messages are the name of the person to whom the message is directed, the name of the person sending the message, the current date and time, the action to be taken, and the time requirement or desired response time. Complete all appropriate blank spaces on a note or message form. Write messages as dictated, or use complete, comprehensible sentences. Write legibly, and verify names and numbers with the caller or person leaving the note.

Memos are transmitted electronically through computer networks. The electronic transmission of memos can shorten the time required for decision-making and problem-solving activities.

QUESTIONS

1. What is meant by this statement: "A good starting point for writing skill improvement is knowing when a document should be written"?

2. Describe the standard and optional parts of a memo.

3. Compare and contrast formal and semiformal memos.

4. Where does the main idea appear in a memo written using the direct approach? the indirect approach?

5. What purpose does a buffer serve in a memo written using the indirect approach?

6. Describe the major components of a persuasive memo.

7. Describe how an electronic mail system can improve internal written communications.

8. What are *electronic mailboxes?*

9. Describe a computer-based message system (CBMS).

10. What is the danger associated with informal electronic communication?

PROBLEM-SOLVING EXPERIENCES

1. Write a memo to Mary Allison telling her about the next Space Utilization Planning Committee meeting. The meeting is scheduled for 2:15 p.m. on Thursday, January 5. Committee members will meet in Conference Room H21.

2. How can the following memo be edited so that the disappointing news is presented in a more positive way? Please assist Mack by rewriting the memo.

Quality Manufacturing Company   **INTEROFFICE MEMORANDUM**

TO: David Snelling

FROM: Mack Pemberton *MP*

DATE: March 6, 19--

SUBJECT: Promotion Request

It is with much regret that I inform you that the promotion you requested has been denied. I looked through your written request and supplementary materials and decided that you are not ready for a promotion from administrative assistant to office manager.

Your work is appreciated. It is evident that you try hard, and you produce. However, employees have to be with the company a minimum of 18 months before they can request a promotion.

Check with me again in November concerning your being promoted. Maybe you will have a better chance of being promoted at that time.

rem

---

3. After deciding that Jennifer Stanton could take vacation on August 11, 12, and 13, Clara Thompson drafted a memo informing Jennifer of her decision. Yesterday Donald Lewis, who will be Jennifer's substitute, informed Clara that he is scheduled for major surgery on August 10. He will be hospitalized from August 9 through 16. Therefore, Jennifer will not be able to take vacation due to the change of events. Write a memo reflecting Clara's new decision.

CASE 12–1

As vice-president of administrative services of Peachtree Industries, you are concerned about the need to reduce telephone costs. Current long-distance costs are double those for the same period last year. You have decided to implement the following steps to control long-distance calling:

- ▲ Each telephone user will keep a daily log of all calls made. Logs will be turned in weekly to department heads. These records will be compared against the monthly telephone invoices to ensure the accuracy of all calls charged to departments.
- ▲ Only authorized personnel will be permitted to place long-distance calls using telephone credit cards.
- ▲ Pay telephones will be installed in the lobby for visitors and employees to make personal long-distance calls.
- ▲ Telephone users should carefully plan each long-distance call in an effort to keep calls short. Long-distance calls that exceed two minutes are of questionable value.

1. Write a memorandum addressed to all department heads. Instruct them to (a) remind all personnel of the need to reduce long-distance costs and (b) inform all personnel of the cost-reducing steps that are to be implemented immediately. Mention that a meeting of department heads will be held next Wednesday at 2 p.m. in the conference room to discuss additional ways to reduce telephone costs.

CASE 12–2

Last week Jim Sluter asked Ben Harper to preside over the April Quality Control Committee meeting since Jim is scheduled to be out of town on business. Ben refused to preside over the meeting, saying he preferred to serve as a group member only. Jim was counting on Ben to conduct the

April meeting. Ben is the senior committee member and the most qualified person to conduct the meeting in Jim's absence. In a last attempt to make him reconsider, Jim plans to write Ben a memo.

1. Write the memo for Jim.

ENDNOTES

[1]James L. Hayes, "Putting It in Writing: A Critical Executive Skill," *Security Management,* Vol. 26, No. 8 (August, 1982), p. 37.

[2]Ibid.

[3]Jo Ann Hennington, "Memorandums—An Executive Communication Tool for Management," *The ABCA Bulletin,* Vol. 41, No. 3 (September, 1978), p. 11.

[4]Ibid.

[5]Mildred S. Myers, "The Manager's Memo as a Strategic Tool," *Management Review,* Vol. 71, No. 6 (June, 1982), pp. 19–20.

[6]Carol Schwalberg, "The Memo Strategies," *Working Woman,* Vol. 8, No. 10 (October, 1983), p. 92.

[7]Ibid.

[8]Myers, op. cit., p. 19.

[9]R. J. Spinrad, "Office Automation," *Science,* Vol. 215, No. 2 (February, 1982), p. 808.

[10]Zane K. Quible and Richard A. Aukerman, "Office Connections," *Management World,* Vol. 12, No. 11 (December, 1983), p. 32.

[11]Bro Uttal, "Linking Computers to Help Managers Manage," *Fortune,* Vol. 108, No. 13 (December 26, 1983), p. 146.

[12]John J. Stallard, E. Ray Smith, and Donald Reese, *The Electronic Office: A Guide for Managers* (Homewood, IL: Dow Jones-Irwin, 1982), pp. 88–89, 217–219.

13

LETTERS

Letters are perhaps the most important of all forms of business writing because they are sent to people outside the company. Potential customers and clients may base their judgment of a business organization on just one letter they receive. Managers who write letters that form a favorable first impression perform a vital function for their organizations.

▲ NATURE OF EXTERNAL WRITTEN COMMUNICATIONS

As soon as a letter is removed from its envelope, the reader forms a favorable or unfavorable impression of its organization. The style, the placement and spacing of the parts, the appearance of the typing, and the design and color of the printed letterhead and envelope are factors sized up by the reader at first sight. The reader is influenced by the overall appearance of the letter before becoming aware of its message.

Attractive letters establish a positive image.

The primary purposes of a letter's format are to create a favorable first impression of the writer and the writer's company and to secure the highest possible level of reader attention and understanding. An effective letter holds the reader's attention, emphasizes the message, and establishes a positive attitude as the message is read.

Letter Parts

Letters are external forms of written communications; that is, they are received by people outside the company. Letters contain eight standard parts and may include eight optional parts.

Standard Parts

There are eight standard letter parts.

Every business letter should have these standard parts: heading, date, inside address, salutation, body, complimentary close, originator's identification, and reference initials.

The *heading* includes the company name, address, and telephone number. Usually the heading appears as a printed letterhead, which refers to the company stationery used for external correspondence. The *date* is typed below the letterhead; it serves as a reference point for both the sender and receiver. On plain paper, the writer's address appears on the two lines above the date.

222

Mr. Joshua B. Schrensington, Jr.
Chairman of the Board
Trenditech Industries International
Newport Beach, CA 92660
Dear Josh: Bug off.

Sincerely, etc.

Source: Reprinted by permission: Tribune Media Services.

The *inside address*—the name, title, and complete mailing address of the receiver—begins on the fourth line below the date. This address should also appear on the envelope. The appropriate two-letter state abbreviation and ZIP Code should be included in the inside address. ZIP Codes should consist of five or nine digits. A nine-digit ZIP Code is used by some companies to reduce mailing costs.

> A nine-digit ZIP Code is used by some companies to reduce mailing costs.

The *salutation* appears a double space below the inside address and is used to greet the receiver. Traditionally the sender greets the receiver by name. A formal greeting including a courtesy title such as Dr., Mr., Mrs., Ms., or Miss is used if the sender is unacquainted or not well acquainted with the receiver. *Dear Ms. Temple* is an example of a formal salutation. An informal greeting which includes only the receiver's first name is used if the sender and receiver know one another. *Dear Chris* is an example of an informal salutation. *Greetings* or *Dear Madam or Sir* may be used as the salutation when the sender is unsure to whom the letter should be sent.

The *body* of a letter represents the message or messages which the sender wishes to convey. The body, which begins a double space below the salutation, consists of three parts—the opening, the middle section,

> The body of a letter contains three parts— an opening, a middle, and a closing.

and the closing. The information contained in these three parts may be presented using a direct or an indirect approach.

A *complimentary close* refers to the farewell or closing of the letter. Expressions such as *Sincerely* or *Cordially* appear a double space below the body. Writers use a complimentary close to end communication in a positive manner.

The *originator's identification,* or name, appears on the fourth line below the complimentary close. A typed or keyboarded originator identification is especially valuable in verifying the sender's name when the sender's signature is not legible. *Reference initials,* the initials of the person who keyboarded the letter for the sender, are typed a double space below the originator's identification at the left margin.

Optional Parts

Optional letter parts include mailing notations, an attention line, a subject line, the typed company name, the originator's title, enclosure notations, copy notations, and a postscript.

Mailing notations, or special mailing instructions, such as *REGISTERED* or *CERTIFIED* should appear a double space below the date and a double space above the inside address. An *attention line* may be used in a letter addressed to a corporation or department so that the letter is routed to a particular person within the organization. The attention line is typed as the second line of the inside address. A *subject line* enables the reader to know the topic of the letter prior to reading it. *SUBJECT:* or *RE:* may be typed before the subject line. The subject line should appear a double space below the salutation and a double space above the body of the letter.

The *typed company name* may be included in a letter when the writer wants to draw special attention to his or her company. Including the typed company name may seem redundant because the letterhead contains the name of the company which the writer represents. The typed company name should appear in all capital letters a double space below the complimentary close and four lines above the originator's identification.

The *originator's title* refers to the business or professional title by which the sender is known. Examples of an originator's title include *Vice-President*, *Department Head*, or *Ph.D.* The originator's title follows the originator's identification.

An *enclosure notation* informs the receiver that additional items are included with the letter. The enclosure notation appears a double space below the reference initials. A *copy notation* identifies the individuals who receive a copy of the letter. A *pc* is used as the copy notation when the letter is photocopied for distribution to others. A copy notation appears a double space below the enclosure notation.

Writers may include eight optional parts in their letters.

The enclosure notation serves as a reminder to the reader.

A *postscript* is used to add an idea or to provide additional information at the end of a letter; it is not a forgotten idea included at the last moment. The postscript is usually treated as a separate paragraph. The postscript may be preceded by *P.S.* or *PS*. The postscript appears a double space below the copy notation.

Figure 13–1 shows the standard and optional parts of a letter. Spacing guides for the different parts of a letter are shown as well.

Punctuation Styles

The most common punctuation styles for letters are the open style and the mixed style. When the open style is used, there is no punctuation after the salutation and complimentary close. When the mixed style is used, a colon follows the salutation and a comma follows the complimentary close.

Second-Page Heading

Letters should be limited to one page in length if possible. However, when a letter runs to two pages, use plain paper of the same size, quality, and color as the letterhead stationery for the second page. The second-page heading should begin on line six from the top of the page. Two common second-page headings are shown here.

A second-page heading is used for lengthy letters.

Mrs. Mary Simcoe
Page 2
December 2, 19—

or

Mrs. Mary Simcoe   2   December 2, 19—

Envelopes

The length of the letter and the size of the letterhead stationery determine the size of envelope used for sending a letter. Properly addressed envelopes include the sender's return address, the receiver's complete address, and any mailing notation contained in the letter. Envelopes may be addressed using the same capitalization, punctuation, and spacing used in the inside address; *or* they may be addressed in all capital letters with no punctuation.

Heading(S)

DIGITAL COMPONENTS
1262 Treemont Way
Atlanta, GA 30303-2403
(404) 555-2974

Date(S)   November 20, 19--
                          (double-space)
Mailing   CERTIFIED
Notation(O)   (double-space)
                 Mr. Terry Allen
Inside   Plant Manager
                 Piedmont Textiles
Address(S)   2391 Winter Way Boulevard
                 Atlanta, GA   30301-2410
                          (double-space)
Salutation(S)   Dear Mr. Allen:
                          (double-space)
Subject Line(O) TICKETS FOR DIGITAL COMPONENTS CLIENT RECEPTION
                          (double-space)
                 Your two complimentary tickets for Digital Components
                 Client Reception at the Atlanta Ritz Carlton on Friday,
                 December 6, are enclosed. You and your wife are cordially
                 invited to attend this special reception.
                          (double-space)
Body(S)   Your company is special to Digital Components. The
                 December 6 reception has been planned to honor preferred
                 clients like you. Mary Kent will call you on Thursday,
                 December 5, to verify whether you and your wife plan to
                 join us at the reception.
                          (double-space)
                 Thank you for doing business with Digital.
                                                          (double-space)
Complimentary Close(S)   Sincerely,
                                                          (double-space)
Typed Company Name(O)   DIGITAL COMPONENTS
                                                          (quadruple-space)
                                           Victor Valdez

Originator's Identification(S)   Victor Valdez
Originator's Title(O)   Marketing Director
                                                          (double-space)
Reference   ks
Initials(S)   (double-space)
Enclosure   Enclosures
Notation(O)   (double-space)
Copy   pc Mary Kent
Notation(O)   (double-space)
Postscript(O)   Please let me know if you need additional tickets for
                 the reception.

                 S = Standard Part
                 O = Optional Part

FIGURE 13–1   Parts of a Letter

If the writer uses an envelope on which the return address is printed, the sender's name should be typed above the return address. If the writer uses a plain envelope, the sender's name and return address should be typed at the top left corner of the envelope. Type special mailing notations two or three lines below the postage on the upper right portion of the envelope. The receiver's complete address should correspond with the inside address of the letter and should be typed slightly left of the horizontal center of the envelope. Figure 13–2 shows two properly addressed envelopes.

Letter Styles

Departmental or company practices usually determine the style used in today's business letters. Differences in culture and custom also affect international business communication practices.[1] Business letters may be arranged in the block style, modified block style, or AMS Simplified style.[2]

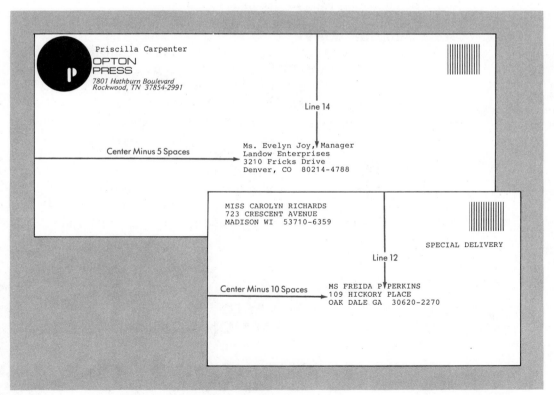

FIGURE 13–2   Properly Addressed Envelopes

Block Style

The block style letter is easy to type and cost effective.

All lines of the *block style letter* begin at the left margin. The block style, illustrated in Figure 13–3, is popular among managers and secretaries because it is easy to keyboard. In view of the high cost of letter production, time saved in keyboarding may become a significant factor when the year's output of letters is considered.[3] Other managers, however, contend that the block style lacks a balanced visual appearance.

Modified Block Style

The modified block letter is a popular style.

The *modified block style letter,* illustrated in Figure 13–4, is a traditional letter style that is widely used in today's correspondence. The date and closing lines usually begin at the horizontal center of the paper. Depending on the design of the letterhead or writer preference, the date line may be centered; or it may end at the right margin. The first line of each paragraph in the body of the letter may begin at the left margin, or it may be indented. The modified block style has maintained its popularity in the business world for many years because it has a balanced, well-shaped appearance that can be arranged in a variety of acceptable forms. However, this style takes longer to produce than the others.

AMS Simplified Style

The AMS Simplified letter is a block style letter without the customary salutation and complimentary close.

The Administrative Management Society (AMS) popularized the Simplified letter style in the 1940s. The *AMS Simplified letter style,* illustrated in Figure 13–5, was designed to improve keyboarding efficiency and to streamline the customary business letter format. As in the block style, all lines of the Simplified style begin at the left margin. The major change is substituting a subject line for the salutation and eliminating the complimentary close. The subject line and the writer's name and title are typed in all capital letters. Notice that the spacing around the subject line is designed to draw the reader's attention immediately to the subject of the letter. The AMS Simplified style, however, may be too innovative and too different for business letter writers and readers who prefer a more conventional form.

▲ ORGANIZATION BASED UPON READER REACTION

The criteria for organizing letters are essentially the same as the criteria for organizing memos in Chapter 12. Managers should use a direct approach if a positive or pleased reader reaction is expected, an indirect

Del Mar
Corporation
100 Marine Drive
Los Angeles, CA 90099-8088
(213)555-6400

October 8, 19--

Mr. Michael E. Campbell
3737 Rogers Road
Birmingham, AL   35202-2501

Dear Mr. Campbell:

Mrs. Cheryl H. Bowman has been appointed sales manager
for the Southern Division. Her office is located in our
Atlanta headquarters.

Mrs. Bowman will supervise the sales of integrated information systems, including microcomputers, printers, and a
wide range of computer supplies and accessories.

Mrs. Bowman will give prompt and efficient attention to
all your computer requirements. She comes to this position with a rich background of sales experience and
accomplishments. She joined our organization five years
ago and has served as the assistant sales manager for
the Eastern Division for the past two years.

Mrs. Bowman and her staff look forward to serving you.

Sincerely,

Carla E. Fuller

Ms. Carla E. Fuller
Vice-President, Sales

ms

FIGURE 13–3   Block Style Letter with Mixed Punctuation (Direct Approach)

SYLVESTER
Office Supplies

690 Sherman Avenue
Denver, CO 80203-7340
(303)555-0106

December 15, 19--

Mr. Thompson Bradford
Universal Sales
123 Gloster Road
Athens, GA   30602-2962

Dear Mr. Bradford

Thank you for buying your dictation equipment from
Sylvester Office Supplies. You are a welcomed addition
to Sylvester's clientele in Clarke County.

Since you made your purchase, I have had an opportunity
to talk with the credit manager concerning your request
for a service contract discount. Sylvester extends service contract discounts to clients who own at least three
dictation systems, eight calculators, or a combination of
one dictation system and five calculators. As soon as
your company owns enough of our equipment, we will be
happy to offer you a service contract.

Your dictation system has a six-month warranty which en-
titles you to free service for defective parts or work-
manship. Sylvester will service your dictation system at
no cost during the six-month warranty period.

Sincerely

Dwight J. Aven
Dwight J. Aven
Marketing Representative

sa

FIGURE 13—4   Modified Block Style Letter with Open Punctuation (Indirect Approach)

SOUTHERN COMMUNICATIONS, INC.

333 Chapman Boulevard
Knoxville, TN 37921-2337
(615) 555-5015

August 8, 19--

Ms. Annabelle Humphrey
Susan's Catering Service
Oak Ridge, TN 37830-2435

SAVING MONEY BY USING ELECTRONIC MAIL

Does your catering service spend excessive time confirming catering arrangements or handling billing?

If your answer is yes, Southern Communications, Inc., can
help you streamline the way your company communicates.
Southern Communications has recently added an electronic
mail service to the list of its many communication services. Our computers can communicate with computers
owned by all the major businesses in metropolitan
Knoxville. In just seconds, Southern Communications can
send an electronic letter confirming catering arrangements with your clients. For less than 10 cents per
contact, Southern Communications can efficiently bill
your clients for you.

A copy of our electronic mail service brochure and an
addressed, stamped postal card are enclosed. Please mail
the postal card to me if you are interested in learning
more about our electronic mail service.

Discover how Southern Communications, Inc., can help you
and your company communicate more efficiently than ever
before.

Paul Junior

PAUL JUNIOR, VICE-PRESIDENT, SALES

bk

Enclosures

FIGURE 13–5   AMS Simplified Style Letter (Persuasive Letter)

approach if a negative reader reaction is expected. As described in Chapter 5, the direct and indirect approaches may also be used to structure oral messages.

Proper organization influences how a message is received. People who receive internal written communications, such as memos, share common organizational goals with the writer. When writing a letter, the writer should use a style that enables the reader to follow the logical flow of the message and to respond properly after reading the letter once. A poorly structured message forces the reader to reread the letter looking for relevant material. Writers should not waste the reader's time with extraneous details or material that is unrelated to the purpose of the letter.

The key purpose in any communication should be the clear exchange of ideas. Writers do not know for sure how a reader will react to a letter, so the letter's organization should be based on anticipated reader response.

Direct Approach

The direct approach is used when sharing pleasant messages.

The direct approach may be used when persuasion is not needed, when a positive response or reaction is expected from the reader, or when presenting technical information. Examples of messages for which the direct approach is appropriate include direct requests or orders, requests for routine action, announcements, good news messages, greetings, inquiries, and letters of congratulation, praise, and thanks. The direct approach is appropriate for initiating and maintaining goodwill and for sharing any pleasant news.

When writing a letter using the direct approach, the main idea is placed in the opening, preferably in the first sentence. Supporting details follow the main idea in the middle section of the letter, either in paragraph or enumerated form. The writer should not waste the reader's time with nonessential details.

A restatement of the main idea in the closing of the body adds emphasis to the letter's theme. A positive reference can also be added to support the main idea or the requested action, but a writer should not use extra emphasis or support that is not necessary to achieve the desired results. Figure 13–3 depicts a letter written in the direct approach.

Indirect Approach

The indirect approach is used to share bad news and persuasive messages.

As with memos, the indirect approach is used to transmit unpleasant messages such as sharing bad news or saying no to requests, favors, or adjustments. A modified indirect approach is used for persuasive letters. Such messages require careful planning, particularly because they are directed to people outside the manager's organization.

Sharing Bad News or Saying No

Most readers can sense when bad news is coming. Placing an unpleasant idea in the opening of a letter creates a barrier to effective reading. This negative mind-set may prompt the reader to stop reading, or just skim the letter, before understanding the reasons or explanations for the bad news or the negative response to a request. With the indirect approach, a neutral buffer statement should appear in the opening. The bad news or negative response should appear in the middle of the body, preceded by an explanation for the undesirable response. Whenever possible, writers should avoid using negative language in stating the unpleasant main idea. Positive or neutral statements should appear in the closing. Figure 13–4 illustrates a letter using the indirect approach.

Persuading the Reader

The indirect approach may also be used in writing persuasive messages. Managers often write persuasive external messages to sell ideas, plans, services, or products. Most readers have a natural aversion to manipulative persuasion. The indirect approach is modified slightly to make persuasion desirable and acceptable. An attention-getting positive or neutral opening is used in a persuasive letter. Attention-getting devices include asking a question, using a quote, providing a statistic, and so forth. The ideas, plans, services, or products "for sale" are introduced in the middle section, along with favorable features of the proposal. In the closing, the writer makes desired action easy for the reader.

The sequencing of information should follow a logical pattern. A listener is forced to wait on the speaker for the main idea; but a reader may scan the letter to find the main idea quickly, skipping over any explanatory material that is not related to the reader's interests. Readers have their own interests and priorities. They may choose not to deal with an organization or individuals who try to manipulate them. Remember that ". . . intelligent use of indirect structure is not as much a matter of psychology as it is a matter of good manners and common sense."[4] Figure 13–5 is an example of a persuasive letter.

▲ ELECTRONIC LETTERS

From the user's standpoint, electronic memos and letters are indistinguishable. Both forms of business communication are based on the concept of the store-and-forward messages described in Chapter 12 and illustrated in Figure 12–9 (page 215). The basic difference between electronic memos and electronic letters is the transmission destination. Electronic memos are transmitted through computer networks between or among employees within an organization; ***electronic letters*** are computer-generated messages that are usually transmitted electronically to one or more individuals outside the organization—messages that would otherwise be sent in conventional letter style through the United States Postal Service.

Electronic letters are usually sent to people outside the company.

Some of the advantages of using electronic letters are

An electronic letter system permits fast, accurate, and convenient communication among users at moderate costs.

▲ *Speed.* Messages are transmitted at high speeds over telephone lines, thereby eliminating postal service delays.
▲ *Access.* People using the system do not have to be on the telephone line at the same time in order to send and receive messages, thereby eliminating telephone tag.
▲ *Convenience.* Video display terminals can either be placed on the desks of managers and secretaries or located in a centralized communication center staffed by trained operators.
▲ *Cost.* The costs are moderate and have been steadily decreasing.

Managers must also understand the potential problems associated with electronic letters in order to use this technology effectively.

Appearance

The appearance of an electronic letter is determined by the type of electronic mail system used.

Whereas an attractive layout is important for conventional letters, the writer loses control over the appearance of electronic letters. Most electronic mail systems use a heading form which dictates the letter style. Writers of electronic letters must emphasize tone, organization, clarity, and grammar in order to create a favorable reader impression of the messages.

Formality

Electronic letters tend to be less formal than conventional letters.

Preliminary research suggests that electronic letters are less formal and less inhibited in tone than conventional letters. Name-calling, swearing, and other forms of slang are often included in the message of an electronic letter. Some writers even attempt to incorporate nonverbal cues into their messages by writing such words as "sigh" (to indicate desperation) or "argh" (to indicate disgust). Also, a sender might write, "I understand you and your friends helped close the nightclubs on Bourbon Street last Saturday. :-)" The symbol :-), representing a smiling face on its side (a colon followed by a hyphen followed by a right parenthesis), is used to indicate a joke.[5] As in traditional forms of letter writing, the level of formality used in writing an electronic letter depends on the writer's purpose and relationship with the reader.

Structure

A one-page letter may consist of up to 54 lines of text (including the letterhead) with one-inch top, side, and bottom margins. By comparison, most video display screens hold only 24 lines of text. If a typical one-page letter was sent by electronic mail, the reader would most likely have to scroll through two or three screens of text to read the entire message. To complicate the issue of screen size, readers who decide to *scan* a traditionally structured message on their video display screens rather than *read* the entire message will probably view only the subject line and one to five lines of text.[6] To increase the probability that an electronic letter will be read, managers must shorten the length of their messages by omitting letter parts such as the letterhead, inside address, and salutation. The return address is replaced by a sender's identification code. Using informative subject lines can shorten reading time. The subject line is a *standard* part of an electronic letter rather than an optional part. Although placing the most important points and ideas at the beginning of the body of an electronic letter may facilitate reading, it can undermine the reader's acceptance of unpleasant or persuasive messages. Whenever possible, writers should use neutral subject lines to introduce unpleasant or persuasive electronic letters. An example of a neutral subject line is shown in Figure 13–5 on page 231.

Electronic letters should be concise.

Editing

Writers of electronic letters usually compose their messages directly at computer terminals. Since many writers lack composition and keyboarding skills and since the editing capabilities of most electronic mail systems are limited, transmitted messages frequently contain grammar, tone, and keyboarding errors. Sloppy, carelessly composed and keyboarded electronic letters may lead to serious misunderstandings and loss of business. Managers must give the same careful consideration to editing electronic letters as they give to conventional letters. Writers with poor keyboarding skills may want to prepare a handwritten first draft of the letter, edit the draft, and then carefully keyboard the message from the edited handwritten copy.

Managers must give special attention to editing electronic letters.

Software and Hardware Compatibility

Hardware used in an electronic mail system must be compatible.

Companies with multiple types of computers and terminals may have problems installing an electronic mail system because of the incompatibility of the software or hardware. It may be advantageous for such companies to use an electronic mail service. It is predicted that electronic mail services will be a multibillion-dollar industry by the end of the 1990s.[7]

Message Transmission Speed

One of the advantages of sending an electronic letter is that the message is transmitted rapidly from writer to reader without being handled by employees and postal workers. The speed of electronic transmission can also be a potential problem, particularly when responding immediately to a controversial message. Human tendency is to react with anger to a negative message. Managers must resist the temptation to send an electronic letter as soon as it is written. As one writer stated, "You cannot put your hand into the mailbox to retrieve a note sent off in the heat of anger or without adequate forethought."[8]

Managers must avoid sending electronic letters written in the heat of anger.

Message Protection

The widespread use of electronic mail has created a major concern about unauthorized computer entry and the invasion of individual privacy. The National Research Council of the National Academy of Sciences states:

> Electronic mail presents potentially serious problems of security and privacy protection. The processing, storage, and transmission of large amounts of data . . . central to electronic mail offer an attractive target for anyone seeking access to individual and corporate information.[9]

The security of most electronic mail systems is inadequate.

Electronic mail systems in current use generally lack adequate security safeguards. Managers must be aware that clever people have had little or no difficulty penetrating the security provisions of computer systems. Because of this, message content must be analyzed carefully. It may be preferable to send highly confidential messages through the postal service.

The technology of electronic letters will permit managers to communicate with more people than ever before. The technology will allow managers access to more information than they may know how to use. Since electronic mail also overcomes some of the limitations found in the delivery systems provided by the postal service and telephone companies, the technology holds the promise of increased productivity. Yet, managers must understand the many potential problems and misuses of electronic mail technology before they can take full advantage of this new form of communication.

SUMMARY

Letters are an important form of business writing because they reach people outside an organization. Letters reflect the commitment, experience, and quality of an organization's management; and good letter writing is a priceless skill for every manager.

The primary purpose of a letter should be the clear, concise exchange of messages. Letters should be limited to one page in length if possible. The physical appearance of a letter is important. The layout, spacing, and type quality influence how the reader receives the message. Poor appearance distracts the reader; attractive appearance catches the reader's attention, emphasizes the message, and helps establish a positive attitude regarding the message.

Standard parts of a business letter are the heading, date, inside address, salutation, body, complimentary close, originator's identification, and reference initials of the person who keyboarded the document. Optional parts of a letter include a mailing notation, attention line, subject line, typed company name, originator's title, enclosure notation, copy notation, and postscript. Address envelopes to include the writer's return address, any special mailing notation, and the receiver's complete address.

Three common letter styles are the block, modified block, and AMS Simplified styles. In the block style, all lines begin at the left margin. The block style is popular because of ease and efficiency of setup. In the modified block style, the closing lines begin at the horizontal center of the page. The date line may start at the horizontal center or may end at the right margin. The first line of each paragraph may be blocked or indented. The modified block style is popular because of its well-balanced appearance. The AMS Simplified style was designed to improve keyboarding efficiency. All lines begin at the left margin, and the salutation and complimentary close are eliminated. A subject line is substituted for the salutation. This style is not as widely used as the block or modified block styles.

Proper organization of a message is critical in letter writing. Readers outside the writer's organization have their own priorities and do not necessarily share common goals with the writer. Letter writers should not waste the reader's time with extraneous information or an illogical order that masks the meaning of the message.

The direct approach is used to convey positive news or routine messages in letters. The indirect approach is used to convey negative news or persuasive messages. Care must be used in the indirect approach to avoid wasting the reader's time.

The electronic transmission of letters has caused some changes in letter preparation. Message construction tends to be less formal, and electronic letters tend to be shorter than traditional letters. The format and style of a message are strongly influenced by the computer software and hardware that are used. Electronic mail systems in current use generally lack adequate security safeguards. Managers must understand the benefits and the potential problems of electronic mail technology before they can maximize the use of this form of communication.

QUESTIONS

1. Identify the standard parts of a letter.
2. What is meant by *originator's identification?*
3. Describe the optional parts of a letter.
4. Describe the similarities of and the differences between the block style letter and the AMS Simplified style letter.
5. Why is the modified block style widely used in today's business correspondence?
6. Why should a writer strive to produce an attractive business letter?
7. How are the criteria for organizing a letter similar to criteria for organizing a memo?
8. Explain the sequencing of information in the body of a letter written in the indirect approach.
9. How can a writer of an electronic letter compensate for the loss of control over the appearance of the letter?
10. What is meant by this statement: "It is best to use electronic letters for simple, short communications"?

PROBLEM-SOLVING EXPERIENCES

1. Assume you are a state government purchasing official. Write a letter to Ronald Garrison, plant manager of Washington Carpet Mill, 2500 Main Street, Lexington, KY 40502–3987. Inform him that his company has been awarded an $89,000 contract for recarpeting the State Capitol. Larry Askew will serve as contract director for the project.

2. Write a letter to Valerie Jacobs, plant manager of Dawson Carpets, 9800 Jefferson Parkway, Louisville, KY 40218–3500. Inform her that although her company submitted a competitive bid for the recarpeting project, the contract will not be awarded because her company lacks experience in handling such projects.

3. Write a persuasive letter to Tina Gay, who owns a small business, promoting the purchase of an electronic mail system designed for her particular hardware. Tina owns Country Charm Antiques in Ridgeville, NC 27603–2666.

CASE 13–1

Jim Brice is the customer support manager for GrassRoots Software. GrassRoots has sold about 100,000 copies of GrowMaster software, a crop-management program. Unfortunately the first version of the program contains a hidden problem that performs incorrect calculations. The error is not immediately obvious to the user. A corrected version of the program is available, and owners of the first version of the program can get a copy for a small upgrade charge; several new features are also included in the corrected version.

Sally Stevenson is the sales manager for GrassRoots. She sent a letter to all registered GrowMaster owners informing them of the need to purchase the upgraded package. Sally's letter was a lot like a sales letter; she described all the new features of the new version. She mentioned that there were some errors in the earlier version that had now been corrected. She also explained in the end of her letter why there was a charge for the new version.

Sales of the upgraded version have been disappointing. Jim is particularly concerned because the rate of service calls is increasing. He is finding that a lot of users do not understand that the new version contains essential corrections. Some people purchased the new version but did not install it.

They were waiting for a convenient installation time, and the old version seemed to work just fine.

Jim and Sally agree that Sally's letter contained all the correct information. Jim believes that most of the GrowMaster users only casually read the letter; he theorizes that they must have thought it was "just another ad."

1. Write a letter for Jim to send to GrowMaster users. Stress the importance of promptly purchasing and installing the new version. Mention the new features. Include essential ordering information.

ENDNOTES

[1]Retha H. Kilpatrick, "International Business Communication Practices," *The Journal of Business Communication*, Vol. 21, No. 4 (Fall, 1984), pp. 33–44.

[2]For a detailed examination of business letter styles, letter parts, and special features, see Clifford R. House and Kathie Sigler, *Reference Manual for Office Personnel* (6h ed.; Cincinnati: South-Western Publishing Co., 1981), pp. 145–179.

[3]The costs of the average business letter have increased from 30 cents in 1930 to $8.52 in 1985. See The Dartnell Institute of Business Research, *Dartnell Target Survey* (Chicago: Dartnell Corporation, Spring, 1985).

[4]Douglas Brent, "Indirect Structure and Reader Response," *The Journal of Business Communication*, Vol. 22, No. 2 (Spring, 1985), pp. 5–8.

[5]Alex Czajkowski and Sara Kiesler, "Computer-Mediated Communication," *National Forum*, Vol. 64, No. 3 (Summer, 1984), pp. 32–33.

[6]Judith Stein and JoAnne Yates, "Electronic Mail: How Will It Change Office Communication? How Can Managers Use It Effectively?" Raymond W. Beswick and Alfred B. Williams (eds.), *Information Systems and Business Communication* (Urbana, IL: American Business Communication Association, 1983), p. 100.

[7]Peggy Straube and Mary Lind, "Electronic Mail: Ready or Not, It's Here to Stay," *PC Week*, Vol. 2, No. 18 (May 7, 1985), p. 53.

[8]Stein and Yates, op. cit., p. 102.

[9]Straube and Lind, op. cit., p. 55.

C H A P T E R

14

EMPLOYMENT
WRITING

When you complete this chapter, you should be able to:

▲ Assess your personal and professional qualifications for employment.

▲ Identify the key documents required for successful employment application.

▲ Draft a résumé and develop an application letter.

▲ Describe the process for evaluating employment documents.

▲ Identify the employment-related documents that managers prepare.

Managers participate in
written employment
communication in three
distinct ways.

Managers assume three distinct roles in written employment communication. First, managers are applicants; they may seek employment or change jobs several times during their careers. Second, managers are reviewers; they may screen employment documents prepared by applicants seeking employment. Third, managers are monitors; they may prepare documents that pertain to the performance, progress, or dismissal of their employees.

▲ APPLYING FOR EMPLOYMENT

Successful employment application requires effective written communication skills. Often a manager's initial contact with a prospective employer is through written communications such as a résumé, application letter, and application form. If an applicant wants to interview for a job, he or she must first look good on paper.

Applicants should conduct a self-assessment prior to starting the employment process. They should develop a sense of direction for their professional and personal lives. Applicants need to know where they are in their professional development, where they would like to be, and what experiences and qualities they need to get there. Adequate planning is essential if applicants are to develop a road map for their individual professional development. Several critical questions need to be answered.

1. Why did I choose my particular occupational field?
2. What kind of employment do I want?
3. What kind of employment do I want five and ten years from now?
4. If I don't get the job I want, what are my second and third choices?
5. What specific skills do I need to obtain the employment I want?
6. How do I acquire these skills?
7. What educational experiences will enable me to obtain the employment I want?
8. What kinds of work experience will enable me to obtain the employment I want?
9. Do my personality traits facilitate my getting the job I want?
10. What personality traits do I need to groom and/or acquire?

Applicants should assess their professional and personal strengths and weaknesses prior to preparing employment application documents. Self-assessment helps applicants clarify information that should be communicated in employment writing and helps them prepare for interview questions.

Specific information about available positions, position requirements, and where to apply can be obtained from several sources. Classified ads in newspapers and trade journals, state employment office listings, and job placement agencies are common sources. Another valuable source is a person who is currently working in the applicant's chosen field; a practitioner may provide insights for job requirements and available positions. Executive search agencies, or headhunters, are another source. Often executive search agencies find applicants through referrals from classified ads in newspapers or trade journals.

Key employment documents which applicants should prepare include a résumé and application letter. Prospective employers may also provide company application forms for applicants to complete. In addition, applicants should prepare thank-you, acceptance, and/or refusal letters as follow-up documents to interviews.

> The résumé and application letter are key employment documents.

Résumé

Detailed information about an applicant's qualifications should be summarized in a *résumé.* The purpose of a résumé is to get an interview. A résumé provides detailed information such as the applicant's career objective, education, work experience, memberships, honors and/or awards, avocational interests, the applicant's address and telephone number, and references.

> The purpose for preparing a résumé is to get an interview.

A precisely stated professional objective or a statement of career interest is important. Candidates often make the mistake of omitting an objective in their résumés. Managers look for objectives that clearly reflect the candidate's immediate- and long-range occupational goals.[1] Many applicants also make the mistake of writing objectives broad enough to encompass all kinds of jobs in all kinds of organizations. It is better to have several versions of a résumé rather than one résumé encompassing all career interests.

Education information shows that the applicant has obtained appropriate training for the desired employment. Work experience shows that current and previously fulfilled job responsibilities qualify the applicant for a particular job.

Memberships and leadership positions held in professional organizations indicate interest in personal development within a career. The inclusion of honors and awards shows special recognition received for exceptional achievement or involvement.

Listing avocational interests indicates that the applicant has interests in addition to work. How applicants spend their leisure time provides some insight about an individual's priorities and values.

Listing a current address and telephone number at which the applicant may be reached makes it easy for the employer to contact prospective interviewees. References indicate who employers may contact to verify or clarify applicant information.

A well-prepared résumé portrays the applicant as a desirable prospective employee, whereas a poorly constructed résumé can seriously impair an applicant's employment opportunities. The résumé should be concise and accurate. If possible, the résumé should be limited to one page. Figure 14–1 shows one résumé designed to attract an employer's attention. Since an applicant must make a good first impression to stand out in a crowd of applicants, the résumé should be structured so that it is easily distinguished from the résumés of other applicants. Applicants should use creativity and innovativeness in designing formats that best present their qualifications; they should not merely copy another's résumé in terms of content, format, or headings. Innovative formatting, contrasting type styles, unique paper selection, use of active voice, and professional packaging can be used to make a positive first impression.[2]

Innovative Formatting

When considering résumé format, applicants should remember that numerous applicants will probably seek the same position within a company. Employers may not have a lot of time to search for or review pertinent applicant information. Résumés should be formatted so that the most important qualifications appear near the beginning of the résumé. Information should be sequenced in logical order based on the applicant's strengths for the job. The applicant's name and career objective should be followed by either work experience or education. Reverse chronological order should be used for listing items in each category so that current information is emphasized. The applicant's address, telephone number, and references should appear near the end of the résumé. In the references category, applicants may wish to list several references and their respective addresses and telephone numbers or mention that references are available through a placement office or upon request.

Whenever possible, information should be in blocked style to facilitate easy reading. Legally, employers are unable to discriminate on the basis of personal information. Consequently, applicants are not obligated to provide information such as sex, marital status, health, age, height, and weight.

Here are ways to make a résumé look distinctive.

Applicants should place their most important qualifications at the beginning of the résumé.

ANDREW JAMES MORGAN

CAREER OBJECTIVE

To assume responsibilities as a branch manager with a progressive bank and to acquire experience that will lead to an upper-level management position.

WORK EXPERIENCE

Position	*Where*	*When*	*Responsibilities*
Assistant Loan Manager	Bank of Oak View 1500 Main Street Nashville, TN 39740-2677	1986-Present	Supervise 11 employees, serve as a loan officer, and provide in-house training programs for all bank personnel.
Collections Manager	Bank of Oak View 1500 Main Street Nashville, TN 39740-2677	1984-86	Handled collection of delinquent loans.

EDUCATION

Degree	*Institution*	*Completion Date*
B.S.	University of Tennessee Knoxville, TN Major: Banking and Finance	June 1984

MEMBERSHIPS

Administrative Management Society, Secretary of Nashville Chapter, 1985-86
American Banking Association

HONORS

Listed in *The Outstanding Young Men of America*, 1984-85
Senator of Student Government Association, University of Tennessee, 1983-84

AVOCATIONAL INTERESTS

Reading, playing golf, gardening

ADDRESS AND TELEPHONE NUMBER

105 Culver Road
Nashville, TN 39740-2675
Telephone: (615) 555-7928

References available upon request

FIGURE 14–1   Résumé

Contrasting Type Styles

Contrasting type styles help highlight the key points and organization of a résumé. The applicant's name should be in the most dominant type style. Headings and subheadings should be used to identify and organize the various parts of a résumé.

Paper Selection

An applicant should use good quality bond paper for each résumé. To make the résumé stand out in a stack of résumés on an employer's desk, the applicant may wish to use pastel-colored paper such as buff or grey. An applicant should avoid bright colors such as pink or orange; pink evokes a feminine connotation, and orange can appear harsh.

Active Voice

Use active voice to describe work experience.

Applicants should use active voice to describe their work experience and activities in a résumé. Active voice helps portray the applicant as a *doer*. Use present tense to express current work responsibilities and past tense to describe former responsibilities.

Packaging

Packaging is another important part of résumé preparation. A well-planned and neatly prepared résumé loses some of its personality when it is folded for mailing. Applicants should use large envelopes—about 9 1/2" × 12"—for mailing résumés to employers. Several copies of the résumé should be sent to an employer in case more than one person participates in the employment selection process. If applicants leave the responsibility of résumé duplication to the employer, the additional copies may look inferior to the original. Also, pastel-colored résumés yield shaded copies on some photocopying equipment.

Application Letter

An *application letter* usually accompanies copies of a résumé sent to a prospective employer. The major purposes of the application letter are to introduce the applicant to the employer, to highlight the applicant's qualifications so the employer will read the detailed information in the résumé, and to make interview arrangements easy. Application letters may be solicited or unsolicited. *Solicited application letters* are written in response to advertisements or requests for applicants. *Unsolicited application letters* are sent to companies in which there are no known job vacancies.

Application letters may be solicited or unsolicited.

Like the résumé, the application letter should offer a neat, high-quality appearance and format. An application letter is in fact a persuasive letter.

As discussed earlier, most persuasive writing follows the indirect approach, in which anticipated reader reaction is not interested. However, applicants should use the direct approach in writing an application letter; the goal of the letter is to "sell" the applicant's skills and qualifications. Anticipated reader reaction is positive because employers are interested in finding qualified individuals.

Use the direct approach to write an application letter.

An attractive, concise application letter invites the employer to learn more about the applicant. An applicant should incorporate the elements of effective writing—thought, appropriateness, correctness, and readability—into an application letter. (These are discussed in Chapter 11.) In most cases, the application letter should be limited to one page; the application letter should not repeat the contents of the résumé. Following the direct approach, the opening of the letter should include a brief description of the position for which one wishes to apply. The middle section should highlight qualifications which make the applicant an excellent candidate for the position. Applicants should highlight previous employment, educational background, interpersonal skills, ability to cope with change, and other positive personal qualities. The closing should offer to provide more detailed information, refer to the enclosed résumé, and indicate the applicant's willingness to discuss employment in an interview. Figure 14–2 illustrates an application letter.

Application Form

Many employers require applicants to complete employment application forms; these forms provide employers with necessary profile information in a standard format. They also serve as tools in assessing an applicant's ability to follow instructions.

Unless other instructions are given, applicants should keyboard or print their responses on the application form. A response should be given for each question or part. *Not applicable,* NA, or a *dash* (—) may be used as a response to questions or parts that are not pertinent to the applicant's individual background. Special attention should be given to the completion of parts which require more than fill-in-the-blank responses. Many employers use indirect or open-ended questions to gain insight into an applicant's writing skills and creativity. Figure 14–3 illustrates a completed employment application form.

Applicants should respond to all parts of an application form.

Many managers are now alert to a rising problem called **_résumé inflation,_** where candidates exaggerate or misrepresent their job qualifications.[3] In view of this problem, managers may focus on the data in the comprehensive employment history sections on application forms.

105 Culver Road
Nashville, TN 39740-2675
May 12, 19--

Mr. Fred Richards
President
Third National Bank
55665 Robinway Boulevard
Nashville, TN 39720-2680

Dear Mr. Richards

Does your bank need a branch manager with diverse banking
experience?

In addition to having coordinated loan transactions totaling
over 34 million dollars, I have supervised loan department
personnel, trained entry-level employees, and coordinated
delinquent loan collections. I am well acquainted with the
various responsibilities assumed by bank personnel, possess
effective communication skills, and am self-motivated.

Work experience and educational details are listed on the
enclosed resume. Additional profile information will be
provided upon request. Please call me at (615) 555-7928 to
arrange an interview.

Sincerely

Andrew James Morgan

Andrew James Morgan

Enclosure

FIGURE 14—2 Application Letter

APPLICATION FOR EMPLOYMENT

3rd National Bank

PLEASE PRINT WITH BLACK INK OR USE TYPEWRITER

AN EQUAL OPPORTUNITY EMPLOYER

NAME (LAST, FIRST, MIDDLE INITIAL)	SOCIAL SECURITY NUMBER	CURRENT DATE
Morgan, Andrew J.	409-94-4733	May 20, 19--

ADDRESS (NUMBER, STREET, CITY, STATE, ZIP CODE)	HOME PHONE NO.
105 Culver Road, Nashville, TN 39740-2675	(615) 555-7928

REACH PHONE NO.	U.S. CITIZEN?	DATE YOU CAN START
(615) 555-7928	X YES NO	August 1, 19--

ARE YOU EMPLOYED NOW?	IF SO, MAY WE INQUIRE OF YOUR PRESENT EMPLOYER?
Yes	Yes

TYPE OF WORK DESIRED	REFERRED BY	SALARY DESIRED
Bank Manager	NA	Negotiable

IF RELATED TO ANYONE IN OUR EMPLOY, STATE NAME AND POSITION   NA

DO YOU HAVE ANY PHYSICAL CONDITION THAT MAY PREVENT YOU FROM PERFORMING CERTAIN KINDS OF WORK?   YES   NO X   IF YES, EXPLAIN

HAVE YOU EVER BEEN CONVICTED OF A FELONY?   YES   NO X   IF YES, EXPLAIN

EDUCATIONAL INSTITUTION	LOCATION (CITY, STATE)	DATES ATTENDED FROM MO. YR.	DATES ATTENDED TO MO. YR.	DIPLOMA, DEGREE, OR CREDITS EARNED	CLASS STANDING (CHK QUARTER) 1	2	3	4	MAJOR SUBJECTS STUDIED
COLLEGE University of Tennessee	Knoxville, TN	09 80	06 84	B.S.					Banking, Finance, Accounting
HIGH SCHOOL Farragut High School	Farragut, TN	08 76	06 80	Diploma					
GRADE SCHOOL Farragut Elementary	Farragut, TN	08 68	06 76						
OTHER									

(E D U C A T I O N)

LIST BELOW THE POSITIONS THAT YOU HAVE HELD (LAST POSITION FIRST)

1. NAME AND ADDRESS OF FIRM
Bank of Oak View
1500 Main Street
Nashville, TN   39740-2677

NAME OF SUPERVISOR
Mr. Boyd Baker

DESCRIBE POSITION RESPONSIBILITIES
Assistant Loan Manager: Supervise 11 employees, serve as a loan officer, and provide in-house training for all bank personnel.

EMPLOYED (MO--YR)
FROM: January 1986   TO: Present

REASON FOR LEAVING
Seek higher position with another institution.

2. NAME AND ADDRESS OF FIRM
Bank of Oak View
1500 Main Street
Nashville, TN   39740-2677

NAME OF SUPERVISOR
Ms. Diane Carpenter

DESCRIBE POSITION RESPONSIBILITIES
Collections Manager: Handled collection of delinquent loans.

EMPLOYED (MO--YR)
FROM: August 1984   TO: January 1986

REASON FOR LEAVING
Promoted within the same bank.

I UNDERSTAND THAT I SHALL NOT BECOME AN EMPLOYEE UNTIL I HAVE SIGNED AN EMPLOYMENT AGREEMENT WITH THE FINAL APPROVAL OF THE EMPLOYER AND THAT SUCH EMPLOYMENT WILL BE SUBJECT TO VERIFICATION OF PREVIOUS EMPLOYMENT, DATA PROVIDED IN THIS APPLICATION, ANY RELATED DOCUMENTS, OR RESUME. I KNOW THAT A REPORT MAY BE MADE THAT WILL INCLUDE INFORMATION CONCERNING ANY

FACTOR THE EMPLOYER MIGHT FIND RELEVANT TO THE POSITION FOR WHICH I AM APPLYING, AND THAT I CAN MAKE A WRITTEN REQUEST FOR ADDITIONAL INFORMATION AS TO THE NATURE AND SCOPE OF THE REPORT IF ONE IS MADE.

Andrew James Morgan

SIGNATURE OF APPLICANT

FIGURE 14–3   Employment Application Form

Follow-Up Letters _____

Successful employment writing results in the applicant getting an interview. During the interview, the applicant should demonstrate effective oral and nonverbal communication skills. Chapters 3 and 4 on listening and Chapters 5 and 6 on speaking provide insights into how these skills can be refined.

A follow-up letter is written after the applicant interviews or receives a job offer.

Generally applicants write one or more follow-up letters before completing the job application process. ***Follow-up letters*** are sent to thank an employer for an interview opportunity, to accept an employment offer, or to refuse an employment offer.

Thank-You Letter

Conscientious applicants capitalize on the thank-you letter as another opportunity to project interest and professionalism. An applicant should send the thank-you letter within several days after the interview. A well-written thank-you letter can be the something extra that makes a difference in employee selection, particularly when employers are unable to identify the best candidate during the interview process. Thank-you letters should be short, individualized expressions of appreciation, which follow the direct approach.

Always use the correct name and title of the interviewer, and include job-related information in the thank-you letter. The thank-you letter should reinforce the application letter, résumé, and interview. Figure 14–4 is an example of a thank-you letter.

Acceptance Letter

An acceptance letter is written when the applicant wants to accept an employment offer. The direct approach should be used to accept the offer and to document the applicant's acceptance of specific employment terms. Salary, employment date, and any other significant terms should be included. Figure 14–5 illustrates how employment terms should be incorporated in an acceptance letter.

Refusal Letter

A refusal letter is written when the applicant chooses to decline an employment offer. An indirect approach is used when constructing a refusal letter because anticipated reader reaction is negative. The applicant should explain significant details which influenced the decision to say no. A refusal letter should be positive and should project the applicant's interest in maintaining goodwill with the employer. Figure 14–6 shows a refusal letter.

105 Culver Road
Nashville, TN 39740-2675
June 3, 19--

Mr. Fred Richards
President
Third National Bank
55665 Robinway Boulevard
Nashville, TN 39720-2680

Dear Mr. Richards

Thank you for talking with me about the branch manager
position with Third National Bank.

I enjoyed my visit with you; Third National's operations
are impressive. I particularly enjoyed your showing me
how your 24-hour teller program works.

My combined work experience and education are a good match
for the requirements of branch manager. The prospect of
working for Third National Bank excites me.

Sincerely

Andrew James Morgan

Andrew James Morgan

FIGURE 14—4   Thank-You Letter

105 Culver Road
Nashville, TN 39740-2675
July 2, 19--

Mr. Fred Richards
President
Third National Bank
55665 Robinway Boulevard
Nashville, TN 39720-2680

Dear Mr. Richards

Yes, I accept your offer for employment as branch manager
of Third National Bank in Nashville, Tennessee.

Your salary offer of $26,500 a year is satisfactory. I
am agreeable to a six-month probationary period after
which time I will be eligible for a salary increase. I
will report to work August 1.

Thank you for selecting me as the branch manager for
Third National's Nashville bank. I look forward to
joining your team.

Sincerely

Andrew James Morgan

Andrew James Morgan

FIGURE 14–5   Acceptance Letter

105 Culver Road
Nashville, TN 39740-2675
July 2, 19--

Mr. Fred Richards
President
Third National Bank
55665 Robinway Boulevard
Nashville, TN 39720-2680

Dear Mr. Richards

Thank you for offering me the job of branch manager for
Third National Bank in Nashville, Tennessee.

The branch manager position is attractive. As I mentioned
in the interview, the $26,500 salary is lower than I
anticipated. Consequently, I am unable to accept your
offer.

Thank you for considering me for employment. I enjoyed
meeting you and your personnel. Perhaps our paths will
cross again in the future.

Sincerely

Andrew James Morgan

Andrew James Morgan

FIGURE 14—6 Refusal Letter

▲ EVALUATING EMPLOYMENT DOCUMENTS

Candidates must prepare their employment documents carefully. From the organization's perspective, these documents must be screened in relation to job requirements. In addition to evaluating employment documents in the employee-selection process, employers often use tests, interviews, physical examinations, and reference checks.

Employment screening is a two-way process: candidates seek organizations and organizations seek candidates. The candidate and the organization make decisions throughout the employment process.

The initial screening of employment documents takes place in the employment, human resources, or personnel departments of most large- and medium-size organizations; managers are limited to cooperating with these departments. The documents of candidates who make it through the preliminary screening process are then forwarded or sent directly to appropriate members of management for evaluation. In small businesses, managers are usually responsible for both screening and evaluating employment documents.

The computer is a useful tool in the hiring process.

Advances in computer technology have prompted organizations where large numbers of candidates are processed to design and implement computer-based systems. Pertinent data from résumés and application forms of candidates are extracted and entered into the computer. Managers seeking new employees can review the computerized data for applicants quickly and request the files of qualified candidates.

Firms use a variety of screening methods in selecting new employees.

The process used to evaluate employment documents varies because evaluation practices differ from manager to manager. Managers tend to evaluate candidates using measures which have proved to be successful in their own business experiences. In some respects, it is as if managers are looking for themselves reflected in the candidates. Most managers, however, base their evaluations on at least four features in employment documents:

Most managers base their evaluations on four features in employment documents.

1. Appearance—The initial screening of résumés may be made solely on appearance and design.
2. A precisely stated professional objective or career interest—Objectives should clearly reflect the candidate's occupational goals.
3. Relevancy of work experience—Work experience should relate to the desired position.
4. Writing skill—Grammar, punctuation, spelling, and keyboarding portray a candidate's image.

A problem associated with initial evaluation is **résumé cloning,** where résumés and cover letters begin to look more and more alike.[4] This trend can be attributed to the widespread use of all-purpose résumés subscribed to by many college placement offices, job-hunting books, and career experts. Since it is becoming more difficult to distinguish one résumé from another, managers look for highly individualized résumés that provide a competitive advantage.

▲ PREPARING EMPLOYMENT-RELATED DOCUMENTS

Managers prepare these employment-related documents: job descriptions, performance appraisals, written reprimands, and discharge letters.

Job Description

A *job description,* or *position description* as it is often called, is a one- or two-page written summary which describes the basic tasks performed on a job. The basis for a job description can vary from a mental image of the job in the manager's mind to a systematic investigation or analysis of the job. Methods that may be used to analyze a job include

The job description summarizes the major duties of a job.

▲ Examining previous job descriptions of the job and/or other job records.
▲ Observing employees while they perform their job tasks.
▲ Interviewing employees and their supervisors to gather information about the job.
▲ Administering questionnaires to employees and their supervisors to collect information about the job.
▲ Examining job logs or diaries kept by the employees.
▲ Recording job tasks on videotape or film.

Several methods may be used to obtain information about a job.

The elements of a job description include the job title, a general description of the job, and the specific duties or activities of the job. Since several persons will use the job description, it should reflect the job accurately in a style that is easily understood. Because jobs tend to change over time, the job description must be kept up-to-date; it may need to be rewritten annually.

To be of any value, job descriptions must be kept up-to-date.

A job specification clarifies the skills and experience needed to perform a job effectively.

Job descriptions are frequently used to develop job specifications. A *job specification* is a written statement listing the qualifications employees need to perform a given job effectively. Job descriptions are also used to recruit employees, to orient new employees toward their jobs, and to serve as references in job evaluation.

Performance Appraisal

A *performance appraisal* is the evaluation of job-related strengths and weaknesses of an employee. Most managers in American business, government, and industry use performance appraisals. Performance appraisals are frequently used for giving individual feedback to employees and for determining promotional opportunities, salary increases, and training needs.

When used properly, performance appraisals are an effective communication link between managers and employees. They aid in building and maintaining a high level of employee morale. Improved morale results in motivating employees to perform their jobs in the most efficient manner possible.

The three common methods of appraisal are rating scales, critical incidents, and narrative essays.

Rating Scales

The rating scale is a widely used method of evaluating job performance.

This method of appraisal includes a number of performance factors or characteristics to be evaluated, such as quality of work, dependability, and attitude. The manager then rates each factor using a rating scale. The simplest type of scale is that in which the manager circles or writes a number, usually from 1 to 5, where 1 is low and 5 is high. Other scales require the manager to place a check mark next to a word or phrase, such as outstanding, good, average, below average, and unsatisfactory. Most rating scales provide space for written comments, enabling the manager to clarify a rating. In many organizations, the manager is required to submit written justification for a high or low rating on any factor.

Rating scales are easy to use and provide a means for comparing job performances among employees. On the other hand, the performance factors on the appraisal instrument, as well as the numerical or verbal ratings, are subject to different interpretations by different managers.

Critical Incidents

This method requires the manager to keep a written record of unusually good or undesirable examples of job performance for each employee.[5] The advantage to the critical incidents method is that the manager can focus on specific examples of job behavior rather than on vaguely defined factors such as initiative or judgment. One serious drawback to this method is that the manager may record a number of desirable or undesirable incidents and neglect to provide immediate feedback to the employee.

Critical incidents focus on good and bad examples of job performance.

Narrative Essays

When this method is used, the manager provides one or more written paragraphs describing an employee's strengths, weaknesses, and potential, together with suggestions for improvement. When narrative essays are well prepared, they can provide detailed feedback to employees regarding their job performance. The disadvantage to the method is that essays vary widely in length and content, which makes comparisons among employees virtually impossible.

The narrative essay describes an employee's performance without making comparisons to other employees.

Progressive Discipline

One of the more unpleasant aspects of a manager's job is that of dealing with employees who fail to comply with job or organization rules. *Progressive discipline,* which specifies that management respond to repeated rule violations with increasingly severe penalties, is widely accepted among organizations. For an employee who has broken a work rule for the first time, an oral warning from the manager is sufficient reprimand. The manager's role at this stage of discipline is to help the employee work out a way to prevent the rule violation from recurring. A sequence of disciplinary actions for subsequent offenses include a written reprimand and a discharge letter.

Oral warning is the first step in progressive discipline.

Written Reprimand

A manager should use the indirect approach for a written reprimand, which documents the employee's undesirable job performance. The reprimand should include a warning of more serious disciplinary action—demotion, suspension, or dismissal—if corrective action is not taken by the employee. End the letter with a statement of the corrective action the manager expects the employee to take. The employee should read and sign the written reprimand; it then becomes part of the employee's company employment record.

The written reprimand becomes part of the employee's employment record.

Discharge Letter

The final disciplinary step for a problem employee is discharge. If all the standardized grievance, complaint, and progressive disciplinary procedures have been adhered to for a chronic violator, management may have just cause for discharge. If such drastic action is deemed necessary,

The ultimate punishment is discharge.

"It's not just *you*, Walker. I'm firing *all* our nincom-poops."

Source: Reprinted by permission: Tribune Media Services.

then the manager will prepare a discharge letter. The letter should cite the work rules or standards violated and the specific circumstances upon which the discharge is based.

Since 1975, the number of lawsuits initiated against organizations by former or current employees has increased substantially.[6] Most lawsuits today are related to employment decision making. If a manager follows good personnel practices and keeps clear-cut documentation of unsatisfactory work performance for each employee, employment-related litigation may be reduced.

> Litigation concerning employment decision making is now commonplace.

SUMMARY

Managers assume three roles in written employment communication: applicant, reviewer, and monitor.

Successful employment application depends on effective written communication skills. Applicants should assess their employability prior to preparing employment documents. The résumé and application letter are key documents that applicants prepare.

A well-developed résumé presents the applicant as a desirable employee; the purpose of a résumé is to get an interview. The résumé should include detailed information about the applicant's career interest, work experience, education, memberships, honors, avocational interests, the applicant's address and telephone number, and references. Applicants can develop distinctive-looking résumés by using innovative formatting, contrasting type styles, good quality paper, active voice, and professional packaging.

The purposes of the application letter are to introduce the applicant to the employer, to highlight the applicant's qualifications so the employer will read the detailed information in the résumé, and to make interview arrangements easy. Application letters may be solicited or unsolicited. The body of an application letter should include (1) a brief description of the position for which one wishes to apply, (2) highlighted qualifications which make the applicant an excellent candidate for employment, (3) an offer to provide more detailed information, (4) a reference to the enclosed résumé, and (5) a statement indicating the applicant's willingness to discuss employment.

In addition to preparing a résumé and letter of application and completing an application form, the applicant generally writes one or more follow-up letters during the application process. A thank-you letter should be sent following an interview with a prospective employer. An acceptance letter should be written when the applicant accepts an employment offer. A refusal letter should be written when the applicant refuses employment.

Employment screening is a two-way process with both the candidate and the organization making decisions during the employment process. Initial employment screening occurs in the employment, human resources, or personnel departments of large- and medium-size firms, after which managers evaluate employment documents. In small companies, managers are responsible for both screening and evaluating employment documents. Managers evaluate documents based on appearance, a precisely stated career objective or career interest, the relevancy of work experience, and writing skill.

Managers prepare these employment-related documents: job descriptions, performance appraisals, written reprimands, and discharge letters. Job descriptions are written summaries which describe job content and requirements. Job descriptions should be updated periodically to reflect changes in employee responsibilities. Managers prepare performance appraisals to evaluate employee job-related strengths and weaknesses. Rating scales, critical incidents, and narrative essays are three methods for documenting employee performance.

Written communication is also important in documenting how management disciplines employees. The concept of progressive discipline is widely accepted among organizations. Progressive discipline specifies that management respond to repeated rule violations with increasingly severe penalties. Oral warnings are issued after a first offense; written documents are prepared for successive offenses. The ultimate or final disciplinary step is documented by a discharge letter.

QUESTIONS

1. Describe the ways in which managers engage in employment writing.

2. What documents do applicants prepare when seeking employment?

3. Describe how an applicant may make a résumé stand out among other applicants' résumés.

4. Explain how an applicant should use the direct approach in preparing an application letter.

5. Describe the purposes of a résumé and application letter.

6. List at least three features of a résumé that a manager usually evaluates.

7. Define *résumé inflation.*

8. What is a *job description?*

9. List three common methods of performance appraisal.

10. What type of disciplinary action is taken by a manager the first time an employee violates a work rule or standard?

PROBLEM-SOLVING EXPERIENCES

1. Prepare a résumé. Use creativity and innovativeness to draw attention to your special qualifications.

2. Select a position with a real company. Write an application letter for that position.

CASE 14–1

Mary Prater is the human resources manager for Elecktra Systems, a rapidly growing office automation systems supplier. The company needs to hire an advertising manager. Advertisements were placed in the appropriate trade journals about a month ago. Applicant response has been good. In fact, Mary has about 300 résumés from interested people. Unfortunately, a union contract negotiation and a major in-plant training program have prohibited Mary from spending much time reviewing the résumés.

David Walters is the marketing vice-president at Elecktra Systems. He would like to hire an advertising manager by the end of the month. David asked Mary for a summary of the qualifications of the top 20 applicants. Mary said she would prepare a summary by late afternoon tomorrow.

1. Describe the process that Mary should go through in screening the 300 résumés to determine the top 20 applicants.

2. Assuming that there is little difference in the work experience of the top 26 applicants, what criteria should Mary use to narrow the choice to 20 applicants?

ENDNOTES

[1]Kevin L. Hutchinson, "Personnel Administrators' Preferences for Résumé Content: A Survey and Review of Empirically Based Conclusions," *The Journal of Business Communication*, Vol. 21, No. 4 (Fall, 1984), p. 8.

[2]Vickie Johnson Stout and James D. Good, "Developing a Competitive Edge in Résumé Writing," *The Ohio Business Teacher*, Vol. 44 (April, 1984), pp. 107–112.

[3]"Résumés: Stretching the Truth?" *Management World*, Vol. 14, No. 6 (June, 1985), p. 4.

[4]"Résumés: Too Many Clones?" *Management World*, Vol. 13, No. 7 (August, 1984), p. 5.

[5]Robert W. Braid, "Exact Evaluation: Guidelines for Precise Performance Appraisals," *Management World*, Vol. 13, No. 10 (November, 1984), p. 37.

[6]George E. Stevens, "Firing Without Fear," *Management World*, Vol. 13, No. 3 (March, 1984), p. 11.

15

GRAPHIC
INFORMATION

When you complete this chapter, you should be able to:

▲ Explain the purpose of graphics.

▲ List the guidelines for table presentation.

▲ Name the main types of figures and explain their essential features.

▲ List the guidelines for figures.

▲ Identify descriptors commonly used to interpret graphics.

▲ Discuss the benefits and primary components of computer graphics.

Statistical data, complex ideas, trends, and relationships are more quickly and easily communicated with graphics than with words. Well-designed graphics illustrate points and help set the mood for a professional presentation. Effective graphics enhance the message managers communicate in their reports and other written documents.

Until recently, most managers were content to give the responsibility for visual illustrations to a graphic arts department or business. Computer technology has changed that by placing the capability to generate graphics in the hands of managers, the dominant users of business graphics.

▲ PURPOSE OF GRAPHIC INFORMATION

Graphic information, the use of visual illustrations in written documents and presentations, makes written and spoken communication more meaningful. Graphics can be used to

▲ Improve reader retention of statistical data by condensing information. Complex numbers and statistics are more easily understood and remembered when narrative material is accompanied by appropriate graphics.[1]

Graphics help improve reader retention of statistical data, ideas, trends, and relationships.

▲ Improve reader retention of complex ideas, trends, and relationships by reducing verbalism. Simple graphics provide the reader with information that can be scanned and digested more quickly than a narrative statement.

▲ Add dramatic impact to business presentations. Graphic information displayed on slides, overhead transparencies, handout materials, and other visual aids will add effectiveness to written and spoken presentations.

Graphics add effectiveness to business presentations.

▲ TYPES OF GRAPHICS

Managers need clear, accurate information for decision making, planning, organizing, leading, and controlling. Well-planned and well-prepared graphics are invaluable communication tools. Graphics should supplement or enhance, rather than replace, spoken and written communications.

How do communicators choose an appropriate medium for communicating information graphically? The type of data to be communicated and the message that the communicator wants to convey influence this decision.[2] Other factors that affect how information is presented graphically include resources, tools, and time.

Tables

A table is a systematic arrangement of information.

Informal tables are often called text tables.

Tables, the systematic arrangement of numbers and/or words in rows and columns, help improve the readability and understanding of information. Tables may be classified as informal and formal.

An *informal table,* sometimes referred to as a text table, is a brief tabulation of information which is inserted into the text of a business document. The informal table does not have a title; its contents are explained in the text. Figure 15–1 illustrates an informal table incorporated into text.

Formal tables stand alone.

A *formal table* usually contains a title, columnar headings, and any explanatory information (the source, notes, or footnotes) which applies to the table. A formal table stands by itself; it does not require text narrative to convey a clear idea to the reader. The format of a properly arranged formal table is shown in Figure 15–2.

Here are guidelines for the proper arrangement of a table.

Here are some helpful guides for table preparation:

1. Number each table consecutively throughout a report.
2. Give each table a clear and complete title. If the title extends beyond one line, the second line should be shorter than the first line. A subheading is used whenever there is a need to further clarify the title or explain units of measurement in the table body.
3. Give each column in the body of the table a concise heading. Generally columnar headings are underlined or placed between ruled lines.
4. Use the same units of measurement (inches, yards, square feet, miles, percentages, etc.) within a column.
5. If appropriate, use a totals line to indicate that column figures have been totaled.
6. Use footnotes to clarify entries in the table. The asterisk symbol (*), the number/pounds symbol (#), superior numbers, or superior lowercase letters are frequently used to key table footnotes. The characters *a, b, c* or *1, 2, 3* indicate the order of priority.
7. Place the footnote(s) before the source note when both are used in the same table.
8. When appropriate, use a source note to identify the source of the information in the table.

The prospective earnings for the next four years of Ace Co. and Hub Inc. are as follows:

	Ace Co.	Hub Inc.
Year 1	$700,000	$600,000
Year 2	300,000	250,000
Year 3	250,000	200,000
Year 4	900,000	750,000

FIGURE 15–1   Informal Table

Table Number	Table 3
Table Title	COMPARISON OF PROMOTIONS BY DEPARTMENTS FOR A TWO-YEAR PERIOD
Subheading	(Lake Point Division)

Department	Last Year	This Year
Accounting	11	12
Information Processing*	10	9
Personnel	3	3
Production	8	10
Research	5	6
Sales	12	15
Totals	49	55

Columnar Headings

Body

Totals Line

Footnote   *Formerly Data and Word Processing

Source Note   Source: Annual Report

FIGURE 15–2   Formal Table

9. Leave adequate space between the table and the text narrative. Also, leave enough space between the columns for ease in reading and comparing data. Do not, however, extend the table into the side margins of the report.

10. Use ruled lines to improve the readability of the table entries. Ruled lines, however, are not a requirement of all tables.

11. Keep the table on a single page if possible. If an extremely long table must be continued on another page, begin the second page with the table number and "Continued" ("Table 3   Continued"). All columnar headings used on the first page must be repeated on the second page.

12. Display wide tables broadside on the page with the top of the table placed against the left margin of the report.

13. Check a style manual for specific rules regarding table construction.

Figures

Graphs and charts are figures.

Figures refer to graphs, charts, illustrations, or other condensed visual representations used to display messages. All figures should include a concisely worded *title* that describes the general contents of the graphic. The following is an example of an appropriate figure title.

AMPAZ Inc. Gross International Sales for 1988

The figure title generally appears below the graphic. Like tables, figures should be numbered consecutively throughout a written document.

Like a table subheading, a *figure subheading* is used to further clarify the main title. A figure subheading may be used to draw attention to the particular time span, population, sample, or unit of measurement shown in the figure. The following example shows how the figure title precedes the subheading. The subheading appears immediately below the figure title.

AMPAZ Inc. Gross International Sales
(in Millions of Dollars)

The source line gives credit to the person who originated the figure.

A legend explains the colors or symbols used in a figure.

A *source line* is included above the figure title to give credit to the person or party who originally prepared the information contained in the figure. A *legend,* or explanatory list of symbols or colors used in a figure, should appear immediately below the graphic and above the figure title if space permits.

Special shading called *cross-hatching* and multiple colors may be used to distinguish the various parts of a figure. A figure's design should enhance the oral or written report in which it is included. The figure's content should be formatted to read from left to right and from top to bottom and should have a balanced appearance. Format of the data may force some features such as the legend to be placed where space is available. However, writers should avoid distorting or illogically arranging data. The illogical arrangement of data causes figures to appear cluttered or messy and impedes reader understanding. Communicators may use these types of figures: pie charts, line charts, bar charts, and pictorials.

Pie Charts

Pie charts are circular figures used to show values and/or percentages that represent parts of a whole. A circle, the pie, is divided into wedges with the size of each wedge representing the value as a fraction of the whole. Pie charts are simple to prepare and used frequently in business presentations and written reports. They are effective in illustrating concepts such as market shares, budgets, and manufacturing costs. An example of a pie chart is shown in Figure 15–3.

Pie charts show parts of a whole.

Construct pie charts so that the divisions start at the twelve o'clock position. Arrange the wedges from largest to smallest in a clockwise direction.

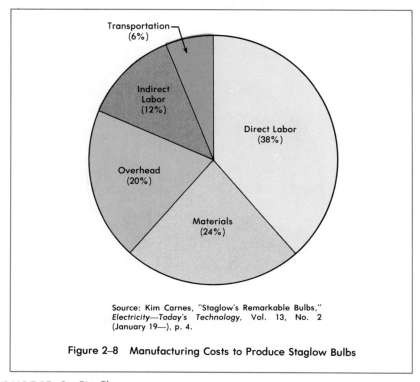

Source: Kim Carnes, "Staglow's Remarkable Bulbs," *Electricity—Today's Technology*, Vol. 13, No. 2 (January 19—), p. 4.

Figure 2–8   Manufacturing Costs to Produce Staglow Bulbs

FIGURE 15–3   Pie Chart

Limit the number of wedges to between five and seven. Identify each wedge with a label and percentage; small amounts may be lumped together as *Miscellaneous.* Be sure that the wedges total 100 percent. A special or important part of the whole can be emphasized by the use of color.

Emphasis may also be achieved by using an ***exploded pie chart,*** in which one wedge is cut away from the pie. The number of exploded slices should be limited to no more than two. Figure 15–4 illustrates an exploded pie chart.

A three-dimensional pie chart is referred to as an ***elongated pie chart.*** Elongating a pie chart causes it to appear oval. An elongated pie chart is shown in Figure 15–5.

A ***multiple pie chart*** is used to compare or contrast the composition of several entities. Figure 15–6 illustrates a multiple pie chart.

Line Charts

Line charts include plotted data points joined by line segments. They are used in oral and written reports to illustrate changes and trends. Line charts are effective for showing the interaction of controllable variables called ***independent variables.*** Typically line charts are used to compare and/or contrast numeric information.

Line charts are used to illustrate trends.

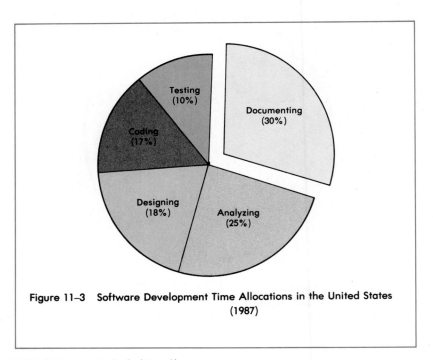

Figure 11–3   **Software Development Time Allocations in the United States**
(1987)

FIGURE 15–4   Exploded Pie Chart

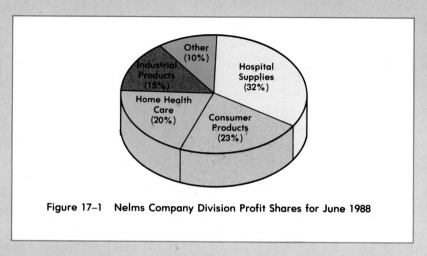

Figure 17–1   Nelms Company Division Profit Shares for June 1988

FIGURE 15–5   Elongated Pie Chart

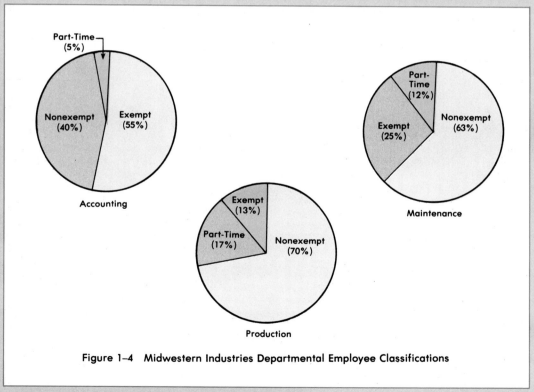

Figure 1–4   Midwestern Industries Departmental Employee Classifications

FIGURE 15–6   Multiple Pie Chart

Dependent variables are uncontrollable; independent variables are controllable.

Line charts are prepared using two axes. The independent variable is usually plotted on the horizontal (X) axis. Often the independent variable is time, particularly when trends or projections are illustrated. Uncontrollable variables, referred to as **dependent variables,** are plotted on the vertical (Y) axis. Divide each axis into equal increments, with values increasing in an upward direction on the Y axis and to the right on the X axis. The vertical axis typically starts at zero. Figure 15–7 displays a line chart.

When more than one dependent variable is illustrated in a line chart, the figure is called a **multiple line chart.** Multiple line charts may be effective, but care must be taken to limit information to a digestible amount. Too much data in a line chart can overwhelm readers and confuse or distort message interpretation. Generally no more than three dependent variables should be plotted on a line chart. Use dots, squares, or other special symbols to illustrate different data points. Or communicators may use different colors or kinds of lines to illustrate the different or multiple dependent variables in a line chart.

Line charts should contain no more than three lines.

Use broken axes to show that increments have been omitted.

So that the points of interest can be shown in a document that is manageable in size, use broken axes to indicate that some increments have been omitted. Use grid lines to add clarity or enhance readability. Figure 15–8 illustrates a multiple line chart with a broken vertical axis.

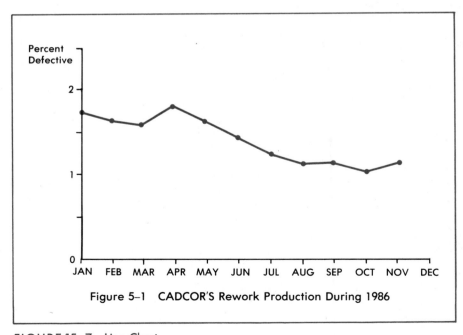

Figure 5–1 CADCOR'S Rework Production During 1986

FIGURE 15–7 Line Chart

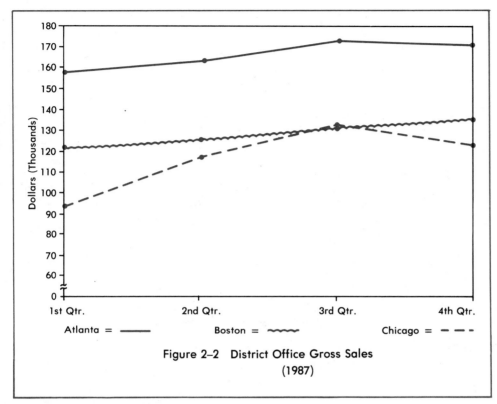

Figure 2–2   District Office Gross Sales
(1987)

FIGURE 15–8   Multiple Line Chart

If exponential relationships are shown, use logarithmic scales and grid lines to show data. More than one vertical axis may be used to illustrate multiple related dependent variables that have different value bases. When multiple scales are used, exercise extreme care to ensure that the data are understandable. When the vertical axis extends below the horizontal axis to show negative quantities, the line figure is referred to as a ***bilateral line chart.*** An example of a bilateral line chart appears in Figure 15–9.

Bar Charts

In addition to pie charts and line charts, bar charts are considered standard graphics in business communications.[3] Bar charts are easy to read and flexible.

Bar charts show comparative information in vertical or horizontal bars. Bar charts may be used to show several variables at once, changes over time in one variable, or the composition of several variables over time.

Bar charts depict comparative information.

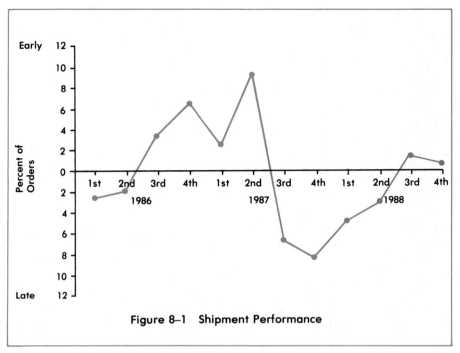

Figure 8-1   Shipment Performance

FIGURE 15–9   Bilateral Line Chart

Bars can be drawn vertically or horizontally; they can show positive and/or negative quantities. Like line charts, bar charts are drawn on two axes. The horizontal (X) axis is used to plot the independent variable, and the vertical (Y) axis is used to plot the dependent variable. Figure 15–10 illustrates a bar chart. A **multiple bar chart,** illustrated in Figure 15–11, shows several variables.

Like pie charts, bar charts may also be used to show the relative size or parts of a whole. In this kind of bar chart, called a **component bar chart** or a stacked bar chart, the bar values are stacked. When using a component bar chart, communicators should make sure that the stacked amounts are easy to read. Figure 15–12 illustrates a component bar chart.

A **bilateral bar chart** is a bar figure that has a vertical axis that extends below the horizontal axis. Like the bilateral line chart, the bilateral bar chart is useful in showing positive and negative quantities. A bilateral bar chart is shown in Figure 15–13.

Pictorials

Pictorials refer to figures that are diagrammed or photographed and are not classified as pie charts, line charts, or bar charts. As with any figure

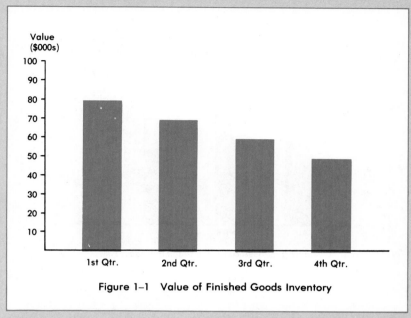

Figure 1–1   Value of Finished Goods Inventory

FIGURE 15–10   Bar Chart

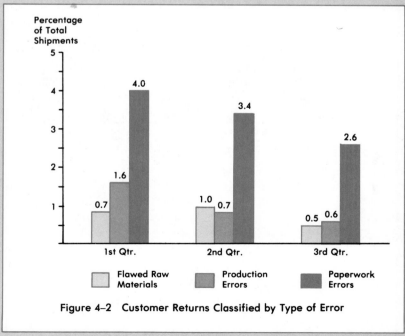

Figure 4–2   Customer Returns Classified by Type of Error

FIGURE 15–11   Multiple Bar Chart

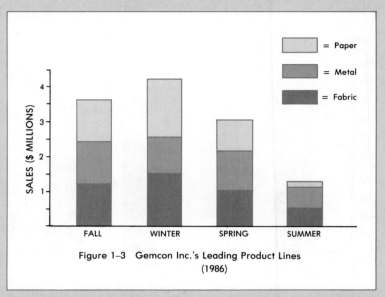

FIGURE 15–12   Component Bar Chart

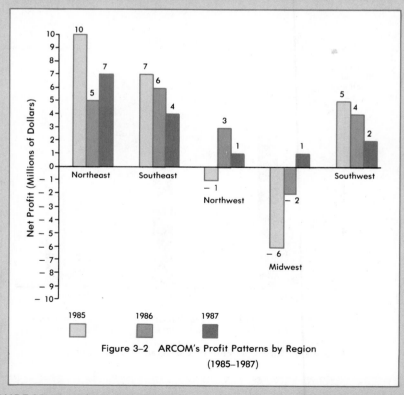

FIGURE 15–13   Bilateral Bar Chart

or table, the amount of detail included in a pictorial should be based on an analysis of the intended audience. Examples of pictorials include pictograms, drawings, photographs, maps, and flowcharts.

Pictograms.   *Pictograms,* or pictographs, are pictorial representations of numerical data or relationships. They resemble bar charts except that parts of a symbol, instead of bars, are used to represent differences in one or more dependent variables. Proportions are clearer when shown by multiples of a symbol rather than by varying sizes of a bar. Figure 15–14 is an example of a pictogram.

Drawings.   *Drawings* refer to diagrams used to communicate the relationship between or among items rather than their relative values. Examples of drawings include organization charts and floor plans. Communicators may use drawings to show the size, shape, or physical location of an object or concept in relation to other objects or concepts. Examples of a floor plan and an organization chart are shown in Figures 15–15 and 15–16, respectively.

Photographs.   *Photographs* are images recorded by a camera and reproduced on a photosensitive surface. They may be used to show shape, relative size, and location.

Figures other than pie, bar, and line charts are called pictorials.

Pictograms resemble bar charts.

Drawings communicate relationships.

Photographs show shape, relative size, and location.

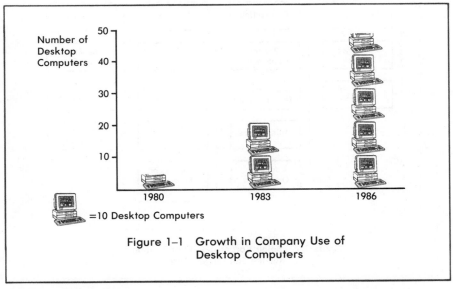

Figure 1–1   Growth in Company Use of Desktop Computers

FIGURE 15–14   Pictogram

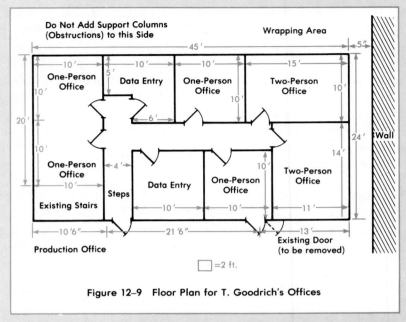

Figure 12–9   Floor Plan for T. Goodrich's Offices

FIGURE 15–15   Drawing—Floor Plan

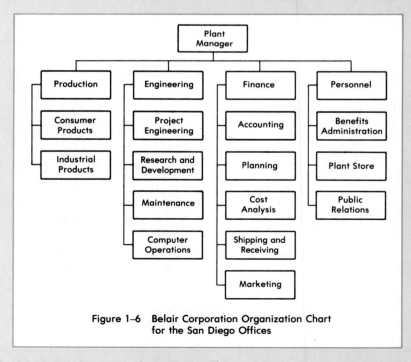

Figure 1–6   Belair Corporation Organization Chart
for the San Diego Offices

FIGURE 15–16   Drawing—Organization Chart

Maps.   *Maps* refer to business drawings used to show positional relationships of geographic regions. An example of a map appears in Figure 15–17.

Flowcharts.   *Flowcharts* are schematic drawings of the logical steps in a sequence of operations. Examples of commonly used flowcharts are computer programs, PERT, and Gantt charts. PERT, the *Program Evaluation Review Technique*, and Gantt charts are special forms of flowcharts used in planning and scheduling business activities. These kinds of flowcharts are particularly helpful in showing work planned and completed side by side in relation to each other and to time. Figure 15–18 illustrates a flowchart.

Maps show positional relationships.

Flowcharts show steps in a sequence.

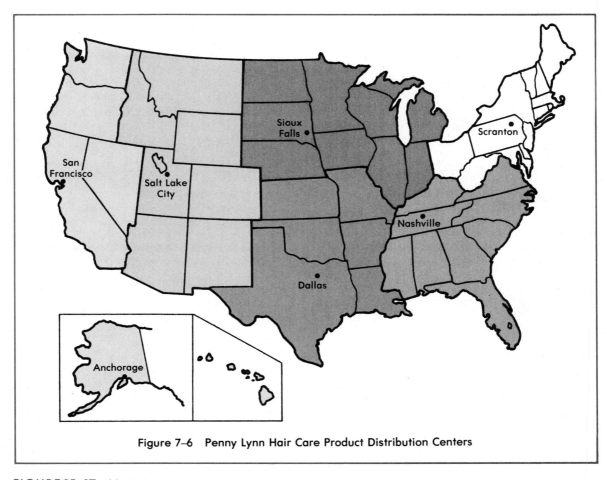

Figure 7–6   Penny Lynn Hair Care Product Distribution Centers

FIGURE 15–17   Map

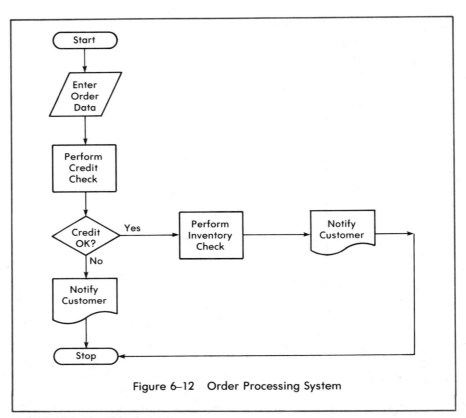

Figure 6–12   Order Processing System

FIGURE 15–18   Flowchart

▲ DESCRIPTORS USED TO EXPLAIN GRAPHICS ▬▬▬

Even though a graphic is generally presented with accompanying spoken or written narrative, a graphic should be understandable and capable of standing alone. Graphics must be introduced in the narrative *before* the graphic appears in the text of a written document. The narrative should explain the graphic rather than merely repeat each detail of the table or figure. For example, the narrative for the bilateral bar chart in Figure 15–13 on page 274 may resemble the following:

> Figure 3–2 shows ARCOM's profit/loss trends by region. Profits have fluctuated in each region. Only the Midwest Region has made continual progress in recovering from a slump. The other regions have experienced declines or have been unstable. However, the greatest dollar amount of profit continues to come from the Northeast Region.

Information used to narrate a graphic should be interpretive. When describing a graphic, communicators should convey the important features of the dependent or uncontrolled variables rather than merely present every feature. Sequencing narratives to interpret graphics in written reports is described in Chapter 16. Some of the most common descriptors used to explain graphics in spoken and written narratives include these terms—mean, median, mode, and range.

The **mean** is the arithmetic average of a set of numbers; it is useful in describing the dependent variable. The mean can be used to describe typical or average behavior and/or results. Knowledge of a mean value or amount can help the reader or listener grasp how data look.

The **median** is the middle value in an array of numbers; it depicts the midpoint of a distribution. The median can provide a more accurate picture of data than the mean since a few extremely low or high values tend to skew the results of arithmetically obtained data. The **mode** identifies data that appear most frequently in a distribution. Communicators can use modal responses to indicate occurrences of identical values or results. The mode is valuable in showing patterns within the data.

The **range** refers to the highest and lowest, or extreme, values in an array of numbers; it is used to describe the best and worst or extreme values among the data. Other exceptions or peculiarities in the data should also be explained.

▲ COMPUTER GRAPHICS

Computer graphics, the creation of figures and tables on computers, are making rapid advances on conventional graphics methods. Several graphics software packages are available which permit the user to create a wide variety of graphics ranging from simple pie charts and maps to complex flowcharts and three-dimensional horizontal bars with inserted labels. Figures 15–19 and 15–20 show examples of computer-generated graphics.

Although business managers are heavy users of graphics, they may not be computer users. To overcome this problem, software is now available which permits managers to create figures by merely using pointing devices on the computer.[4]

Once a graphic has been created on the computer, it may be printed on either plain paper or transparency film. For the highest-quality color graphics, a pen plotter is needed. Most plotters are compatible with the popular microcomputers and graphics software packages. One such plotter offers ten color fiber-tipped pens for paper and seven for transparency printing. It prints at a maximum speed of 15 inches per second.[5]

Discuss the features of the dependent variable in the narrative of a figure or table.

The mean, median, mode, and range are descriptors commonly used to describe graphics.

A wide variety of graphics software packages are now available.

A pen plotter is the key to high-quality color graphics.

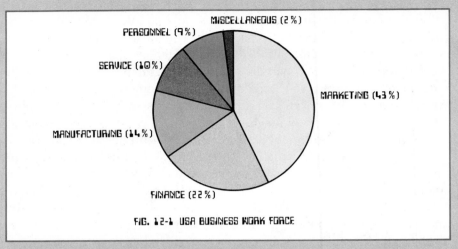

FIGURE 15–19   Computer-Generated Pie Chart

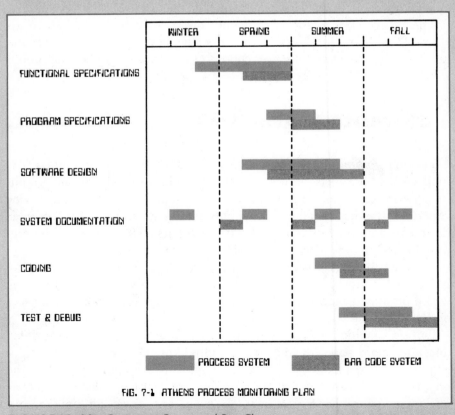

FIGURE 15–20   Computer-Generated Bar Chart

Cost and time savings are the primary advantages of using computer-generated graphics over conventional graphics methods. Commercially prepared graphics can be expensive. Time savings, however, may be more important to busy and preoccupied managers than cost savings. It often takes several days to get results from a graphic arts department, whereas computer-generated graphics can be produced in a matter of minutes or hours.

The main advantages of using computer graphics are cost and time savings.

Although computer technology is revolutionizing the graphics market, managers still need an understanding of basic design principles to use computer graphics effectively. Computers don't automatically produce high-impact graphics. Someone must create the design.[6]

Users of computer graphics need an understanding of basic design principles.

SUMMARY

Graphic information is the use of visual illustrations in written documents and presentations. By using well-designed graphics, statistical data, complex ideas, trends, and relationships are more quickly and easily communicated than with words. Graphics can improve reader retention and understanding of statistical data and complex ideas, as well as add dramatic impact to business presentations.

Tables, the systematic arrangement of numbers and/or words in rows and columns, may be used to improve the readability and understanding of information. Tables may be classified as informal and formal. Informal tables do not have titles. Their content is explained in the text of a report. Formal tables contain headings and can stand alone. When preparing tables, communicators should number each table consecutively throughout a report, give each table a clear title, and give each column in the body of the table a concise heading.

A figure is a graph, chart, or other condensed visual representation used to illustrate a message. All figures should include a concisely worded title that describes the general contents of the graphic. The figure title generally appears below the figure. A source line is included above the figure title to give credit to the person or party who originally prepared the information contained in the figure. A legend should be used to explain symbols or colors used in a figure. If a legend is used, it should appear immediately below the graphic and above the figure title if space permits. The most common types of figures are pie charts, line charts, bar charts, and pictorials.

Although a graphic is usually presented with a spoken or written narrative, the graphic should be understandable and capable of standing alone. The narrative should include a reference to the graphic and an explanation of its main ideas and/or significant details. Information used to narrate a graphic should be interpretive. Important features of the dependent or uncontrolled variables should be described. Descriptors commonly used to explain graphics in spoken and written narratives are mean, median, mode, and range. Exceptions or peculiarities in the data should also be explained.

Computer graphics, or the creation of figures and tables on computers, are making rapid advances on conventional graphics methods. Business managers are heavy users of graphics even though they may not be computer users.

QUESTIONS

1. What is the primary purpose for using graphics?
2. What is the purpose of a subheading in a table?
3. A report has three tables, three charts, one pictogram, and two maps. How would you number these visual aids?
4. What are four figures commonly used in business?
5. Identify two factors which influence the type of graphic used to display data.
6. What kind of figure is used to show percentages or parts of a whole?
7. Define *dependent variable*.
8. On which axis is the dependent variable plotted in a bar or line chart?
9. What descriptors are often used to explain data?
10. What are the two main advantages of computer graphics?

PROBLEM-SOLVING EXPERIENCES

1. Using the following information, create a figure and determine the narrative that should be used to describe it and why. In 1985, Corrine

Plastics employed 3,000 workers in the United States. One thousand employees were stationed in New York, 535 in Seattle, 465 in Kansas City, 270 in Dallas, and 730 in Orlando. Only 2,600 employees worked for Corrine in 1984. These employees were located in the following cities: 980 in New York, 400 in Seattle, 250 in Kansas City, 128 in Dallas, and 842 in Orlando.

2. The following statistics are based on percentages, compiled from Jekyll Company's annual report, for five types of investments for last year and this year, respectively. Prepare a ruled table for these data. The table will be the last of six tables included in a financial report for top-level management.

STRUCTURAL ANALYSIS OF TYPES OF INVESTMENTS FOR A TWO-YEAR PERIOD, JEKYLL COMPANY (Golden Island Division)

Short-Term Investments, 6%, 5%; Bonds, 59%, 60%; Common Stocks, 30%, 32%; Mortgages and Other Secured Notes, 4%, 2%; Real Estate, 1%, 1%.

3. Using the following employee absenteeism data for the months of January through June, prepare a figure and write the narrative that should accompany the figure in a written report.

Mary Stober	five absences
Trent Stein	seven absences
Sarah Greenway	no absences
Mitch Skilley	one absence
Miles Jordan	no absences
Helen Bell	three absences
Tippy Moore	ten absences
Clara Timpen	six absences

4. The following Continuing Education Units (CEUs) were awarded to 45 employees of the Callaway Company from 1982–1987. (Employee 1 received 41 CEUs, Employee 2 received 66 CEUs, and so on.) From these data, prepare a formal table. Divide the CEUs into seven equal groups, the first group containing 10–19 CEUs. Also, indicate the percentage of employees who obtained each group of CEUs. List the percentages rounded to two decimal places (represent 22.222% as 22.22%).

41	58	50	26	30	55	29	34	49
66	33	43	38	45	40	59	68	52
22	43	47	44	57	37	35	45	31
15	20	62	56	39	51	42	53	40
45	36	74	65	48	46	78	32	25

CASE 15–1

Rachel Greenway of Quinolta Tire Service Company is responsible for maintaining growth and decline data for each of Quinolta's service centers in the Southeastern Region of the United States. At the end of each fiscal year, she is required to give a presentation and submit a report about the company's growth patterns. She will give her presentation at the upcoming national sales conference to be held in Boston. Total company sales for the last fiscal year were 3.5 million dollars, or $300,000 greater than total sales of the previous year. However, sales in Florida were $610,000, or $40,000 less than last year. In Georgia, sales were $490,000, down $10,000 from last year. North Carolina and South Carolina also had decreased sales, from $800,000 to $780,000 and $550,000 to $520,000, respectively. Only the centers in Tennessee had increased sales over the previous year—$1.1 million, up from $700,000.

Rachel is in a quandary about how she can accurately report Quinolta's increase in total sales and also show that there are growth problems in some of the states. She plans to prepare a pie chart, bar chart, *or* table showing the sales for the fiscal year.

1. Which graphic will best illustrate the changes in sales?
2. Prepare the figure or table that best illustrates the data.
3. What descriptors should Rachel use to explain the graphic information in her presentation?
4. Write the narrative which will accompany the graphic data.

ENDNOTES

[1]Becky K. Peterson, "Tables and Graphs Improve Reader Performance and Reader Reaction," *The Journal of Business Communication*, Vol. 20, No. 2 (Spring, 1983), p. 48.

[2]David Benchley, "Presentation Pointers," *PC World*, Vol. 4, No. 2 (February, 1986), p. 134.

[3]Ibid., p. 133.

[4]Winn L. Rosch, "Graphics Seen as Key to Expanding PC's Role," *PC Week*, Vol. 2, No. 27 (July 9, 1985), p. 95.

[5]*LVP16 Color Graphics Plotter* (Brochure published by Digital Equipment Corporation, 1985), p. 2.

[6]Benchley, op. cit., p. 134.

16

REPORTS

The need for reports has increased proportionally with the increased complexity of business organizations. The coordination of activities among managers is necessary if an organization is to gain maximum efficiency at the minimum expense of human effort. Reports aid in achieving the coordination and successful operation of the business organization.

Reports are written and read so that specific actions are rationally undertaken. Managers have a responsibility to present their reports in both content and format so that all readers are fully served. Reports should not be "pulled together" but must be shaped for the purpose of conveying and explaining information to readers who want and need ideas.

▲ PURPOSE OF A REPORT

Successful managers at all levels are decision makers. Indeed, management experts contend that decision making is the most important activity performed by managers. At times, these decisions are simple and uncomplicated, such as deciding to hire a temporary employee. Other decisions that managers face are more difficult and complex, such as deciding the best geographical location for a corporate office. All decisions, simple or difficult, should be made only after examining and evaluating relevant information.

A report conveys information from one person to another and assists the decision-making process.

A basic source of information for decision making is the report. Generally a **business report** provides individual managers or groups of people (committees, study teams, task forces, and so forth) with facts and/or ideas for making decisions.

Since reports are an essential part of management communication, the ability to write an effective report is a fundamental skill required of all responsible managers. As with letters and memos, the manager must think through the purpose for writing a report. Before beginning to write a report, the manager must assess the reader's needs and desires. Essentially, the effectiveness of any report depends on how useful it is to the reader.

A report must meet the needs of the reader.

For example, if the reader wants information on copier-duplicator equipment, the writer needs to know if the information is to be used to select a specific machine. If so, the writer is obligated to expand the report beyond a listing of equipment models, functions, capabilities, and prices and provide information related to buying, renting, and leasing.

Reports are among the most important contacts many organizations have with their customers—often the only ones. In some areas of business, for example, customers may receive only a report for their money. In a sense, then, reports reflect an organization's capability as well as its image or reputation.

The need to know the central purpose of a business report is crucial. The following questions will help a writer establish the primary purpose of a report:

1. Who will read it?
2. What reaction or response is expected from the reader?

▲ RESEARCH CONDUCTED FOR REPORT WRITING

The main objective of most reports is to provide information for answering a question or solving a problem. Although most reports are internal documents used for decision making within an organization, reports may be prepared as external documents for audiences outside the organization.

Someone other than the writer may ask the question or pose the problem. Or the writer may anticipate the question and provide a response before the question is asked or the problem is addressed. If someone other than the writer requests that a report be prepared, the initiator of the report should tell the writer the intended purpose of the report.

A writer should follow these steps of the problem-solving process when conducting research for report writing:

1. Recognize that a problem exists.
2. Define the problem.
3. Collect relevant information.
4. Analyze the information.
5. Develop plausible solutions for eliminating the problem and preventing similar problems in the future.
6. Select an appropriate solution.
7. Implement the selected solution.
8. Evaluate the effectiveness of the selected solution.

Generally research is conducted to answer the question or solve the problem and subsequently fulfill the purpose of writing the report. Two kinds of research may be used for report writing.

Primary research is first-hand investigation of a topic.

Primary research data are obtainable through experimentation, observation, and survey.

Secondary research refers to indirectly investigating a topic.

Primary research refers to first-hand investigation of a topic or to research that has not been conducted previously. Primary data are obtained directly from an original source in three different ways. **Experimentation** involves determining whether the change in one factor causes a change in another factor. **Observation** consists of watching the actions of a particular person or group or watching the results of an event or series of events. **Survey** study pertains to collecting data from others by conducting face-to-face or intermediary interviews or by using a questionnaire. Primary research may also consist of a combination of experimentation, observation, and survey.

Secondary research refers to second-hand or indirect investigation of a topic. Writers who conduct secondary research are expected to document the indirect sources from which data are obtained. Sources include association publications, encyclopedias, trade journals, government documents, books, indexes, computer data bases, dictionaries, abstracts, handbooks, recordings, video material, almanacs, microfilm, microfiche, and company records.

▲ REPORT WRITING MECHANICS

The fundamentals of the writing process and the elements of effective writing mentioned in Chapter 11 should also be implemented in report writing. Communicators should plan, organize, draft, and edit their reports to meet the needs of the intended audience. Consideration should be given to the direction in which the report will be sent, whether the report is an internal or external document. Also, special attention should be given to the correctness of the report as reflected by accuracy, grammar, spelling, punctuation, format, and coherence.

Attractive, well-written reports are vital to business.

Reports should be prepared so that the sender's writing style enhances readability. A positive or pleasant tone should be used. When possible, active, concrete, concise, and objective language should be used. Ideas should be arranged in a digestible sequence, and appropriate vocabulary should be employed.

▲ TYPES OF REPORTS

The type of report a writer prepares depends on the purpose for which the report is written. Other factors that affect the type of report a writer prepares include the time of year, progress or lack of progress to date, inquiries from clients, or questions and directives from higher management. Although the major reasons for communication are to inform, to persuade, and to entertain, business reports are rarely written to entertain the reader. Rather, the writer prepares a report to inform or persuade the reader. The two types of reports are informational and analytical.

Usually business reports are written to inform or to persuade.

Informational Reports

An *informational report* provides data for the reader to analyze and interpret. This type of report is based primarily on secondary research, writer experience, or writer knowledge. Examples of informational reports include committee reports, annual reports, credit reports, progress reports, periodic reports, sales reports, specification reports, one-time directives, meeting minutes, and personnel reports.

Informational reports provide data but do not provide the analysis or interpretation.

Analytical Reports

An *analytical report* not only provides data for the reader but also includes data analysis, conclusions or interpretations of findings, and recommendations. The writer presents recommendations to aid the reader in making decisions. In addition to interpreting the data for the reader, making recommendations is a major factor which distinguishes an analytical report from an informational report.[1] Problem-solving skills are needed to write an analytical report. Examples of analytical reports include research reports, budget reports, feasibility reports, proposals, market analyses, justification reports, and sales analyses.

Writers try to influence readers in analytical reports.

▲ REPORT WRITING APPROACHES

As with any written communication, report writing is influenced by expected reader reaction.

Report writing is influenced by expected reader reaction.

Direct Approach

Any type of report may be written in direct order. However, a direct approach is generally used when the writer initiates the report to share information that will please or interest others. Typically, informational reports are written using a direct approach. If anticipated reader reaction is positive, the writer should position the main ideas or recommendations first. Next, significant details and background information are provided. In conclusion, the writer may restate the main ideas or use some other positive closing. Data included in informational reports may be arranged according to sequence, time, importance, spatial relations, geographic designations, or categories.

The direct approach may be used in an analytical report when someone other than the writer initiates the report in order to get the writer's recommendations on a topic. Some executives expect recommendations or conclusions near the beginning of the report.

Indirect Approach

An indirect approach is generally used when the writer initiates the report and anticipated reader reaction is negative or when reader persuasion is needed. Persuasion is used when the writer wants the reader to accept specified hypotheses, conclusions, or recommendations. When the indirect approach is used, recommendations appear after explanations and other persuasive information have been supplied.

"I'm sorry I didn't get the projected sales figures finished on time, Mr. Emmett. Here's an excuse from my wife."

Source: Reprinted by permission: Tribune Media Services.

▲ REPORT PARTS

The type of report a writer chooses to prepare determines the parts included in the report. Reports may include several standard and optional parts.

Standard Parts

The two standard parts of a report are the title and body. The **title** is the main heading of the report. It concisely describes the subject or topic of the report. The **body** is the core of the report; it may contain headings, text, and graphics.

The writer declares the purpose of the report in the body. The writer identifies a question to be answered or a problem to be solved, defines the question or problem, and defines the scope and limitations of the report. The writer should explain why a question was asked or how a problem was identified by discussing briefly the background or situation that led to the question or problem. The writer should describe the methods used for collecting and analyzing the data and then present the data or findings. The key findings should be presented in a summary. A writer should include conclusions or deductions based on the findings along with recommendations that answer the original question or solve the original problem stated at the outset of the report. Depending on the length and scope of the report, the body may be divided into several sections. Decisions concerning the division and order of the sections within a report are based on the writer's interpretation of the reader's interest and needs as well as on standardized formats.

The title and body are standard parts of a report.

Optional Parts

Optional parts include the cover or title page, an abstract, a preface, a contents page, a list of tables or figures, headings, reference citations, a reference list, an appendix, and an index.

The title page, abstract, preface, contents page, list of tables, and list of figures are optional preliminary parts of a report; they are positioned before the body of the report. The **cover** or **title page** lists the title of the report, the identification of the person who authorized the report (if applicable), the writer, and the date. An **abstract** is a brief description or synopsis of the topics addressed in the report. Abstracts are often limited to a few paragraphs and are seldom over a page long. Businesses that routinely enter abstracts into computerized document data bases may limit

The title page, abstract, preface, contents page, list of tables, and list of figures appear before the body.

abstracts to 100 words and require the writers to provide a key word or descriptor list to identify major topics in a report. A *preface* is a short statement used to introduce the report. It follows the title page but precedes the contents page. The *contents page* or table of contents is an outline of the report, with corresponding page numbers for locating the various sections within the report. It helps the reader find specific sections of interest quickly. The contents page is prepared after the report is completely written so that correct page numbers are used. The *list of tables* or *list of figures* is a sequential itemization of the tables or figures included in the report. The list usually includes the number, title, and page number of each table or figure.

Headings and reference citations appear in the body of a report.

Headings and reference citations are optional parts which appear in the body of the report. *Headings* or topic titles may be used to identify related information grouped in sections. Headings help the communicator organize information, and they help the reader locate and read information within a report. All headings in the body must also appear in the contents page. *Reference citations* or entries used to give credit to the original source of quoted, paraphrased, or text material are included in the body of a report when applicable.

The reference list, appendix, and index appear after the body.

The reference list, appendix, and index are optional parts which succeed or follow the body of the report. The *reference list* is an alphabetic array of sources whose information was used in the report or related to the report topic. An *appendix* is a collection of supplemental material related to the report; it usually appears before the index at the end of a report. Material included in an appendix may interest some readers, but such material is not essential to understanding the findings or recommendations in the body of an analytical report. In many reports, data are summarized in the body; and the bulky details, such as supplemental graphics and step-by-step analytical procedures, are placed in an appendix. A report may have several appendixes. Generally materials are grouped; related or grouped materials appear in the same appendix. The *index* is an alphabetic listing of key topics or items that are mentioned in the report and the page numbers indicating where they can be found in the report. Indexes are helpful aids for finding information on a specific topic, but they are not often included in reports because they are time-consuming to prepare.

▲ COMMON REPORT FORMATS

Reports vary in length and formality. The longer the report, the more parts it generally contains. Likewise, the more parts a report contains, the more formal it is. Reports may be classified as informal or formal.

Informal Reports _____

Research shows managers use short informational reports more frequently than any other form of report.[2] Managers also write short reports more often than they write long reports. Short reports tend to be routine; they help managers perform their respective planning and controlling functions. Three kinds of informal reports are form, memorandum, and letter reports.

Form, memorandum, and letter reports are examples of informal reports.

Form Report

The *form report* is the most streamlined report format; it involves the reporting of standardized, routine, and/or repetitive data on a printed sheet. The purpose and scope of a form report are defined by the blanks that are to be completed. The title of the report should be printed on the form. Examples of data commonly reported in a form report are expense reports and medical insurance claim reports.

Memorandum Report

A *memorandum report* is a short report prepared in memorandum format for use within an organization. Figure 16–1 is an example of a memorandum report. The title of the report is placed in the *Subject* line. The receiver and the preparer are identified in the *To* and *From* lines. Memorandum reports are widely used for brief communications such as status reports and responses to specific queries.

The title of a memorandum report appears in the *Subject* line.

Usually paragraphs of a memorandum report are short, and the writer's tone is informal. First- and second-person pronouns are commonly used.[3] The direct or indirect approach may be used depending on whether the primary purpose is to inform or to persuade. Specific references to secondary research sources are omitted.

Letter Report

A *letter report* is a short report prepared in letter format for audiences external to the organization. A letter report is often more substantial and systematic than a letter. Often headings are used to identify different sections in the letter report. Introductory and summary sections are common. Figure 16–2 on page 296 is an example of a letter report.

Headings may be used in letter reports.

Formal Report _____

A *formal report* is a manuscript report which usually includes a combination of standard and optional parts. It is usually prepared for upper management within an organization, but it may be prepared for other readers as well. A formal report should be prepared as a complete, independent

Kadell Desh Company

INTEROFFICE MEMORANDUM

TO: Trent Stober, Project Engineer

FROM: Jill Cowley, Project Engineer   *JC*

DATE: March 4, 19--

SUBJECT: Morange-Rill Tag Printer Acquisition

The Project Engineering Department has just acquired a Morange-Rill Tag Printer. This system is part of our new inventory tracking system. Ned Stein and Chess Grogan will be conducting a test program on the system over the next few weeks.

Major features of the Morange-Rill Tag System are as follows:

Hardware Description

The printer system consists of an operator interface device with a 20-character alphanumeric display, a 16-button keypad, and a dot matrix tag printer. This equipment is configured near the roll winder and is connected to one of the on-line programmable controllers.

General Operating Description

The printer system can track in-process inventory and automatically produce finished roll, box, and pallet tags. The proposed tag can carry two kinds of information: clear (human readable) data for plant personnel and bar-coded data for other processes.

Clear data. Clear data are information printed for roll identification. These data include the roll number, date and time, roll length, operator code, roll width, and product code.

Bar-coded data. Bar-coded data include the Code 39 start character, roll number, and product code. These data also include roll width, roll length, and the Code 39 stop character.

Tag Print Routine

In normal operation the roll tags are printed automatically, starting as soon as the roll cut is made. The program produces two tags, one for the roll and a second for the laboratory sample. The program checks for the operator-entered data and does not continue its print routine if these data are omitted.

FIGURE 16–1 Memorandum Report

Trent Stober   2   March 4, 19--

Tag Reprint Routine

The operator can call for a reprint of the last set of tags
by entering '3' at the '(*)CODE(*)?' display (13). The
program then reprints the range roll tag set using the most
recent input. This routine may be used if the first set of
tags is damaged or if it contains incorrect product code or
roll-width data. Entering the correct data and calling for
a reprint will produce a correct set of tags.

Summary

We will begin the testing of the recently acquired Morange-
Rill Tag System next week and complete it within a few weeks.
We will evaluate these main system characteristics: the
operator interface, tag printing, and tag readability.

mas

pc Ned Stein
   Chess Grogan

FIGURE 16–1   (Continued)

Custom Material Handling

1821 Tremont Stelley Street
Lancaster, CA 93402-8322
(415) 555-4820

April 3, 19--

Mr. Trace Roseman, President
Acme Distributors, Inc.
9810 Jerome Road
Cincinnati, OH 45218-4450

Dear Mr. Roseman:

WAREHOUSE PROJECT FIRST QUARTER STATUS REPORT

Work on the design of the Acme Distributors warehouse continues to go well. We anticipate completing the design of your Cleveland warehouse by the end of the year.

System Hardware

System layout drawings were approved during the February design review meeting. Our drafting department is slightly behind schedule; but we still expect to have the mechanical, structural, and electrical drawings ready for the May design review meeting.

System Software

Software design is ahead of schedule. Your personnel did an excellent job in preparing a functional specification. Since the February design meeting, we have completed the design of the operator screens and procedures. Next week we will send you copies of these completed designs. We have started coding the approved inventory management functions.

Demonstration Facility

The Laser bar-coded scanners have finally arrived and have passed the prescribed quality acceptance tests. We plan to work some overtime at our expense to catch up and be ready for the demonstration facility's June 1 start-up date.

Summary

The project is essentially on schedule and within budget. The next milestone is the May design review meeting.

Please let me know if you have any questions about the progress during the first quarter. I look forward to seeing you at the May meeting.

Sincerely,

George Westbrook

George Westbrook, Project Engineer

jeb

FIGURE 16–2 Letter Report

business document. However, a **transmittal memo** or **transmittal letter** usually accompanies a formal report when it is transmitted to the reader. Figure 16–3 illustrates a transmittal memo.

Formal reports may range from short to long. A short report has ten or fewer pages.[4] Figure 16–4 represents a formal informational report. It contains both standard report parts and several of the optional parts commonly included in a formal report.

Optional preliminary parts in many formal reports are a title page and a contents page. A list of tables or figures is included if there are multiple graphics in the report.

The body of a formal report opens with an introduction. Typically, the introduction provides some background information, describes the purpose of the report, sets the limits of the report, and explains the presentation of data.

In a formal report written in the direct approach, the introduction contains the primary and secondary sources of information and provides a recommended solution to the problem or recommended courses of action.

> Formal reports may be short or long.

Milicent Industries   **INTEROFFICE MEMORANDUM**

TO: Wilma Underwood, Personnel Manager

FROM: Jon Creech, Associate Systems Analyst JC

DATE: June 2, 19--

SUBJECT: Transmittal of Corporate Education Report

Here is the report you asked me to write concerning corporate education. In the report, I provide a recommendation for our company, synthesize trends of consequence, describe the corporate university, and review the relationship between academia and business.

Please let me know if additional information is needed pertaining to this topic. I am eager to get your feedback about the report.

mp

Attachment

FIGURE 16–3 Transmittal Memo

CORPORATE EDUCATION OF THE FUTURE

Jon Creech

Milicent Industries

June 2, 19--

Source: Kenneth H. Hess, Jr., "Corporate Education of the Future" (Unpublished manuscript, The University of Georgia, March, 1986).

FIGURE 16–4   Formal Report

CONTENTS

FIGURE 16–4   (Continued)

CORPORATE EDUCATION OF THE FUTURE

As our company prepares to start its own educational program, I suggest that management take a close look at trends which affect education in general. Secondary sources of information were used for this report. American education has seen a major participant in its educational system become its largest participant in recent years. This participant in American education is the corporation. For a number of reasons, corporations in this country have found their way into the educational circles of our nation. Their investments into education have reached the rate of billions of dollars per year, and every indication points to a continuation and growth of this investment.

Trends of Consequence

As we consider the future role that corporations will play in American education, we must consider several trends. It is these trends that will place pressure upon both public and private sectors of education and, thus, will direct their futures.

The first trend that will greatly affect corporate education is the recent number of mergers and buy outs within the corporations of America. Large and small businesses alike have been involved in corporate mergers. In 1983 alone, some 2,533 mergers took place (Butler, 1984, 42). These mergers involved $73.1 billion (Butler, 1984, 42). The number of mergers is likely to increase. Pending legislation is before the House of Representatives in Washington, DC, which will allow such mergers to take place more easily. The simple fact that corporations are merging is not the important fact, but the consequences of these mergers is. As these corporate mergers continue to occur, larger corporate giants are created. In the past, it has been the corporate giants who have led the way in the area of private-sector education. With more and more of these very large corporations in existence, it is most predictable that corporate education will continue to grow.

Due to the growing number of corporate giants, competition between these large companies becomes greater. Competition increases for larger shares of the marketplace and for the better employees. As competition grows, corporations become aware of the need to protect and invest in their "human capital." Thus, the second trend is the new awareness of the value of the employee as an asset and resource. Although no dollar value can be placed on the value of the employee, it is now being recognized as the corporation's number one asset. It is this asset, if made creative and visionary, that will provide a corporation

FIGURE 16—4   (Continued)

2

with a lead over other like companies. That is why corporations have invested in excess of $40 billion per year in employee education (Eurich, 1985, 8).

A third trend that has had a profound effect on corporate education is the status of public education. Throughout the 1970s and early 1980s, American education produced an inferior product. Corporations found themselves hiring individuals who could hardly read or write, and who had difficulty in communicating with other employees and customers. Corporations have spent millions of dollars on such classes as remedial reading, remedial math, introduction to writing, and effective speech (Eurich, 1985, 48). It should be noted that corporations did not seek to get involved in the educational field but had to out of necessity. It was due to such deficiencies in employees that corporations were forced to create such classes. Despite the successes of corporate classes, corporations still do not seek to enter the educational field to be in direct competition with the public sector of education.

Some may argue that recent reports such as "A Nation at Risk" and other ideas such as the "Minnesota Plan" will result in an improved product on the part of public education. But history need only remind us of the past Sputnik push in our educational system. Faced with the threat of Russian superiority, we cried for a "back to the basics" emphasis. Within a decade we had seen the pendulum swing away from that emphasis and enter a more creative and permissive type of education, which has resulted in today's inferior product. Reality tells us that such a trend will occur again in the next few years.

A fourth trend is the reality of a growing global market. American corporations must compete against the likes of Japan, Europe, and South America. Our employees must compete with the employees of those corporations represented in those countries. Currently our employees are not superior by any means. In 1980, 95 percent of Japanese teenagers graduated from high school, while only 74 percent of Americans did (Burke, 1985, 149). Europeans spend longer days and more total days per year in school than Americans. If our public system does not bridge the gap between our system and the systems of other nations, the corporation will have to do it for itself. Along with the internationalization of business comes the need for training employees how to deal with these other countries. Corporations must be able to send effective employees abroad to handle business transactions and other dealings for their country. The employee must be able to understand foreign governments, foreign priorities, and foreign languages in order to be effective for his or her company. Some training must take place before this can happen.

A fifth trend that will affect corporate education is the federal efforts to balance the budget. If billions of dollars are to be cut, it is unlikely that more money will be available to spend

FIGURE 16—4   (Continued)

3

on new educational programs, student loans, and improved instruction. These deficiencies, as well, will have to be picked up by the
private sector. This will not only affect corporate education but
will also increase the amount of contributions that will be needed
from the business sector to meet the needs of the public schools and
colleges.

A sixth trend is the continued growth and explosion of new
technology in the business field. Almost daily, new equipment is
introduced into the business world. It is difficult for public
education to keep up with these changes due to restrictions on fund-
ing. Therefore, the corporation finds it necessary to train its own
people on the newly developed equipment. Time considerations also
tell us that businesses cannot possibly wait until the public sector
trains these people. This is one situation that is not likely to
change any time soon.

The individual effect of any one of these trends would be significant when considering corporate education of the future. But
when all six of these trends are considered, the result is profound.
Out of these trends, two major events will occur: the growth of
corporate universities and the closer association of business with
public education. Most corporations will only be involved with one
of these two events. Larger corporations will find it to their
benefit to develop large corporate schools for themselves. Medium
and small corporations will find it best to cooperate with the
public sector.

The Corporate University

The fact that American workers are going back to school is not
new by any means. American workers have been going back to school
for years. Only the scope and location of this training are new.
Millions of adults are now involved in some type of schooling, a lot
of which takes place within the corporation. Figure 1 shows the
growth in American corporation educational expenses over the last
four decades. In-house corporate education has quietly grown into
a major educational institution. In 1982, it was estimated that
total corporate enrollment reached the total enrollment of America's
public and private four-year colleges and universities (Eurich,
1985, 1).

Such companies as AT&T ($1.7 billion in 1980) and IBM ($500
million in 1982) enroll a combined one million employees per year
in corporate classes (Eurich, 1985, 6). Other companies, like
McDonald's, Holiday Inn, and Xerox, have created their own universities with complete campuses and elaborate facilities (Eurich, 1985,
6). The Wang Institute of Graduate Studies has a 200-acre campus
in Massachusetts. Xerox's Learning Center, located in Leesburg,
Virginia, serves more than 3,000 students at one time (Eurich,
1985, 6).

FIGURE 16–4   (Continued)

4

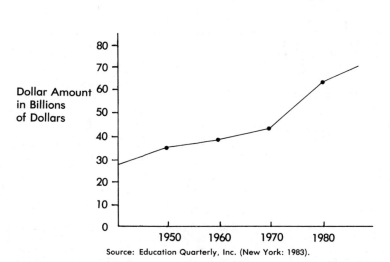

Source: Education Quarterly, Inc. (New York: 1983).

Figure 1 American Corporation Educational Expenses

    The most traditional type of education in the corporation has
been company-oriented education. This type of education is used to
indoctrinate both old and new employees to the particular ways of
that corporation. Compensatory education is used to make up for
deficiencies in employee skills such as reading, writing, and math.
Some companies even use corporate education as a recruiting tool,
offering employees opportunity for degrees in exchange for signing
on with their company. Most all of these classes are taught by
corporate instructors, thus allowing that particular corporation
to retain control of all input. Many instructors serve part-time
as managers and part-time as instructors.

    Curriculum includes basic skills instruction, management and
executive training, technical study, service and customer training,
and just general education. General courses include such topics as
interpersonal relations, self-assessment, and personal finance.
Other courses have been developed to help the employee deal with
self-image problems, such as how to handle growing old. Many corporate institutions now offer their own degrees. The Rand Graduate
Institute offers its own Ph.D., which is a well-respected program
(Eurich, 1985, 8). The Wang Institute of Graduate Studies offers
a Masters of Software Engineering (MSE) (Eurich, 1985, 48).

    <u>The future of corporate schools</u>. The future of corporate
colleges and universities is bright. In a recent speech by Lloyd
B. Dennis, senior vice-president of the First Interstate Bank of
California, he stated that by 1989, 13 more corporations will offer

FIGURE 16–4   (Continued)

5

a combined total of 28 more college level degree programs (Frey, 1984, 639). With this rate of growth, it is not unlikely that we could see as many as 100 or more new corporate schools by the year 2010 (Frey, 1984, 639). There is little doubt that corporate presidents and managers are discovering that they can produce a better product in the workplace than they can by giving outside sources a prerequisite for the student and hoping for the best results.

    <u>The future of corporate curriculum</u>. Curriculum in the corporate school will expand in a few areas, but will remain fairly similar to the five areas discussed earlier. One area of expansion will be in the area of international training. Employees will need to understand other languages, cultures, and governments. As the global market expands, so will the need for this type of instruction.

The Academic-Business Relationship

    The largest single change in the next 25 years affecting corporations will occur in the relationship that businesses have with post-secondary public institutions. This will be most evident in the realm of small- to medium-sized corporations. Large corporations will continue to develop their own colleges and universities, but the smaller corporations will seek a different road due to lack of enormous amounts of capital with which to develop their own schools. Some experts estimate that nearly half the current work force will need retraining by the turn of the century. Medium- and small-sized corporations do not have the in-house means by which to retrain all their people. They will be forced to seek an outside source for this training.

    Joint efforts between business and academia have been suggested and tried in the past. Success has been limited for several reasons: (1) businesses have not been satisfied with the product that academia has been able to produce; (2) academia has failed to listen to business needs; (3) there has been a difference in purpose and philosophy; (4) there has been a difference in goals (profit versus knowledge and truth). The second two will be difficult to overcome, but there are also reasons why these two are likely to be conquered (Burke, 1985, 149).

    Corporations and public academic centers need to cooperate with one another. Both need some of the benefits that the other party has to offer. Corporations need the training and people that public institutions have to offer. Academia needs enrollment and funding for equipment from businesses. With declining enrollment in public post-secondary schools, public colleges and universities will seek to increase their enrollments via the corporation's efforts to train their employees. Public colleges and universities could develop specific programs for a corporation by seeking just what the corporation needed to accomplish with its employees. Such joint programs could be developed to benefit both sides. Until now,

FIGURE 16–4 (Continued)

6

businesses have generally given grants for equipment and scholar-
ships. But the future will need more than just money for equipment.

Something new has begun to happen between corporations and
post-secondary public colleges and universities. For the first
time, a corporation and a community technical college have become
involved in a joint venture to benefit each other. In Greenville,
South Carolina, the Michelin Tire Corporation and the Greenville
Technical College have joined in a venture to build a training
facility. Michelin and Greenville TEC plan to build an $800,000
building on the campus of Greenville TEC (Greenville News, March 4,
1986, B1). The building will be used by both parties. Michelin
will pay $500,000 of the building cost, plus provide the equipment
and furnishings for the building (Greenville News, March 4, 1986,
B1). Greenville TEC will make up the remaining $300,000 (Greenville
News, March 4, 1986, B1). Michelin will use the facility as a
technical training center for its manufacturing division. Michelin
employs between 6,000 and 7,000 employees in South Carolina, most
of whom require ongoing training (Greenville News, March 4, 1986,
B1). Greenville TEC will use the facility as its training and
retraining center (Greenville News, March 4, 1986, B1). This is
just one way in which both parties can benefit by cooperating with
one another.

Summary

American education has seen the corporation become its largest
participant. These trends place pressure upon the public and
private sectors of education. These trends include the recent
number of mergers and buy outs in American corporations, new awareness of the value of the employee, the status of public education,
the reality of a growing global market, federal efforts to balance
the budget, and continued growth and explosion of new technology in
business. As a result of these trends, two major events will occur:
the growth of corporate universities and the closer association of
business with public education. Large corporations will develop
corporate schools while medium- and small-sized corporations will
cooperate with the public sector.

FIGURE 16–4   (Continued)

7

REFERENCES

Aburdene, Patricia, and Naisbitt, John. <u>Re-inventing the Corpora-</u>
     <u>tion</u>. New York: Warner Books, Inc., 1985.

Anderson, Wayne C. "Academia and Business." <u>Vital Speeches of the</u>
     <u>Day</u>, October 1, 1985, 57-60.

Breakey, John. "When Companies Tell Business Schools What to
     Teach." <u>Business Week</u>, February 10, 1986, 60-61.

Burke, Joseph C. "The Academic-Business Partnership." <u>Vital</u>
     <u>Speeches of the Day</u>, November 15, 1985, 148-150.

Butler, David. "How the New Merger Boom Will Benefit the Economy."
     <u>Business Week</u>, February 6, 1984, 42-43.

Dennis, Lloyd B. "Bridging the Gap Between Corporate Public Affairs
     and Academia." <u>Vital Speeches of the Day</u>, January 15, 1986,
     758-761.

Eurich, Nell P. <u>Corporate Classrooms: The Learning Business</u>.
     Lawrenceville: Princeton University Press, 1985.

Frey, Donald N. "Developing Corporate Classrooms." <u>Vital Speeches</u>
     <u>of the Day</u>, August 1, 1984, 637-640.

Johnson, C. W. "Meeting Technology and Human Resource Needs."
     <u>Vital Speeches of the Day</u>, February 1, 1986, 719-722.

Manasee, Geoff. "Business Schools Try to Churn Out Entrepreneurs."
     <u>Business Week</u>, March 5, 1984, 102.

"Michelin TEC to Build Training Center." <u>Greenville News</u>, 4 March
     1986, B1.

Naisbitt, John. <u>Megatrends</u>. New York: Warner Books, Inc., 1982.

Ruffin, Santee C. "School-Business Partnerships." <u>Education</u>
     <u>Digest</u>, March 1984, 57-60.

FIGURE 16–4   (Continued)

Limitations or constraints experienced when conducting or interpreting the research may be included in the introduction. In addition, the writer may wish to incorporate assumptions or premises on which the findings are based and special definitions which clarify the terms used in the report. An overview of the major sections of the report may also be included in the introduction.

In analytical formal reports, the solution or recommendation is usually withheld until the end of the body; if the solution or recommendation *is* stated in the introduction, it appears in the form of a hypothesis to be tested or a question to be answered. However, analytical reports *can* be written in direct order: introduction, conclusions, discussion, and findings.

The remaining body of a formal report contains findings and details of the research conducted for the report. Headings are used to divide the body into related sections. Reference citations may be used throughout the body to indicate sources of secondary research data. The body may include graphics as well as text. Graphics mentioned in the text should be introduced prior to their appearance in the report; they are usually referred to by number and/or title. Text descriptions of graphics should highlight their contents.

A formal report may end after sharing the researched findings. Generally the body of a long report ends with a **summary** or brief restatement of the major findings. Some writers choose to include conclusions and recommendations at the end of the body. Conclusions are inferences or decisions reached based on the findings or facts; recommendations are preferred solutions or courses of action. When the direct approach is used in a long formal report, recommendations appear in the introduction so that only a summary and/or conclusions need appear at the end of the body. When the indirect approach is used, the writer should structure the end of a formal report so that it includes a summary, conclusions, and recommendations.

A reference list should appear after the body of a formal report. Other optional parts such as an appendix and an index may be included after the references of a long report.

▲ GUIDELINES FOR REPORT PREPARATION

Reports should not only be well written but also well arranged. The appearance of a finished report should reflect favorably on the professionalism of the writer. An attractive report which fits a page like a picture in a

Well-arranged reports give impressions of competency.

Numerous formats may be used to present the information in a report.

These guidelines provide for an effective report layout.

frame will help communicate the message as well as leave the reader with a positive image of the writer's company.

While style manuals describe a variety of acceptable report formats, the following guidelines provide some basic information for the layout of a conventional report:

1. *Side margins.* As a general rule, 1-inch side margins are used for all pages. If the report is to be bound along the left edge, a 1 1/2-inch left margin is recommended.

2. *Top margin.* The first page of a report should have a top margin of about 2 inches. The second and subsequent pages of the report should have a top margin of about 1 inch. If the report is to be bound along the top edge, an extra 1/2 inch should be provided at the top of all pages to allow for binding.

3. *Pagination.* The first page of a report is usually not numbered. On the second and subsequent pages, the page number is placed on line 6 at the right margin; the text continues on line 8.

4. *Main heading.* The main heading or title of a report is centered 2 inches below the top edge of the first page. The heading is displayed in capital letters. If the heading extends beyond one line, the second line should be shorter than the first line; the lines may either be single-spaced or double-spaced. The main heading also appears on the title page.

5. *Body.* The body or text of the report begins three blank lines below the main heading. The paragraphs of the body are usually double-spaced to improve readability; however, some organizations prefer to use single-spacing, particularly for long reports. In the latter format, double-spacing is used between paragraphs.

6. *Side headings.* Side headings indicate the major subdivisions of the main heading. They are placed on separate lines at the left margin with a double space above and below them. They are shown in capital-and-lowercase letters (first and important words capitalized) and are underlined for emphasis.

7. *Paragraph headings.* Paragraph headings indicate subdivisions of the main idea presented by the side heading. They are indented five spaces from the left margin, are shown with only the first and proper names capitalized, are underlined, and end with a period. The text of the report follows the heading on the same line two spaces after the period.

8. *Reference citations.* Three methods for citing sources consulted or quoted in the body of a report are widely used: internal citation/reference list, endnotes, and footnotes/bibliography.

Internal citations include the last name(s) of the author(s), the year of publication, and the page number(s) in parentheses. If the citation appears at the end of a sentence, a period is placed after the closing parenthesis:

> Tardiness and absenteeism are serious problems for the administrative manager (Kelling and Kallaus, 1983, 282).

If the author's name appears in the text, only the date and page number(s) in parentheses are used:

> According to Smith, Alexander, and Medley (1986, 95–96), "Manual filing systems, then, are maintained for backup and to meet legal record-keeping requirements."

For more than three authors, the following style is used:

> A carefully written report requires one or more rough drafts (Popham et al., 1983, 481).

When the internal citation method is used, a section entitled *REFERENCES* is provided at the end of the report. The references are arranged alphabetically by the author's last name or by the first important word in the title if there are no authors. Figure 16–4 shows the internal citation/reference list method.

In the endnotes method, superior (raised) reference figures are used throughout the text. The number-matched notes are listed numerically at the end of the report in a section entitled *ENDNOTES*. Endnote referencing is used in each chapter of this book.

The footnotes/bibliography method requires the use of superior (raised) footnote reference figures at appropriate points within the text. The matching-number footnotes are listed at the bottom of the page on which the reference figures appear. All references cited in the footnotes (plus relevant general references) are arranged alphabetically at the end of the report in a section entitled *BIBLIOGRAPHY*.

▲ INFLUENCE OF TECHNOLOGY ON REPORT PREPARATION

Information processing technology has simplified the task of report preparation. From the early 1970s to the early 1980s, word processing functions were performed on **dedicated word processing,** equipment designed only to process text material. In the early 1980s, microcomputer-based word

Ways of producing written reports are changing.

processing took a giant leap forward to replace dedicated equipment. Microcomputers are popular in the business sector because of their low cost and their ability to handle both word processing and data processing applications.

A wide variety of word processing software packages are now available for most types of microcomputers. These software packages are designed for the manipulation of text material before being printed. Some of the special features of word processing software systems allow the user to

Word processing improves the efficiency of report preparation.

▲ Automatically move the text from one spot in a report to another spot.
▲ Quickly change or delete errors in the report.
▲ Automatically locate and replace words or phrases that are repeated throughout a report and that must be changed.
▲ Automatically align or justify the right margin of a report as it is printed.
▲ Automatically number the pages of a report.
▲ Automatically generate the index of a report.
▲ Locate misspelled words with a programmed spelling dictionary.
▲ Place in alphabetical or numerical order columns or lists of information.
▲ Automatically renumber and reposition revised footnotes.
▲ Quickly change the format of a report.

Microcomputer systems now make it easy to produce high-quality reports with both text and graphics.

Report preparation systems are now available which make it easy to produce documents containing text, data, and graphics. These systems not only produce typeset-quality reports, but they also perform electronic filing, printing, and mailing functions all at the same workstation.[5]

SUMMARY

Reports are written and read so that people have information for making decisions. Report writing requires thinking; thought must be given to the purpose for writing, the reader's needs, and the reader's desires.

The main objective of most reports is to provide information for answering a question or solving a problem. Either the writer or a reader may initiate a report. If someone other than the writer requests that a report be prepared, the initiator of the report should tell the writer the intended purpose of the report.

Generally research is conducted to answer the question or solve the problem and subsequently fulfill the purpose of writing a report. Writers may conduct primary or secondary research in report writing. Primary research is first-hand research or research that has not been conducted previously. Data may be obtained through experimentation, observation, or survey study. Secondary research involves indirect investigation of a topic. Writers who conduct secondary research may obtain data through a variety of printed, audio, and video sources.

Report writing should incorporate the fundamentals of the writing process and the elements of effective writing. When possible, reports should use active, concrete, concise, and objective language.

The type of report a writer prepares depends on the purpose for which the report is written. Other variables such as time of year, progress or lack of progress to date, client inquiries, or questions and directives from higher management may also affect the type of report that a writer prepares. Generally the writer prepares a report to inform or to persuade the reader.

Writers may prepare informational or analytical reports. An informational report provides data for the reader to analyze and interpret. This type of report is based primarily on secondary research, writer experience, or writer knowledge. An analytical report provides the reader with data, data analysis, conclusions, and recommendations. Problem-solving skills are needed for writing an effective analytical report.

Report writing is influenced by expected reader reaction. Although any type of report may be written in direct order, a direct approach is usually used when preparing informational reports. An indirect approach is typically used for analytical reports. An analytical report may be written using a direct approach if someone other than the writer initiates the report based on needing or wanting to know the writer's recommendations on a topic. However, an indirect approach is generally used when the writer initiates the report and anticipated reader reaction is negative or when reader persuasion is needed.

Standard report parts are the title and body. Optional report parts include the cover or title page, an abstract, a preface, a contents page, a list of tables or figures, headings, reference citations, a reference list, an appendix, and an index.

Report formats range from informal to formal. Popular informal report formats are the form report, the memorandum report, and the letter report. These informal formats contain standard report parts. Writers may also prepare short formal reports and long formal reports which consist of various combinations of standard and optional parts.

Reports should be well written and well arranged. The appearance of the formal report should reflect favorably on the professionalism of the writer.

Technology continues to simplify report preparation. A wide variety of information processing software packages have been designed and are now available for manipulation of text material prior to printing a report. Many of the stages of report preparation previously considered complicated and time-consuming have been made simple and time efficient. Report preparation systems are now available to produce and assemble documents containing text, data, and graphics.

QUESTIONS

1. What is a business report?
2. What is meant by this statement: "The effectiveness of any report depends on how useful it is to the reader"?
3. Describe the kinds of research conducted for report writing.
4. Contrast informational reports and analytical reports.
5. List and define the standard parts of a report.
6. Identify the optional parts of a report.
7. How do memorandum reports and letter reports differ from formal reports?
8. What purpose do paragraph headings serve?
9. What is the difference between footnotes and endnotes?
10. What is the advantage of producing a report on information processing equipment?

PROBLEM-SOLVING EXPERIENCES

1. Prepare a memorandum report for your instructor. Use your progress or status thus far in the communication class as your report topic.
2. Prepare a short formal report describing your proposed occupation. Include the following optional parts in your report: a cover page, a con-

tents page, and a reference list. Also, incorporate one figure or table in your report.

3. Prepare a letter report describing the highlights of your proposed occupation. Write the letter to a person interested in your occupational area of study. Use the following headings: job description, work environment, areas of specialization, employment trends, and summary. Include a figure showing employment data for 1960–1990.

CASE 16–1

Susan Cortez is a tour coordinator for Dream Trips Travel in New York City. She has been asked to conduct primary research and put together a vacation plan for Mr. Jennings Brady, an important client company's vice-president. (His address is DeRanch International, DeRanch Tower, Suite 18731, Little Rock, AR 72204–6900.) Mr. Brady will spend a week in the local area on business; he plans to bring his wife and combine a vacation with the business trip.

Susan has written local businesses asking for information on accommodations, unique restaurants, and attractions. She indicated that Mr. Brady is particularly interested in historical sites and natural scenery.

1. Assuming that you are Susan, write a letter report describing the facilities and room rates for at least three hotels in the area. Also provide brief descriptions of three interesting restaurants and at least three attractions that are within an hour's drive of the city.

ENDNOTES

[1]Marie E. Flatley, "A Comparative Analysis of the Written Communication of Managers at Various Organizational Levels in the Private Business Sector," *The Journal of Business Communication*, Vol. 19, No. 3 (Summer, 1982), p. 43.

[2]Ibid., pp. 44–45.

[3]March C. Bromage, *Writing for Business* (Ann Arbor: The University of Michigan Press, 1980), p. 83.

[4]Ibid., p. 75.

[5]Two high-performance, single-user workstations designed to support a variety of report applications are the Xerox 6085 Professional Computer System and the NBI Integrated Workstation.

17

M A N U A L S

Well-designed, well-written manuals are important communication tools in today's complex organizations. Research shows that manuals are a practical way of communicating large amounts of detailed, work-related information to employees over long periods of time.[1]

▲ THE IMPORTANCE OF MANUALS

A *manual* is a guidebook that gives instructions or reference information. Manuals are important to organizations; they communicate standardized information to employees and external audiences such as clients or consumers with whom the organization interrelates. Manuals encourage a common understanding of information. Sharing standardized information in manual form can reduce duplication of that information in other written communications. When properly used, a manual can enhance the continuity and uniformity of an organization's operations through effective communication.

Manuals communicate standardized information.

An organization may use manuals to provide instructions to its members on how to function properly within the organization. Manuals usually identify the organization's responsibilities to its members and its members' responsibilities to the organization. Management can also use manuals to specify the organization's official operating policies in matters such as ethics, structure and management, personnel evaluation and compensation, employee benefits, employment policies and procedures, health and safety, and methods for resolving grievances.

Many organizations use manuals as training tools, textbooks, or references in educational programs. These manuals generally focus on specialized topics relevant to specific persons or groups. They are used to train persons in new skill areas or to teach greater efficiency and professionalism in existing areas. Manuals may be designed for client use as well. Many organizations use manuals to instruct clients in using their products or services.

Although managers primarily write manuals for others to use, they also rely on manuals for fulfilling managerial functions. Manuals are valuable guides for planning, organizing, leading, and controlling an organization's performance.[2]

Manuals are useful tools for fulfilling managerial functions.

▲ CHARACTERISTICS OF MANUALS

When preparing manual material, managers should incorporate the elements of effective writing described in Chapter 11. The purpose for writing a manual is restrictive. Unlike memos, letters, and reports which may be written for the purposes of informing, persuading, or entertaining, manuals are written *only* for the purpose of informing.

Manuals inform.

In addition, anticipated reader reaction is less critical in the development of manuals than in the development of other written communications. Employees and clients read manuals because they need to know particular information. Therefore, the direct approach is used for writing manuals.

A direct approach is used for writing manuals.

Manuals are generally longer than other written communications; consequently, they are not read in their entirety during a single session. Rather, users read only a particular part or group of parts when specific information is needed. For example, an employee who needs to know how to complete a travel expense form will read the travel expense reimbursement section of the procedures manual instead of reading the entire manual. Manual writing should be clear and concise so that each section is understandable.

Manuals are also more durable than other written documents. Typically a company will use a manual for years, whereas an individual will write a letter, memo, or report to satisfy an immediate need. Manuals are written for use by many people; consequently, an impersonal tone should be used for manual writing. Because manuals must withstand repeated use over several years, the physical construction of a manual should be planned carefully. Durable materials such as a strong binding, paper, and dividers or index tabs should be used.

Content

Manuals provide documented standards or criteria that help users comply with recommended action. Clear standards help ensure that the quality of work performed is uniform, regardless of who performs the work; time is not wasted *redeciding* how to accomplish a task.

The content of a manual is based on several variables.

A manager determines the content of a manual by the nature of the organization, the intended users, the type of manual, and the information needed by the users. The manager should define the scope of the manual carefully in order to avoid preparing an all-purpose manual which covers a wide variety of topics. In addition, the manager should write the manual so that it has current and futuristic relevance.

Organizations may wish to copyright their manuals that have potential value for external groups or organizations such as competitors. Copyrighting helps an organization maintain control over the external distribution of a manual.

Manuals may be copyrighted.

Having potential users participate in determining the kinds of information to include in a manual is important; it broadens managerial understanding of users' needs and reading abilities. Although many people may participate in preliminary manual development, the responsibility for manual writing should rest with management. Often human resource or personnel department managers will prepare manuals for their organization. However, the responsibility for manual writing varies within organizations depending on the type of manual being prepared. Only one manager should assume the responsibility of coordinating group input and conceptualizing manual content.

Readability

The readability of a manual should match the reading and interest levels of its readers. Users must be able to get information from a manual without being confused by complex structures. Lengthy manuals may warrant separate sections or versions written for different users. For example, some users may require only a summary of information, while other users may need detailed operating instructions or maintenance procedures.

As described in Chapter 11, managers should write using active voice whenever possible. Manual writing should specify who is to fulfill the instructions. Harmon recommends that managers use precise and unpretentious terms that focus on the message rather than draw attention to the writing style. Managers should express mandatory procedures in the imperative mood.[3] Figure 17–1 demonstrates how to write mandatory instructions using infinitives with *you* understood as the subject.

Write mandatory procedures using the imperative mood.

A manager should use graphics, such as tables or figures, for support or clarification when appropriate. (Examples of various graphics are shown in Chapter 15.) Instructions for properly completing business forms often appear in manuals. Completed forms may be coded using letters or numbers so users can recognize easily key parts and the instructions which correspond to those parts.

Organization

Managers should write manuals so that the topics are easy to locate. As shown in the outline section of Chapter 11, the information should be organized in logical order. Manuals may be organized in alphabetical or

Topics should be easily located in a manual.

COMPLETING A PETTY CASH VOUCHER FORM

1. Keyboard borrower's name in appropriate space on the voucher form.

2. Keyboard borrower's department.

3. Keyboard current date.

4. Keyboard amount borrowed from petty cash.

5. Obtain signature of borrower.

6. Have borrower initial amount withdrawn from petty cash.

7. Submit form in triplicate.

FIGURE 17–1   Instructions in the Imperative Mood

functional order. Reference manuals are often organized in alphabetical order; examples include computer command manuals, dictionaries, and telephone books. Tutorial or instructional manuals are often organized based on the sequential order in which steps or functions are performed. Sequential information is easier to update and revise than information arranged without any apparent organization. A manual's contents page serves as the user's guide for understanding the sequencing of information within the manual. (The parts of a contents page are shown in Chapter 16.) A manual should also contain an introduction which describes the purpose, scope, and organization of the material. If the manual is lengthy, an index may be required to help the user locate information.

Format

A manager should determine the format of a manual before the writing begins but after the organization process. Since format affects readability, the manual's format should support or enhance the intended use of the manual. Appropriate format will result in an easy-to-use manual for the user.

Managers should give special attention to margins, type sizes, and type styles. To draw attention to important points, use boldface printing, underlining, variations in type style, and shaded sections. Small print and multiple columns are acceptable for some specialty manuals such as dictionaries, in which the reader only reads a small section at a time. However, printing a reference manual in a type size that is too large could produce a document that is unusable because of its size. As a rule, companies should prepare training manuals using larger print than reference manuals because longer sections are read during a single session.

Paragraphs may be blocked with white space left between paragraphs to make material easier to read. Block indentation may be used for each level of manual text. Thus, numbers and letters used for part/section identification are easily seen.[4] Use either numeric or alphanumeric section coding and devise the format to limit the levels of detail.

Manual sections should be easily identified.

In most cases, step-by-step listing is preferred instead of long narrative paragraphs. Lengthy paragraphs can be monotonous and cause the user to lose interest in finishing a passage. Some managers use playscript to simplify manual format and enhance readability. **Playscript** refers to the listing of procedures in sequential order with each participant's part distinguished from other participants' parts by using separate rows, columns, or labels. Figure 17–2 shows how playscript can enhance manual format.

Using playscript makes procedures easy to read.

Since a manual may be updated numerous times, its format should facilitate updating. Binding a manual in a loose-leaf binder makes it easy to change pages that are affected by amendments, deletions, or additions. With this format, an individual may use manual pages while out of the main binder, and a company may issue updated pages separate from the master document. Therefore, managers may wish to include identification information in a standardized heading at the top or bottom of each page of a manual.

A standardized heading may be used at the top or bottom of manual pages.

Person Responsible for Action	Action
Employee	1. Draft expense reimbursement form (Form 1098-A).
Secretary	2. Keyboard form.
Supervisor	3. Approve expense reimbursement by signing form.
Secretary	4. Submit completed form to Accounting Department.
Accounting Officer	5. Verify form.
Accounting Officer	6. Authorize reimbursement check.
Finance Officer	7. Write check.
Finance Clerk	8. Mail check to employee.

FIGURE 17–2 Playscript

A standardized heading and pagination can help users organize manual material if pages become jumbled or out of sequence. Information commonly included in a standardized page heading are the company logo, the title of the manual, the title of the document or section, the page number, the department issuing the document, and the issue or effective date. Figure 17–3 shows an acceptable method for arranging standardized page heading information.

PROCEDURES MANUAL

SECTION TITLE External Written Communications		SECTION NO. 12	
DEPARTMENT ISSUING Administrative Services		DATE ISSUED 04-03-87	PAGE 12-1

FIGURE 17–3   Page Heading

Consecutive pagination in each section adds flexibility.

A manual may have consecutive page numbers either throughout the manual or within the individual sections. Consecutive pagination throughout a manual is somewhat restrictive; it lacks flexibility for adding updated information unless additions occur only at the end of the manual. Consecutively numbering pages within each individual section allows for more flexibility. For example, the second page of Section 13 is numbered 13–2. One way to add pages without having to completely renumber or reindex a manual is to insert material that is paginated using alphanumeric characters. The characters 13–2a may be used to represent a new page added following page 13–2.

Electronic manuals are now available.

On-line electronic manuals are replacing some paper manuals. Formatting for electronic manuals is generally limited to the features of the software. However, format should be tailored as much as possible to fit the intended use of the manual.

Indexing

The index appears at the end of a manual.

An index is an alphabetized listing of names, terms, and subjects included in a printed document. A manual's index lists the page or pages on which key terms and subjects are mentioned within the manual. The index should appear at the end of the manual. The contents page and index help users locate specific information. A common complaint about an ineffective manual is that there is little or no relationship between the manual's organization or format and the index.[5]

Commonly understood terms should be used in manual text material, and those same terms should appear in the index. The time spent making a thorough index is time well spent. An effective index includes cross-references to similar terms and topics. Some word processing software packages are capable of generating indexes.

An index should also contain commonly used topics and operations in addition to the terms that appear in the manual text. For instance, the control codes for changing a printer's speed might be indexed as *control codes*. However, a user interested in changing the printer's speed might look under *speed* or *printer, speed* first.

A *glossary* or list of complex or specialized words and their definitions may precede the index of a manual. The glossary is a valuable tool for improving the usability of an index and the overall readability of the manual. It provides users with definitions of unfamiliar terms. The glossary may be prepared as manual material is being prepared or after the manual is completed.

> A glossary provides manual users with definitions of unfamiliar terms.

▲ TYPES OF MANUALS

A wide variety of manuals is used throughout both large and small organizations. Some organizations prefer to maintain their manuals as separate documents, while other organizations combine the information from two or more manuals in one binder.[6] The most commonly used manuals are policy manuals, procedures manuals, organization manuals, and specialty manuals.

Policy Manuals

A *policy manual* provides a written record of the regulations that employees are expected to follow. Policy manuals frequently state management's concepts and philosophies with respect to the operation of business affairs.

> A policy manual states the regulations of an organization.

A policy manual is usually a compromise between comprehensive and sketchy treatment. According to Bloom and Dold, "A policy statement can never cover every contingency. A well-written policy should cover *most* possibilities. Policies should not be so broad as to be meaningless, and not so narrow as to stifle initiative."[7]

When policies are formally documented, four major benefits result. The company finds it easier to

▲ Further agreement among management, employees, and units in the organization.

▲ Delegate authority on a sound and clearly understood basis.

▲ Ensure consistency in interpreting the desires of management.
▲ Orient new employees more quickly to the organization and its requirements.

Policy statements should be written such that they are understood by all readers in the same way. The writer should use a simple, readable style. Several employee users should read a policy statement before it is finalized and evaluate the clarity of its contents.

Here are two examples of well-written policy statements:

Please have your personal mail delivered to your home or residence address. Personal mail delivered to the Company may be opened by mistake or delayed in reaching you.

Classified information shall not be transmitted by telephone, by intercommunications systems, or by other means of electronic transmission.

A page from the accounting policy manual of the E. I. Du Pont de Nemours & Company is shown in Figure 17–4.

Procedures Manuals

A *procedures manual* describes how to perform certain work tasks.

A *procedures manual* provides a written explanation of the steps involved in performing certain work tasks. An effective procedural statement is tailored for the end user. For example, "While an engineer may be comfortable with a flowchart, the typical employee prefers a step-by-step format."[8]

There are two general kinds of procedures manuals: one with wide application throughout the organization and the other with specialized application. Examples of organization-wide procedures include filling out a travel request, making local and long-distance telephone calls, and procuring printed forms. Examples of specialized procedures are adding a new account to the general ledger; purchasing tires, tubes, and batteries; and providing legal counsel to employees. Organizations achieve the following results from using procedures manuals:

1. Ensuring consistency in performing repetitive tasks.
2. Improving the training of new employees or experienced employees who have to perform unfamiliar tasks.
3. Enhancing the understanding of the interrelationship between an employee's activities and those of others.

Since procedures are concerned with getting specific jobs done, usually in a series of steps, procedures statements should be precisely and clearly

I. INTRODUCTION

A. Objective and Purpose

The objective of this manual is to establish minimum standards for a satisfactory system of accounting controls applicable to Du Pont locations worldwide. The purpose of such standards is to assist those responsible for establishing and maintaining a system of internal accounting controls at the various sites. Conoco's standards for accounting controls as documented in the manual, "Internal Control Guidelines for Domestic and International Operations," are similar to and consistent with the standards contained in this manual. Accounting controls and related responsibilities for such control systems are discussed below.

B. Accounting Controls

Accounting controls are defined by the American Institute of Certified Public Accountants as follows:

"Accounting controls comprise the plan of organization and the procedures and records that are concerned with the safeguarding of assets and the reliability of financial records and consequently are designed to provide reasonable assurance that:

1. Transactions are executed in accordance with management's general or specific authorization.

2. Transactions are recorded as necessary (1) to permit preparation of financial statements in conformity with generally accepted accounting principles or any other criteria applicable to such statements and (2) to maintain accountability for assets.

3. Access to assets is permitted only in accordance with management's authorization.

4. The recorded accountability for assets is compared with the existing assets at reasonable intervals and appropriate action is taken with respect to any differences."

C. Responsibility

Accounting controls in Du Pont are the responsibility of the Vice President and Comptroller as part of his broad responsibility to the Senior Vice President—Finance for operation of the Company's accounting system.

Source: Finance Department Accounting Control Standards Manual (Wilmington, DE: E. I. Du Pont de Nemours & Company, 1985), p. 1000.

FIGURE 17—4   Policy Manual

stated. Statements should be written at the reader's level of understanding. Before procedures statements are finalized, they should be read and evaluated by several people who will use them.

Here are two examples of well-written procedures statements:

In the presence of a notary public, enter the date and sign your name. The notary public should complete this section, sign his or her name, and affix his or her seal.

Check the proper time and classification in this section. If an employee works less than full-time (40 hours per week), please indicate the percentage of time of employment. For example, twenty hours per week would be 50 percent, thirty hours per week would be 75 percent, and so on.

The procedures followed by The University of Georgia in preparing a job request form for central duplicating service is shown in Figure 17–5.

Organization Manuals

An *organization manual,* sometimes referred to as a company manual, provides a written description of the formal structure of a company. Or-

Procedure Number   .000-5   Preparation Instructions
                                  for ''Job Request for Central Duplicating Service''

The job request form must be prepared by the requesting department. This form should be completed according to the following instructions:

1. Enter requesting department.

2. Enter *correct* account number.

3. Enter the requested information. Check the ''Pick up'' space if you wish the completed work to be held in Central Duplicating for you. Enter the name of someone familiar with the job request.

4. Enter desired delivery date. This date should be realistic and should allow as much time as possible for production. Do not use ASAP (as soon as possible), since it indicates routine processing.

5. Leave this space blank.

Department _____1._____

Account No._____2._____

Room # _____ Bldg._____3._____

Phone No._____

Deliver _____ Pick up _____

JOB REQUEST

For

CENTRAL DUPLICATING SERVICE

Date _____4._____

(For Central Duplicating Use Only)

Job No. _____5._____

Date Promised _____

Date Delivered _____

Source: *Administrative Policies and Procedures Manual,* Business and Finance (Athens, GA: The University of Georgia, 1984), Vol. 2, pp. 552Q–552R.

FIGURE 17–5 Procedures Manual

ganizations use these manuals because it is more efficient to communicate information of this nature in written rather than oral form.

An organization manual explains the company structure.

Organization manuals may contain the following information about a company:

1. Historical information.
2. Organization objectives.
3. Organization charts.
4. Job descriptions for key personnel.
5. Pay plans.
6. Products manufactured or services provided.
7. Fringe benefits.

Organization manuals are often used to help new employees become better acquainted with their company and to show employees how their jobs relate to other jobs. Here are two well-written statements for an organization manual:

The pay plan is a schedule of pay rates arranged in ranges and steps. Each employee is assigned to a range and step based on the job he or she performs.

Under the prescription drug plan, you pay a $3 co-payment per prescription or prescription refill, and the Purple Cross of Oregon pays the balance.

An excerpt from the *Clarke County Employee Handbook,* an organization manual, is shown in Figure 17–6.

PENSION PLAN

You are eligible after one year of employment, for inclusion in the pension plan. The County pays 100% of the cost of your Pension Plan. You may choose:

—*Normal* retirement at age 60 or 62, with 25 years of service.

—*Early* retirement within 5 to 7 years of your normal retirement date and at least 10 years of service.

You should notify the Personnel Department of your intent to retire at least 60 to 90 days in advance. A Pension Plan Book will be provided for you. Please read it carefully. If you should have any questions, be sure to contact the Personnel Department.

Source: *Clarke County Employee Handbook* (Athens, GA: Clarke County, 1986), p. 12.

FIGURE 17–6 Organization Manual

Specialty Manuals _____

A specialty manual contains information about a particular function.

A *specialty manual* contains detailed information about a particular function or process. Specialty manuals are usually unique to a specific department or audience. Examples of specialty manuals are

▲ Training manuals.
▲ Technical manuals.
▲ Computer systems documentation manuals.
▲ Accounting manuals.
▲ Marketing manuals.
▲ Safety manuals.
▲ Security manuals.
▲ Records control manuals.
▲ Assembly manuals.
▲ Operating manuals.
▲ Diagnostic manuals.
▲ Specifications manuals.

A page from a specialty manual of the E. I. Du Pont de Nemours & Company is shown in Figure 17–7.

SUMMARY

A manual is a guidebook that gives instructions or reference information. It communicates standardized information to people inside and outside the organization.

A manager should apply the elements of effective writing in preparing manuals. Unlike other written communications, manuals are written only for the purpose of informing. Usually manuals are not read in their entirety; users read only a particular part when specific information is needed. Consequently, managers should write manuals using a direct approach. Manuals are more durable than other written documents; through updating, their life spans are unlimited.

Determine the content of a manual by the nature of the organization, the intended users, the type of manual, and the information needed by the users. Manuals may be copyrighted so that the organization can maintain control over the external distribution of their

INPUT RECORDS

Introduction	The Stores Management System receives data via 80 character input records or "cards."
Different Record Types	There are 25 different standard input record types. For installations with extra features, such as we-invoicing, there are additional input record types.
How to Input	The Input Transactions section of the manual describes: • when to use the input records • what entries are made to each field in the input records
How to Change Contents of a Field	All input records on SMS can have new data entered to a field simply by entering another input record of the same type having: • the item code (or vendor code) • new entries to any fields that need to be changed OR X's to blank out the field • a "C" or "CM" to the action or change indicator fields • the input record type NOTE: It is not possible to change a field on an item if it is being set up in the same run.

Source: *Information Systems Department Manual,* Stores Management System (Wilmington, DE: E. I. Du Pont de Nemours & Company, 1986), p. 3–1–2.

FIGURE 17–7   Specialty Manual

manuals. Having potential users assist in determining information to include in a manual is important; it broadens managerial understanding of users' needs and reading abilities. The ultimate responsibility for manual writing rests with management.

The readability of a manual should match the reading and interest levels of its users. Write manuals so that the information is organized in logical order. Since format affects readability, the manual's format should support or enhance the intended use of the manual.

The format should also facilitate updating. Managers may include identification information in a standardized heading at the top or bottom of each page of a manual. Formatting for electronic manuals is generally limited to the features of the software.

An index should appear at the end of a manual. The index and contents page help users locate information. A glossary or list of complex or specialized words and their definitions may precede the index of a manual.

The four major types of manuals are policy manuals, procedures manuals, organization manuals, and specialty manuals. A policy manual provides a written record of the regulations that employees should follow. A procedures manual gives written explanations of the steps involved in performing certain work tasks. An organization manual, or a company manual, provides written descriptions of the formal organization. A specialty manual contains detailed information about a particular function or process.

QUESTIONS

1. Why are manuals important?
2. How does the content of a manual differ from the content of a memo, letter, or report?
3. How can playscript simplify manual format?
4. Why is a glossary included in a manual?
5. Define *index*.
6. What are some of the benefits of using policy manuals?
7. What is the difference between a policy and a procedure?
8. What are some of the advantages of using a procedures manual?
9. What type of information may be included in an organization manual?
10. What are some examples of specialty manuals?

PROBLEM-SOLVING EXPERIENCES

1. The Houston Company has the following policy on the use of business telephones:

The telephone is an excellent communication tool, but it is often misused. Good telephone manners are essential at all times to the image of the Company.

Based on this policy statement and on the suggestions in Chapter 6 for using the telephone, write a step-by-step procedure for answering the telephone and taking a message.

2. Zebco Associates wants to reduce tension between management and employees by instituting an employee grievance policy. Write a grievance policy statement to include in *Zebco Associates Policy Manual.* Include a rationale for having a fair-treatment policy that addresses employee dissatisfaction.

CASE 17–1

BSC does not have a master plan for integrating word processing in its offices. Each department has selected its own computer system without considering whether available software is compatible with other systems already in the plant. Unfortunately the various word processing software programs do not implement the same features with equal ease. Dana Pelham, plant manager, has noticed that several formats are used in company memos. Dana prefers that a standardized format be used for internal written communications. It is not feasible to supervise all the word processing operators in a centralized area so that a single format can be enforced. Therefore, Dana has asked you to develop a specialty manual that addresses internal written communications.

1. Using Chapter 12 as a reference, write a memorandum preparation section for the manual.

2. Provide step-by-step procedures for memo preparation.

ENDNOTES

[1]Robert E. Harmon, *Improving Administrative Manuals* (New York: Research and Information Services, American Management Associations, 1982), p. 25.

[2]The authors express appreciation to B. L. Johnson, Sr., of Martin Marietta Energy Systems, Inc., Oak Ridge, TN, for contributing to "The Importance of Manuals" section of this chapter.

[3]Harmon, op. cit., p. 32.

[4]Susan Z. Diamond, *Preparing Administrative Manuals* (New York: AMACOM, a division of American Management Associations, 1981), p. 3.

[5]Harmon, op. cit., p. 28.

[6]Diamond, loc. cit.

[7]Stuart P. Bloom and Evan L. Dold, "A Guide to Developing a Policies and Procedures Manual," *Management World*, Vol. 10, No. 6 (June, 1981), p. 31.

[8]Ibid.

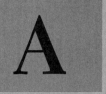
SELECTED READINGS

THE MANAGER'S JOB: FOLKLORE AND FACT

HENRY MINTZBERG

If you ask a manager what he does, he will most likely tell you that he plans, organizes, coordinates, and controls. Then watch what he does. Don't be surprised if you can't relate what you see to these four words.

When he is called and told that one of his factories has just burned down, and he advises the caller to see whether temporary arrangements can be made to supply customers through a foreign subsidiary, is he planning, organizing, coordinating, or controlling? How about when he presents a gold watch to a retiring employee? Or when he attends a conference to meet people in the trade? Or on returning from that conference, when he tells one of his employees about an interesting product idea he picked up there?

The fact is that these four words, which have dominated management vocabulary since the French industrialist Henri Fayol first introduced them in 1916, tell us little about what managers actually do. At best, they indicate some vague objectives managers have when they work.

The field of management, so devoted to progress and change, has for more than half a century not seriously addressed the basic question: What do managers do? Without a proper answer, how can we teach management? How can we design planning or information systems for managers? How can we improve the practice of management at all?

Our ignorance of the nature of managerial work shows up in various ways in the modern organization—in the boast by the successful manager that he never spent a single day in a management training program; in the turnover of corporate planners who never quite understood what it was the manager wanted; in the computer consoles gathering dust in the back room because the managers never used the fancy on-line MIS some analyst thought they

needed. Perhaps most important, our ignorance shows up in the inability of our large public organizations to come to grips with some of their most serious policy problems.

Somehow, in the rush to automate production, to use management science in the functional areas of marketing and finance, and to apply the skills of the behavioral scientist to the problem of worker motivation, the manager—that person in charge of the organization or one of its subunits—has been forgotten.

My intention in this article is simple: to break the reader away from Fayol's words and introduce him to a more supportable, and what I believe to be a more useful, description of managerial work. This description derives from my review and synthesis of the available research on how various managers have spent their time.

In some studies, managers were observed intensively ("shadowed" is the term some of them used); in a number of others, they kept detailed diaries of their activities; in a few studies, their records were analyzed. All kinds of managers were studied—foremen, factory supervisors, staff managers, field sales managers, hospital administrators, presidents of companies and nations, and even street gang leaders. These "managers" worked in the United States, Canada, Sweden, and Great Britain. In the ruled insert on pages 334–335 is a brief review of the major studies that I found most useful in developing this description, including my own study of five American chief executive officers.

A synthesis of these findings paints an interesting picture, one as different from Fayol's classical view as a cubist abstract is from a Renaissance painting. In a sense, this picture will be obvious to anyone who has ever spent a day in a manager's office, either in front of the desk or behind it. Yet, at the same time, this picture may turn out to be revolutionary, in that it throws into doubt so much of the folklore that we have accepted about the manager's work.

I first discuss some of this folklore and contrast it with some of the discoveries of systematic research—the hard facts about how managers spend their time. Then I synthesize these research findings in a description of ten roles that seem to describe the essential content of all managers' jobs. In a concluding section, I discuss a number of implications of this synthesis for those trying to achieve more effective management, both in classrooms and in the business world.

SOME FOLKLORE AND FACTS ABOUT MANAGERIAL WORK

There are four myths about the manager's job that do not bear up under careful scrutiny of the facts.

1. FOLKLORE: *The manager is a reflective, systematic planner.* The evidence on this issue is overwhelming, but not a shred of it supports this statement.

FACT: *Study after study has shown that managers work at an unrelenting pace, that their activities are characterized by brevity, variety, and discontinuity, and that they are strongly oriented to action and dislike reflective activities.* Consider this evidence:

▲ Half the activities engaged in by the five chief executives of my study lasted less than nine minutes, and only 10% exceeded one hour.[1] A study of 56 U.S. foremen found that they averaged 583 activities per eight-hour shift, an average of 1 every 48 seconds.[2] The work pace for both chief executives and foremen was unrelenting. The chief executives met a steady stream of callers and mail from the moment they arrived in the morning until they left in the evening. Coffee breaks and lunches were inevitably work related, and ever-present subordinates seemed to usurp any free moment.

▲ A diary study of 160 British middle and top managers found that they worked for a half hour or more without interruption only about once every two days.[3]

▲ Of the verbal contacts of the chief executives in my study, 93% were arranged on an ad hoc basis.

Only 1% of the executives' time was spent in open-ended observational tours. Only 1 out of 368 verbal contacts was unrelated to a specific issue and could be called general planning. Another researcher finds that "in *not one single case* did a manager report the obtaining of important external information from a general conversation or other undirected personal communication."[4]

▲ No study has found important patterns in the way managers schedule their time. They seem to jump from issue to issue, continually responding to the needs of the moment.

Is this the planner that the classical view describes? Hardly. How, then, can we explain this behavior? The manager is simply responding to the pressures of his job. I found that my chief executives terminated many of their own activities, often leaving meetings before the end, and interrupted their desk work to call in subordinates. One president not only placed his desk so that he could look down a long hallway but also left his door open when he was alone—an invitation for subordinates to come in and interrupt him.

Clearly, these managers wanted to encourage the flow of current information. But more significantly, they seemed to be conditioned by their own work loads. They appreciated the opportunity cost of their own time, and they were continually aware of their ever-present obligations—mail to be answered, callers to attend to, and so on. It seems that no matter what he is doing, the manager is plagued by the possibilities of what he might do and what he must do.

When the manager must plan, he seems to do so implicitly in the context of daily actions, not in some abstract process reserved for two weeks in the organization's mountain retreat. The plans of the chief executives I studied seemed to exist only in their heads—as flexible, but often specific, intentions. The traditional literature notwithstanding, the job of managing does not breed reflective planners; the manager is a real-time responder to stimuli, an individual who is conditioned by his job to prefer live to delayed action.

RESEARCH ON MANAGERIAL WORK

Considering its central importance to every aspect of management, there has been surprisingly little research on the manager's work, and virtually no systematic building of knowledge from one group of studies to another. In seeking to describe managerial work, I conducted my own research and also scanned the literature widely to integrate the findings of studies from many diverse sources with my own. These studies focused on two very different aspects of managerial work. Some were concerned with the characteristics of the work—how long managers work, where, at what pace and with what interruptions, with whom they work, and through what media they communicate. Other studies were more concerned with the essential content of the work—what activities the managers actually carry out, and why. Thus, after a meeting, one researcher might note that the manager spent 45 minutes with three government officials in their Washington office, while another might record that he presented his company's stand on some proposed legislation in order to change a regulation. A few of the studies of managerial work are widely known, but most have remained buried as single journal articles or isolated books. Among the more important ones I cite (with full references in the footnotes) are the following:

▲ Sune Carlson developed the diary method to study the work characteristics of nine Swedish managing directors. Each kept a detailed log of his activities. Carlson's results are reported in his book *Executive Behavior*. A number of British researchers, notably Rosemary Stewart, have subsequently used Carlson's method. In *Managers and Their Jobs*, she describes the study of 160 top and middle managers of British companies during four weeks, with particular attention to the differences in their work.

▲ Leonard Sayles's book *Managerial Behavior* is another important reference. Using a method he refers to as "anthropological," Sayles studied the work content of middle- and lower-level managers in a large U.S. corporation. Sayles moved

---

2. FOLKLORE: The effective manager has no regular duties to perform. Managers are constantly being told to spend more time planning and delegating, and less time seeing customers and engaging in negotiations. These are not, after all, the true tasks of the manager. To use the popular analogy, the good manager, like the good conductor, carefully orchestrates everything in advance, then sits back to enjoy the fruits of his labor, responding occasionally to an unforeseeable exception.

But here again the pleasant abstraction just does not seem to hold up. We had better take a closer look at those activities managers feel compelled to engage in before we arbitrarily define them away.

FACT: In addition to handling exceptions, managerial work involves performing a number of regular duties, including ritual and ceremony, negotiations, and processing of soft information that links the organization with its environment. Consider some evidence from the research studies:

▲ A study of the work of the presidents of small companies found that they engaged in routine activities because their companies could not afford

freely in the company, collecting whatever information struck him as important.

▲ Perhaps the best-known source is *Presidential Power*, in which Richard Neustadt analyzes the power and managerial behavior of Presidents Roosevelt, Truman, and Eisenhower. Neustadt used secondary sources—documents and interviews with other parties—to generate his data.

▲ Robert H. Guest, in *Personnel*, reports on a study of the foreman's working day. Fifty-six U.S. foremen were observed and each of their activities recorded during one eight-hour shift.

▲ Richard C. Hodgson, Daniel J. Levinson, and Abraham Zaleznik studied a team of three top executives of a U.S. hospital. From that study they wrote *The Executive Role Constellation*. These researchers addressed in particular the way in which work and socioemotional roles were divided among the three managers.

▲ William F. Whyte, from his study of a street gang during the Depression, wrote *Street Corner Society*. His findings about the gang's leadership, which George C. Homans analyzed in *The Human Group*, suggest some interesting similarities of job content between street gang leaders and corporate managers.

My own study involved five American CEOs of middle- to large-sized organizations—a consulting firm, a technology company, a hospital, a consumer goods company, and a school system. Using a method called "structural observation," during one intensive week of observation for each executive I recorded various aspects of every piece of mail and every verbal contact. My method was designed to capture data on both work characteristics and job content. In all, I analyzed 890 pieces of incoming and outgoing mail and 368 verbal contacts.

---

staff specialists and were so thin on operating personnel that a single absence often required the president to substitute.[5]

▲ One study of field sales managers and another of chief executives suggest that it is a natural part of both jobs to see important customers, assuming the managers wish to keep those customers.[6]

▲ Someone, only half in jest, once described the manager as that person who sees visitors so that everyone else can get his work done. In my study, I found that certain ceremonial duties—meeting visiting dignitaries, giving out gold watches, presiding at Christmas dinners—were an intrinsic part of the chief executive's job.

▲ Studies of managers' information flow suggest that managers play a key role in securing "soft" external information (much of it available only to them because of their status) and in passing it along to their subordinates.

3. FOLKLORE: The senior manager needs aggregated information, which a formal management information system best provides. Not too long ago, the words *total information system* were everywhere in the management literature. In keeping with the classical view of the manager as that individual perched on the apex of a regulated, hierarchical system, the literature's manager was to receive all his important information from a giant, comprehensive MIS.

But lately, as it has become increasingly evident that these giant MIS systems are not working—that managers are simply not using them—the enthusiasm has waned. A look at how managers actually process information makes the reason quite clear. Managers have five media at their command—documents, telephone calls, scheduled and unscheduled meetings, and observational tours.

FACT: Managers strongly favor the verbal media—namely, telephone calls and meetings. The evidence comes from every single study of managerial work. Consider the following:

▲ In two British studies, managers spent an average of 66% and 80% of their time in verbal (oral) communication.[7] In my study of five American chief executives, the figure was 78%.

▲ These five chief executives treated mail processing as a burden to be dispensed with. One came in Saturday morning to process 142 pieces of mail in just over three hours, to "get rid of all the stuff." This same manager looked at the first piece of "hard" mail he had received all week, a standard cost report, and put it aside with the comment, "I never look at this."

▲ These same five chief executives responded immediately to 2 of the 40 routine reports they received during the five weeks of my study and to four items in the 104 periodicals. They skimmed most of these periodicals in seconds, almost ritualistically. In all, these chief executives of good-sized organizations initiated on their own—that is, not in response to something else—a grand total of 25 pieces of mail during the 25 days I observed them.

An analysis of the mail the executives received reveals an interesting picture—only 13% was of specific and immediate use. So now we have another piece in the puzzle: not much of the mail provides live, current information—the action of a competitor, the mood of a government legislator, or the rating of last night's television show. Yet this is the information that drove the managers, interrupting their meetings and rescheduling their workdays.

Consider another interesting finding. Managers seem to cherish "soft" information, especially gossip, hearsay, and speculation. Why? The reason is its timeliness; today's gossip may be tomorrow's fact. The manager who is not accessible for the telephone call informing him that his biggest customer was seen golfing with his main competitor may read about a dramatic drop in sales in the next quarterly report. But then it's too late.

To assess the value of historical, aggregated, "hard" MIS information, consider two of the manager's prime uses for his information—to identify problems and opportunities[8] and to build his own mental models of the things around him (e.g., how his organization's budget system works, how his customers buy his product, how changes in the economy affect his organization, and so on). Every bit of evidence suggests that the manager identifies decision situations and builds models not with the aggregated abstractions an MIS provides, but with specific tidbits of data.

Consider the words of Richard Neustadt, who studied the information-collecting habits of Presidents Roosevelt, Truman, and Eisenhower:

"It is not information of a general sort that helps a President see personal stakes; not summaries, not surveys, not the *bland amalgams*. Rather . . . it is the odds and ends of *tangible detail* that pieced together in his mind illuminate the underside of issues put before him. To help himself he must reach out as widely as he can for every scrap of fact, opinion, gossip, bearing on his interests and relationships as President. He must become his own director of his own central intelligence."[9]

The manager's emphasis on the verbal media raises two important points:

First, verbal information is stored in the brains of people. Only when people write this information down can it be stored in the files of the organization—whether in metal cabinets or on magnetic tape—and managers apparently do not write down much of what they hear. Thus the strategic data bank of the organization is not in the memory of its computers but in the minds of its managers.

Second, the manager's extensive use of verbal media helps to explain why he is reluctant to delegate tasks. When we note that most of the manager's important information comes in verbal form and is stored in his head, we can well appreciate his reluctance. It is not as if he can hand a dossier over to someone; he must take the time to "dump memory"—to tell that someone all he knows about the subject. But this could take so long that the manager may find it easier to do the task himself. Thus the manager is damned by his own information system to a "dilemma of delegation"—to do too much himself or to delegate to his subordinates with inadequate briefing.

4. FOLKLORE: Management is, or at least is quickly becoming, a science and a profession. By almost any definitions of *science* and *profession*, this statement is false. Brief observation of any manager will quickly lay to rest the notion that managers practice a science. A science involves the enaction of systematic, analytically determined procedures or programs. If we do not even know what procedures managers use, how can we prescribe them by scientific analysis? And how can we call management a profession if we cannot specify what managers are to learn? For after all, a profession involves "knowledge of some department of learning or science" (*Random House Dictionary*).[10]

FACT: The managers' programs—to schedule time, process information, make decisions, and so on—remain locked deep inside their brains. Thus, to describe these programs, we rely on words like *judgment* and *intuition*, seldom stopping to realize that they are merely labels for our ignorance.

I was struck during my study by the fact that the executives I was observing—all very competent by any standard—are fundamentally indistinguishable from their counterparts of a hundred years ago (or a

thousand years ago, for that matter). The information they need differs, but they seek it in the same way—by word of mouth. Their decisions concern modern technology, but the procedures they use to make them are the same as the procedures of the nineteenth-century manager. Even the computer, so important for the specialized work of the organization, has apparently had no influence on the work procedures of general managers. In fact, the manager is in a kind of loop, with increasingly heavy work pressures but no aid forthcoming from management science.

Considering the facts about managerial work, we can see that the manager's job is enormously complicated and difficult. The manager is overburdened with obligations; yet he cannot easily delegate his tasks. As a result, he is driven to overwork and is forced to do many tasks superficially. Brevity, fragmentation, and verbal communication characterize his work. Yet these are the very characteristics of managerial work that have impeded scientific attempts to improve it. As a result, the management scientist has concentrated his efforts on the specialized functions of the organization, where he could more easily analyze the procedures and quantify the relevant information.[11]

But the pressures of the manager's job are becoming worse. Where before he needed only to respond to owners and directors, now he finds that subordinates with democratic norms continually reduce his freedom to issue unexplained orders, and a growing number of outside influences (consumer groups, government agencies, and so on) expect his attention. And the manager has had nowhere to turn for help. The first step in providing the manager with some help is to find out what his job really is.

BACK TO A BASIC DESCRIPTION OF MANAGERIAL WORK

Now let us try to put some of the pieces of this puzzle together. Earlier, I defined the manager as that person in charge of an organization or one of its subunits. Besides chief executive officers, this definition would include vice presidents, bishops, foremen, hockey coaches, and prime ministers. Can all of these people have anything in common? Indeed they can. For an important starting point, all are vested with formal authority over an organizational unit. From formal authority comes status, which leads to various interpersonal relations, and from these comes access to information. Information, in turn, enables the manager to make decisions and strategies for his unit.

The manager's job can be described in terms of various "roles," or organized sets of behaviors identified with a position. My description, shown in Exhibit I, comprises ten roles. As we shall see, formal authority gives rise to the three interpersonal roles, which in turn give rise to the three informational roles; these two sets of roles enable the manager to play the four decisional roles.

INTERPERSONAL ROLES. Three of the manager's roles arise directly from his formal authority and involve basic interpersonal relationships.

1. First is the *figurehead* role. By virtue of his position as head of an organizational unit, every manager must perform some duties of a ceremonial nature. The president greets the touring dignitaries, the foreman attends the wedding of a lathe operator, and the sales manager takes an important customer to lunch.

   The chief executives of my study spent 12% of their contact time on ceremonial duties; 17% of their incoming mail dealt with acknowledgments and requests related to their status. For example, a letter to a company president requested free merchandise for a crippled schoolchild; diplomas were put on the desk of the school superintendent for his signature.

   Duties that involve interpersonal roles may sometimes be routine, involving little serious communication and no important decision making. Nevertheless, they are important to the smooth functioning of an organization and cannot be ignored by the manager.

2. Because he is in charge of an organizational unit, the manager is responsible for the work of the people of that unit. His actions in this regard constitute the *leader* role. Some of these actions in-

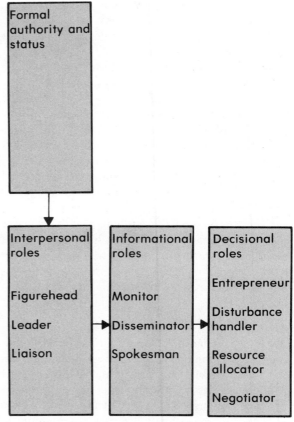

EXHIBIT I The Manager's Roles

volve leadership directly—for example, in most organizations the manager is normally responsible for hiring and training his own staff.

In addition, there is the indirect exercise of the leader role. Every manager must motivate and encourage his employees, somehow reconciling their individual needs with the goals of the organization. In virtually every contact the manager has with his employees, subordinates seeking leadership clues probe his actions: "Does he approve?" "How would he like the report to turn out?" "Is he more interested in market share than high profits?"

The influence of the manager is most clearly seen in the leader role. Formal authority vests him with great potential power; leadership determines in large part how much of it he will realize.

3. The literature of management has always recognized the leader role, particularly those aspects of it related to motivation. In comparison, until recently it has hardly mentioned the *liaison* role, in which the manager makes contacts outside his vertical chain of command. This is remarkable in light of the finding of virtually every study of managerial work that managers spend as much time with peers and other people outside their units as they do with their own subordinates—and, surprisingly, very little time with their own superiors.

In Rosemary Stewart's diary study, the 160 British middle and top managers spent 47% of their time with peers, 41% of their time with people outside their unit, and only 12% of their time with their superiors. For Robert H. Guest's study of U.S. foremen, the figures were 44%, 46%, and 10%. The chief executives of my study averaged 44% of their contact time with people outside their organizations, 48% with subordinates, and 7% with directors and trustees.

The contacts the five CEOs made were with an incredibly wide range of people: subordinates; clients, business associates, and suppliers; and peers—managers of similar organizations, government and trade organization officials, fellow directors on outside boards, and independents with no relevant organizational affiliations. The chief executives' time with and mail from these groups is shown in Exhibit II on page 340. Guest's study of foremen shows, likewise, that their contacts were numerous and wide ranging, seldom involving fewer than 25 individuals, and often more than 50.

As we shall see shortly, the manager cultivates such contacts largely to find information. In effect, the liaison role is devoted to building up the manager's own external information system—informal, private, verbal, but, nevertheless, effective.

INFORMATIONAL ROLES.   By virtue of his interpersonal contacts, both with his subordinates and with his network of contacts, the manager emerges as the nerve center of his organizational unit. He may not know everything, but he typically knows more than any member of his staff.

Studies have shown this relationship to hold for all managers, from street gang leaders to U.S. presidents. In *The Human Group*, George C. Homans explains how, because they were at the center of the information flow in their own gangs and were also in close touch with other gang leaders, street gang leaders were better informed than any of their followers.[12] And Richard Neustadt describes the following account from his study of Franklin D. Roosevelt:

"The essence of Roosevelt's technique for information-gathering was competition. 'He would call you in,' one of his aides once told me, 'and he'd ask you to get the story on some complicated business, and you'd come back after a couple of days of hard labor and present the juicy morsel you'd uncovered under a stone somewhere, and *then* you'd find out he knew all about it, along with something else you *didn't* know. Where he got this information from he wouldn't mention, usually, but after he had done this to you once or twice you got damn careful about *your* information.' "[13]

We can see where Roosevelt "got this information" when we consider the relationship between the interpersonal and informational roles. As leader, the manager has formal and easy access to every member of his staff. Hence, as noted earlier, he tends to know more about his own unit than anyone else does. In addition, his liaison contacts expose the manager to external information to which his subordinates often lack access. Many of these contacts are with other managers of equal status, who are themselves nerve centers in their own organization. In this way, the manager develops a powerful data base of information.

The processing of information is a key part of the manager's job. In my study, the chief executives spent 40% of their contact time on activities devoted exclusively to the transmission of information; 70% of their incoming mail was purely informational (as opposed to requests for action). The manager does not leave meetings or hang up the telephone in or-

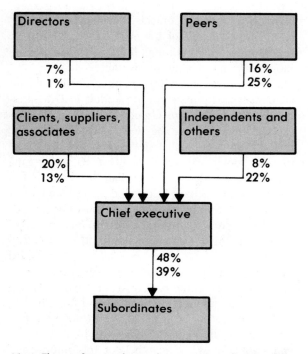

Note: The top figure indicates the proportion of total contact time spent with each group and the bottom figure, the proportion of mail from each group.

EXHIBIT II The Chief Executives' Contacts

der to get back to work. In large part, communication *is* his work. Three roles describe these informational aspects of managerial work.

1. As *monitor*, the manager perpetually scans his environment for information, interrogates his liaison contacts and his subordinates, and receives unsolicited information, much of it as a result of the network of personal contacts he has developed. Remember that a good part of the information the manager collects in his monitor role arrives in verbal form, often as gossip, hearsay, and speculation. By virtue of his contacts, the manager has a natural advantage in collecting this soft information for his organization.

2. He must share and distribute much of this information. Information he gleans from outside personal contacts may be needed within his organization. In his *disseminator* role, the manager

passes some of his privileged information directly to his subordinates, who would otherwise have no access to it. When his subordinates lack easy contact with one another, the manager will sometimes pass information from one to another.

3. In his *spokesman* role, the manager sends some of his information to people outside his unit—a president makes a speech to lobby for an organization cause, or a foreman suggests a product modification to a supplier. In addition, as part of his role as spokesman, every manager must inform and satisfy the influential people who control his organizational unit. For the foreman, this may simply involve keeping the plant manager informed about the flow of work through the shop.

The president of a large corporation, however, may spend a great amount of his time dealing with a host of influences. Directors and shareholders must be advised about financial performance; consumer groups must be assured that the organization is fulfilling its social responsibilities; and government officials must be satisfied that the organization is abiding by the law.

DECISIONAL ROLES. Information is not, of course, an end in itself; it is the basic input to decision making. One thing is clear in the study of managerial work: the manager plays the major role in his unit's decision-making system. As its formal authority, only he can commit the unit to important new courses of action; and as its nerve center, only he has full and current information to make the set of decisions that determines the unit's strategy. Four roles describe the manager as decision-maker.

1. As *entrepreneur*, the manager seeks to improve his unit, to adapt it to changing conditions in the environment. In his monitor role, the president is constantly on the lookout for new ideas. When a good one appears, he initiates a development project that he may supervise himself or delegate to an employee (perhaps with the stipulation that he must approve the final proposal).

There are two interesting features about these development projects at the chief executive level. First, these projects do not involve single decisions or even unified clusters of decisions. Rather, they emerge as a series of small decisions and actions sequenced over time. Apparently, the chief executive prolongs each project so that he can fit it bit by bit into his busy, disjointed schedule and so that he can gradually come to comprehend the issue, if it is a complex one.

Second, the chief executives I studied supervised as many as 50 of these projects at the same time. Some projects entailed new products or processes; others involved public relations campaigns, improvement of the cash position, reorganization of a weak department, resolution of a moral problem in a foreign division, integration of computer operations, various acquisitions at different stages of development, and so on.

The chief executive appears to maintain a kind of inventory of the development projects that he himself supervises—projects that are at various stages of development, some active and some in limbo. Like a juggler, he keeps a number of projects in the air; periodically, one comes down, is given a new burst of energy, and is sent back into orbit. At various intervals, he puts new projects on-stream and discards old ones.

2. While the entrepreneur role describes the manager as the voluntary initiator of change, the *disturbance handler* role depicts the manager involuntarily responding to pressures. Here change is beyond the manager's control. He must act because the pressures of the situation are too severe to be ignored: strike looms, a major customer has gone bankrupt, or a supplier reneges on his contract.

It has been fashionable, I noted earlier, to compare the manager to an orchestra conductor, just as Peter F. Drucker wrote in *The Practice of Management*:

"The manager has the task of creating a true whole that is larger than the sum of its parts, a productive entity that turns out more than the sum of the resources put into it. One analogy is the conductor of a symphony orchestra, through whose effort, vision and leadership individual in-

strumental parts that are so much noise by themselves become the living whole of music. But the conductor has the composer's score; he is only interpreter. The manager is both composer and conductor."[14]

Now consider the words of Leonard R. Sayles, who has carried out systematic research on the manager's job:

"[The manager] is like a symphony orchestra conductor, endeavouring to maintain a melodious performance in which the contributions of the various instruments are coordinated and sequenced, patterned and paced, while the orchestra members are having various personal difficulties, stage hands are moving music stands, alternating excessive heat and cold are creating audience and instrument problems, and the sponsor of the concert is insisting on irrational changes in the program."[15]

In effect, every manager must spend a good part of his time responding to high-pressure disturbances. No organization can be so well run, so standardized, that it has considered every contingency in the uncertain environment in advance. Disturbances arise not only because poor managers ignore situations until they reach crisis proportions, but also because good managers cannot possibly anticipate all the consequences of the actions they take.

3. The third decisional role is that of *resource allocator*. To the manager falls the responsibility of deciding who will get what in his organizational unit. Perhaps the most important resource the manager allocates is his own time. Access to the manager constitutes exposure to the unit's nerve center and decision-maker. The manager is also charged with designing his unit's structure, that pattern of formal relationships that determines how work is to be divided and coordinated.

Also, in his role as resource allocator, the manager authorizes the important decisions of his unit before they are implemented. By retaining this power, the manager can ensure that decisions are interrelated; all must pass through a single brain. To fragment this power is to encourage discontinuous decision making and a disjointed strategy.

There are a number of interesting features about the manager's authorizing others' decisions. First, despite the widespread use of capital budgeting procedures—a means of authorizing various capital expenditures at one time—executives in my study made a great many authorization decisions on an ad hoc basis. Apparently, many projects cannot wait or simply do not have the quantifiable costs and benefits that capital budgeting requires.

Second, I found that the chief executives faced incredibly complex choices. They had to consider the impact of each decision on other decisions and on the organization's strategy. They had to ensure that the decision would be acceptable to those who influence the organization, as well as ensure that resources would not be overextended. They had to understand the various costs and benefits as well as the feasibility of the proposal. They also had to consider questions of timing. All this was necessary for the simple approval of someone else's proposal. At the same time, however, delay could lose time, while quick approval could be ill considered and quick rejection might discourage the subordinate who had spent months developing a pet project.

One common solution to approving projects is to pick the man instead of the proposal. That is, the manager authorizes those projects presented to him by people whose judgment he trusts. But he cannot always use this simple dodge.

4. The final decisional role is that of *negotiator.* Studies of managerial work at all levels indicate that managers spend considerable time in negotiations: the president of the football team is called in to work out a contract with the holdout superstar; the corporation president leads his company's contingent to negotiate a new strike issue; the foreman argues a grievance problem to its conclusion with the shop steward. As Leonard Sayles puts it, negotiations are a "way of life" for the sophisticated manager.

These negotiations are duties of the manager's job; perhaps routine, they are not to be shirked. They are an integral part of his job, for only he has the authority to commit organizational resources in "real time," and only he has the nerve center information that important negotiations require.

THE INTEGRATED JOB.   It should be clear by now that the ten roles I have been describing are not easily separable. In the terminology of the psychologist, they form a gestalt, an integrated whole. No role can be pulled out of the framework and the job be left intact. For example, a manager without liaison contacts lacks external information. As a result, he can neither disseminate the information his employees need nor make decisions that adequately reflect external conditions. (In fact, this is a problem for the new person in a managerial position, since he cannot make effective decisions until he has built up his network of contacts.)

Here lies a clue to the problems of team management.[16] Two or three people cannot share a single managerial position unless they can act as one entity. This means that they cannot divide up the ten roles unless they can very carefully reintegrate them. The real difficulty lies with the informational roles. Unless there can be full sharing of managerial information—and, as I pointed out earlier, it is primarily verbal—team management breaks down. A single managerial job cannot be arbitrarily split, for example, into internal and external roles, for information from both sources must be brought to bear on the same decisions.

To say that the ten roles form a gestalt is not to say that all managers give equal attention to each role. In fact, I found in my review of the various research studies that

. . . sales managers seem to spend relatively more of their time in the interpersonal roles, presumably a reflection of the extrovert nature of the marketing activity;

. . . production managers give relatively more attention to the decisional roles, presumably a reflection of their concern with efficient work flow;

. . . staff managers spend the most time in the informational roles, since they are experts who manage departments that advise other parts of the organization.

Nevertheless, in all cases the interpersonal, informational, and decisional roles remain inseparable.

TOWARD MORE EFFECTIVE MANAGEMENT

What are the messages for management in this description? I believe, first and foremost, that this description of managerial work should prove more important to managers than any prescription they might derive from it. That is to say, *the manager's effectiveness is significantly influenced by his insight into his own work.* His performance depends on how well he understands and responds to the pressures and dilemmas of the job. Thus managers who can be introspective about their work are likely to be effective at their jobs. The ruled insert on pages 344–345 offers 14 groups of self-study questions for managers. Some may sound rhetorical; none is meant to be. Even though the questions cannot be answered simply, the manager should address them.

Let us take a look at three specific areas of concern. For the most part, the managerial logjams—the dilemma of delegation, the data base centralized in one brain, the problems of working with the management scientist—revolve around the verbal nature of the manager's information. There are great dangers in centralizing the organization's data bank in the minds of its managers. When they leave, they take their memory with them. And when subordinates are out of convenient verbal reach of the manager, they are at an informational disadvantage.

1. *The manager is challenged to find systematic ways to share his privileged information.* A regular debriefing session with key subordinates, a weekly memory dump on the dictating machine, the maintaining of a diary of important information

for limited circulation, or other similar methods may ease the logjam of work considerably. Time spent disseminating this information will be more then regained when decisions must be made. Of course, some will raise the question of confidentiality. But managers would do well to weigh the risks of exposing privileged information against having subordinates who can make effective decisions.

If there is a single theme that runs through this article, it is that the pressures of his job drive the manager to be superficial in his actions—to overload himself with work, encourage interruption, respond quickly to every stimulus, seek the tangible and avoid the abstract, make decisions in small increments, and do everything abruptly.

2. *Here again, the manager is challenged to deal consciously with the pressures of superficiality by giving serious attention to the issues that require it, by stepping back from his tangible bits of information in order to see a broad picture, and by making use of analytical inputs.* Although effective managers have to be adept at responding quickly to numerous and varying problems, the danger in managerial work is that they will respond to every issue equally (and that means abruptly) and that they will never work the tangible bits and pieces of informational input into a comprehensive picture of their world.

As I noted earlier, the manager uses these bits of information to build models of his world. But the manager can also avail himself of the models of the specialists. Economists describe the functioning of markets, operations researchers simulate financial flow processes, and behavioral scientists explain the needs and goals of people. The best of these models can be searched out and learned.

In dealing with complex issues, the senior manager has much to gain from a close relationship with the management scientists of his own organization. They have something important that he lacks—time to probe complex issues. An

SELF-STUDY QUESTIONS FOR MANAGERS

1. Where do I get my information, and how? Can I make greater use of my contacts to get information? Can other people do some of my scanning for me? In what areas is my knowledge weakest, and how can I get others to provide me with the information I need? Do I have powerful enough mental models of those things I must understand within the organization and in its environment?

2. What information do I disseminate in my organization? How important is it that my subordinates get my information? Do I keep too much information to myself because dissemination of it is time-consuming or inconvenient? How can I get more information to others so they can make better decisions?

3. Do I balance information collecting with action taking? Do I tend to act before information is in? Or do I wait so long for all the information that opportunities pass me by and I become a bottleneck in my organization?

4. What pace of change am I asking my organization to tolerate? Is this change balanced so that our operations are neither excessively static nor overly disrupted? Have we sufficiently analyzed the impact of this change on the future of our organization?

5. Am I sufficiently well informed to pass judgment on the proposals that my subordinates make? Is it possible to leave final authorization for more of the proposals with subordinates? Do we have problems of coordination because subordinates in fact now make too many of these decisions independently?

6. What is my vision of direction for this organization? Are these plans primarily in my own mind in loose form? Should I make them explicit in order to guide the decisions of others in the organization better? Or do I need flexibility to change them at will?

7. How do my subordinates react to my managerial style? Am I sufficiently sensitive to the powerful influence my actions have on them? Do I fully understand their reactions to my actions? Do I find an appropriate balance between encouragement and pressure? Do I stifle their initiative?

8. What kind of external relationships do I maintain, and how? Do I spend too much of my time maintaining these relationships? Are there certain types of people whom I should get to know better?

9. Is there any system to my time scheduling, or am I just reacting to the pressures of the moment? Do I find the appropriate mix of activities, or do I tend to concentrate on one particular function or one type of problem just because I find it interesting? Am I more efficient with particular kinds of work at special times of the day or week? Does my schedule reflect this? Can someone else (in addition to my secretary) take responsibility for much of my scheduling and do it more systematically?

10. Do I overwork? What effect does my work load have on my efficiency? Should I force myself to take breaks or to reduce the pace of my activity?

11. Am I too superficial in what I do? Can I really shift moods as quickly and frequently as my work patterns require? Should I attempt to decrease the amount of fragmentation and interruption in my work?

12. Do I orient myself too much toward current, tangible activities? Am I a slave to the action and excitement of my work, so that I am no longer able to concentrate on issues? Do key problems receive the attention they deserve?

Should I spend more time reading and probing deeply into certain issues? Could I be more reflective? Should I be?

13. Do I use the different media appropriately? Do I know how to make the most of written communication? Do I rely excessively on face-to-face communication, thereby putting all but a few of my subordinates at an informational disadvantage? Do I schedule enough of my meetings on a regular basis? Do I spend enough

time touring my organization to observe activity at first hand? Am I too detached from the heart of my organization's activities, seeing things only in an abstract way?

14. How do I blend my personal rights and duties? Do my obligations consume all my time? How can I free myself sufficiently from obligations to ensure that I am taking this organization where I want it to go? How can I turn my obligations to my advantage?

---

effective working relationship hinges on the resolution of what a colleague and I have called "the planning dilemma."[17] Managers have the information and the authority; analysts have the time and the technology. A successful working relationship between the two will be effected when the manager learns to share his information and the analyst learns to adapt to the manager's needs. For the analyst, adaptation means worrying less about the elegance of the method and more about its speed and flexibility.

It seems to me that analysts can help the top manager especially to schedule his time, feed in analytical information, monitor projects under his supervision, develop models to aid in making choices, design contingency plans for disturbances that can be anticipated, and conduct "quick-and-dirty" analysis for those that cannot. But there can be no cooperation if the analysts are out of the mainstream of the manager's information flow.

3. *The manager is challenged to gain control of his own time by turning obligations to his advantage and by turning those things he wishes to do into obligations.* The chief executives of my study initiated only 32% of their own contacts (and another 5% by mutual agreement). And yet to a considerable extent they seemed to control their time. There were two key factors that enabled them to do so.

First, the manager has to spend so much time discharging obligations that if he were to view them as just that, he would leave no mark on his organization. The unsuccessful manager blames failure on the obligations; the effective manager turns his obligations to his own advantage. A speech is a chance to lobby for a cause; a meeting is a chance to reorganize a weak department; a visit to an important customer is a chance to extract trade information.

Second, the manager frees some of his time to do those things that he—perhaps no one else—

thinks important by turning them into obligations. Free time is made, not found, in the manager's job; it is forced into the schedule. Hoping to leave some time open for contemplation or general planning is tantamount to hoping that the pressures of the job will go away. The manager who wants to innovate initiates a project and obligates others to report back to him; the manager who needs certain environmental information establishes channels that will automatically keep him informed; the manager who has to tour facilities commits himself publicly.

THE EDUCATOR'S JOB.   Finally, a word about the training of managers. Our management schools have done an admirable job of training the organization's specialists—management scientists, marketing researchers, accountants, and organizational development specialists. But for the most part they have not trained managers.[18]

Management schools will begin the serious training of managers when skill training takes a serious place next to cognitive learning. Cognitive learning is detached and informational, like reading a book or listening to a lecture. No doubt much important cognitive material must be assimilated by the manager-to-be. But cognitive learning no more makes a manager than it does a swimmer. The latter will drown the first time he jumps into the water if his coach never takes him out of the lecture hall, gets him wet, and gives him feedback on his performance.

In other words, we are taught a skill through practice plus feedback, whether in a real or a simulated situation. Our management schools need to identify the skills managers use, select students who show potential in these skills, put the students into situations where these skills can be practiced, and then give them systematic feedback on their performance.

My description of managerial work suggests a number of important managerial skills—developing peer relationships, carrying out negotiations, motivating subordinates, resolving conflicts, establishing information networks and subsequently disseminating information, making decisions in conditions of extreme ambiguity, and allocating resources. Above all, the manager needs to be introspective about his work so that he may continue to learn on the job.

Many of the manager's skills can, in fact, be practiced, using techniques that range from role playing to videotaping real meetings. And our management schools can enhance the entrepreneurial skills by designing programs that encourage sensible risk taking and innovation.

No job is more vital to our society than that of the manager. It is the manager who determines whether our social institutions serve us well or whether they squander our talents and resources. It is time to strip away the folklore about managerial work, and time to study it realistically so that we can begin the difficult task of making significant improvements in its performance.

[1] All the data from my study can be found in Henry Mintzberg, *The Nature of Managerial Work* (New York: Harper & Row, 1973).

[2] Robert H. Guest, "Of Time and the Foreman," *Personnel*, May 1956, p. 478.

[3] Rosemary Stewart, *Managers and Their Jobs* (London: Macmillan, 1967); see also Sune Carlson, *Executive Behaviour* (Stockholm: Strömbergs, 1951), the first of the diary studies.

[4] Francis J. Aguilar, *Scanning the Business Environment* (New York: Macmillan, 1967), p. 102.

[5] Unpublished study by Irving Choran, reported in Mintzberg, *The Nature of Managerial Work*.

[6] Robert T. Davis, *Performance and Development of Field Sales Managers* (Boston: Division of Research, Harvard Business School, 1957); George H. Copeman, *The Role of the Managing Director* (London: Business Publications, 1963).

[7] Stewart, *Managers and Their Jobs*; Tom Burns, "The Directions of Activity and Communication in a Departmental Executive Group," *Human Relations* 7, no. 1 (1954): 73.

[8] H. Edward Wrapp, "Good Managers Don't Make Policy Decisions," HBR September–October 1967, p. 91; Wrapp refers to this as spotting opportunities and relationships in the stream of operating problems and decisions; in his article Wrapp raises a number of excellent points related to this analysis.

[9] Richard E. Neustadt, *Presidential Power* (New York: John Wiley, 1960), pp. 153–154; italics added.

[10] For a more thorough, though rather different, discussion of this issue, see Kenneth R. Andrews, "Toward Professionalism in Business Management," HBR March–April 1969, p. 49.

[11] C. Jackson Grayson, Jr., in "Management Science and Business Practice," HBR July–August 1973, p. 41, explains in similar terms why, as chairman of the Price Commission, he did not use those very techniques that he himself promoted in his earlier career as a management scientist.

[12] George C. Homans, *The Human Group* (New York: Harcourt, Brace & World, 1950), based on the study by William F. Whyte entitled *Street Corner Society*, rev. ed. (Chicago: University of Chicago Press, 1955).

[13] Neustadt, *Presidential Power*, p. 157.

[14] Peter F. Drucker, *The Practice of Management* (New York: Harper & Row, 1954), pp. 341–342.

[15] Leonard R. Sayles, *Managerial Behavior* (New York: McGraw-Hill, 1964), p. 162.

[16] See Richard C. Hodgson, Daniel J. Levinson, and Abraham Zaleznik, *The Executive Role Constellation* (Boston: Division of Research, Harvard Business School, 1965), for a discussion of the sharing of roles.

[17] James S. Hekimian and Henry Mintzberg, "The Planning Dilemma," *The Management Review*, May 1968, p. 4.

[18] See J. Sterling Livingston, "Myth of the Well-Educated Manager," HBR January–February 1971, p. 79.

BARRIERS AND GATEWAYS TO COMMUNICATION

CARL R. ROGERS AND F. J. ROETHLISBERGER

Communication among human beings has always been a problem. But it is only fairly recently that management and management advisers have become so concerned about it and the way it works or does not work in industry. Now, as the result of endless discussion, speculation, and plans of action, a whole cloud of catchwords and catch-thoughts has sprung up and surrounded it.

The Editors of the Review therefore welcome the opportunity to present the following two descriptions of barriers and gateways to communication, in the thought that they may help to bring the problem down to earth and show what it means in terms of simple fundamentals. First Carl R. Rogers analyzes it from the standpoint of human behavior generally (Part I); then F. J. Roethlisberger illustrates it in an industrial context (Part II).

—*The Editors*

PART I

It may seem curious that a person like myself, whose whole professional effort is devoted to psychotherapy, should be interested in problems of communication. What relationship is there between obstacles to communication and providing therapeutic help to individuals with emotional maladjustments?

Actually the relationship is very close indeed. The whole task of psychotherapy is the task of dealing with a failure in communication. The emotionally

Editors' Note: Mr. Rogers' and Mr. Roethlisberger's observations are based on their contributions to a panel discussion at the Centennial Conference on Communications, Northwestern University, October 1951. A complete report of this conference may be secured by writing to the Publications Office, Northwestern University, Evanston, Illinois.

maladjusted person, the "neurotic," is in difficulty, first, because communication within himself has broken down and, secondly, because as a result of this his communication with others has been damaged. To put it another way, in the "neurotic" individual parts of himself which have been termed unconscious, or repressed, or denied to awareness, become blocked off so that they no longer communicate themselves to the conscious or managing part of himself; as long as this is true, there are distortions in the way he communicates himself to others, and so he suffers both within himself and in his interpersonal relations. The task of psychotherapy is to help the person achieve, through a special relationship with a therapist, good communication within himself. Once this is achieved, he can communicate more freely and more effectively with others. We may say then that psychotherapy is good communication, within and between men. We may also turn that statement around and it will still be true. Good communication, free communication, within or between men, is always therapeutic.

It is, then, from a background of experience with communication in counseling and psychotherapy that I want to present two ideas: (1) I wish to state what I believe is one of the major factors in blocking or impeding communication, and then (2) I wish to present what in our experience has proved to be a very important way of improving or facilitating communication.

BARRIER: THE TENDENCY TO EVALUATE. I should like to propose, as a hypothesis for consideration, that the major barrier to mutual interpersonal communication is our very natural tendency to judge, to evaluate, to approve (or disapprove) the statement of the other person or the other group. Let me illustrate my meaning with some very simple examples. Suppose someone, commenting on this discussion, makes the statement, "I didn't like what that man said." What will you respond? Almost invariably your reply will be either approval or disapproval of the attitude expressed. Either you respond, "I didn't either; I thought it was terrible," or else you tend to reply, "Oh, I thought it was really good." In other words, your primary reaction is to evaluate it from *your* point of view, your own frame of reference.

Or take another example. Suppose I say with some feeling, "I think the Republicans are behaving in ways that show a lot of good sound sense these days." What is the response that arises in your mind? The overwhelming likelihood is that it will be evaluative. In other words, you will find yourself agreeing, or disagreeing, or making some judgment about me such as "He must be a conservative," or "He seems solid in his thinking." Or let us take an illustration from the international scene. Russia says vehemently, "The treaty with Japan is a war plot on the part of the United States." We rise as one person to say, "That's a lie!"

This last illustration brings in another element connected with my hypothesis. Although the tendency to make evaluations is common in almost all interchange of language, it is very much heightened in those situations where feelings and emotions are deeply involved. So the stronger our feelings, the more likely it is that there will be no mutual element in the communication. There will be just two ideas, two feelings, two judgments, missing each other in psychological space.

I am sure you recognize this from your own experience. When you have not been emotionally involved yourself and have listened to a heated discussion, you often go away thinking, "Well, they actually weren't talking about the same thing." And they were not. Each was making a judgment, an evaluation, from his own frame of reference. There was really nothing which could be called communication in any genuine sense. This tendency to react to any emotionally meaningful statement by forming an evaluation of it from our own point of view is, I repeat, the major barrier to interpersonal communication.

GATEWAY: LISTENING WITH UNDER-STANDING. Is there any way of solving this prob-lem, of avoiding this barrier? I feel that we are making exciting progress toward this goal, and I should like to present it as simply as I can. Real communication occurs, and this evaluative tendency is avoided, when we listen with understanding. What does that mean? It means to see the expressed idea and attitude from the other person's point of view, to sense how it feels to him, to achieve his frame of reference in regard to the thing he is talking about.

Stated so briefly, this may sound absurdly simple, but it is not. It is an approach which we have found extremely potent in the field of psychotherapy. It is the most effective agent we know for altering the basic personality structure of an individual and for improving his relationships and his communications with others. If I can listen to what he can tell me, if I can understand how it seems to him, if I can see its personal meaning for him, if I can sense the emotional flavor which it has for him, then I will be releasing potent forces of change in him.

Again, if I can really understand how he hates his father, or hates the company, or hates Communists—if I can catch the flavor of his fear of insanity, or his fear of atom bombs, or of Russia—it will be of the greatest help to him in altering those hatreds and fears and in establishing realistic and harmonious relationships with the very people and situations toward which he has felt hatred and fear. We know from our research that such empathic understanding—understanding *with* a person, not *about* him—is such an effective approach that it can bring about major changes in personality.

Some of you may be feeling that you listen well to people and yet you have never seen such results. The chances are great indeed that your listening has not been of the type I have described. Fortunately, I can suggest a little laboratory experiment which you can try to test the quality of your understanding. The next time you get into an argument with your wife, or your friend, or with a small group of friends, just stop the discussion for a moment and, for an experiment, institute this rule: "Each person can speak up for himself only *after* he has first restated the ideas and feelings of the previous speaker accurately and to that speaker's satisfaction."

You see what this would mean. It would simply mean that before presenting your own point of view, it would be necessary for you to achieve the other speaker's frame of reference—to understand his thoughts and feelings so well that you could summarize them for him. Sounds simple, doesn't it? But if you try it, you will discover that it is one of the most difficult things you have ever tried to do. However, once you have been able to see the other's point of view, your own comments will have to be drastically revised. You will also find the emotion going out of the discussion, the differences being reduced, and those differences which remain being of a rational and understandable sort.

Can you imagine what this kind of an approach would mean if it were projected into larger areas? What would happen to a labor-management dispute if it were conducted in such a way that labor, without necessarily agreeing, could accurately state management's point of view in a way that management could accept; and management, without approving labor's stand, could state labor's case in a way that labor agreed was accurate? It would mean that real communication was established, and one could practically guarantee that some reasonable solution would be reached.

If, then, this way of approach is an effective avenue to good communication and good relationships, as I am quite sure you will agree if you try the experiment I have mentioned, why is it not more widely tried and used? I will try to list the difficulties which keep it from being utilized.

Need for Courage.   In the first place it takes courage, a quality which is not too widespread. I am indebted to Dr. S. I. Hayakawa, the semanticist, for pointing out that to carry on psychotherapy in this fashion is to take a very real risk, and that courage is required. If you really understand another person in this way, if you are willing to enter his private world and see the way life appears to him, without any attempt to make evaluative judgments, you run the risk of being changed yourself. You might see it his way; you might find yourself influenced in your attitudes or your personality.

This risk of being changed is one of the most frightening prospects many of us can face. If I enter, as fully as I am able, into the private world of a neurotic or psychotic individual, isn't there a risk that I might become lost in that world? Most of us are afraid to take that risk. Or if we were listening to a Russian Communist, or Senator Joe McCarthy, how many of us would dare to try to see the world from each of their points of view? The great majority of us could not *listen*; we would find ourselves compelled to *evaluate*, because listening would seem too dangerous. So the first requirement is courage, and we do not always have it.

Heightened Emotions.   But there is a second obstacle. It is just when emotions are strongest that it is most difficult to achieve the frame of reference of the other person or group. Yet it is then that the attitude is most needed if communication is to be established. We have not found this to be an insuperable obstacle in our experience in psychotherapy. A third party, who is able to lay aside his own feelings and evaluations, can assist greatly by listening with understanding to each person or group and clarifying the views and attitudes each holds.

We have found this effective in small groups in which contradictory or antagonistic attitudes exist. When the parties to a dispute realize that they are being understood, that someone sees how the situation seems to them, the statements grow less exaggerated and less defensive, and it is no longer necessary to maintain the attitude, "I am 100% right and you are 100% wrong." The influence of such an understanding catalyst in the group permits the members to come closer and closer to the objective truth involved in the relationship. In this way mutual communication is established, and some type of agreement becomes much more possible.

So we may say that though heightened emotions make it much more difficult to understand *with* an opponent, our experience makes it clear that a neutral, understanding, catalyst type of leader or therapist can overcome this obstacle in a small group.

Size of Group.   That last phrase, however, suggests another obstacle to utilizing the approach I have described. Thus far all our experience has been with small face-to-face groups—groups exhibiting industrial tensions, religious tensions, racial tensions, and therapy groups in which many personal tensions are present. In these small groups our experience, confirmed by a limited amount of research, shows that this basic approach leads to improved communication, to greater acceptance of others and by others, and to attitudes which are more positive and more problem-solving in nature. There is a decrease in defensiveness, in exaggerated statements, in evaluative and critical behavior.

But these findings are from small groups. What about trying to achieve understanding between larger groups that are geographically remote, or between face-to-face groups that are not speaking for themselves but simply as representatives of others, like the delegates at Kaesong? Frankly we do not know the answers to these questions. I believe the situation might be put this way: As social scientists we have a tentative test-tube solution of the problem of breakdown in communication. But to confirm the validity of this test-tube solution and to adapt it to the enormous problems of communication breakdown between classes, groups, and nations would involve additional funds, much more research, and creative thinking of a high order.

Yet with our present limited knowledge we can see some steps which might be taken even in large groups to increase the amount of listening *with* and decrease the amount of evaluation *about*. To be imaginative for a moment, let us suppose that a therapeutically oriented international group went to the Russian leaders and said, "We want to achieve a genuine understanding of your views and, even more important, of your attitudes and feelings toward the United States. We will summarize and resummarize these views and feelings if necessary, until you agree that our description represents the situation as it seems to you."

Then suppose they did the same thing with the leaders in our own country. If they then gave the widest possible distribution to these two views, with the feelings clearly described but not expressed in name-calling, might not the effect be very great? It

would not guarantee the type of understanding I have been describing, but it would make it much more possible. We can understand the feelings of a person who hates us much more readily when his attitudes are accurately described to us by a neutral third party than we can when he is shaking his fist at us.

Faith in Social Sciences.   But even to describe such a first step is to suggest another obstacle to this approach of understanding. Our civilization does not yet have enough faith in the social sciences to utilize their findings. The opposite is true of the physical sciences. During the war when a test-tube solution was found to the problem of synthetic rubber, millions of dollars and an army of talent were turned loose on the problem of using that finding. If synthetic rubber could be made in milligrams, it could and would be made in the thousands of tons. And it was. But in the social science realm, if a way is found of facilitating communication and mutual understanding in small groups, there is no guarantee that the finding will be utilized. It may be a generation or more before the money and the brains will be turned loose to exploit that finding.

SUMMARY.   In closing, I should like to summarize this small-scale solution to the problem of barriers in communication, and to point out certain of its characteristics.

I have said that our research and experience to date would make it appear that breakdowns in communication, and the evaluative tendency which is the major barrier to communication, can be avoided. The solution is provided by creating a situation in which each of the different parties comes to understand the other from the *other's* point of view. This has been achieved, in practice, even when feelings run high, by the influence of a person who is willing to understand each point of view empathically, and who thus acts as a catalyst to precipitate further understanding.

This procedure has important characteristics. It can be initiated by one party, without waiting for the other to be ready. It can even be initiated by a neutral third person, provided he can gain a minimum of cooperation from one of the parties.

This procedure can deal with the insincerities, the defensive exaggerations, the lies, the "false fronts" which characterize almost every failure in communication. These defensive distortions drop away with astonishing speed as people find that the only intent is to understand, not to judge.

This approach leads steadily and rapidly toward the discovery of the truth, toward a realistic appraisal of the objective barriers to communication. The dropping of some defensiveness by one party leads to further dropping of defensiveness by the other party, and truth is thus approached.

This procedure gradually achieves mutual communication. Mutual communication tends to be pointed toward solving a problem rather than toward attacking a person or group. It leads to a situation in which I see how the problem appears to you as well as to me, and you see how it appears to me as well as to you. Thus accurately and realistically defined, the problem is almost certain to yield to intelligent attack; or if it is in part insoluble, it will be comfortably accepted as such.

This then appears to be a test-tube solution to the breakdown of communication as it occurs in small groups. Can we take this small-scale answer, investigate it further, refine it, develop it, and apply it to the tragic and well-nigh fatal failures of communication which threaten the very existence of our modern world? It seems to me that this is a possibility and a challenge which we should explore.

PART II

In thinking about the many barriers to personal communication, particularly those that are due to differences of background, experience, and motivation, it seems to me extraordinary that any two persons can ever understand each other. Such reflections provoke the question of how communication is

Author's Note: For the concepts I use to present my material I am greatly indebted to some very interesting conversations I have had with my friend, Irving Lee. —F.J.R.

possible when people do not see and assume the same things and share the same values.

On this question there are two schools of thought. One school assumes that communication between A and B, for example, has failed when B does not accept what A has to say as being fact, true, or valid; and that the goal of communication is to get B to agree with A's opinions, ideas, facts, or information.

The position of the other school of thought is quite different. It assumes that communication has failed when B does not feel free to express his feelings to A because B fears they will not be accepted by A. Communication is facilitated when on the part of A or B or both there is a willingness to express and accept differences.

As these are quite divergent conceptions, let us explore them further with an example. Bill, an employee, is talking with his boss in the boss's office. The boss says, "I think, Bill, that this is the best way to do your job." Bill says, "Oh, yeah!" According to the first school of thought, this reply would be a sign of poor communication. Bill does not understand the best way of doing his work. To improve communication, therefore, it is up to the boss to explain to Bill why his way is the best.

From the point of view of the second school of thought, Bill's reply is a sign neither of good nor of bad communication. Bill's response is indeterminate. But the boss has an opportunity to find out what Bill means if he so desires. Let us assume that this is what he chooses to do, i.e., find out what Bill means. So this boss tries to get Bill to talk more about his job while he (the boss) listens.

For purposes of simplification, I shall call the boss representing the first school of thought "*Smith*" and the boss representing the second school of thought "*Jones*." In the presence of the so-called same stimulus each behaves differently. Smith chooses to *explain*; Jones chooses to *listen*. In my experience Jones's response works better than Smith's. It works better because Jones is making a more proper evaluation of what is taking place between him and Bill than Smith is. Let us test this hypothesis by continuing with our example.

WHAT SMITH ASSUMES, SEES, AND FEELS.
Smith assumes that he understands what Bill means when Bill says, "Oh yeah!" so there is no need to find out. Smith is sure that Bill does not understand why this is the best way to do his job, so Smith has to tell him. In this process let us assume Smith is logical, lucid, and clear. He presents his facts and evidence well. But, alas, Bill remains unconvinced. What does Smith do? Operating under the assumption that what is taking place between him and Bill is something essentially logical, Smith can draw only one of two conclusions: either (1) he has not been clear enough, or (2) Bill is too damned stupid to understand. So he either has to "spell out" his case in words of fewer and fewer syllables or give up. Smith is reluctant to do the latter, so he continues to explain. What happens?

If Bill still does not accept Smith's explanation of why this is the best way for him to do his job, a pattern of interacting feelings is produced of which Smith is often unaware. The more Smith cannot get Bill to understand him, the more frustrated Smith becomes and the more Bill becomes a threat to his logical capacity. Since Smith sees himself as a fairly reasonable and logical chap, this is a difficult feeling to accept. It is much easier for him to perceive Bill as uncooperative or stupid. This perception, however, will affect what Smith says and does. Under these pressures Bill comes to be evaluated more and more in terms of Smith's values. By this process Smith tends to treat Bill's values as unimportant. He tends to deny Bill's uniqueness and difference. He treats Bill as if he had little capacity for self-direction.

Let us be clear. Smith does not see that he is doing these things. When he is feverishly scratching hieroglyphics on the back of an envelope, trying to explain to Bill why this is the best way to do his job, Smith is trying to be helpful. He is a man of goodwill, and he wants to set Bill straight. This is the way Smith sees himself and his behavior. But it is for this very reason that Bill's "Oh yeah!" is getting under Smith's skin.

"How dumb can a guy be?" is Smith's attitude, and unfortunately Bill will hear that more than

Smith's good intentions. Bill will feel misunderstood. He will not see Smith as a man of goodwill trying to be helpful. Rather he will perceive him as a threat to his self-esteem and personal integrity. Against this threat Bill will feel the need to defend himself at all cost. Not being so logically articulate as Smith, Bill expresses this need, again, by saying, "Oh yeah!"

WHAT JONES ASSUMES, SEES, AND FEELS.
Let us leave this sad scene between Smith and Bill, which I fear is going to terminate by Bill's either leaving in a huff or being kicked out of Smith's office. Let us turn for a moment to Jones and see what he is assuming, seeing, hearing, feeling, doing, and saying when he interacts with Bill.

Jones, it will be remembered, does not assume that he knows what Bill means when he says, "Oh yeah!" so he has to find out. Moreover, he assumes that when Bill said this, he had not exhausted his vocabulary or his feelings. Bill may not necessarily mean one thing; he may mean several different things. So Jones decides to listen.

In this process Jones is not under any illusion that what will take place will be eventually logical. Rather he is assuming that what will take place will be primarily an interaction of feelings. Therefore, he cannot ignore the feelings of Bill, the effect of Bill's feelings on him, or the effect of his feelings on Bill. In other words, he cannot ignore his relationship to Bill; he cannot assume that it will make no difference to what Bill will hear or accept.

Therefore, Jones will be paying strict attention to all of the things Smith has ignored. He will be addressing himself to Bill's feelings, his own, and the interactions between them.

Jones will therefore realize that he has ruffled Bill's feelings with his comment, "I think, Bill, this is the best way to do your job." So instead of trying to get Bill to understand him, he decides to try to understand Bill. He does this by encouraging Bill to speak. Instead of telling Bill how he should feel or think, he asks Bill such questions as, "Is this what you feel?" "Is this what you see?" "Is this what you assume?" Instead of ignoring Bill's evaluations as irrelevant, not valid, inconsequential, or false, he tries to understand Bill's reality as he feels it, perceives it, and assumes it to be. As Bill begins to open up, Jones's curiosity is piqued by this process.

"Bill isn't so dumb; he's quite an interesting guy" becomes Jones's attitude. And that is what Bill hears. Therefore Bill feels understood and accepted as a person. He becomes less defensive. He is in a better frame of mind to explore and re-examine his own perceptions, feelings, and assumptions. In this process he perceives Jones as a source of help. Bill feels free to express his differences. He feels that Jones has some respect for his capacity for self-direction. These positive feelings toward Jones make Bill more inclined to say, "Well, Jones, I don't quite agree with you that this is the best way to do my job, but I'll tell you what I'll do. I'll try to do it that way for a few days, and then I'll tell you what I think."

CONCLUSION.   I grant that my two orientations do not work themselves out in practice in quite so simple or neat a fashion as I have been able to work them out on paper. There are many other ways in which Bill could have responded to Smith in the first place. He might even have said, "O.K., boss, I agree that your way of doing my job is better." But Smith still would not have known how Bill felt when he made this statement or whether Bill was actually going to do his job differently. Likewise, Bill could have responded to Jones in a way different from my example. In spite of Jones's attitude, Bill might still be reluctant to express himself freely to his boss.

The purpose of my examples has not been to demonstrate the right or wrong way of communicating. My purpose has been simply to provide something concrete to point to when I make the following generalizations:

1. Smith represents to me a very common pattern of misunderstanding. The misunderstanding does not arise because Smith is not clear enough in expressing himself. It arises because of Smith's misevaluation of what is taking place when two people are talking together.

2. Smith's misevaluation of the process of personal communication consists of certain very common assumptions, e.g., (a) that what is taking place is something essentially logical; (b) that words in themselves apart from the people involved mean something; and (c) that the purpose of the interaction is to get Bill to see things from Smith's point of view.

3. Because of these assumptions, a chain reaction of perceptions and negative feelings is engendered which blocks communication. By ignoring Bill's feelings and by rationalizing his own, Smith ignores his relationship to Bill as one of the most important determinants of the communication. As a result, Bill hears Smith's attitude more clearly than the logical content of Smith's words. Bill feels that his individual uniqueness is being denied. His personal integrity being at stake, he becomes defensive and belligerent. As a result, Smith feels frustrated. He perceives Bill as stupid. So he says and does things which only provoke more defensiveness on the part of Bill.

4. In the case of Jones, I have tried to show what might possibly happen if we made a different evaluation of what is taking place when two people are talking together. Jones makes a different set of assumptions. He assumes (a) that what is taking place between him and Bill is an interaction of sentiments; (b) that Bill—not his words in themselves—means something; (c) that the object of the interaction is to give Bill an opportunity to express freely his differences.

5. Because of these assumptions, a psychological chain reaction of reinforcing feelings and perceptions is set up which facilitates communication between Bill and him. When Jones addresses himself to Bill's feelings and perceptions from Bill's point of view, Bill feels understood and accepted as a person; he feels free to express his differences. Bill sees Jones as a source of help; Jones sees Bill as an interesting person. Bill in turn becomes more cooperative.

6. If I have identified correctly these very common patterns of personal communication, then some interesting hypotheses can be stated:

(a) Jones's method works better than Smith's, not because of any magic, but because Jones has a better map than Smith of the process of personal communication.

(b) The practice of Jones's method, however, is not merely an intellectual exercise. It depends on Jones's capacity and willingness to see and accept points of view different from his own, and to practice this orientation in a face-to-face relationship. This practice involves an emotional as well as an intellectual achievement. It depends in part on Jones's awareness of himself, in part on the practice of a skill.

(c) Although our colleges and universities try to get students to appreciate intellectually points of view different from their own, very little is done to help them to implement this general intellec-tual appreciation in a simple face-to-face relationship—at the level of a skill. Most educational institutions train their students to be logical, lucid, and clear. Very little is done to help them to listen more skillfully. As a result, our educated world contains too many Smiths and too few Joneses.

(d) The biggest block to personal communication is man's inability to listen intelligently, understandingly, and skillfully to another person. This deficiency in the modern world is widespread and appalling. In our universities as well as elsewhere, too little is being done about it.

7. In conclusion, let me apologize for acting toward you the way Smith did. But who am I to violate a long-standing academic tradition!

LISTENING TO PEOPLE

RALPH G. NICHOLS AND
LEONARD A. STEVENS

Recently the top executives of a major manufacturing plant in the Chicago area were asked to survey the role that listening plays in their work. Later, an executive seminar on listening was held. Here are three typical comments made by participants:

▲ "Frankly, I had never thought of listening as an important subject by itself. But now that I am aware of it, I think that perhaps 80% of my work depends on my listening to someone, or on someone else listening to me."

▲ "I've been thinking back about things that have gone wrong over the past couple of years, and I suddenly realized that many of the troubles have resulted from someone not hearing something, or getting it in a distorted way."

▲ "It's interesting to me that we have considered so many facets of communication in the company, but have inadvertently overlooked listening. I've about decided that it's the most important link in the company's communications, and it's obviously also the weakest one."

These comments reflect part of an awakening that is taking place in a number of management circles. Business is tied together by its systems of communication. This communication, businessmen are discovering, depends more on the spoken word than it does on the written word; and the effectiveness of the spoken word hinges not so much on how people talk as on how they listen.

Authors' Note: The material for this article comes from our forthcoming book, *Are You Listening?* (New York, McGraw-Hill Book Company, Inc., scheduled for publication in September, 1957).

THE UNUSED POTENTIAL

It can be stated, with practically no qualification, that people in general do not know how to listen. They have ears that hear very well, but seldom have they acquired the necessary aural skills which would allow those ears to be used effectively for what is called *listening*.

For several years we have been testing the ability of people to understand and remember what they hear. At the University of Minnesota we examined the listening ability of several thousand students and of hundreds of business and professional people. In each case the person tested listened to short talks by faculty members and was examined for his grasp of the content.

These extensive tests led us to this general conclusion: immediately after the average person has listened to someone talk, he remembers only about half of what he has heard—no matter how carefully he thought he was listening.

What happens as time passes? Our own testing shows—and it has been substantiated by reports of research at Florida State University and Michigan State University[1]—that two months after listening to a talk, the average listener will remember only about 25% of what was said. In fact, after we have barely learned something, we tend to forget from one-half to one-third of it *within eight hours*; it is startling to realize that frequently we forget more in this first short interval than we do in the next six months.

GAP IN TRAINING. Behind this widespread inability to listen lies, in our opinion, a major oversight in our system of classroom instruction. We have focused attention on reading, considering it the primary medium by which we learn, and we have practically forgotten the art of listening. About six years are devoted to formal reading instruction in our school systems. Little emphasis is placed on speaking, and almost no attention has been given to the skill of listening, strange as this may be in view of the fact that so much lecturing is done in college. Listening training—if it could be called training—has often consisted merely of a series of admonitions extending from the first grade through college: "Pay attention!" "Now get this!" "Open your ears!" "Listen!"

Certainly our teachers feel the need for good listening. Why then have so many years passed without educators developing formal methods of teaching students to listen? We have been faced with several false assumptions which have blocked the teaching of listening. For example:

1. We have assumed that listening ability depends largely on intelligence, that "bright" people listen well, and "dull" ones poorly. There is no denying that low intelligence has something to do with inability to listen, but we have greatly exaggerated its importance. A poor listener is not necessarily an unintelligent person. To be good listeners we must apply certain skills that are acquired through either experience or training. If a person has not acquired these listening skills, his ability to understand and retain what he hears will be low. This can happen to people with both high and low levels of intelligence.

2. We have assumed that learning to read will automatically teach one to listen. While some of the skills attained through reading apply to listening, the assumption is far from completely valid. Listening is a different activity from reading and requires different skills. Research has shown that reading and listening skills do not improve at the same rate when only reading is taught.

   This means that in our schools, where little attention is paid to the aural element of communication, reading ability is continually upgraded while listening ability, left to falter along on its own, actually degenerates. As a fair reader and a bad listener, the typical student is graduated into a society where the chances are high that he will have to listen about three times as much as he reads.

The barriers to listening training that have been built up by such false assumptions are coming down.

Educators are realizing that listening is a skill that can be taught. In Nashville, for example, the public school system has started training in listening from elementary grades through high school. Listening is also taught in the Phoenix school system, in Cincinnati, and throughout the state of North Dakota. About two dozen major universities and colleges in the country now provide courses in listening.

At the University of Minnesota we have been presenting a course in listening to a large segment of the freshman class. Each group of students that has taken listening training has improved at least 25% in ability to understand the spoken word. Some of the groups have improved as much as 40%. We have also given a course in listening for adult education classes made up mostly of business and professional people. These people have made some of the highest gains in listening ability of any that we have seen. During one period, 60 men and women nearly doubled their listening test scores after working together on this skill one night a week for 17 weeks.

WAYS TO IMPROVEMENT

Any course or any effort that will lead to listening improvement should do two things:

1. Build awareness to factors that affect listening ability.

2. Build the kind of aural experience that can produce good listening habits.

At least a start on the first of these two educational elements can be made by readers of this article; a certain degree of awareness is developed by merely discussing factors that affect listening ability. Later we shall discuss some steps that might be taken in order to work at the second element.

TRACKS & SIDETRACKS. In general, people feel that concentration while listening is a greater problem than concentration during any other form of personal communication. Actually, listening concentration *is* more difficult. When we listen, concentration must be achieved despite a factor that is peculiar to aural communication, one of which few people are aware.

Basically, the problem is caused by the fact that we think much faster than we talk. The average rate of speech for most Americans is around 125 words per minute. This rate is slow going for the human brain, which is made up of more than 13 billion cells and operates in such a complicated but efficient manner that it makes the great, modern digital computers seem slow-witted. People who study the brain are not in complete agreement on how it functions when we think, but most psychologists believe that the basic medium of thought is language. Certainly words play a large part in our thinking processes, and the words race through our brains at speeds much higher than 125 words per minute. This means that, when we listen, we ask our brain to receive words at an extremely slow pace compared with its capabilities.

It might seem logical to slow down our thinking when we listen so as to coincide with the 125-word-per-minute speech rate, but slowing down thought processes seems to be a very difficult thing to do. When we listen, therefore, we continue thinking at high speed while the spoken words arrive at low speed. In the act of listening, the differential between thinking and speaking rates means that our brain works with hundreds of words in addition to those that we hear, assembling thoughts other than those spoken to us. To phrase it another way, we can listen and still have some spare time for thinking.

The use, or misuse, of this spare thinking time holds the answer to how well a person can concentrate on the spoken word.

Case of the Disenchanted Listener.   In our studies at the University of Minnesota, we find most people do not use their spare thinking time wisely as they listen. Let us illustrate how this happens by describing a familiar experience:

A, the boss, is talking to B, the subordinate, about a new program that the firm is planning to launch. B is a poor listener. In this instance, he tries to listen well, but he has difficulty concentrating on what A has to say.

A starts talking and B launches into the listening process, grasping every word and phrase that comes into his ears. But right away B finds that, because of A's slow rate of speech, he has time to think of things other than the spoken line of thought. Subconsciously, B decides to sandwich a few thoughts of his own into the aural ones that are arriving so slowly. So B quickly dashes out onto a mental sidetrack and thinks something like this: "Oh, yes, before I leave I want to tell A about the big success of the meeting I called yesterday." Then B comes back to A's spoken line of thought and listens for a few more words.

There is plenty of time for B to do just what he has done, dash away from what he hears and then return quickly, and he continues taking sidetracks to his own private thoughts. Indeed, he can hardly avoid doing this because over the years the process has become a strong aural habit of his.

But, sooner or later, on one of the mental sidetracks, B is almost sure to stay away too long. When he returns, A is moving along ahead of him. At this point it becomes harder for B to understand A, simply because B has missed part of the oral message. The private mental sidetracks become more inviting than ever, and B slides off onto several of them. Slowly he misses more and more of what A has to say.

When A is through talking, it is safe to say that B will have received and understood less than half of what was spoken to him.

RULES FOR GOOD RECEPTION.   A major task in helping people to listen better is teaching them to use their spare thinking time efficiently as they listen. What does "efficiently" mean? To answer this question, we made an extensive study of people's listening habits, especially trying to discover what happens when people listen well.

We found that good listeners regularly engage in four mental activities, each geared to the oral discourse and taking place concurrently with that oral discourse. All four of these mental activities are neatly coordinated when listening works at its best.

They tend to direct a maximum amount of thought to the message being received, leaving a minimum amount of time for mental excursions on sidetracks leading away from the talker's thought. Here are the four processes:

1. The listener thinks ahead of the talker, trying to anticipate what the oral discourse is leading to and what conclusions will be drawn from the words spoken at the moment.

2. The listener weighs the evidence used by the talker to support the points that he makes. "Is this evidence valid?" the listener asks himself. "Is it the complete evidence?"

3. Periodically the listener reviews and mentally summarizes the points of the talk completed thus far.

4. Throughout the talk, the listener "listens between the lines" in search of meaning that is not necessarily put into spoken words. He pays attention to nonverbal communication (facial expressions, gestures, tone of voice) to see if it adds meaning to the spoken words. He asks himself, "Is the talker purposely skirting some area of the subject? Why is he doing so?"

The speed at which we think compared to that at which people talk allows plenty of time to accomplish these four mental tasks when we listen; however, they do require practice before they can become part of the mental agility that makes for good listening. In our training courses we have devised aural exercises designed to give people this practice and thereby build up good habits of aural concentration.

LISTENING FOR IDEAS. Another factor that affects listening ability concerns the reconstruction of orally communicated thoughts once they have been received by the listener. To illustrate:

The newspapers reported not too long ago that a church was torn down in Europe and shipped stone by stone to America, where it was reassembled in its original form. The moving of the church is analogous to what happens when a person speaks and is understood by a listener. The talker has a thought. To transmit his thought, he takes it apart by putting it into words. The words, sent through the air to the listener, must then be mentally reassembled into the original thought if they are to be thoroughly understood. But most people do not know what to listen *for*, and so cannot reconstruct the thought.

For some reason many people take great pride in being able to say that above all they try to "get the facts" when they listen. It seems logical enough to do so. If a person gets all the facts, he should certainly understand what is said to him. Therefore, many people try to memorize every single fact that is spoken. With such practice at "getting the facts," the listener, we can safely assume, will develop a serious bad listening habit.

Memorizing facts is, to begin with, a virtual impossibility for most people in the listening situation. As one fact is being memorized, the whole, or part, of the next fact is almost certain to be missed. When he is doing his very best, the listener is likely to catch only a few facts, garble many others, and completely miss the remainder. Even in the case of people who *can* aurally assimilate all the facts that they hear, one at a time as they hear them, listening is still likely to be at a low level; they are concerned with the pieces of what they hear and tend to miss the broad areas of the spoken communication.

When people talk, they want listeners to understand their *ideas*. The facts are useful chiefly for constructing the ideas. Grasping ideas, we have found, is the skill on which the good listener concentrates. He remembers facts only long enough to understand the ideas that are built from them. But then, almost miraculously, grasping an idea will help the listener to remember the supporting facts more effectively than does the person who goes after facts alone. This listening skill is one which definitely can be taught, one in which people can build experience leading toward improved aural communication.

EMOTIONAL FILTERS. In different degrees and in many different ways, listening ability is affected by our emotions.[2] Figuratively we reach up and mentally turn off what we do not want to hear. Or, on the other hand, when someone says what we especially want to hear, we open our ears wide, accepting everything—truths, half-truths, or fiction. We might say, then, that our emotions act as aural filters. At times they in effect cause deafness, and at other times they make listening altogether too easy.

If we hear something that opposes our most deeply rooted prejudices, notions, convictions, mores, or complexes, our brains may become overstimulated, and not in a direction that leads to good listening. We mentally plan a rebuttal to what we hear, formulate a question designed to embarrass the talker, or perhaps simply turn to thoughts that support our own feelings on the subject at hand. For example:

The firm's accountant goes to the general manager and says: "I have just heard from the Bureau of Internal Revenue, and . . . ." The general manager suddenly breathes harder as he thinks, "That blasted bureau! Can't they leave me alone? Every year the government milks my profits to a point where . . . ." Red in the face, he whirls and stares out the window. The label "Bureau of Internal Revenue" cuts loose emotions that stop the general manager's listening.

In the meantime, the accountant may go on to say that here is a chance to save $3,000 this year if the general manager will take a few simple steps. The fuming general manager may hear this—if the accountant presses hard enough—but the chances are he will fail to comprehend it.

When emotions make listening too easy, it usually results from hearing something which supports the deeply rooted inner feelings that we hold. When we hear such support, our mental barriers are dropped and everything is welcomed. We ask few questions about what we hear; our critical faculties are put out of commission by our emotions. Thinking drops to a minimum because we are hearing thoughts that we have harbored for years in support of our inner feelings. It is good to hear someone else think those thoughts, so we lazily enjoy the whole experience.

What can we do about these emotional filters? The solution is not easy in practice, although it can be summed up in this simple admonition: *hear the man out.* Following are two pointers that often help in training people to do this:

1. *Withhold evaluation*—This is one of the most important principles of learning, especially learning through the ear. It requires self-control, sometimes more than many of us can muster, but with persistent practice it can be turned into a valuable habit. While listening, the main object is to comprehend each point made by the talker. Judgments and decisions should be reserved until after the talker has finished. At that time, and only then, review his main ideas and assess them.

2. *Hunt for negative evidence*—When we listen, it is human to go on a militant search for evidence which proves us right in what we believe. Seldom do we make a search for evidence to prove ourselves wrong. The latter type of effort is not easy, for behind its application must lie a generous spirit and real breadth of outlook. However, an important part of listening comprehension is found in the search for negative evidence in what we hear. If we make up our minds to seek out the ideas that might prove us wrong, as well as those that might prove us right, we are less in danger of missing what people have to say.

BENEFITS IN BUSINESS

The improvement of listening, or simply an effort to make people aware of how important their listening ability is, can be of great value in today's business. When people in business fail to hear and understand each other, the results can be costly. Such things as numbers, dates, places, and names are especially easy to confuse, but the most straightforward agreements are often subjects of listening errors, too. When these mistakes are compounded, the resulting cost and inefficiency in business communication become serious. Building awareness of the importance of listening among employees can eliminate a large percentage of this type of aural error.

What are some of the specific problems which better listening can help solve?

LESS PAPER WORK.   For one thing, it leads to economy of communication. Incidents created by poor listening frequently give businessmen a real fear of oral communication. As a result, they insist that more and more communication should be put into writing. A great deal of communication needs to be on the record, but the pressure to write is often carried too far. The smallest detail becomes "memoed." Paper work piles higher and higher and causes part of the tangle we call red tape. Many times less writing and more speaking would be advisable—*if* we could plan on good listening.

Writing and reading are much slower communication elements than speaking and listening. They require more personnel, more equipment, and more space than do speaking and listening. Often a stenographer and a messenger are needed, to say nothing of dictating machines, typewriters, and other writing materials. Few people ever feel it is safe to throw away a written communication; so filing equipment is needed, along with someone to do the filing.

In oral communication there are more human senses at work than in the visual; and if there is good listening, more can often be communicated in one message. And, perhaps most important of all, there is the give-and-take feature of oral communication. If the listener does not understand a message, he has the opportunity to straighten matters out then and there.

UPWARD COMMUNICATION.   The skill of listening becomes extremely important when we talk about "upward communication." There are many avenues through which management can send messages downward through a business organization, but there are few avenues for movement of information in the upward direction. Perhaps the most obvious of the upward avenues is the human chain of people talking to people: the man working at the bench talks to his foreman, the foreman to his superintendent, the superintendent to his boss; and,

relayed from person to person, the information eventually reaches the top.

This communication chain has potential, but it seldom works well because it is full of bad listeners. There can be failure for at least three reasons:

▲ Without good listeners, people do not talk freely and the flow of communication is seldom set in motion.

▲ If the flow should start, only one bad listener is needed to stop its movement toward the top.

▲ Even if the flow should continue to the top, the messages are likely to be badly distorted along the way.

It would be absurd to assume that these upward communication lines could be made to operate without hitches, but there is no reason to think that they cannot be improved by better listening. But the first steps must be taken by top management people. More and better listening on their part can prime the pumps that start the upward flow of information.

HUMAN RELATIONS.   People in all phases of business need to feel free to talk to their superiors and to know they will be met with sympathetic understanding. But too many superiors—although they announce that their doors are always open—fail to listen; and their subordinates, in the face of this failure, do not feel free to say what they want to say. As a result, subordinates withdraw from their superiors more and more. They fail to talk about important problems that should be aired for both parties' benefit. When such problems remain unaired, they often turn into unrealistic monsters that come back to plague the superior who failed to listen.

The remedy for this sort of aural failure—and it should be applied when subordinates feel the need to talk—is what we have called "nondirective listening." The listener hears, really tries to understand, and later shows understanding by taking action if it is required. Above all, during an oral discourse, the listener refrains from firing his own thoughts back at the person talking or from indicating his displeasure or disapproval by his mannerisms or gestures; he speaks up only to ask for clarification of a point.

Since the listener stands the chance of hearing that his most dearly held notions and ideas may be wrong, this is not an easy thing to do. To listen nondirectively without fighting back requires more courage than most of us can muster. But when nondirective listening can be applied, the results are usually worth the effort. The persons talking have a chance to unburden themselves. Equally important, the odds are better that the listener can counsel or act effectively when the time comes to make a move.

Listening is only one phase of human relations, only one aspect of the administrator's job; by itself it will solve no major problems. Yet the past experience of many executives and organizations leaves no doubt, in our opinion, that better listening can lead to a reduction of the human frictions which beset many businesses today.

LISTENING TO SELL.   High-pressure salesmanship is rapidly giving way to low-pressure methods in the marketing of industrial and consumer goods. Today's successful salesman is likely to center his attention on the customer-problem approach of selling.

To put this approach to work, the skill of listening becomes an essential tool for the salesman, while his vocal agility becomes less important. *How* a salesman talks turns out to be relatively unimportant because *what* he says, when it is guided by his listening, gives power to the spoken word. In other words, the salesman's listening becomes an on-the-spot form of customer research that can immediately be put to work in formulating any sales talk.

Regardless of the values that listening may hold for people who live by selling, a great many sales organizations seem to hold to the conviction that glibness has magic. Their efforts at improvement are aimed mainly at the talking side of salesmanship. It is our conviction, however, that with the typical salesman the ability to talk will almost take care of itself, but the ability to listen is something in real need of improvement.

IN CONFERENCE.   The most important affairs in business are conducted around conference tables. A great deal has been said and written about how to

talk at a conference, how to compromise, how to get problem-centered, and how to cope with certain types of individuals. All these things can be very important, but too frequently the experts forget to say, "First and foremost you must learn to listen at a conference."

The reason for this is simple when we think of the basic purpose for holding almost any conference. People get together to contribute their different viewpoints, knowledge, and experience to members of the group, which then seeks the best of all the conferees' thinking to solve a common problem. If there is far more talking than listening at a conference, however, the oral contributions made to the group are hardly worth the breath required to produce them.

More and better listening at any conference is certain to facilitate the exchange of ideas so important to the success of a meeting. It also offers many other advantages; for example, when participants do a good job of listening, their conference is more likely to remain centered on the problem at hand and less likely to go off on irrelevant tangents.

The first steps toward improved conference listening can be taken by the group leader. If he will simply make an opening statement calling attention to the importance of listening, he is very likely to increase the participants' aural response. And if the leader himself does a good job of listening, he stands the chance of being imitated by the others in his group.

CONCLUSION

Some businessmen may want to take steps to develop a listening improvement program in their companies. Here are 14 suggestions designed to carry on what we hope this article has already started to do—build awareness of listening.

1. Devote an executive seminar, or seminars, to a discussion of the roles and functions of listening as a business tool.

2. Use the filmed cases now becoming available for management training programs.[3] Since these cases present the problem as it would appear in

reality, viewers are forced to practice good listening habits in order to be sure of what is going on—and this includes not only hearing the sound track but also watching the facial mannerisms, gestures, and motions of the actors.

3. If possible, bring in qualified speakers and ask them to discuss listening with special reference to how it might apply to business. Such speakers are available at a number of universities where listening is being taught as a part of communication training.

4. Conduct a self-inventory by the employees regarding their listening on the job. Provide everyone with a simple form divided into spaces for each hour of the day. Each space should be further divided to allow the user to keep track of the amount of time spent in reading, writing, speaking, and listening. Discuss the results of these forms after the communication times have been totaled. What percentage of the time do people spend listening? What might improved listening mean in terms of job effectiveness?

5. Give a test in listening ability to people and show them the scores that they make. There is at least one standardized test for this purpose.[4] Discuss the meaning of the scores with the individuals tested.

6. Build up a library of spoken-word records of literature, speeches, and so forth (many can be purchased through record stores), and make them available in a room that has a record player. Also, lend the records to employees who might wish to take them home to enjoy them at their leisure. For such a library, material pertinent to the employees' jobs might be recorded so that those who are interested can listen for educational purposes.

7. Record a number of actual briefing sessions that may be held by plant superintendents or others. When new people go to work for the company, ask them to listen to these sessions as part of their initial training. Check their comprehension of what they hear by means of brief objec-

tive tests. Emphasize that this is being done because listening is important on the new jobs.

8. Set up role-playing situations wherein executives are asked to cope with complaints comparable to those that they might hear from subordinates. Ask observers to comment on how well an executive seems to listen. Do his remarks reflect a good job of listening? Does he keep himself from becoming emotionally involved in what the subordinate says? Does the executive listen in a way which would encourage the subordinate to talk freely?

9. Ask salesmen to divide a notebook into sections, one for each customer. After making a call, a salesman should write down all useful information received aurally from the customer. As the information grows, he should refer to it before each return visit to a customer.

10. Where a sales organization has a number of friendly customers, invite some of the more articulate ones to join salesmen in a group discussion of sales techniques. How do the customers feel about talking and listening on the part of salesmen? Try to get the customers to make listening critiques of salesmen they encounter.

11. In a training session, plan and hold a conference on a selected problem and tape-record it. Afterwards, play back the recording. Discuss it in terms of listening. Do the oral contributions of different participants reflect good listening? If the conference should go off the track, try to analyze the causes in terms of listening.

12. If there is time after a regularly scheduled conference, hold a listening critique. Ask each member to evaluate the listening attention that he received while talking and to report his analysis of his own listening performance.

13. In important management meetings on controversial issues try Irving J. Lee's "Procedure for 'Coercing' Agreement."[5] Under the ground rules for this procedure, which Lee outlined in detail in his article, the chairman calls for a pe-

riod during which proponents of a hotly debated view can state their position without interruption; the opposition is limited to (a) the asking of questions for clarification, (b) requests for information concerning the peculiar characteristics of the proposal being considered; and (c) requests for information as to whether it is possible to check the speaker's assumptions or predictions.

14. Sponsor a series of lectures for employees, their families, and their friends. The lectures might be on any number of interesting topics that have educational value as well as entertainment features. Point out that these lectures are available as part of a listening improvement program.

Not all of these suggestions are applicable to every situation, of course. Each firm will have to adapt them to its own particular needs. The most important thing, however, may not be what happens when a specific suggestion is followed, but rather simply what happens when people become aware of the problem of listening and of what improved aural skills can do for their jobs and their businesses.

[1]See E. J. J. Kramar and Thomas R. Lewis, "Comparison of Visual and Nonvisual Listening," *Journal of Communication*, November 1951, p. 16; and Arthur W. Heilman, "An Investigation in Measuring and Improving Listening Ability of College Freshmen," *Speech Monographs*, November 1951, p. 308.

[2]See Wendell Johnson, "The Fateful Process of Mr. A Talking to Mr. B," HBR January–February 1953, p. 49.

[3]See George W. Gibson, "The Filmed Case in Management Training," HBR May–June 1957, p. 123.

[4]Brown-Carlsen Listening Comprehension Test (Yonkers-on-Hudson, World Book Company).

[5]HBR January–February 1954, p. 39.

HOW TO RUN A MEETING

ANTONY JAY

Why have a meeting anyway? Why indeed? A great many important matters are quite satisfactorily conducted by a single individual who consults nobody. A great many more are resolved by a letter, a memo, a phone call, or a simple conversation between two people. Sometimes five minutes spent with six people separately is more effective and productive than a half-hour meeting with them all together.

Certainly a great many meetings waste a great deal of everyone's time and seem to be held for historical rather than practical reasons; many long-established committees are little more than memorials to dead problems. It would probably save no end of managerial time if every committee had to discuss its own dissolution once a year, and put up a case if it felt it should continue for another twelve months. If this requirement did nothing else, it would at least refocus the minds of the committee members on their purposes and objectives.

But having said that, and granting that "referring the matter to a committee" can be a device for diluting authority, diffusing responsibility, and delaying decisions, I cannot deny that meetings fulfill a deep human need. Man is a social species. In every organization and every human culture of which we have record, people come together in small groups at regular and frequent intervals, and in larger "tribal" gatherings from time to time. If there are no meetings in the places where they work, people's attachment to the organizations they work for will be small, and they will meet in regular formal or informal gatherings in associations, societies, teams, clubs, or pubs when work is over.

This need for meetings is clearly something more positive than just a legacy from our primitive hunting past. From time to time, some technomaniac or other comes up with a vision of the executive who never leaves his home, who controls his whole operation from an all-electronic, multichannel, microwave, fiber-optic video display dream console in his living room. But any manager who has ever had to make an organization work greets this vision with a smile that soon stretches into a yawn.

There is a world of science fiction, and a world of human reality; and those who live in the world of human reality know that it is held together by face-to-face meetings. A meeting still performs functions that will never be taken over by telephones, teleprinters, Xerox copiers, tape recorders, television monitors, or any other technological instruments of the information revolution.

FUNCTIONS OF A MEETING

At this point, it may help us understand the meaning of meetings if we look at the six main functions that meetings will always perform better than any of the more recent communication devices:

1. In the simplest and most basic way, a meeting defines the team, the group, or the unit. Those present belong to it; those absent do not. Everyone is able to look around and perceive the whole group and sense the collective identity of which he or she forms a part. We all know who we are—whether we are on the board of Universal International, in the overseas sales department of Flexitube, Inc., a member of the school management committee, on the East Hampton football team, or in Section No. 2 of Platoon 4, Company B.

2. A meeting is the place where the group revises, updates, and adds to what it knows *as a group*. Every group creates its own pool of shared knowledge, experience, judgment, and folklore. But the pool consists only of what the individuals have experienced or discussed as a group—i.e., those things which every individual knows that all the others know, too. This pool not only helps

all members to do their jobs more intelligently, but it also greatly increases the speed and efficiency of all communications among them. The group knows that all special nuances and wider implications in a brief statement will be immediately clear to its members. An enormous amount of material can be left unsaid that would have to be made explicit to an outsider.

But this pool needs constant refreshing and replenishing, and occasionally the removal of impurities. So the simple business of exchanging information and ideas that members have acquired separately or in smaller groups since the last meeting is an important contribution to the strength of the group. By questioning and commenting on new contributions, the group performs an important "digestive" process that extracts what's valuable and discards the rest.

Some ethologists call this capacity to share knowledge and experience among a group "the social mind," conceiving it as a single mind dispersed among a number of skulls. They recognize that this "social mind" has a special creative power, too. A group of people meeting together can often produce better ideas, plans, and decisions than can a single individual, or a number of individuals, each working alone. The meeting can of course also produce worse outputs or none at all, if it is a bad meeting.

However, when the combined experience, knowledge, judgment, authority, and imagination of a half dozen people are brought to bear on issues, a great many plans and decisions are improved and sometimes transformed. The original idea that one person might have come up with singly is tested, amplified, refined, and shaped by argument and discussion (which often acts on people as some sort of chemical stimulant to better performance), until it satisfies far more requirements and overcomes many more objections than it could in its original form.

3. A meeting helps every individual understand both the collective aim of the group and the way in which his own and everyone else's work can contribute to the group's success.

4. A meeting creates in all present a commitment to the decisions it makes and the objectives it pursues. Once something has been decided, even if you originally argued against it, your membership in the group entails an obligation to accept the decision. The alternative is to leave the group, but in practice this is very rarely a dilemma of significance. Real opposition to decisions within organizations usually consists of one part disagreement with the decision to nine parts resentment at not being consulted before the decision. For most people on most issues, it is enough to know that their views were heard and considered. They may regret that they were not followed, but they accept the outcome.

And just as the decision of any team is binding on all the members, so the decisions of a meeting of people higher up in an organization carry a greater authority than any decision by a single executive. It is much harder to challenge a decision of the board than of the chief executive acting on his own. The decision-making authority of a meeting is of special importance for long-term policies and procedures.

5. In the world of management, a meeting is very often the only occasion where the team or group actually exists and works as a group, and the only time when the supervisor, manager, or executive is actually perceived as the leader of the team, rather than as the official to whom individuals report. In some jobs the leader does guide his team through his personal presence—not just the leader of a pit gang or construction team, but also the chef in the hotel kitchen and the maître d'hôtel in the restaurant, or the supervisor in a department store. But in large administrative headquarters, the daily or weekly meeting is often the only time when the leader is ever perceived to be guiding a team rather than doing a job.

6. A meeting is a status arena. It is no good to pretend that people are not or should not be concerned with their status relative to the other members in a group. It is just another part of

human nature that we have to live with. It is a not insignificant fact that the word *order* means (a) hierarchy or pecking order; (b) an instruction or command; and (c) stability and the way things ought to be, as in "put your affairs in order," or "law and order." All three definitions are aspects of the same idea, which is indivisible.

Since a meeting is so often the only time when members get the chance to find out their relative standing, the "arena" function is inevitable. When a group is new, has a new leader, or is composed of people like department heads who are in competition for promotion and who do not work in a single team outside the meeting, "arena behavior" is likely to figure more largely, even to the point of dominating the proceedings. However, it will hardly signify with a long-established group that meets regularly.

Despite the fact that a meeting can perform all of the foregoing main functions, there is no guarantee that it will do so in any given situation. It is all too possible that any single meeting may be a waste of time, an irritant, or a barrier to the achievement of the organization's objectives.

WHAT SORT OF MEETING?

While my purpose in this article is to show the critical points at which most meetings go wrong, and to indicate ways of putting them right, I must first draw some important distinctions in the size and type of meetings that we are dealing with.

Meetings can be graded by *size* into three broad categories: (1) the assembly—100 or more people who are expected to do little more than listen to the main speaker or speakers; (2) the council—40 or 50 people who are basically there to listen to the main speaker or speakers but who can come in with questions or comments and who may be asked to contribute something on their own account; and (3) the committee—up to 10 (or at the most 12) people, all of whom more or less speak on an equal footing under the guidance and control of a chairman.

We are concerned in this article only with the "committee" meeting, though it may be described as a committee, a subcommittee, a study group, a project team, a working party, a board, or by any of dozens of other titles. It is by far the most common meeting all over the world, and can perhaps be traced back to the primitive hunting band through which our species evolved. Beyond doubt it constitutes the bulk of the 11 million meetings that—so it has been calculated—take place every day in the United States.

Apart from the distinction of size, there are certain considerations regarding the *type* of meeting that profoundly affect its nature. For instance:

1. *Frequency*—A daily meeting is different from a weekly one, and a weekly meeting from a monthly one. Irregular, ad hoc, quarterly, and annual meetings are different again. On the whole, the frequency of meetings defines—or perhaps even determines—the degree of unity of the group.

2. *Composition*—Do the members work together on the same project, such as the nursing and ancillary staff on the same ward of a hospital? Do they work on different but parallel tasks, like a meeting of the company's plant managers or regional sales managers? Or are they a diverse group—strangers to each other, perhaps—united only by the meeting itself and by a common interest in realizing its objectives?

3. *Motivation*—Do the members have a common objective in their work, like a football team? Or do they to some extent have a competitive working relationship, like managers of subsidiary companies at a meeting with the chief executive, or the heads of research, production, and marketing discussing finance allocation for the coming year? Or does the desire for success through the meeting itself unify them, like a neighborhood action group or a new product design committee?

4. *Decision process*—How does the meeting group ultimately reach its decisions? By a general consensus, "the feeling of the meeting"? By a majority vote? Or are the decisions left entirely to the chairman himself, after he has listened to the facts, opinions, and discussions?

KINDS OF MEETINGS. The experienced meeting-goer will recognize that, although there seem to be five quite different methods of analyzing a meeting, in practice there is a tendency for certain kinds of meetings to sort themselves out into one of three categories. Consider:

The *daily meeting,* where people work together on the same project with a common objective and reach decisions informally by general agreement.

The *weekly* or *monthly meeting,* where members work on different but parallel projects and where there is a certain competitive element and a greater likelihood that the chairman will make the final decision himself.

The *irregular, occasional,* or *"special project" meeting,* composed of people whose normal work does not bring them into contact and whose work has little or no relationship to the others'. They are united only by the project the meeting exists to promote and motivated by the desire that the project should succeed. Though actual voting is uncommon, every member effectively has a veto.

Of these three kinds of meetings, it is the first—the workface type—that is probably the most common. It is also, oddly enough, the one most likely to be successful. Operational imperatives usually ensure that it is brief, and the participants' experience of working side by side ensures that communication is good.

The other two types are a different matter. In these meetings all sorts of human crosscurrents can sweep the discussion off course, and errors of psychology and technique on the chairman's part can defeat its purposes. Moreover, these meetings are likely to bring together the more senior people and to produce decisions that profoundly affect the efficiency, prosperity, and even survival of the whole organization. It is, therefore, toward these higher-level meetings that the lessons of this article are primarily directed.

BEFORE THE MEETING

The most important question you should ask is: "What is this meeting intended to achieve?" You can ask it in different ways—"What would be the likely consequences of not holding it?" "When it is over, how shall I judge whether it was a success or a failure?"—but unless you have a very clear requirement from the meeting, there is a grave danger that it will be a waste of everyone's time.

DEFINING THE OBJECTIVE. You have already looked at the six main functions that all meetings perform, but if you are trying to use a meeting to achieve definite objectives, there are in practice only certain types of objectives it can really achieve. Every item on the agenda can be placed in one of the following four categories, or divided up into sections that fall into one or more of them:

1. *Informative-digestive*—Obviously, it is a waste of time for the meeting to give out purely factual information that would be better circulated in a document. But if the information should be heard from a particular person, or if it needs some clarification and comment to make sense of it, or if it has deep implications for the members of the meeting, then it is perfectly proper to introduce an item onto the agenda that requires no conclusion, decision, or action from the meeting; it is enough, simply, that the meeting should receive and discuss a report.

   The "informative-digestive" function includes progress reports—to keep the group up to date on the current status of projects it is responsible for or that affect its deliberations—and review of completed projects in order to come to a collective judgment and to see what can be learned from them for the next time.

2. *Constructive-originative*—This "What shall we do?" function embraces all items that require something new to be devised, such as a new policy, a new strategy, a new sales target, a new product, a new marketing plan, a new procedure, and so forth. This sort of discussion asks people to contribute their knowledge, experience, judgment, and ideas. Obviously, the plan will probably be inadequate unless all relevant parties are present and pitching in.

3. *Executive responsibilities*—This is the "How shall we do it?" function, which comes after it has been decided what the members are going to do;

at this point, executive responsibilities for the different components of the task have to be distributed around the table. Whereas in the second function the contributors' importance is their knowledge and ideas, here their contribution is the responsibility for implementing the plan. The fact that they and their subordinates are affected by it makes their contribution especially significant.

It is of course possible to allocate these executive responsibilities without a meeting, by separate individual briefings, but several considerations often make a meeting desirable:

First, it enables the members as a group to find the best way of achieving the objectives.

Second, it enables each member to understand and influence the way in which his own job fits in with the jobs of the others and with the collective task.

Third, if the meeting is discussing the implementation of a decision taken at a higher level, securing the group's consent may be of prime importance. If so, the fact that the group has the opportunity to formulate the detailed action plan itself may be the decisive factor in securing its agreement, because in that case the final decision belongs, as it were, to the group. Everyone is committed to what the group decides and is collectively responsible for the final shape of the project, as well as individually answerable for his own part in it. Ideally, this sort of agenda item starts with a policy, and ends with an action plan.

4. *Legislative framework*—Above and around all considerations of "What to do" and "How to do it," there is a framework—a departmental or divisional organization—and a system of rules, routines, and procedures within and through which all the activity takes place. Changing this framework and introducing a new organization or new procedures can be deeply disturbing to committee members and a threat to their status and long-term security. Yet leaving it unchanged can stop the organization from adapting to a changing world. At whatever level this change happens, it

must have the support of all the perceived leaders whose groups are affected by it.

The key leaders for this legislative function must collectively make or confirm the decision; if there is any important dissent, it is very dangerous to close the discussion and make the decision by decree. The group leaders cannot expect quick decisions if they are seeking to change the organization framework and routines that people have grown up with. Thus they must be prepared to leave these items unresolved for further discussion and consultation. As Francis Bacon put it—and it has never been put better—"Counsels to which time hath not been called, time will not ratify."

MAKING PREPARATIONS. The four different functions just discussed may of course be performed by a single meeting, as the group proceeds through the agenda. Consequently, it may be a useful exercise for the chairman to go through the agenda, writing beside each item which function it is intended to fulfill. This exercise helps clarify what is expected from the discussion and helps focus on which people to bring in and what questions to ask them.

People. The value and success of a committee meeting are seriously threatened if too many people are present. Between 4 and 7 is generally ideal, 10 is tolerable, and 12 is the outside limit. So the chairman should do everything he can to keep numbers down, consistent with the need to invite everyone with an important contribution to make.

The leader may have to leave out people who expect to come or who have always come. For this job he may need tact; but since people generally preserve a fiction that they are overworked already and dislike serving on committees, it is not usually hard to secure their consent to stay away.

If the leader sees no way of getting the meeting down to a manageable size, he can try the following devices: (a) analyze the agenda to see whether everyone has to be present for every item (he may be able to structure the agenda so that some people can leave at half time and others can arrive); (b) ask himself whether he doesn't really need two separate, smaller meetings rather than one big one; and (c) determine whether one or two groups can be asked to thrash some of the topics out in advance so that only one of them needs to come in with its proposals.

Remember, too, that a few words with a member on the day before a meeting can increase the value of the meeting itself, either by ensuring that an important point is raised that comes better from the floor than from the chair or by preventing a time-wasting discussion of a subject that need not be touched on at all.

Papers.   The agenda is by far the most important piece of paper. Properly drawn up, it has a power of speeding and clarifying a meeting that very few people understand or harness. The main fault is to make it unnecessarily brief and vague. For example, the phrase "development budget" tells nobody very much, whereas the longer explanation "To discuss the proposal for reduction of the 1976-1977 development budget now that the introduction of our new product has been postponed" helps all committee members to form some views or even just to look up facts and figures in advance.

Thus the leader should not be afraid of a long agenda, provided that the length is the result of his analyzing and defining each item more closely, rather than of his adding more items than the meeting can reasonably consider in the time allowed. He should try to include, very briefly, some indication of the reason for each topic to be discussed. If one item is of special interest to the group, it is often a good idea to single it out for special mention in a covering note.

The leader should also bear in mind the useful device of heading each item "For information," "For discussion," or "For decision" so that those at the meeting know where they are trying to get to.

And finally, the chairman should not circulate the agenda too far in advance, since the less organized members will forget it or lose it. Two or three days is about right—unless the supporting papers are voluminous.

Other 'paper' considerations: The order of items on the agenda is important. Some aspects are obvious—the items that need urgent decision have to come before those that can wait till next time. Equally, the leader does not discuss the budget for the reequipment program before discussing whether to put the reequipment off until next year. But some aspects are not so obvious. Consider:

▲ The early part of a meeting tends to be more lively and creative than the end of it, so if an item needs mental energy, bright ideas, and clear heads, it may be better to put it high up on the list. Equally, if there is one item of great interest and concern to everyone, it may be a good idea to hold it back for a while and get some other useful work done first. Then the star item can be introduced to carry the meeting over the attention lag that sets in after the first 15 to 20 minutes of the meeting.

▲ Some items unite the meeting in a common front while others divide the members one from another. The leader may want to start with unity before entering into division, or he may prefer the other way around. The point is to be aware of the choice and to make it consciously, because it is apt to make a difference to the whole atmosphere of the meeting. It is almost always a good idea to find a unifying item with which to end the meeting.

▲ A common fault is to dwell too long on trivial but urgent items, to the exclusion of subjects of fundamental importance whose significance is long-term rather than immediate. This can be remedied by putting on the agenda the time at which discussion of the important long-term issue will begin—and by sticking to it.

▲ Very few business meetings achieve anything of value after two hours, and an hour and a half is enough time to allocate for most purposes.

▲ It is often a good idea to put the finishing time of a meeting on the agenda as well as the starting time.

▲ If meetings have a tendency to go on too long, the chairman should arrange to start them one hour before lunch or one hour before the end of work. Generally, items that ought to be kept brief can be introduced ten minutes from a fixed end point.

▲ The practice of circulating background or proposal papers along with the minutes is, in principle, a good one. It not only saves time, but it also helps in formulating useful questions and considerations in advance. But the whole idea is sabotaged once the papers get too long; they should be brief or provide a short summary. If they are circulated, obviously the chairman has to read them, or at least must not be caught not having read them. (One chairman, more noted for his cunning than his conscientiousness, is said to have spent 30 seconds before each meeting going through all the papers he had not read with a thick red pen, marking lines and question marks in the margins at random, and making sure these were accidentally made visible to the meeting while the subject was being discussed.) ·

▲ If papers are produced at the meeting for discussion, they should obviously be brief and simple, since everyone has to read them. It is a supreme folly to bring a group of people together to read six pages of closely printed sheets to themselves. The exception is certain kinds of financial and statistical papers whose function is to support and illustrate verbal points as reference documents rather than to be swallowed whole: these are often better tabled at the meeting.

▲ All items should be thought of and thought about in advance if they are to be usefully discussed. Listing "Any other business" on the agenda is an invitation to waste time. This does not absolutely preclude the chairman's announcing an extra agenda item at a meeting if something really urgent and unforeseen crops up or is suggested to him by a member, provided it is fairly simple and straightforward. Nor does it preclude his leaving time for general unstructured discussion after the close of the meeting.

▲ The chairman, in going through the agenda items in advance, can usefully insert his own brief notes of points he wants to be sure are not omitted from the discussion. A brief marginal scribble of "How much notice?" or "Standby arrangements?" or whatever is all that is necessary.

THE CHAIRMAN'S JOB

Let's say that you have just been appointed chairman of the committee. You tell everyone that it is a bore or a chore. You also tell them that you have been appointed "for my sins." But the point is that you tell them. There is no getting away from it: some sort of honor or glory attaches to the chairman's role. Almost everyone is in some way pleased and proud to be made chairman of something. And that is three quarters of the trouble.

MASTER OR SERVANT? Their appointment as committee chairman takes people in different ways. Some seize the opportunity to impose their will on a group that they see themselves licensed to dominate. Their chairmanship is a harangue, interspersed with demands for group agreement.

Others are more like scoutmasters, for whom the collective activity of the group is satisfaction enough, with no need for achievement. Their chairmanship is more like the endless stoking and fueling of a campfire that is not cooking anything.

And there are the insecure or lazy chairmen who look to the meeting for reassurance and support in their ineffectiveness and inactivity, so that they can spread the responsibility for their indecisiveness among the whole group. They seize on every expression of disagreement or doubt as a justification for avoiding decision or action.

But even the large majority who do not go to those extremes still feel a certain pleasurable tumescence of the ego when they take their place at the head of the table for the first time. The feeling is no sin: the sin is to indulge it or to assume that the pleasure is shared by the other members of the meeting.

It is the chairman's self-indulgence that is the greatest single barrier to the success of a meeting. His first duty, then, is to be aware of the temptation and of the dangers of yielding to it. The clearest of the danger signals is hearing himself talking a lot during a discussion.

One of the best chairmen I have ever served under makes it a rule to restrict her interventions to a single sentence, or at most two. She forbids herself ever to contribute a paragraph to a meeting she is chairing. It is a harsh rule, but you would be hard put to find a regular attender of her meetings (or anyone else's) who thought it was a bad one.

There is, in fact, only one legitimate source of pleasure in chairmanship, and that is pleasure in the achievements of the meeting—and to be legitimate, it must be shared by all those present. Meetings are *necessary* for all sorts of basic and primitive human reasons, but they are *useful* only if they are seen by all present to be getting somewhere—and somewhere they know they could not have gotten to individually.

If the chairman is to make sure that the meeting achieves valuable objectives, he will be more effective seeing himself as the servant of the group rather than as its master. His role then becomes that of assisting the group toward the best conclusion or decision in the most efficient manner possible: to interpret and clarify; to move the discussion forward; and to bring it to a resolution that everyone understands and accepts as being the will of the meeting, even if the individuals do not necessarily agree with it.

His true source of authority with the members is the strength of his perceived commitment to their combined objective and his skill and efficiency in helping and guiding them to its achievement. Control and discipline then become not the act of imposing his will on the group but of imposing the group's will on any individual who is in danger of diverting or delaying the progress of the discussion and so from realizing the objective.

Once the members realize that the leader is impelled by his commitment to their common objective, it does not take great force of personality for him to control the meeting. Indeed, a sense of urgency and a clear desire to reach the best conclusion as quickly as possible are a much more effective disciplinary instrument than a big gavel. The effective chairman can then hold the discussion to the point by indicating that there is no time to pursue a particular idea now, that there is no time for long speeches, that the group has to get through this item and on to the next one, rather than by resorting to pulling rank.

There are many polite ways the chairman can indicate a slight impatience even when someone else is speaking—by leaning forward, fixing his eyes on the speaker, tensing his muscles, raising his eyebrows, or nodding briefly to show the point is taken. And when replying or commenting, the chairman can indicate by the speed, brevity, and finality of his intonation that "we have to move on." Conversely, he can reward the sort of contribution he is seeking by the opposite expressions and intonations, showing that there is plenty of time for that sort of idea, and encouraging the speaker to develop the point.

After a few meetings, all present readily understand this nonverbal language of chairmanship. It is the chairman's chief instrument of educating the group into the general type of "meeting behavior" that he is looking for. He is still the servant of the group, but like a hired mountain guide, he is the one who knows the destination, the route, the weather signs, and the time the journey will take. So if he suggests that the members walk a bit faster, they take his advice.

This role of servant rather than master is often obscured in large organizations by the fact that the chairman is frequently the line manager of the members: this does not, however, change the reality of the role of chairman. The point is easier to see in, say, a neighborhood action group. The question in that case is, simply, "Through which person's chairmanship do we collectively have the best chance of getting the children's playground built?"

However, one special problem is posed by this definition of the chairman's role, and it has an extremely interesting answer. The question is: How can the chairman combine his role with the role of a member advocating one side of an argument?

The answer comes from some interesting studies by researchers who sat in on hundreds of meetings to find out how they work. Their consensus finding is that most of the effective discussions have, in fact, two leaders: one they call a "team," or "social," leader; the other a "task," or "project," leader.

Regardless of whether leadership is in fact a single or a dual function, for our purposes it is enough to say that the chairman's best role is that of social leader. If he wants a particular point to be strongly advocated, he ensures that it is someone else who leads off the task discussion, and he holds back until much later in the argument. He might indeed change or modify his view through hearing the discussion, but even if he does not it is much easier for him to show support for someone else's point later in the discussion, after listening to the arguments. Then, he can summarize in favor of the one he prefers.

The task advocate might regularly be the chairman's second-in-command, or a different person might advocate for different items on the agenda. On some subjects, the chairman might well be the task advocate himself, especially if they do not involve conflict within the group. The important point is that the chairman has to keep his "social leadership" even if it means sacrificing his "task leadership." However, if the designated task advocate persists in championing a cause through two or three meetings, he risks building up quite a head of antagonism to him among the other members. Even so, this antagonism harms the group less by being directed at the "task leader" than at the "social leader."

STRUCTURE OF DISCUSSION. It may seem that there is no right way or wrong way to structure a committee meeting discussion. A subject is raised, people say what they think, and finally a decision is reached, or the discussion is terminated. There is some truth in this. Moreover, it would be a mistake to try and tie every discussion of every item down to a single immutable format.

Nevertheless, there is a logical order to a group discussion, and while there can be reasons for not following it, there is no justification for not being aware of it. In practice, very few discussions are inhibited, and many are expedited, by a conscious adherence to the following stages, which follow exactly the same pattern as a visit to the doctor:

"What seems to be the trouble?" The reason for an item being on a meeting agenda is usually like the symptom we go to the doctor with: "I keep getting this pain in my back" is analogous to "Sales have risen in Germany but fallen in France." In both cases it is clear that something is wrong and that something ought to be done to put it right. But until the visit to the doctor, or the meeting of the European marketing committee, that is about all we really know.

"How long has this been going on?" The doctor will start with a case history of all the relevant background facts, and so will the committee discussion. A solid basis of shared and agreed-on facts is the best foundation to build any decision on, and a set of pertinent questions will help establish it. For example, when did French sales start to fall off? Have German sales risen exceptionally? Has France had delivery problems, or less sales effort, or weaker advertising? Have we lost market share, or are our competitors' sales falling too? If the answers to all these questions, and more, are not established at the start, a lot of discussion may be wasted later.

"Would you just lie down on the couch?" The doctor will then conduct a physical examination to find out how the patient is now. The committee, too, will want to know how things stand at this moment. Is action being taken? Do long-term orders show the same trend? What are the latest figures? What is the current stock position? How much money is left in the advertising budget?

"You seem to have slipped a disc." When the facts are established, you can move toward a diagnosis. A doctor may seem to do this quickly, but that is the result of experience and practice. He is, in fact, rapidly eliminating all the impossible or far-fetched explanations until he leaves himself with a short list. The committee, too, will hazard and eliminate a variety of diagnoses until it homes in on the most probable—for example, the company's recent energetic and highly successful advertising campaign in Germany plus new packaging by the market leader in France.

"Take this round to the druggist." Again, the doctor is likely to take a shortcut that a committee meeting may be wise to avoid. The doctor comes out

with a single prescription, and the committee, too, may agree quickly on a single course of action.

But if the course is not so clear, it is better to take this step in two stages: (a) construct a series of options—do not, at first, reject any suggestions outright but try to select and combine the promising elements from all of them until a number of thought-out, coherent, and sensible suggestions are on the table; and (b) only when you have generated these options do you start to choose among them. Then you can discuss and decide whether to pick the course based on repackaging and point-of-sale promotion, or the one based on advertising and a price cut, or the one that bides its time and saves the money for heavier new-product promotion next year.

If the item is at all complex or especially significant, it is important for the chairman not only to have the proposed course of the discussion in his own head, but also to announce it so that everyone knows. A good idea is to write the headings on an easel pad with a felt pen. This saves much of the time wasting and confusion that result when people raise items in the wrong place because they were not privy to the chairman's secret that the right place was coming up later on in the discussion.

CONDUCTING THE MEETING

Just as the driver of a car has two tasks, to follow his route and to manage his vehicle, so the chairman's job can be divided into two corresponding tasks, dealing with the subject and dealing with the people.

DEALING WITH THE SUBJECT. The essence of this task is to follow the structure of discussion as just described in the previous section. This, in turn, entails listening carefully and keeping the meeting pointed toward the objective.

At the start of the discussion of any item, the chairman should make it clear where the meeting should try to get to by the end. Are the members hoping to make a clear decision or firm recommendation? Is it a preliminary deliberation to give the members something to go away with and think about? Are they looking for a variety of different lines to be pursued outside the meeting? Do they have to approve the proposal, or merely note it?

The chairman may give them a choice: "If we can agree on a course of action, that's fine. If not, we'll have to set up a working party to report and recommend before next month's meeting."

The chairman should make sure that all the members understand the issue and why they are discussing it. Often it will be obvious, or else they may have been through it before. If not, then he or someone he has briefed before the meeting should give a short introduction, with some indication of the reason the item is on the agenda; the story so far; the present position; what needs to be established, resolved, or proposed; and some indication of lines of inquiry or courses of action that have been suggested or explored, as well as arguments on both sides of the issue.

If the discussion is at all likely to be long or complex, the chairman should propose to the meeting a structure for it with headings (written up if necessary), as I stated at the end of the section on "Structure of discussion." He should listen carefully in case people jump too far ahead (e.g., start proposing a course of action before the meeting has agreed on the cause of the trouble), or go back over old ground, or start repeating points that have been made earlier. He has to head discussion off sterile or irrelevant areas very quickly (e.g., the rights and wrongs of past decisions that it is too late to change, or distant prospects that are too remote to affect present actions).

It is the chairman's responsibility to prevent misunderstanding and confusion. If he does not follow an argument or understand a reference, he should seek clarification from the speaker. If he thinks two people are using the same word with different meanings, he should intervene (e.g., one member using *promotion* to mean point-of-sale advertising only, and another also including media publicity).

He may also have to clarify by asking people for facts or experience that perhaps influence their view but are not known to others in the meeting. And he should be on the lookout for points where an interim summary would be helpful. This device frequently takes only a few seconds, and acts like a life belt to some of the members who are getting out of their depth.

Sometimes a meeting will have to discuss a draft document. If there are faults in it, the members should agree on what the faults are and the chairman should delegate someone to produce a new draft later. The group should never try to redraft around the table.

Perhaps one of the most common faults of chairmanship is the failure to terminate the discussion early enough. Sometimes chairmen do not realize that the meeting has effectively reached an agreement, and consequently they let the discussion go on for another few minutes, getting nowhere at all. Even more often, they are not quick enough to close a discussion *before* agreement has been reached.

A discussion should be closed once it has become clear that (a) more facts are required before further progress can be made, (b) discussion has revealed that the meeting needs the views of people not present, (c) members need more time to think about the subject and perhaps discuss it with colleagues, (d) events are changing and likely to alter or clarify the basis of the decision quite soon, (e) there is not going to be enough time at this meeting to go over the subject properly, or (f) it is becoming clear that two or three of the members can settle this outside the meeting without taking up the time of the rest. The fact that the decision is difficult, likely to be disputed, or going to be unwelcome to somebody, however, is not a reason for postponement.

At the end of the discussion of each agenda item, the chairman should give a brief and clear summary of what has been agreed on. This can act as the dictation of the actual minutes. It serves not merely to put the item on record, but also to help people realize that something worthwhile has been achieved. It also answers the question "Where did all that get us?" If the summary involves action by a member of the meeting, he should be asked to confirm his acceptance of the undertaking.

DEALING WITH THE PEOPLE. There is only one way to ensure that a meeting starts on time, and that is to start it on time. Latecomers who find that the meeting has begun without them soon learn the lesson. The alternative is that the prompt and punctual members will soon realize that a meeting never starts until ten minutes after the advertised time, and they will also learn the lesson.

Punctuality at future meetings can be wonderfully reinforced by the practice of listing late arrivals (and early departures) in the minutes. Its ostensible and perfectly proper purpose is to call the latecomer's attention to the fact that he was absent when a decision was reached. Its side effect, however, is to tell everyone on the circulation list that he was late, and people do not want that sort of information about themselves published too frequently.

There is a growing volume of work on the significance of seating positions and their effect on group behavior and relationships. Not all the findings are generally agreed on. What does seem true is that:

▲ Having members sit face to face across a table facilitates opposition, conflict, and disagreement, though of course it does not turn allies into enemies. But it does suggest that the chairman should think about whom he seats opposite himself.

▲ Sitting side by side makes disagreements and confrontation harder. This in turn suggests that the chairman can exploit the friendship-value of the seats next to him.

▲ There is a "dead man's corner" on the chairman's right, especially if a number of people are seated in line along from him (it does not apply if he is alone at the head of the table).

▲ As a general rule, proximity to the chairman is a sign of honor and favor. This is most marked when he is at the head of a long, narrow table. The greater the distance, the lower the rank—just as the lower-status positions were "below the salt" at medieval refectories.

Control the Garrulous. In most meetings someone takes a long time to say very little. As chairman, your sense of urgency should help indicate to him the need for brevity. You can also suggest that if he is going to take a long time it might be better for him to write a paper. If it is urgent to stop him in full flight, there is a useful device of picking on a phrase (it really doesn't matter what phrase) as he utters it as an excuse for cutting in and offering it to someone else: "Inevitable decline—that's very interesting. George, do you agree that the decline is inevitable?"

Draw Out the Silent.   In any properly run meeting, as simple arithmetic will show, most of the people will be silent most of the time. Silence can indicate general agreement, or no important contribution to make, or the need to wait and hear more before saying anything, or too good a lunch, and none of these need worry you. But there are two kinds of silence you must break:

1. The silence of diffidence. Someone may have a valuable contribution to make but be sufficiently nervous about its possible reception to keep it to himself. It is important that when you draw out such a contribution, you should express interest and pleasure (though not necessarily agreement) to encourage further contributions of that sort.

2. The silence of hostility. This is not hostility to ideas, but to you as the chairman, to the meeting, and to the process by which decisions are being reached. This sort of total detachment from the whole proceedings is usually the symptom of some feeling of affront. If you probe it, you will usually find that there is something bursting to come out, and that it is better out than in.

Protect the Weak.   Junior members of the meeting may provoke the disagreement of their seniors, which is perfectly reasonable. But if the disagreement escalates to the point of suggesting that they have no right to contribute, the meeting is weakened. So you may have to take pains to commend their contribution for its usefulness, as a pre-emptive measure. You can reinforce this action by taking a written note of a point they make (always a plus for a member of a meeting) and by referring to it again later in the discussion (a double-plus).

Encourage the Clash of Ideas.   But, at the same time, discourage the clash of personalities. A good meeting is not a series of dialogues between individual members and the chairman. Instead, it is a crossflow of discussion and debate, with the chairman occasionally guiding, mediating, probing, stimulating, and summarizing, but mostly letting the others thrash ideas out. However, the meeting must be a contention of *ideas*, not people.

If two people are starting to get heated, widen the discussion by asking a question of a neutral member of the meeting, preferably a question that requires a purely factual answer.

Watch Out for the Suggestion-Squashing Reflex.   Students of meetings have reduced everything that can be said into questions, answers, positive reactions, and negative reactions. Questions can only seek, and answers only supply, three types of response: information, opinion, and suggestion.

In almost every modern organization, it is the suggestions that contain the seeds of future success. Although very few suggestions will ever lead to anything, almost all of them need to be given every chance. The trouble is that suggestions are much easier to ridicule than facts or opinions. If people feel that making a suggestion will provoke the negative reaction of being laughed at or squashed, they will soon stop. And if there is any status-jostling going on at the meeting, it is all too easy to use the occasion of someone's making a suggestion as the opportunity to take him down a peg. It is all too easy and a formula to ensure sterile meetings.

The answer is for you to take special notice and show special warmth when anyone makes a suggestion, and to discourage as sharply as you can the squashing-reflex. This can often be achieved by requiring the squasher to produce a better suggestion on the spot. Few suggestions can stand up to squashing in their pristine state: your reflex must be to pick out the best part of one and get the other committee members to help build it into something that might work.

Come to the Most Senior People Last.   Obviously, this cannot be a rule, but once someone of high authority has pronounced on a topic, the less senior members are likely to be inhibited. If you work up the pecking order instead of down it, you are apt to get a wider spread of views and ideas. But the juniors who start it off should only be asked for contributions within their personal experience and competence. ("Peter, you were at the Frankfurt Exhibition—what reactions did you pick up there?")

Close on a Note of Achievement. Even if the final item is left unresolved, you can refer to an earlier item that was well resolved as you close the meeting and thank the group.

If the meeting is not a regular one, fix the time and place of the next one before dispersing. A little time spent with appointment diaries at the end, especially if it is a gathering of five or more members, can save hours of secretarial telephoning later.

FOLLOWING THE MEETING

Your secretary may take the minutes (or better still, one of the members), but the minutes are your re-sponsibility. They can be very brief, but they should include these facts:

▲ The time and date of the meeting, where it was held, and who chaired it.

▲ Names of all present and apologies for absence.

▲ All agenda items (and other items) discussed and all decisions reached. If action was agreed on, record (and underline) the name of the person responsible for the assignment.

▲ The time at which the meeting ended (important, because it may be significant later to know whether the discussion lasted 15 minutes or 6 hours).

▲ The date, time, and place of the next committee meeting.

In the busy routine of everyday living, the best way to find time for enrichment through reading is by increasing your reading rate. If you have never tried to improve your reading skill, you will be surprised to discover how much you can increase your speed and still understand what you read. In the reading laboratory of Air University, it is not unusual for students to show a substantial increase in reading speed after only one or two training periods. These first periods take up the reader's slack, indicating that most people can read much faster than they do.

This article is concerned with some of the principles upon which a reading improvement program is based and offers some suggestions that you can try for yourself without laboratory equipment.

COMPREHENSION

Comprehension is the most important factor in reading. All of us are careful not to read any faster than we can understand, but most of us can understand much faster than we usually read. Being abstract, comprehension is relatively hard to measure. Defined as "the ability to understand what is seen or heard," it is based on the sum total of the individual's experience and education. Comprehension is of two kinds, receptive and reflective.

Receptive comprehension of written material involves literal understanding of the author's meaning. To understand fully, you must have an adequate vocabulary, you must be able to get the intended significance from the author's words and sentences, and you must be able to concentrate. The words should convey the author's surface information to you.

Reflective comprehension of written material involves the ability to determine the full meaning which may be intended by the author—the ability to draw the inferences the author wishes you to draw and to apply these ideas to new situations. Of course, you must first understand the surface information before you can determine its purpose and significance. Reflective comprehension involves comparing what you already know about a subject with the author's statement and deciding which

points you will accept or reject. You must be alert to draw inferences or detect depth of meaning when the author intends you to—for example, when the author gives an illustration but lets you decide how it supports the main idea.

Since comprehension involves the sum total of your education and experience to date, you cannot expect rapid improvement in this element. The more you see, read, and hear and the more you understand of the world and people, the more quickly and deeply you comprehend. But receptive understanding can be considerably sharpened by increased awareness of it as an important part of communication. Obviously, it depends to a great degree upon your concentration in reading and upon the manner in which you receive and store ideas in your mind.

Many skilled readers use a three-step approach to improve their reading comprehension.

IDENTIFICATION. In preparing to read a book, try to condense the theme of the book into a single statement or short paragraph. Publishers and authors provide signposts that highlight objectives in titles, on book jackets, and in forewords, prefaces, and introductions. Next, analyze the major parts and divisions of the book. The table of contents provides an outline of what is to be read, and a study of chapter titles and subtitles enables you to identify the author's organizational framework. Finally, scan the material in the first chapter. Usually, in the initial chapter, the author establishes the pattern of thought and development followed in subsequent chapters. The writer notes the importance of the subject, relates it to other areas, defines terms, establishes principles, and indicates the style of writing. Identification with the author will assist you in adapting to the author's ideas and the framework used to present those ideas.

INTERPRETATION. The second step in the approach to reading is the reader's search for meaning. This involves recognizing an author's frame of reference, major propositions, and the supporting evidence.

Frame of Reference. Knowledge of the author's background will help to determine the probable viewpoint of a book. Obviously, a book on the North Atlantic Treaty Organization written by a former chief marshal of the Royal Air Force would present a British viewpoint. Examine the summary on the book jacket of the author's background and experience. Learn all you can about the author's previous works, usually listed opposite the title page. Then turn to the index and select a few topics of personal interest. By reading these passages and noting the author's treatment of the subject, you can quickly determine the point of view and establish a frame of reference for reading the remainder of the book.

Determine Author's Propositions. Whatever the book, you must find the propositions that support the thesis of the book. For example, an analysis of Major Alexander de Seversky's *Air Power: Key to Survival* provides several propositions in support of his theme. The author comments on the speed and mobility of our Armed Forces and the destructive power of nuclear weapons.

Find Supporting Evidence. Good writers support their major propositions. Facts, statistics, and reasoning are the evidence that supports main ideas. Major de Seversky comments that the Army and Navy do not move fast enough to counteract all enemy military situations; he concludes that only a strong Air Force is a major deterrent factor. One aid in finding supporting facts is to recognize that the paragraph is a cluster of sentences around a central idea. Most writers state the key proposition in the initial sentence and then use the rest of the paragraph for development.

EVALUATION. As the final step in charting your reading, you should evaluate the written material on the basis of your understanding of the book. Decide whether or not you accept the main thesis of the book. Did the author use illogical reasoning? Were the facts and statistics inaccurate and outdated? Were generalizations based on small samplings? When you answer these questions to your satisfaction, make a final decision as to whether you agree or disagree with the writer. The three-step method for effective, critical reading is then complete.

SPEED

While speed is secondary to comprehension, it is still very important. Administrative and executive positions require a great deal of reading. Obviously, if you can attain a speed of 600 words per minute, you can get through far more paper work than the person who never reads anything faster than 200 words per minute.

Statistics show that in 20 hours' practice in the reading laboratory of Air University, some students are able to increase their average speed 60 to 70 percent on professional books, such as Seversky's *Air Power* and Tedder's *Air Power in War*. Others achieve more than a 100-percent improvement in speed in 36 hours of laboratory work. However, sustained improvement represents much hard work and practice. Gains in speed are easier to achieve under instruction, but substantial gains are possible without equipment or supervision. By understanding how you read and by practicing with determination, you can increase your speed.

You do not read by a continuous sweep of the eyes across the page. Your eyes move and pause several times as they cross a line, and you read only when they stop between movements. The frequency of these stops, or "fixations," is determined by your eye span, or "span of recognition." To increase your reading speed, you must do these things:

▲ Increase your span of recognition and reduce the time of your fixations.

▲ Work to eliminate the habits of regression and subvocalizing.

▲ Constantly strive to overcome vocabulary difficulties.

INCREASING THE SPAN OF RECOGNITION. Your span of recognition is the amount of material you can read at a single fixation. If you can increase this span, you will make fewer fixations per line and thus read faster. A fast reader will make only two fixations per line in *Time* magazine, reading with full comprehension; a poor reader may make five. The fast reader takes in three or four words per fixation; the slow reader may stop on every word.

With practice, you can increase your span of recognition. In the laboratory, this is done by means of exercises with a reading pacer. You can do similar exercises in one of the self-improvement books such as Spache and Berg, *The Art of Efficient Reading.* You can also practice on the daily paper. Newspapers are printed in narrow columns, and you may find that you are reading them at three fixations per line. Try to bring this down to two fixations per line, and now and then try one fixation per line; that is, try reading straight down the column.

Another good exercise is trying to read the columns in *Time* or *Newsweek* with two fixations per line. Daily practice of this kind increases your span of recognition.

The slow reader not only makes more fixations than the fast reader: he also takes more time on each fixation. By pushing yourself to read faster than is actually comfortable, you force yourself to cut down your fixation time. In the laboratory, the pacing machines can be set to do this for you. Away from a laboratory, you can time yourself with a watch. Time yourself in minutes and seconds as you read a page of narrative such as a history or a biography and then see if you can read the next few pages at a faster pace. You will soon find that you can attain excellent comprehension while reading faster than your usual rate.

ELIMINATING REGRESSION. The elimination of the two slow-down habits—regressing and subvocalizing—is the surest way to improve your reading skills.

When your eyes move back to the left and fix again on a word you have already read, you have made a regression. Regressing holds down reading speed. If you read too slowly, you become bored and probably will develop an aversion to reading. The good reader makes few regressions; the slow reader usually makes many. Of course, some regressions are made because of unfamiliar words or confusing sentence structure. Only an increased skill in the use of words and rhetoric can help the reader overcome this problem.

A common habit is letting the mind wander and then regressing to pick up what was missed. In the laboratory the pacing machine prevents you from regressing. By pushing yourself and by concentrating so intently that your mind stays on the track, you can control the regression habit. Pace is closely connected with regressing. If you read too slowly to keep your mind occupied, you forget what you have read. Then you have to regress to pick up the thread. The good reader keeps himself interested. Since he does not have time for woolgathering, he does not make unnecessary regressions.

ELIMINATING SUBVOCALIZING. Another serious reading fault that is common in adults is subvocalizing. This habit develops as we learn to read. Most of us were first taught to read aloud. When we began to read silently, we vocalized silently. Some of you may have taken college courses that required much supplementary reading, and you learned to read rapidly. Others of you may have taken technical courses that required you to analyze and evaluate each sentence. As a result, you may have remained a slow reader. Many people pronounce each word silently and therefore can read no faster silently than aloud. Few adult readers actually form syllables with the lips, but many either form the syllables in their throats or pronounce the sounds mentally. Thus their speed in silent reading is limited to the rate at which they can form or "listen" to spoken words. Since few people can read aloud faster than 250 to 300 words per minute, the subvocalizer is tied down to that speed.

A series of tests at Air University has shown that many students read at an average of 220 to 240 words per minute. This is a slow rate for light reading material. Increased reading rates would give these students the ability to handle quickly much of the paper work that is a part of their day's work.

Let's see how subvocalizing can be overcome. In vocalizing, you are taking three steps for the reading process, using eye, throat, and brain. Actually, the good reader takes only two steps, eye and brain. Put your finger on your throat muscles as you read. If you feel any vibration, you are using those muscles to say the words to yourself. If you continue to vocalize after trying to avoid it, chew gum or hum to yourself as you read, but constantly push yourself. When you get up to or above 400 words per minute, you will find that you vocalize less often. Continued practice at high speeds will eventually free you of this restraining habit.

OVERCOMING VOCABULARY DIFFICULTIES. Finally, work at building your vocabulary. Readers with a poor vocabulary must constantly regress to guess at meanings, and unfamiliar words cause them to take long fixations.

There are several ways to improve vocabulary. Probably the best way is to read widely. New words often become clear in context, and this is also true of new meanings for old words. Another way to build a vocabulary is to list unfamiliar words as you read, look them up in a dictionary, and then use them often enough to be sure of them. New words and new meanings for old words help you read steadily and swiftly only if they have become an active part of your reading vocabulary. It is usually futile to memorize lists of new words from books that promise you a large vocabulary. Words are functions of thoughts, and as you learn to handle complicated thoughts in reading, you also strengthen and develop your useful vocabulary.

ADAPTABILITY

Adaptability, the real key to effective reading, is the ability to adjust your speed to the level of your reading material. Neither speed nor comprehension should be your goal; rather it should be a flexibility in gearing your speed to the importance and the difficulty of the material. Some students read the comics and their school asssignments at the same plodding rate. The habit of reading everything at the same speed is one sign of the immature reader. Check constantly to be sure that you are adapting your speed and comprehension to the material and to your purpose in reading.

Adaptability and discrimination go hand in hand. Discrimination is knowing what is worth reading and how to read it for best results. Of course, in Air Force schools you are given some guidance in what you are to read. But when the decision rests with you, choose carefully so that you do not waste your time. Decide what you want to take away from your reading *before* you read. Then read in the most efficient manner to fill this need. Do not read fast just to get through material, and do not read so slowly that you waste valuable time that could be put to other uses. If you are studying school materials or regulations that you must understand thoroughly, slow down and read with critical attention to detail. Of if you enjoy a certain style or description, slow down and think about it—savor it. But if you are reading for general information and feel that you have a good control of the content as you proceed, then speed up and save time for more important activities.

Skimming is a useful technique for comprehending quickly the sense of a passage. It is useful in taking an overview of an article before reading thoroughly and in looking for particular material. Proficient skimming takes considerable practice. The following suggestions will help you develop a good technique. First, look at the table of contents if there is one. Then riffle through the book, giving most of your attention to chapter headings and section heads. When you skim, look for topic sentences and summary sentences. Connectives such as *if, so, therefore,* and *finally* may point up these important sentences. Of course, you will watch for words that are underlined or italicized, and you will want to pay special attention to the initial and closing paragraphs. When you feel that you have an overview of the author's main ideas and outline, ask yourself a few study questions and plunge into rapid, fruitful reading.

SUMMARY

Most people have the capability to read much faster than they actually do. You can use your reading time to much better advantage if you follow helpful suggestions to increase your reading speed and retain comprehension. The main causes of slow reading are short span of recognition, regression, subvocalizing, and poor vocabulary. By overcoming these handicaps, you can make surprising gains in speed that will enable you to handle paper work much more efficiently. The key is adaptability. Adapt your speed to what you are reading. Be the master of your reading habits, not the slave!

"WHAT DO YOU MEAN I CAN'T WRITE?"

JOHN FIELDEN

What do businessmen answer when they are asked, "What's the most troublesome problem you have to live with?" Frequently they reply, "People just can't write! What do they learn in college now? When I was a boy . . . !"

There is no need to belabor this point; readers know well how true it is. HBR subscribers, for example, recently rated the "ability to communicate" as the prime requisite of a promotable executive (see Exhibit 1).[1] And, of all the aspects of communication, the written form is the most troublesome, if only because of its formal nature. It is received cold, without the communicator's tone of voice or gesture to help. It is rigid; it cannot be adjusted to the recipients' reactions as it is being delivered. It stays "on the record," and cannot be undone. Further, the reason it is in fact committed to paper is usually that its subject is considered too crucial or significant to be entrusted to casual, short-lived verbal form.

Businessmen know that the ability to write well is a highly valued asset in a top executive. Consequently, they become ever more conscious of their writing ability as they consider what qualities they need in order to rise in their company.

They know that in big business today ideas are not exchanged exclusively by word of mouth (as they might be in smaller businesses). And they know that even if they get oral approval for something they wish to do, there will be the inevitable "give me a memo on it" concluding remark that will send them back to their office to oversee the writing of a carefully documented report.

They know, too, that as they rise in their company, they will have to be able to supervise the writing of subordinates—for so many of the memos, reports, and letters written by subordinates will go out over their signature, or be passed on to others in the company and thus reflect on the caliber of work done under their supervision.

Even the new data-processing machines will not make business any less dependent on words. For while the new machines are fine for handling tabular or computative work, someone must write up an eventual analysis of the findings in the common parlance of the everyday executive.

TIME FOR ACTION

Complaints about the inability of managers to write are a very common and justifiable refrain. But the problem this article poses—and seeks to solve—is that it is of very little use to complain about something and stop right there. I think it is about time for managers to begin to do something about it. And the first step is *to define what "it"—what good business writing—really is.*

Suppose you are a young managerial aspirant who has recently been told: "You simply can't write!" What would this mean to you? Naturally, you would be hurt, disappointed, perhaps even alarmed to have your *own* nagging doubts about your writing ability put uncomfortably on the line. "Of course," you say, "I know I'm no stylist. I don't even pretend to be a literarily inclined person. But how can I improve my writing on the job? Where do I begin? Exactly what *is* wrong with my writing?" But nobody tells you in specific, meaningful terms.

Does this mean that you can't spell or punctuate or that your grammar is disastrous? Does it mean that you can't think or organize your thoughts? Or does it mean that even though you are scrupulously correct in grammar and tightly organized in your thinking, a report or letter from you is always completely unreadable; that reading it, in effect, is like trying to butt one's head through a brick wall? Or does it mean that you are so tactless and boorish in the human relations aspect of communication that your messages actually build resentment and resistance? Do you talk "down" too much or do you talk

382

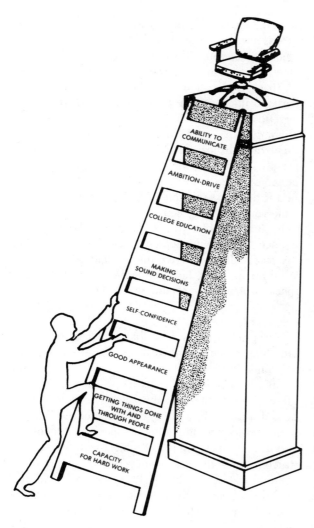

Source: Taken from Exhibit III, Garda W. Bowman, "What Helps or Harms Promotability?" (Problems in Review), HBR January–February 1964, p. 14.

EXHIBIT I Qualities That Characterize Promotable Executives

"over your reader's head"? Just what do you do wrong?

Merely being told that you can't write is so basically meaningless and so damaging to your morale that you may end up writing more ineffectually than ever before. What you need to know is: "What are the elements of good business writing? And in which

of these elements am I proficient? In which do I fall down?" If only the boss could break his complaint down into a more meaningful set of components, you could begin to do something about them.

Now let's shift and assume that you are a high-ranking manager whose job it is to supervise a staff of assistants. What can you do about upgrading the writing efforts of your men? You think of the time lost by having to do reports and letters over and over before they go out, the feasibility reports which did not look so feasible after having been befogged by an ineffectual writer, the letters presented for your signature that would have infuriated the receiver had you let them be mailed. But where are you to start?

Here is where the interests of superior and subordinate meet. Unless both arrive at a common understanding, a shared vocabulary that enables them to communicate with one another about the writing jobs that need to be done, nobody is going to get very far. No oversimplified, gimmicky slogans (such as, "Every letter is a sales letter"; "Accentuate the positive, eliminate the negative"; or "Write as you speak") are going to serve this purpose. No partial view is either—whether that of the English teacher, the logician, or the social scientist—since good business writing is not just grammar, or clear thinking, or winning friends and influencing people. It is some of each, the proportion depending on the purpose.

TOTAL INVENTORY. To know what effective business writing is, we need a total inventory of all its aspects, so that:

▲ Top managers can say to their training people, "Are you sure our training efforts in written communications are not tackling just part of the problem? Are we covering all aspects of business writing?"

▲ A superior can say to an assistant, "Here, look; this is where you are weak. See? It is one thing when you write letters that you sign, another when you write letters that I sign. The position and power of the person we are writing to make a lot of difference in *what* we say and *how* we say it."

▲ The young manager can use the inventory as a guide to self-improvement (perhaps even ask his superior to go over his writing with him, using the writing inventory as a means of assuring a common critical vocabulary).

▲ The superior may himself get a few hints about how he might improve his own performance.

Such an inventory appears in Exhibit II. Notice that it contains four basic categories—*readability, correctness, appropriateness,* and *thought.* Considerable effort has gone into making these categories (and the subtopics under them) as mutually exclusive as possible, although some overlap is inevitable. But even if they are not completely exclusive, they are still far less general than an angry, critical remark, such as, "You cannot write."

Furthermore, you should understand that these four categories are not listed in order of importance, since their importance varies according to the abilities and the duties of each individual. The same thing is true of the subtopics; I shall make no attempt to treat each of them equally, but will simply try to do some practical, commonsense highlighting. I will begin with readability, and discuss it most fully, because this is an area where half-truths abound and need to be scotched before introducing the other topics.

READABILITY

What is *readability?* Nothing more than a clear style of writing. It does not result absolutely (as some readability experts would have you believe) from mathematical counts of syllables, of sentence length, or of abstract words. These inflexible approaches to readability assume that all writing is being addressed to a general audience. Consequently, their greatest use is in forming judgments about the readability of such things as mass magazine editorial copy, newspaper communications, and elementary textbooks.

To prove this point, all you need do is to pick up a beautifully edited magazine like the *New England Journal of Medicine* and try to read an article in it. You as a layman will probably have trouble. On the other hand, your physician will tell you that the article is a masterpiece of readable exposition. But, on second look, you will still find it completely unreadable. The reason, obviously, is that you do not have the background or the vocabulary necessary to understand it. The same thing would hold true if you were to take an article from a management science quarterly, say, one dealing with return on investment or statistical decision making, and give it to the physician. Now he is likely to judge this one to be completely incomprehensible, while you may find it the most valuable and clear discussion of the topic you have ever seen.

In situations like this, it does not make much difference whether the sentences are long or short; if the reader does not have the background to understand the material, he just doesn't. And writing such specialized articles according to the mathematical readability formulas is not going to make them clearer.

Nevertheless, it is true that unnecessarily long, rambling sentences are wearing to read. Hence you will find these stylistic shortcomings mentioned in Exhibit II. The trick a writer has to learn is to judge the complexity and the abstractness of the material he is dealing with, and to cut his sentences down in those areas where the going is especially difficult. It also helps to stick to a direct subject-verb-object construction in sentences wherever it is important to communicate precisely. Flights of unusually dashing style should be reserved for those sections which are quite general in nature and concrete in subject matter.

What about paragraphs? The importance of "paragraph construction" is often overlooked in business communication, but few things are more certain to make the heart sink than the sight of page after page of unbroken type. One old grammar book rule would be especially wise to hark back to, and that is the topic sentence. Not only does placing a topic sentence at the beginning of each paragraph make it easier for the reader to grasp the content of the communication quickly; it also serves to discipline the writer into including only one main idea in each paragraph. Naturally, when a discussion of one idea

1. READABILITY

READER'S LEVEL

☐ Too specialized in approach

☐ Assumes too great a knowledge of subject

☐ So underestimates the reader that it belabors the obvious

SENTENCE CONSTRUCTION

☐ Unnecessarily long in difficult material

☐ Subject-verb-object word order too rarely used

☐ Choppy, overly simple style (in simple material)

PARAGRAPH CONSTRUCTION

☐ Lack of topic sentences

☐ Too many ideas in single paragraph

☐ Too long

FAMILIARITY OF WORDS

☐ Inappropriate jargon

☐ Pretentious language

☐ Unnecessarily abstract

READER DIRECTION

☐ Lack of "framing" (i.e., failure to tell the reader about purpose and direction of forthcoming discussion)

☐ Inadequate transitions between paragraphs

☐ Absence of subconclusions to summarize reader's progress at end of divisions in the discussion

FOCUS

☐ Unclear as to subject of communication

☐ Unclear as to purpose of message

2. CORRECTNESS

MECHANICS

☐ Shaky grammar

☐ Faulty punctuation

FORMAT

☐ Careless appearance of documents

☐ Failure to use accepted company form

COHERENCE

☐ Sentences seem awkward owing to illogical and ungrammatical yoking of unrelated ideas

☐ Failure to develop a logical progression of ideas through coherent, logically juxtaposed paragraphs

3. APPROPRIATENESS

A. UPWARD COMMUNICATIONS

TACT

☐ Failure to recognize differences in position between writer and receiver

☐ Impolitic tone—too brusk, argumentative, or insulting

SUPPORTING DETAIL

☐ Inadequate support for statements

☐ Too much undigested detail for busy superior

OPINION

☐ Adequate research but too great an intrusion of opinions

☐ Too few facts (and too little research) to entitle drawing of conclusions

☐ Presence of unasked for but clearly implied recommendations

ATTITUDE

☐ Too obvious a desire to please superior

☐ Too defensive in face of authority

☐ Too fearful of superior to be able to do best work

B. DOWNWARD COMMUNICATIONS

DIPLOMACY

☐ Overbearing attitude toward subordinates

☐ Insulting and/or personal references

☐ Unmindfulness that messages are representative of management group or even of company

CLARIFICATION OF DESIRES

☐ Confused, vague instructions

☐ Superior is not sure of what is wanted

☐ Withholding of information necessary to job at hand

MOTIVATIONAL ASPECTS

☐ Orders of superior seem arbitrary

☐ Superior's communications are manipulative and seemingly insincere

4. THOUGHT

PREPARATION

☐ Inadequate thought given to purpose of communication prior to its final completion

☐ Inadequate preparation or use of data known to be available

COMPETENCE

☐ Subject beyond intellectual capabilities of writer

☐ Subject beyond experience of writer

FIDELITY TO ASSIGNMENT

☐ Failure to stick to job assigned

☐ Too much made of routine assignment

☐ Too little made of assignment

ANALYSIS

☐ Superficial examination of data leading to unconscious overlooking of important pieces of evidence

☐ Failure to draw obvious conclusions from data presented

☐ Presentation of conclusions unjustified by evidence

☐ Failure to qualify tenuous assertions

☐ Failure to identify and justify assumptions used

☐ Bias, conscious or unconscious, which leads to distorted interpretation of data

PERSUASIVENESS

☐ Seems more convincing than facts warrant

☐ Seems less convincing than facts warrant

☐ Too obvious an attempt to sell ideas

☐ Lacks action-orientation and managerial viewpoint

☐ Too blunt an approach where subtlety and finesse called for

EXHIBIT II   Written Performance Inventory.

means the expenditure of hundreds (or thousands) of words, paragraphs should be divided according to subdivisions of the main idea. In fact, an almost arbitrary division of paragraphs into units of four or five sentences is usually welcomed by the reader.

As for jargon, the only people who complain about it seriously are those who do not understand it. Moreover, it is fashionable for experts in a particular field to complain about their colleagues' use of jargon, but then to turn right around and use it themselves. The reason is that jargon is no more than shop talk. And when the person being addressed fully understands this private language, it is much more economical to use it than to go through laborious explanations of every idea that could be communicated in the shorthand of jargon. Naturally, when a writer knows that his message is going to be read by persons who are not familiar with the private language of his trade, he should be sure to translate as much of the jargon as he can into common terms.

The same thing holds true for simplicity of language. Simplicity is, I would think, always a "good." True, there is something lost from our language when interesting but unfamiliar words are no longer used. But isn't it true that the shrines in which these antiquities should be preserved lie in the domain of poetry or the novel, and not in business communciations—which, after all, are not baroque cathedrals but functional edifices by which a job can be done?

The simplest way to say it, then, is invariably the best in business writing. But this fact the young executive does not always understand. Often he is eager to parade his vocabulary before his superiors, for fear his boss (who has never let him know that he admires simplicity, and may indeed adopt a pretentious and ponderous style himself) may think less of him.

LEADING THE READER. But perhaps the most important aspect of readability is the one listed under the subtopic "reader direction." The failure of writers to seize their reader by the nose and lead him carefully through the intricacies of his communication is like an epidemic. The job that the writer must do is to develop the "skeleton" of the docu-

ment that he is preparing. And, at the very beginning of his communication, he should identify the skeletal structure of his paper; he should, in effect, frame the discussion which is to follow.

You will see many of these frames at the beginning of articles published by HBR, where the editors take great pains to tell the reader quickly what the article is about and what specific areas will come under discussion during its progress. In every business document this initial frame, this statement of purpose and direction, should appear. Furthermore, in lengthy reports there should be many such frames; indeed, most major sections of business reports should begin with a new frame.

There should also be clear transitions between paragraphs. The goal should be that of having each element in a written message bear a close relationship to those elements which have preceded and those which follow it. Frequently a section should end with a brief summary, plus a sentence or two telling the reader the new direction of the article. These rather mechanical signposts, while frequently the bane of literary stylists, are always of valuable assistance to readers.

The final aspect of readability is the category that I call "focus." This term refers to the fact that many communications seem diffuse and out of focus, much like a picture on a television screen when the antennas are not properly directed. Sometimes in a report it seems as if one report has been superimposed on another, and that there are no clear and particular points the writer is trying to make. Thus the burden is put on the reader to ferret out the truly important points from the chaos.

If a writer wants to improve the readability of his writing, he must make sure that he has thought things through sufficiently, so that he can focus his readers' attention on the salient points.

CORRECTNESS

The one thing that flies to a writer's mind when he is told he cannot write is *correctness*. He immediately starts looking for grammar and punctuation mistakes in things that he has written.

But mistakes like these are hardly the most important aspects of business writing. The majority of executives are reasonably well educated and can, with a minimum of effort, make themselves adequately proficient in the "mechanics" of writing. Furthermore, as a man rises in his company, his typing (at least) will be done by a secretary, who can (and should) take the blame if a report is poorly punctuated and incorrect in grammar, not to mention being presented in an improper "format."

Then what is the most important point? Frequently, the insecure writer allows small mistakes in grammar and punctuation to become greatly magnified, and regards them as reflections on his education and, indeed, his social acceptability. A careless use of "he don't" may seem to be as large a disgrace in his mind as if he attended the company banquet in his shorts. And in some cases this is true. But he should also realize (as Exhibit II shows) that the ability to write *correctly* is not synonymous with the ability to write *well*. Hence, everyone should make sure that he does not become satisfied with the rather trivial act of mastering punctuation and grammar.

It is true, of course, that, in some instances, the inability to write correctly will cause a lack of clarity. We can all think of examples where a misplaced comma has caused serious confusion—although such instances, except in contracts and other legal documents, are fortunately rather rare.

A far more important aspect of correctness is "coherence." Coherence means the proper positioning of elements within a piece of writing so that it can be read clearly and sensibly. Take one example:

▲ *Incoherent:* "I think it will rain. However, no clouds are showing yet. Therefore, I will take my umbrella."

▲ *Coherent:* "Although no clouds are showing, I think it will rain. Therefore, I will take my umbrella."

Once a person has mastered the art of placing related words and sentences as close as possible to each other, he will be amazed at how smooth his formerly awkward writing becomes. But that is just the beginning. He will still have to make sure that he has placed paragraphs which are related in thought next to one another, so that the ideas presented do not have to leapfrog over any intervening digressions.

APPROPRIATENESS

I have divided the category *appropriateness* into two sections reflecting the two main types of internal business communications—those going upward in the organization and those going downward. This distinction is one that cannot be found in textbooks on writing, although the ideas included here are commonplace in the human relations area.

There is an obvious difference between the type of communication that a boss writes to his subordinate and the type that the subordinate can get away with when he writes to his boss (or even the type that he drafts for his boss's signature). I suspect that many managers who have had their writing criticized had this unpleasant experience simply because of their failure to recognize the fact that messages are affected by the relative positions of the writer and the recipient in the organizational hierarchy.

UPWARD COMMUNICATIONS. Let us roughly follow the order of the subtopics included under upward communications in Exhibit II. "Tact" is important. If a subordinate fails to recognize his role and writes in an argumentative or insulting tone, he is almost certain to reap trouble for himself (or for his boss if the document goes up under the boss's actual or implied signature). One of the perennially difficult problems facing any subordinate is how to tell a superior he is wrong. If the subordinate were the boss, most likely he *could* call a spade a spade; but since he is not, he has problems. And, in today's business world, bosses themselves spend much time figuring out how to handle problem communications with discretion. Often tender topics are best handled orally rather than in writing.

Two other subtopics—"supporting detail" and "opinion"—also require a distinction according to the writer's role. Since the communication is going upward, the writer will probably find it advisable to support his statements with considerable detail. On the other hand, he may run afoul of superiors who will be impatient if he gives too much detail and not enough generalization. Here is a classic instance where a word from above as to the amount of detail required in a particular assignment would be of inestimable value to the subordinate.

The same holds true for "opinion." In some cases, the subordinate may be criticized for introducing too many of his personal opinions—in fact, often for giving any recommendation at all. If the superior wishes the subordinate to make recommendations and to offer his own opinions, the burden is on the superior to tell him. If the superior fails to do so, the writer can at least try to make it clear where facts cease and opinions begin; then the superior can draw his own conclusions.

The writer's "attitude" is another important factor in upward communications. When a subordinate writes to his boss, it is almost impossible for him to communicate with the blandness that he might use if he were writing a letter to a friend. There may be many little things that he is doing throughout his writing that indicate either too great a desire to impress the boss or an insecurity which imparts a feeling of fearfulness, defensiveness, or truculence in the face of authority.

DOWNWARD COMMUNICATIONS.

While the subordinate who writes upward in the organization must use "tact," the boss who writes down to his subordinates must use "diplomacy." If he is overbearing or insulting (even without meaning to be), he will find his effectiveness as a manager severely limited. Furthermore, it is the foolish manager who forgets that, when he communicates downward, he speaks as a representative of management or even of the entire company. Careless messages have often played an important part in strikes and other corporate human relations problems.

It is also important for the superior to make sure that he has clarified in his own mind just what it is he wishes to accomplish. If he does not, he may give confused or vague instructions. (In this event, it is unfair for him to blame a subordinate for presenting a poorly focused document in return.) An-

other requirement is that the superior must make sure that he has supplied any information which the subordinate needs but could not be expected to know, and that he has sufficiently explained any points which may be misleading.

Motivation is important, too. When a superior gives orders, he will find that over the long run he will not be able to rely on mere power to force compliance with his requests. It seems typically American for a subordinate to resent and resist what he considers to be arbitrary decisions made for unknown reasons. If at all possible, the superior not only should explain the reasons why he gives an order but should point out (if he can) why his decision can be interpreted as being in the best interests of those whom it affects.

I am not, however, suggesting farfetched explanations of future benefits. In the long run, those can have a boomerang effect. Straight talk, carefully and tactfully couched, is the only sensible policy. If, for example, a subordinate's request for a new assignment has been denied because he needs further experience in his present assignment, he should be told the facts. Then, if it is also true that getting more experience may prepare him for a better position in the future, there is no reason why this information should not be included to "buffer" the impact of the refusal of a new assignment.

THOUGHT

Here—a most important area—the superior has a tremendous vested interest in the reporting done by his subordinates. There is no substitute for the thought content of a communication. What good is accomplished if a message is excellent in all the other respects we have discussed—if it is readable, correct, and appropriate—yet the content is faulty? It can even do harm if the other aspects succeed in disguising the fact that it is superficial, stupid, or biased. The superior receiving it may send it up through the organization with his signature, or, equally serious, he may make an important (and disastrous) decision based on it.

Here is the real *guts* of business writing—intelligent content, something most purveyors of business writing gimmicks conveniently forget. It is also something that most training programs shortchange. The discipline of translating thoughts into words and organizing these thoughts logically has no equal as intellectual training. For there is one slogan that is true: "Disorganized, illogical writing reflects a disorganized, illogical (and untrained) mind."

That is why the first topic in this section is "preparation." Much disorganized writing results from insufficient preparation, from a failure to think through and isolate the purpose and the aim of the writing job. Most writers tend to think as they write; in fact, most of us do not even know what it is we think until we have actually written it down. The inescapability of making a well-thought-out outline before dictating seems obvious.

A primary aspect of *thought*, consequently, is the intellectual "competence" of the writer. If a report is bad merely because the subject is far beyond the experience of the writer, it is not his fault. Thus his superior should be able to reject the analysis and at the same time accept the blame for having given his assistant a job that he simply could not do. But what about the many cases where the limiting factor *is* basically the intellectual capacity of the writer? It is foolish to tell a man that he cannot *write* if in effect he simply does not have the intellectual ability to do the job that has been assigned to him.

Another aspect of thought is "fidelity to the assignment." Obviously the finest performance in the world on a topic other than the one assigned is fruitless, but such violent distortions of the assignment fortunately are rare. Not so rare, unfortunately, are reports which subtly miss the point, or wander away from it. Any consistent tendency on the part of the writer to drag in his pet remedies or favorite villains should be pointed out quickly, as should persistent efforts to grind personal axes.

Another lapse of "fidelity" is far more forgivable. This occurs when an eager subordinate tends to make too much of a routine assignment and consistently turns memos into 50-page reports. On the other hand, some subordinates may consistently make too little of an assignment and tend to do superficial and poorly researched pieces of work.

Perhaps the most important aspect of thought is the component "analysis." Here is where the highly intelligent are separated from those less gifted, and those who will dig from those who content themselves with superficial work. Often subordinates who have not had the benefit of experience under a strict taskmaster (either in school or on the job) are at a loss to understand why their reports are considered less than highly effective. Such writers, for example, may fail to draw obvious conclusions from the data that they have presented. On the other hand, they may offer conclusions which are seemingly unjustified by the evidence contained in their reports.

Another difficulty is that many young managers (and old ones, too) are unsophisticated in their appreciation of just what constitutes evidence. For example, if they base an entire report on the fact that sales are going to go up the next year simply because one assistant sales manager thinks so, they should expect to have their conclusions thrown out of court. They may also find themselves in difficulty if they fail to identify and justify assumptions which have been forced on them by the absence of factual data. Assumptions, of course, are absolutely necessary in this world of imperfect knowledge—especially when we deal with future developments—but it is the writer's responsibility to point out that certain assumptions have been made and that the validity of his analysis depends on whether or not these assumptions prove to be justified.

Another serious error in "analysis" is that of bias. Few superiors will respect a communication which is consciously or unconsciously biased. A writer who is incapable of making an objective analysis of all sides of a question, or of all alternatives to action, will certainly find his path to the top to be a dead end. On the other hand, especially in many younger writers, bias enters unconsciously, and it is only by a patient identification of the bias that the superior will be able to help the subordinate develop a truly objective analytical ability.

PERSUASIVENESS. This discussion of bias in reporting raises the question of "persuasiveness." "Every letter is a sales letter of some sort," goes the refrain. And it is true that persuasiveness in writing can range from the "con man" type of presentation to that which results from a happy blending of the four elements of business writing I have described. While it would be naive to suggest that it is not often necesssary for executives to write things in manipulative ways to achieve their ends *in the short run*, it would be foolish to imply that this type of writing will be very effective with the same people (if they are reasonably intelligent) *over the long run*. Understandably, therefore, the "con man" approach will not be particularly effective in the large business organization.

On the other hand, persuasiveness is a necessary aspect of organizational writing. Yet it is difficult to describe the qualities which serve to make a communication persuasive. It could be a certain ring of conviction about the way recommendations are advanced; it could be enthusiasm, or an understanding of the reader's desires, and a playing up to them. One can persuade by hitting with the blunt edge of the axe or by cutting finely with the sharp edge to prepare the way. Persuasion could result from a fine sense of discretion, of hinting but not stating overtly things which are impolitic to mention; or it could result from an action-orientation that conveys top management's desire for results rather than a more philosophical approach to a subject. In fact, it could be many things.

In an organization, the best test to apply for the propriety of persuasiveness is to ask yourself whether you would care to take action on the basis of what your own communication presents. In the long run, it is dangerous to assume that everyone else is stupid and malleable; so, if you would be offended or damaged in the event that you were persuaded to take the action suggested, you should restate the communication. This test eliminates needless worry about slightly dishonest but well-meaning letters of congratulation, or routine progress reports written merely for a filing record, and the like. But it does bring into sharp focus those messages that cross the line from persuasiveness to bias; these are the ones that will injure others and so eventually injure you.

CONCLUSION

No one can honestly estimate the billions of dollars that are spent in U.S. industry on written communications, but the amount must be staggering. By contrast, the amount of thinking and effort that goes into improving the effectiveness of business writing is tiny—a mouse invading a continent. A written performance inventory (like Exhibit II) in itself is not the answer. But a checklist of writing elements should enable executives to speak about writing in a common tongue and hence be a vehicle by which individual and group improvement in writing can take place.

By executives' own vote, no aspect of a manager's performance is of greater importance to his success than communication, particularly written communication. By the facts, however, no part of business practice receives less formal and intelligent attention. What this article asserts is that when an individual asks, "What do you mean I can't write?"— and has every desire to improve—his company owes him a sensible and concrete answer.

[1]See also, C. Wilson Randle, "How to Identify Promotable Executives," HBR May–June 1956, p. 122.

GLOSSARY

Abstract A brief description of the topics addressed in a report.

Acronym A word formed from the first letters of a name.

Administrative Management Society (AMS) Simplified letter style A block style letter in which the salutation is replaced by a subject line in all capital letters, the complimentary close is eliminated, and the writer's name and title are in all capital letters.

Aggressive listeners Listeners who are so intent on receiving the correct message that they intimidate the sender.

Analytical report A type of report which provides data for the reader and also includes data analysis, conclusions or interpretations of findings, and recommendations.

Appendix A collection of supplemental material which usually appears before the index at the end of a report.

Application letter A letter which accompanies copies of a résumé sent to a prospective employer. It introduces the applicant to the employer, highlights the applicant's qualifications, and makes interview arrangements easy.

Applied comprehension A level of comprehension involving the expression of opinions about and drawing insights and new ideas from text material based on the reader's existing knowledge.

Appropriateness The structure of a message—its emphasis and formality—based on whether the message is an upward, lateral, or downward internal communication or an external communication.

Assembly A group of 51 or more people.

Attention line An optional letter part that is used in a letter addressed to a corporation or department so that the letter is routed to a particular person within the organization.

Attentive listening A type of listening in which the main idea and the significant details of a message are retained. The subject matter to which a person listens is less complex or less abstract than in concentrated listening.

Audio conferencing A voice-only meeting between people at two or more locations linked via telephones or microphones and loud speakers.

Audiographics Graphic devices added to an audio conference when participants find it necessary to illustrate information with slides, drawings, or writing.

Autocratic leader A leader who makes decisions without the advice of workers.

Bar charts Figures that show comparative information in vertical or horizontal bars.

Barriers Factors that hinder the communication process.

Bilateral bar chart A bar figure that has a vertical axis that extends below the horizontal axis.

Bilateral line chart A line figure in which the vertical axis extends below the horizontal axis to show negative quantities.

Block style letter A letter style in which all lines of the letter begin at the left margin.

Body A standard letter or memo part that represents the message or messages which the sender wishes to convey; also, the core of a report.

Bridge A system that interconnects telephone lines from more than two locations.

Business-related messages Messages which relate to the attainment of organization and employee goals within an organization.

Business report A communication document generally written by one person who has compiled information to share with another person who will use that information to make a decision or take a course of action.

Buzz words The specialized language of a trade or professional group.

Careful reading A type of reading which involves the comprehension and retention of main ideas and significant details for either short or long periods of time.

Casual listening Listening for overall content in which only the main idea or gist of a message is retained.

Cellular radio telephone systems Small hand-held mobile telephones that use scarce radio frequencies that permit mobile communication from anywhere in the world.

Centralized station A type of output unit that features several centrally located transcription stations attached to a single storage unit.

Central recording system A type of input unit that enables several people to dictate simultaneously from different locations to a central transcription area.

Chain of command The means of transmitting authority from the top level through successive levels of management to workers at the lowest level.

Channel The medium through which the response to a message travels.

Climate The atmosphere of the company.

Closed system A self-contained system that does not interact with the environment in which it exists.

Cluster chain The most common grapevine channel in which information is selectively distributed.

Committee A group of 12 or fewer people.

Committee organization A form of organization in which authority and responsibility are jointly held by a group of people rather than by a single manager.

Communication The process of passing knowledge from person to person.

Communication system The orderly arranged parts of the communication process.

Communication training Training in which communicators learn to identify and eliminate barriers.

Complimentary close The farewell or closing of a letter.

Component bar chart A bar figure that shows the relative size or parts of a whole; it is sometimes called a stacked bar chart.

Comprehension Understanding.

Computer-based message system (CBMS) A method used by managers to deliver electronic memos and messages in which the managers input their memos at their terminals and send the memos over wires or cables to a main computer.

Computer conferencing A form of conference based entirely on transmitting data through terminals or personal computers connected by telephone lines to a central store-and-forward computer.

Computer graphics The creation of figures and tables on computers.

Computer-telephone A computer and a telephone housed in a single desktop unit. It permits the simultaneous transmission of both computer data and voice data.

Concentrated listening Comprehending and retaining the main ideas and significant details of complex or abstract information.

Conflict Disharmony.

Consensus The collective agreement or acceptance of a general opinion.

Contents page An outline of a report; it contains corresponding page numbers for locating the various sections within the report.

Controlling A function of management consisting of measuring or evaluating progress made toward planned goals and objectives.

Controls Policies, rules, and regulations that monitor the various components of a system.

Copy notation An optional letter or memo part which identifies the individuals who receive a copy of the letter or memo.

Cordless telephone A radio-operated base unit (which plugs into the telephone line) and a portable battery-powered handset.

Correctness The process of adhering to the commonly accepted practices of writing.

Council A group of 13 to 50 people.

Cover page A page devoted to listing the title of the report, the identification of the person who authorized the report, the writer, and the date.

Cross-hatching Special shading used to distinguish the various parts of a figure.

Daily practice One of the "Three D's" of good listening.

Date **line** A standard memo part which indicates the date the memo was prepared.

Decoding The process of deciding what a message really means.

Dedicated word processing Equipment designed

only to process text material.

Democratic leader A leader who involves workers in making decisions.

Dependent variable The uncontrollable variable which is plotted on the vertical axis.

Desire One of the "Three *D's*" of good listening.

Desktop model A type of input unit that generally rests on the top of a workstation and uses continuous-loop or cassette tapes to record dictation.

Direct approach An approach used when sharing a positive or routine message.

Discipline One of the "Three *D's*" of good listening.

Discrete medium Any type of magnetic tape, disk, or belt that can be removed from an input unit.

Discussants Group members.

Downward written communications Written messages sent to subordinates.

Drawings Diagrams used to communicate the relationship between or among items rather than their relative values.

Editing The critical thinking phase of the writing process during which the writer analyzes and scrutinizes what has been written.

Electronic blackboard A device that displays on a TV screen at one site whatever is being written on the electronic blackboard at another site.

Electronic cueing A process used by many input units to mark the beginning and end of dictated material.

Electronic letters Computer-generated messages that are usually transmitted electronically to one or more individuals outside the organization.

Electronic mail The transmission of a written message using a computer system which is responsible for routing and delivering the message.

Elongated pie chart A three-dimensional pie chart.

Enclosure notation An optional letter or memo part which informs the receiver that additional items are included with the letter or memo.

Encoding The process of selecting or converting thoughts into a message.

Endless-loop medium A continuous-loop magnetic tape housed in a central tanklike device that cannot be handled or removed from the machine.

Esteem needs The need to feel important and to receive recognition from others.

Experimentation The determination of whether the change in one factor causes a change in another factor.

Exploded pie chart A pie figure in which one wedge is cut away from the pie to indicate special emphasis.

Extemporaneous speech A carefully planned, thoroughly researched and rehearsed presentation.

External factors Outside factors such as organization structure, surroundings, circumstances, and communication resources which have the potential for becoming communication barriers.

External written communications Written documents that a company sends to or receives from its outside environment.

Face-to-face speaking A type of person-to-person speaking in which two people converse while in one another's presence.

Facsimile (FAX) device A machine used to relay printed material, pictures, or figures to distant sites.

Feedback Information about the quality, quantity, and cost of the goods or services produced in a system.

Feedback speaker The person who responds or reacts to a message.

Fidgeters Nervous listeners who move or fidget while the sender transmits a message.

Figure A graph, chart, or other condensed visual representation used to illustrate a message.

Filtering The mental process of interpreting information by focusing on some input and ignoring other input.

First-line managers Supervisory managers who engage in short-range planning.

Flowcharts Schematic drawings of the logical steps in a sequence of operations.

Follower A manager's role which refers to the relationship between the manager and his or her boss.

Follow-up letters Letters sent after the interview to thank an employer for an interview opportunity, to accept an employment offer, or to refuse an employment offer.

Formality The degree of structure of a speech.

Formal memo A memo sent to a superior or colleague with whom the sender is unacquainted or not well acquainted.

Formal report A manuscript report which usually includes a combination of standard and optional parts.

Formal table A table that contains a title, columnar headings, and any explanatory information which applies to the table; it can stand by itself and does not require text narrative to convey a clear idea to the reader.

Form report A report format which involves the reporting of standardized, routine, and/or repetitive data on a printed sheet.

Frame of reference A communicator's background or life experiences.

From **line** A standard memo part which contains the writer's name.

Functional organization A form of organization in which each manager has line authority over all employees in the work unit.

Glossary A list of complex or specialized words and their definitions.

Gobbledygook Nonsensical wording.

Grapevine The informal communication network that exists in every firm.

Graphic information The use of visual illustrations in written documents and presentations.

Group leader The person who guides the group in performing its responsibilities.

Group member A person who provides and obtains information in a meeting.

Heading A standard letter part which includes the company name, address, and telephone number.

Headings Topic titles used to identify related information grouped in sections of a report.

Impromptu speech A speech which occurs when the speaker is called upon to deliver a few words on the spur of the moment with little or no time for preparation.

Inaccurate listeners Listeners who alter the messages they receive and who do not retain the complete message.

Independent variable The controllable variable which is plotted on the horizontal axis.

Index An alphabetic listing of key topics or items that are mentioned in the report and the page numbers indicating where they can be found in the report.

Indirect approach An approach used whenever unpleasant news must be given.

Individual transcription station A type of output unit which is equipped with a machine that holds the magnetic medium, a headset for listening to the dictation, and foot or thumb controls to regulate the playback speed.

Inference comprehension A level of comprehension which requires the reader to interpret what a writer means in order to answer a question.

Informal memo A memo in which the sender and receiver communicate on a first-name basis.

Informal table A brief tabulation of information which is inserted into the text of a business document; it is sometimes referred to as a text table.

Informational report A type of report which provides data for the reader to analyze and interpret.

Initial speaker The person who initiates conversation.

Input The elements that enter a system from the external environment.

Inside address A standard letter part which includes the name, title, and complete mailing address of the receiver of a letter.

Interactive theory of reading A reading theory which maintains that comprehension depends upon an interaction between the text and the reader.

Intermediary speaking A type of person-to-person speaking in which two people separated by distance converse through an electronic device.

Internal factors Factors existing within the sender and/or receiver such as prejudice, close-mindedness, lack of trust, and physical impairments which have the potential for becoming communication barriers.

Internal written communications Written documents that are sent and received within an organization.

Interoffice memorandums Memorandums that are sent between or among employees of different work units.

Intimate zone Personal space of zero up to two feet from an individual.

Intraoffice memorandums Memorandums that are sent between or among employees of the same work unit.

Jargon The specialized language of a trade or professional group.

Job description A one- or two-page written summary which describes the basic tasks performed on a job.

Job specification A written statement listing the qualifications employees need to perform a given job effectively.

Lateral written communications Written messages sent to peers and colleagues.

Leadership The means used to achieve company goals by motivating and controlling workers to high levels of performance.

Leading The managerial function that encompasses staffing and directing.

Legend An explanatory list of symbols or colors used in a figure.

Letter report A short report prepared in letter format for audiences external to the organization.

Line-and-staff organization A form of organization which combines the direct flow of authority of the line organization with the specialized feature of the functional organization.

Line charts Figures that include plotted data points joined by line segments.

Line organization A form of organization in which direct authority flows downward from top-level managers, through middle-level managers, to lower-level managers and workers.

Listening follow-up The component of the communication system in which information is processed, filtered, and interpreted.

Listening habits The usual manner in which a person listens.

Listening mind-set One's mental attitude or disposition to listening.

Listening process A process that involves three stages of listening activity: prelistening, actual listening, and postlistening.

List of figures A sequential itemization of the figures included in a report.

List of tables A sequential itemization of the tables included in a report.

Mailing notations Special mailing instructions, such as *REGISTERED* or *CERTIFIED*.

Manager A person in charge of or having authority over an organization or one of its units.

Managerial functions The major areas of responsibility assumed by managers.

Manual A guidebook that gives instructions or reference information.

Maps Business drawings used to show positional relationships of geographic regions.

Matrix organization A dual command system which involves full-time or part-time workers participating on a complex project while remaining in their functional groups.

Mean The arithmetic average of a set of numbers.

Median The middle value in an array of numbers.

Meeting People gathering together for a purpose.

***Memorandum* heading** The label that appears on a memorandum when a preprinted form is not used.

Memorandum report A short report prepared in memorandum format for use within an organization.

Memorized speech A speech that occurs when the speaker commits to memory every word of a written presentation.

Microcassettes The smallest cassettes available, which hold up to 60 minutes of recorded material.

Middle-level managers Managers who are responsible for intermediate-range planning.

Minicassettes A type of media which is smaller than a standard-size cassette and provides 30 to 60 minutes of recording time.

Mode The most frequently appearing number in a distribution.

Modified block style letter A letter style in which the date and closing lines begin at the horizontal center of the paper.

Multiple bar chart A bar figure that shows several variables.

Multiple line chart A line figure which illustrates more than one dependent variable.

Multiple pie chart A pie figure used to compare or contrast the composition of several entities.

Observation The process of watching the actions of a particular person or group or watching the results of an event or series of events.

Open system A type of system whose operation requires the interaction of the system with the environment.

Organizational manuals Manuals which provide a written description of the formal structure of a company.

Organizing The orderly arrangement of resources needed to achieve what has been planned.

Originator's identification A standard letter part which indicates the sender's name.

Originator's title The business or professional title by which the sender of a letter is known.

Output The goods and/or services produced by a company.

Overly passive listeners Listeners who are physically present to hear a message but absent in spirit.

Peer A co-worker or colleague of roughly equal rank or status.

Performance appraisal The evaluation of job-related strengths and weaknesses of an employee.

Personal space The invisible boundaries of a person's private domain.

Personal zone Personal space ranging from two to four feet from an individual.

Person-to-group speaking A type of speaking in which communication occurs in a group situation.

Person-to-person speaking A type of speaking in which communication occurs with one person at a time.

Photographs Images recorded by a camera and reproduced on a photosensitive surface.

Pictorials Figures that are diagrammed or photographed and are not classified as pie charts, line charts, or bar charts.

Pictograms Pictorial representations of numerical data or relationships; they are sometimes called pictographs.

Pie charts Circular figures used to show values and/or percentages that represent parts of a whole.

Planning A managerial function that involves developing goals and objectives to be attained by the company under the manager's control.

Playscript The listing of procedures in sequential order with each participant's part distinguished from other participants' parts by using separate rows, columns, or labels.

Policy manuals Manuals which provide a written record of the regulations that employees are expected to follow.

Portable models Hand-held, battery-powered input units that have built-in microphones and use cassettes for recording.

Position description A one- or two-page written summary which describes the basic tasks performed on a job.

Postscript An optional letter part which is used to add an idea or to provide additional information at the end of a letter.

Preface A short statement used to introduce a report.

Primary research First-hand investigation of a topic.

Procedures manuals Manuals which provide a written explanation of the steps involved in performing various work tasks.

Process The phase of a system that changes inputs into outputs.

Progressive discipline Management's response to repeated rule violations with increasingly severe penalties.

Proxemics The physical distance between communicators.

Pseudo-intellectual listeners Listeners who inhibit the sending of messages because they listen only to facts and consider feelings and opinions of little value.

Public speaking Speaking to a massive audience.

Public zone Personal space of twelve or more feet between communicators.

Range The highest and lowest, or extreme, values in an array of numbers.

Readability The reader's ability to read a message and extract the intended meaning.

Reader-centered theory of reading A reading theory in which readers use their existing knowledge and expectations to make sense out of what they read.

Reading The process of extracting information and meaning from the text copy.

Reading habits The manner in which a person reads.

Recall comprehension A level of comprehension that involves getting the facts as stated by the writer of the material.

Reference citations Entries used to give credit to the original source of quoted, paraphrased, or text material.

Reference initials The initials of the person who keyboarded the letter or memo for the sender.

Reference list An alphabetic array of sources whose information was used in the report or related to the report topic.

Résumé A summary of detailed information about an applicant's qualifications.

Résumé cloning A problem in which résumés and cover letters begin to look more and more alike.

Résumé inflation A problem in which candidates exaggerate or misrepresent their job qualifications.

Retention Remembering information that is received during the communication process.

Safety needs The needs for economic security, for protection from physical dangers, and for the desire for an orderly, predictable environment.

Salutation A standard letter part which is used to greet the receiver.

Scan reading A type of reading which requires readers to search for specific information which is to be retained for a short period.

Secondary research Second-hand or indirect investigation of a topic.

Selectivity in perception Choosing what is perceived.

Selectivity in retention Choosing what is retained.

Selectivity in transmission Choosing what is transmitted.

Self-actualization The need to realize one's full potential.

Semiformal memo A memo that is sent to a superior or colleague with whom the sender is acquainted.

Sentence outline A type of outline in which each entry is written as a complete sentence.

Serial communication Several messages grouped together in a single message.

Skim reading A type of reading which consists of finding information known to be in the material or quickly finding important information without reading irrelevant material.

Slow scan television (SSTV) A type of teleconferencing system which consists of equipment designed to store images at one site and to transmit the images over telephone lines to SSTV units at other sites.

Social messages Messages which focus on topics other than the attainment of organization or employee goals.

Social zone Personal space of four to twelve feet between communicators.

Solicited application letters Application letters written in response to advertisements or requests for applicants.

Source line A part of a figure which appears above the figure title to give credit to the person or party who originally prepared the information contained in the figure.

Span of control The number of workers who are directly managed by one person.

Speaking The exchange of thoughts, opinions, or information from one person to another through the use of spoken words and nonverbal signals.

Speaking to entertain Speaking for the purpose of amusing the receiver.

Speaking to inform The sharing of information with or obtaining information from another person.

Speaking to persuade The selling of an idea, goods, or services.

Specialty manuals Manuals which contain detailed information about a particular function or process.

Speech A requested address or talk given before a group.

Standard cassettes Cassettes which are standard in size and provide from 30 to 180 minutes of recording time.

Subject line A letter or memo part that enables the reader to know the topic of the message prior to reading it.

Subsystems Smaller systems within a super system.

Summary A brief restatement of a report's major findings.

Super system A whole or complete entity composed of smaller parts or units.

Supervisory managers First-line managers who engage in short-range planning.

Survey The collection of data from others by conducting face-to-face or intermediary interviews or by using a questionnaire.

System The orderly arranged parts of a whole.

Tables The systematic arrangement of numbers and/or words in rows and columns.

Teleconferencing An electronic method of communication between two or more people at two or more locations.

Telephone-answering machine A machine which permits a person to receive voice messages while attending to other matters.

Telephone tag The time-wasting activity of making repeated, unsuccessful attempts to reach another person by phone.

Text-centered theory of reading A reading theory which emphasizes that a reader's ability to understand the meaning of text material is directly related to the structure or organization of the text itself.

Thought A product of thinking as it relates to structuring a message.

"Three *D's*" of good listening Desire, discipline, and daily practice.

Title The main heading of a report.

Title page A page devoted to listing the title of the report, the identification of the person who authorized the report, the writer, and the date.

To line A standard memo part which indicates the name of the person to whom the memo is written.

Top-level managers Managers who assume responsibility for long-range planning.

Topic outline A type of outline in which each entry is expressed as a word, a few words, or a short phrase.

Transmittal letter A letter that usually accompanies a formal report when it is transmitted to a reader outside the organization.

Transmittal memo A memo that usually accompanies a formal report when it is transmitted to a reader inside the organization.

Typed company name The line of a letter which lists in all capital letters the name of the company which the writer represents.

Unity of command A principle which states that a worker should report to only one boss.

Unity of functions A principle which states that all parts of a firm must work and communicate with one another if mutual goals are to be realized.

Unsolicited application letters Application letters sent to companies in which there are no known job vacancies.

Uplink device A device that receives a TV signal from the originating site and then transmits that signal to a satellite, which then transmits the signal to the receiver site.

Upward communication The flow of information from lower levels (employees) to higher levels (managers).

Upward written communications Documents sent to superiors.

Video conferencing Systems that combine TV-quality images and high-quality audio in specially constructed rooms.

Videocassette A videotape completely enclosed in a plastic container.

Videocassette recorder (VCR) A playback device for videocassettes. It is designed for use by the non-technical person.

Visual aids Graphic or written materials used to convey a messsage or to reinforce a spoken message.

Written speech A speech that occurs when the speaker presents a subject to an audience by reading word for word from a written manuscript.

INDEX